# The Exilic Code

# The Exilic Code

*Ciphers, Word Links, and Dating in Exilic and Post-Exilic Biblical Literature*

PRESTON KAVANAGH

☙PICKWICK *Publications* • Eugene, Oregon

THE EXILIC CODE
Ciphers, Word Links, and Dating in Exilic and Post-Exilic Biblical Literature

Copyright © 2009 Preston Kavanagh. All rights reserved. Except for brief quotations in critical publications or reviews, no part of this book may be reproduced in any manner without prior written permission from the publisher. Write: Permissions, Wipf and Stock Publishers, 199 W. 8th Ave., Suite 3, Eugene, OR 97401.

Pickwick Publications
A Division of Wipf and Stock Publishers
199 8th Ave., Suite 3
Eugene, OR 97401

www.wipfandstock.com

Scripture quotations contained herein (unless otherwise noted) are from the New Revised Standard Version of the Bible, copyright © 1989 by the National Council of Churches of Christ in the USA. Used by permission. All rights reserved.

Scripture quotations marked RSV are from the Revised Standard Version of the Bible, copyright © 1946, 1952, and 1971 by the National Council of Churches of Christ in the USA. Used by permission. All rights reserved.

Part of chapter 1 was originally published as "The Jehoiachin Code in Scripture's Priestly Benediction" in *Biblica* 88 (2007) 234–44. It is reprinted with permission of *Biblica*, and appears here in an expanded form.

ISBN 13: 978-1-55635-070-2

*Cataloging-in-Publication data:*

Kavanagh, Preston
The exilic code : ciphers, word links, and dating in exilic and post-exilic biblical literature / Preston Kavanagh.

xiv + 316 p.; 23 cm. Includes bibliography.

ISBN 13: 978-1-55635-070-2

1. Bible. O.T.—Criticism, interpretation, etc. 2. Jews—History—Babylonian captivity, 598-515 B.C. 3. Jews—History—586 B.C. to 70 A.D. 3. Ciphers in the Bible. 4. Bible. O.T.—Data processing. I. Title.

BS1197 K38 2009

Manufactured in the U.S.A.

# Contents

*Acknowledgments / vii*

*Abbreviations / ix*

*Tables and Figures / xii*

1. The Jehoiachin Code in Scripture's Priestly Benediction / 1
2. Extending the Bible Code / 21
3. The Word-Link King of Babylon / 42
4. Second Isaiah's Identity / 62
5. Coding Revelations of Psalm Fifty-One / 85
6. The Suffering Servant and the Son of Man / 107
7. The Breadth of Exilic Coding / 134

APPENDIX ONE—Athbash Letter Exchanges / 173

APPENDIX TWO—2 Kings 25:27—30: 468 Word Links / 174

APPENDIX THREE—Coding in Psalm 51 / 177

    Part A: Names with Higher Coding / 177

    Part B: Selected Coded Spellings from Psalm 51 / 189

APPENDIX FOUR—Coding of Exilic Names in Hebrew Scripture / 221

*Bibliography / 299*

*Index of Modern Authors / 303*

*Index of Scripture / 305*

# Acknowledgments

MANY PEOPLE ADVISED, ENCOURAGED, and assisted me during the several decades it has taken to bring *The Exilic Code* to publication. Herman Chernoff (now Professor of Statistics emeritus at Harvard University) showed me how to identify exceptional coding values. His patience, skepticism, and genius were exactly what I needed. Simo Parpola's scholarship provided the basis for solving the riddle of the Suffering Servant. Harry White kept my aged computers humming. Jim Rotholz and Wade Pugh spent endless hours compiling data. The insight and judgment of K. C. Hanson, editor-in-chief at Wipf & Stock, brought *The Exilic Code* into being. And Elisabeth Bruno applied both stylistic rigor and good counsel to this book. I also am indebted to librarians at a score of institutions in the Chicago, Boston, and Washington areas. God bless those librarians, Professors Chernoff and Parpola, K. C. Hanson, Harry White, Jim Rotholz, Wade Pugh, and Elisabeth Bruno. And, of course, God bless Lois, my infinitely patient wife.

# Abbreviations

| | |
|---|---|
| AB | Anchor Bible |
| *ABD* | *Anchor Bible Dictionary*, 6 vols., edited by David Noel Freedman |
| *AfO* | *Archiv fur Orientforschung* |
| *ANET* | *Ancient Near Eastern Texts Relating to the Old Testament*, 3rd ed., edited by James B. Pritchard |
| *AnSt* | *Anatolian Studies* |
| *Ant* | Josephus *Antiquities* |
| AOAT | Alter Orient und Altes Testament |
| *Apion* | Josephus *Against Apion* |
| *Aug* | Suetonius *Divus Augustus* |
| *b.* | *Babylonian Talmud tractate* |
| *B. Bat.* | *Baba Batra* |
| BCE | Before Common Era |
| *B. Qam.* | *Baba Qamma* |
| BA | *Biblical Archaeologist* |
| BASOR | *Bulletin of the American Schools of Oriental Research* |
| *Ber.* | *Berakhot* |
| Bib | *Biblica* |
| BR | *Bible Review* |
| BZAW | Beiheft zur Zeitschrift fur die alttestamentliche Wissenschaft |
| CE | Common Era |
| CW | Coded Word |
| DH | Deuteronomistic History |
| Dtr | Deuteronomistic Historian, seventh century |
| Dtr² | Deuteronomistic Historian, sixth century |

| | |
|---|---|
| *EncJud* | *Encyclopaedia Judaica*, corrected edition, 17 vols., edited by Cecil Roth and Geoffrey Wigoder |
| ETL | *Ephemerides Theologicae Lovanienses* |
| *Gen. Rab.* | *Genesis Rabbah* |
| IDB | *Interpreter's Dictionary of the Bible*, 4 vols., edited by George A. Buttrick |
| *Int* | *Interpretation* |
| *JBL* | *Journal of Biblical Literature* |
| *JBQ* | *Jewish Bible Quarterly* |
| *JNES* | *Journal of Near Eastern Studies* |
| *JSS* | *Journal of Semitic Studies* |
| *Julius* | Suetonius *Divus Julius* |
| *Lev. Rab.* | *Leviticus Rabbah* |
| *Mak.* | *Makkot* |
| *Mid. Ps.* | *Midrash Psalms* |
| MT | Masoretic Text |
| NT | New Testament |
| OT | Old Testament |
| Parpola I | Simo Parpola, *Letters from Assyrian Scholars to the Kings Esarhaddon and Assurbanipal: Texts* |
| Parpola II | Simo Parpola, *Letters from Assyrian Scholars to the Kings Esarhaddon and Assurbanipal: Commentary and Appendices* |
| *Pesaḥ.* | *Pesaḥim* |
| *Qidd.* | *Qiddushin* |
| *Sanh.* | *Sanhedrin* |
| *Shabb.* | *Shabbath* |
| *Song Rab.* | *Song of Songs Rabbah* |
| *StatSci* | *Statistical Science* |
| TA | *Tel Aviv* |
| *Targ. Yer.* | *Targum Yerushalmi* |
| *TynBul* | *Tyndale Bulletin* |
| VT | *Vetus Testamentum* |

*Abbreviations*

| | |
|---|---|
| VTSup | Vetus Testamentum Supplements |
| WL | Word Link |
| *WTJ* | *Westminster Theological Journal* |
| *ZAW* | *Zeitschrift für die alttestamentliche Wissenschaft* |

# Tables and Other Figures

## TABLES

1.1  Jehoiachin (יויכין) Spellings Concealed within Priestly Benediction
1.2  Personal Names of High Value Concealed within Priestly Benediction
1.3  Comparing Jehoiachin-Sarpuhi Coded Spellings for Priestly Benediction Only and for Benediction with Adjacent Verses
1.4  Jehoiachin-Sarpuhi Coded Spellings for the Priestly Benediction and Its Adjacent Verses (Num 6:23–27)
2.1  Sarpuhi-Jehoiachin Athbash Codes in Ezekiel 9
2.2  Values of Cyrus Athbash Spellings Concealed within Isaiah 41:1–13
2.3  Word Link Example
4.1  Shared Words in Isaiah 49:1–3, 5 and Genesis 25:21–26
4.2  Jacob-Israel IDs in Hebrew Scripture
5.1  Coding Frequencies in Psalm 51 Ranked by Place among 929 Chapters
5.2  Coded Psalm 51 Spellings Suitable for Replication
5.3  Names with Higher Coding in Psalm 51
5.4  "Cyrus King of Babylon" Coded in Psalm 51
6.1  Ezekiel Coding in Isaiah 52:13—53:12
6.2  Substitute-King Motif in the Synoptic Gospels:
A. Kingly Rule
B. Rebellion and Trials
C. Death
7.1  Coding in 1 Kings 1–16

*Tables and Other Figures*

7.2  Coding in Proverbs 7–21
7.3  Coding in Joshua 9–23
7.4  Candidates for Subject or Authorship of Job, Proverbs, and Songs
7.5  Candidates for Subject or Authorship of Individual Psalms
7.6  Candidates for Subject or Authorship of Sections of the Book of Isaiah
7.7  Density of Exilic Coding in Hebrew Scripture
7.8  Candidates for Subject or Authorship of Job, Proverbs, Songs, and Minor Prophets
7.9  Twenty-Eight Chapters Containing Highest Daniel Coding

## OTHER FIGURES

Chart of Jehoiachin-Coded Spellings in Five Hundred Fifteen-Word Passages and in Priestly Benediction / 14
Graph of Coded Names in Psalm / 90

# 1

# The Jehoiachin Code in Scripture's Priestly Benediction

## THE CASE FOR BIBLICAL CODES

ACCORDING TO HISTORIAN DAVID Kahn, the use of codes is as ancient and widespread as civilization. He says, "It must be that as soon as culture has reached a certain level, probably measured by its literacy, cryptography appears spontaneously . . . Human needs for privacy . . . must inevitably lead to cryptography wherever men thrive and wherever they write."[1] There are numerous examples.

A Mesopotamian tablet dating from 1500 BCE employed special writing symbols to guard pottery-glazing secrets.[2] Neo-Babylonian scribes often used a cryptogram substituting numbers for characters when they affixed their names to documents.[3] The *Kama Sutra*, an early Hindu work, listed coding and deciphering as arts women should practice.[4] An Indian text from the fourth century BCE advised ambassadors to employ cryptanalysis to obtain intelligence.[5] Both Augustus and Julius Caesar used ciphers.[6] A system in which letters are replaced by others further down the alphabet is still known as a Caesar code.[7] A lengthy fourth-century BCE Egyptian papyrus written in demotic script proved to have been an Aramaic cryptogram pertaining to a Syrian mystery cult.[8]

---

1. Kahn, *Codebreakers*, 84.
2. Gadd and Thompson, "Middle-Babylonian Text," 87–96.
3. Leichty, "Colophon," 152.
4. *Kama Sutra*, under Study of Arts and Sciences: Intellectual Pastimes.
5. Shamasastry, *Kautilya's Arthasastra*, I, 12:21, 16:31.
6. Suetonius, "Julius" 56; "Augustus" 88.
7. Kahn, *Codebreakers*, 84.
8. Bowman, "Text in Cryptogram," 219–27.

In the fifth century BCE the Spartans used batons of various thicknesses called skytales.[9] The sender wrote his message on a strip of parchment or leather wrapped around the baton. The recipient decoded the message by winding it around a skytale of the same thickness.

The Babylonian Exile began when Nebuchadnezzar captured Jerusalem and deported its leading citizens. After he returned to punish a revolt eleven years later, the Babylonians spent several years leisurely ravaging the land. When the smoke had cleared from Judah's charred cities, Judeans were spread across the Near East. They fled to Egypt and to neighboring Moab, Ammon, and Edom. The presence of Judean tribes in Arabia could date from this time. Many Judeans made it to nearby Samaria, which did not participate in Judah's revolt. Trade may further have expanded the dispersion that war had begun. As the Exile wore on, Judean merchants, centered in Babylonia and elsewhere, might in their travels have crisscrossed the ancient world. This supposition gains support from a trove of documents from Nippur. An archive of the Murashu family shows Judeans were heavily involved in commercial activities during the century following the Exile.[10]

In a few years the Judeans had passed from a settled to a scattered people. That physical dispersion makes coded communication plausible, since those in the Diaspora would have wanted important questions answered. How soon would God liberate his exiles? What alliance was forming against Babylon? On which projects were captives laboring? Could Tyre withstand its siege or Egypt expel its invaders? Was King Jehoiachin in prison, and could David's line endure? What was the state of worship at Jerusalem's ruined temple and which priestly group held control? On an even more personal basis, virtually every refugee now had a relative someplace else. He or she would have been eager for news of that relative and that someplace else. These were questions of lively interest that often could not have been openly addressed.

How would information have been gathered? It is possible Judeans had access to official sources within the Egyptian and Babylonian courts. A Joseph or a Daniel who had risen to high position could have contributed, as could scribes, merchants, travelers, and domestic servants. One

---

9. Plutarch, *Lives* "Lysander" 19.
10. Weisburg, "Murashu's Sons," 529.

can even imagine a network of couriers with stops and sources spanning the Fertile Crescent.

Assuming there was a code, if writers *en*coded scripture, others would have had to *de*code it. Few exiles would likely have had the training to decode any scripture bulletins their communities might receive. That would have been a task for experts—scribes, priests, and Levites. Any deciphering would have called for lots of counting and tabulation, and also for layout boards and word lists. Decoding would have been difficult and tedious labor, best done by careful people working individually. Once decoded, the information would have been widely shared, though with due care to conceal that there *was* a code. If synagogues got their start during the Exile, they could have become centers of this work.

Some of the kingdoms bordering Judah welcomed fugitive Judeans, some tolerated them, and a few may have enslaved them or turned them away. But whatever the reception, the refugees' new rulers were foreign rulers. To complicate matters, some of the places to which Judeans fled were either governed by Babylon or allied with it. Nearby Samaria was a Babylonian province. Syria, to its north, had already fallen to Nebuchadnezzar. Edom had joined the Babylonians in their campaign against Judah. Whatever the extent of Babylonian influence, local officials would not have welcomed openly anti-Babylonian sentiments from Judean refugees. Coded scripture was a way for the exiles to express such views while staying on the better sides of their hosts.

In Babylonia itself the risk must have been especially high. Ezekiel, King Jehoiachin, and other exiles lived under the eye of Nebuchadnezzar's officials and informers, and perhaps were held directly responsible for events in distant Judah. Surely Judeans in Babylon absorbed punishment for Zedekiah's revolt and for any others. Second Isaiah wrote, "This is a people robbed and plundered, all of them are trapped in holes and hidden in prisons" (Isa 42:22). These were dangerous times, times calling for riddles and ciphers. Certainly those writing scripture for circulation in Nebuchadnezzar's Babylon had strong incentives to use coded language.

Before the Babylonians leveled Solomon's temple, worship at Jerusalem had been a focus of Judean religious life. But with the temple gone, what could then bond God's people? The answer was a profusion of scripture. In the sixth century the amount of scripture may have doubled. Second Isaiah, Jeremiah, Ezekiel, the Deuteronomistic Historian (Dtr), perhaps the Priestly source (P), and others sent forth entire books of hope and judgment. More than any other nation, the Jews in exile became the people of the book. And what better medium for coding than scripture itself, the thing that commanded the attention of every displaced Judean? This very reliance upon scripture makes coding within scripture credible. Readers should not think coding means only baffling gibberish. It can also come in a plain wrapper, concealed within sense-making language. And the language conveying information to the exiles would have been biblical Hebrew.

Coding would certainly have added weight to the word of the Lord. Moderns separate word and act, but in the ancient world there was less distinction. And until recent times, in the Near East that still held true. To illustrate, an Arab accompanied by his son chose to walk away from an argument with another man. But when his antagonist began to shout insults, the father pulled his son to the ground and threw his cloak over him. He had to protect the boy from the bullet-like impact of the words. In the mouths of the prophets, the word of God was heavy, unstoppable, and never returned without accomplishment. Coding underneath God's words would have added still more weight.

Finally, here is the best reason to suspect coding within scripture. So much of the Bible is exasperatingly unspecific. Consider the books of Ecclesiastes, Isaiah, Job, Joel, Jonah, Malachi, Obadiah, Proverbs, Psalms, Song of Solomon, and Zephaniah. Address to these the journalistic questions of who, what, when, and where. Scholars posing those questions have received scant satisfaction, though common sense suggests that somewhere within those texts are who-what-when-where answers. Coding would have supplied them.

How was the biblical code found? Several decades ago, using word associations, I detected the name of Second Isaiah, the anonymous prophet of the Exile. (Second Isaiah's identity is treated in chapter 4 below.) I then used that name to see how the author might have signed his work. Eventually, patterns emerged of a letter per text word from words at regular intervals. Next, a customized computer program was acquired to speed searches, but it lacked a sound basis for evaluating output. Herman Chernoff, then Professor of Statistics at Harvard University, helped remedy the problem. Drawing upon his years of experience, Professor Chernoff kindly identified the sampling and probability elements needed to produce more understandable search results. By 1992, when Gabriel Barkay published news of the Ketef Hinnom finds, I had become aware that the

MT of the Priestly Benediction concealed Jehoiachin values. And after reading the Barkay group's 2004 *BASOR* article, I realized that I could introduce the code to scholars by using it to help establish the age of the amulets. Thus this chapter came to be.

## THE KETEF HINNOM AMULETS

In 1979 excavations led by Gabriel Barkay at Ketef Hinnom uncovered two silver amulets containing the earliest citations of scripture ever found. These were unearthed in a family tomb below Jerusalem's Old City walls. Portions of Num 6:24–26, called the Priestly Benediction, are inscribed upon the two amulets. In this chapter I argue that coding within that passage's benediction helps to establish the date of these amulets.

The Priestly Benediction is among the best-loved passages in all of scripture, and today those who conduct Jewish and Christian worship use the words often. Here are the NRSV and MT texts:

> [24] The Lord bless you and keep you;
> [25] the Lord make his face to shine upon you, and be gracious to you;
> [26] the Lord lift up his countenance upon you, and give you peace.

> יברכך יהוה וישמרך
>
> יאר יהוה פניו אליך ויחנך
>
> ישא יהוה פניו אליך וישם לך שלום

Though the amulets have made headlines, controversy has accompanied the find. The problem centers upon when the plaques were made. In 1992 Barkay gave the opinion that the amulets date from the late seventh century BCE.[11] Then, a dozen years later he and three coauthors concluded, "We can reaffirm with confidence that the late pre-exilic period is the proper chronological context for the artifacts."[12] Elsewhere in the 2004 article they said the plaques "date from the horizon of the end of the Judean monarchy—or a palaeographic date of the late seventh century BCE to early sixth century BCE."[13] Ada Yardeni, by analyzing writing

---

11. Barkay, "Priestly Benediction," 147, 174.
12. Barkay et al., "Amulets," 41.
13. Ibid. 42.

# The Exilic Code

styles, dates the plaques at the dawn of the sixth century, which is close to the Barkay group's estimate.[14] Johannes Renz, however, places the work in the Hellenistic period.[15] Finally, John Rogerson and Philip Davies conclude that paleography by itself does not allow certainty in such dating.[16]

When experts disagree, others do well to listen quietly—though perhaps some may venture a change of approach. To explore dating of the amulets, this chapter will concentrate upon the biblical text rather than the artifacts themselves. Barkay and others think it highly likely that scripture's Priestly Benediction predated the amulets and not vice versa.[17] Assuming this, the earliest possible time that scribes could have cut the blessing into the plaques was just after what became Num 6:24–26 was written. And when was that?

## CODED NAMES IN THE BENEDICTION

Discovery of the Ketef Hinnom amulets offers an occasion to test what the MT's Priestly Benediction might conceal. The possible system of concealment—if system it is—is simple. The author might have used letters from regularly spaced text words, one letter per word. The interval can range from one (letters taken from consecutive text words), to four (a letter from every fourth text word). Suppose the author wished to conceal a four-letter word while using an interval of two. He or she would have employed single letters from text words one, three, five, and seven. Any letter within the proper Hebrew word could be used. There seems to have been just one other general rule: letters could fall in any sequence. Thus *cat* could also be spelled *cta*, *act*, *atc*, *tca*, and *tac*.

In summary, to form coded words a biblical author could:

- use one letter per text word
- employ text words spaced at regular intervals
- arrange letters in any sequence.

Under the rules outlined above, the benediction's fifteen Hebrew words conceal fourteen spellings of Jehoiachin, יויכן. The Bible has only one

---

14. Yardeni, "Ancient Amulets," 180.
15. Renz and Rollig, *Handbuch*, 447–56.
16. Rogerson and Davies, "Siloam Tunnel," 146.
17. Barkay, "Priestly Benediction," 177; Waaler, "Revised Date," 43.

## The Jehoiachin Code in Scripture's Priestly Benediction

Jehoiachin, and it clearly establishes his dates. Jehoiachin briefly reigned over Judah before his exile in March of 597 BCE (2 Kgs 24:12). Thirty-seven years later, in late March (Jer 51:31) or early April (2 Kgs 25:27) of 561, the Judean king emerged from a Babylonian prison. One could add a few post-prison years to establish the span during which Jehoiachin might have influenced scripture. That period between 597 and, say, 558 BCE sets the probable limit for the Priestly Benediction's composition. It would have been created during or slightly after Jehoiachin's lifetime—that is, if the coded Jehoiachin spellings are not coincidental. This table shows how the author by accident or intent worked those fourteen coded spellings into the benediction.

### TABLE 1.1—JEHOIACHIN (יויכין) SPELLINGS CONCEALED WITHIN PRIESTLY BENEDICTION

|    | Letter Sequence | Word Interval | Start Verse-Word | End Verse-Word |
|----|-----------------|---------------|------------------|----------------|
| 1  | כויייין         | 1             | 24-1             | 25-3           |
| 2  | יויכין          | 2             | 24-1             | 26-3           |
| 3  | ויייניך         | 1             | 24-2             | 25-4           |
| 4  | ייניך           | 2             | 24-2             | 26-4           |
| 5  | כייוין          | 1             | 24-3             | 25-5           |
| 6  | כוייני          | 2             | 24-3             | 26-5           |
| 7  | יונכיי          | 1             | 25-1             | 26-1           |
| 8  | יניויך          | 2             | 25-1             | 26-6           |
| 9  | יכיניו          | 2             | 25-2             | 26-7           |
| 10 | נכוייי          | 1             | 25-3             | 26-3           |
| 11 | כנייי           | 1             | 25-4             | 26-4           |
| 12 | ייינכו          | 1             | 25-5             | 26-5           |
| 13 | ייניך           | 1             | 26-1             | 26-6           |
| 14 | ינייכו          | 1             | 26-2             | 26-7           |

The *Letter Sequence* column shows the scrambled order of the Hebrew spellings. They are like anagrams, except that letters are drawn from more than one text word. Notice that only item 2 gives the true letter sequence for this version of Jehoiachin, which is יויכן. The *Word Interval* column recognizes how the writer spaced the letters of the concealed words. A 1 indicates he or she drew a letter from six consecutive text words, while a 2 means the writer used every second word. The other columns give the starting and ending text words for each spelling.

Here are details about two of the table's encodings. Item 1 shows a letter sequence of בויין and an interval of one. This coding begins at the first word of Num 6:24, the start of the Priestly Benediction, and ends at the third word of 6:25. יְבָרֶכְךָ יהוה וְיִשְׁמְרֶךָ יָאֵר יהוה פָּנָיו has the words with the letters of the Jehoiachin spelling underlined. Item 2 in the table offers another example. The coded word begins on the same text word, but has an interval of two. That is, the author draws a letter from every other text word, starting with the first. A six-letter coded word requires eleven text words. The appropriate letters of יויכן are shown in underline: יְבָרֶכְךָ יהוה וְיִשְׁמְרֶךָ יָאֵר יהוה פָּנָיו אֵלֶיךָ וִיחֻנֶּךָּ יִשָּׂא יהוה פָּנָיו. These examples illustrate how simply the biblical writer might have conveyed information—should this prove to be an authentic code. Readers are invited to verify the other spellings shown in the table.

The benediction numbers fifteen text words, and it conceals fourteen spellings of Jehoiachin. This is just one short of what a passage of this length could accommodate. Based upon this, it seemed likely that the Priestly Benediction was intended to honor the exiled king of Judah. When a draft of this chapter was shown to Herman Chernoff, Emeritus Professor of Statistics at Harvard University, his first question was: What other names are coded in the benediction? To answer that query, a list was assembled of every personal Hebrew name in scripture, including all spelling variations. To this were added names from rabbinic writings, drawn principally from Marcus Jastrow's *Dictionary*.[18] Archaeology also made its contribution with previously unknown Hebrew names discovered on signature seals.[19] The final list of Hebrew personal names totaled 1,302, ninety-four percent of which are found in the Bible. The list of biblical names is exhaustive, though those from rabbinic writings and archaeology are not (and perhaps cannot be).

The Priestly Benediction contains but thirteen of the twenty-two letters in the Hebrew alphabet. This permits elimination of names con-

---

18. Jastrow, *Dictionary of Targumim, Talmud, and Midrashic Literature*.
19. For example, Avigad, *Hebrew Bullae*.

taining any of the absent letters, leaving 456 names that could have been spelled within the benediction.[20] Many of scripture's personal names have multiple spellings, and Jehoiachin with six variations has more than any. An additional fact is that in 1928 William F. Albright discovered a jar handle with a possible seventh variation, one that does not appear in the Bible.[21] Six of the seven Jehoiachin spellings are included among the 456 Hebrew personal names that could find concealment in the benediction. (The seventh Jehoiachin variation is יכניהו, but since it contains the same letters as יכוניה, it need not be considered.)

The 456 had previously been calibrated as to frequency by running them against a large, randomly drawn sample of scripture.[22] The measure of frequency was the number of coded spellings a single passage contained divided by its opportunities to make such spellings. The next step was to run these 456 names against the text of Num 6:24–26. Table 1.2 shows the results.

20. Of the 456 personal Hebrew names, 427 (93.6 percent) come from the Bible, twenty-seven from archaeological finds, and two from rabbinic sources.

21. Albright, "Seal of Eliakim," 81; "Joiachin in Exile," 50. The following challenge identifying יוכן with Jehoiachin: Malamat, "Judah in the Maelstrom," 138 n. 34; Ussishkin, "Private Seal Impressions," 11.

22. The random sample contains 499 passages. Its mean is twenty-seven words, and it has a fifteen-word minimum and a fifty-word maximum. It includes 885 verses, ninety-eight percent of which come from two-verse passages. (The benediction has three short verses.) The random sample's search program selects the best ratio of spellings to opportunities within passages. The result is that the average lengths of the higher s/o ratios are close to fifteen words, which is the number of words in the Priestly Benediction. The program's minimum for determining opportunities is fifteen words.

## TABLE 1.2—PERSONAL NAMES OF HIGH VALUE CONCEALED WITHIN PRIESTLY BENEDICTION

|   | Personal Name | Hebrew Spelling | Biblical Occurrences | Spellings/ Opportunities | Search Value |
|---|---|---|---|---|---|
| 1 | Cushi | כושי | 4 | 17/30 | A |
| 2 | Shecaniah | שכניהו | 2 | 13/15 | A |
| 3 | Jehoiachin | יויכין | 1 | 14/15 | A |
| 4 | Jehoiachin | יבניה | 6 | 13/21 | A |
| 5 | Jehoiachin | יכוניה | 1 | 14/15 | A |
| 6 | Jehoiachin | כניהו | 6 | 15/21 | B |
| 7 | Jehoiachin | יהויכין | 9 | 10/12 | B |
| 8 | Jehoiachin | יוכן | 0 | 21/30 | B |
| 9 | Jecoliah | יכליהו | 1 | 13/15 | B |

This table displays the nine names that the computer search program selected from the 456 run against the Priestly Benediction. The table's first two columns give the English and Hebrew versions of the names with highest values. Cushi, Shecaniah, and Jecoliah have one appearance, while Jehoiachin has six. The center column shows how often each version appears in Hebrew Scripture. Biblical occurrences range from zero (the jar-handle version of Jehoiachin) to nine.

The table's next column gives the ratios of coded spellings to opportunities within Num 6:24–26. Item 3 of that column summarizes what we already have seen in the prior table. Jehoiachin (יויכין) has fourteen encoded spellings in fifteen opportunities. The spellings/opportunities column is only half the story. Unseen is how common or rare the coded name might be within scripture as a whole. Note that Shecaniah with a 13/15 ratio has an A value while Jecoliah with the same 13/15 ratio draws a B. The reason is that Shecaniah has a less-usual coded spelling, which the computer took account of when assigning the A value.

This brings us to the *Search Value* column. In examining 456 names, the computer selected the nine with highest values: five of them with A and four with B. Cushi, Shecaniah, and three versions of Jehoiachin earned an A. Each had a *Spellings/Opportunities* ratio in the Priestly Benediction that was equal to or higher than its top value in computerized searches of the large sample. An A means the ratio is at least as good as the best ratio in the sample; B is the same or better than the second-best ratio. It is easiest to think of them simply as best and second-best. In this study, five names are best, four are second-best, and 447 are also-rans.

The run of Jehoiachin variations is extraordinary. All six Jehoiachin variations (and just three other names) reach the top nine in a field of 456. If the author acted intentionally, it is hard to say which version he or she wished to emphasize. The Jehoiachin spellings each possessed at least three of the same Hebrew letters, so commonality might have had a little to do with this abundance.[23] But the author would have been as aware as we are that Jehoiachin could be written many ways, and he or she seems to have selected the benediction's words, spacing, and grammar to give maximum play to every Jehoiachin variation.

Examining individual spellings, two Jehoiachin versions—יכוניה and יויכין—convert fourteen of fifteen opportunities into coded spellings. Fourteen of fifteen! For this performance each of those wins an A. For other versions, the ratios are ten of twelve, and thirteen and fifteen of twenty-one. The shortest encoding is יובן. It comes from the jar-handle inscription, and rates a B value for its twenty-one spellings in thirty opportunities. Chapter 6 of Numbers is bare of any A or B Jehoiachin values except for those within the benediction. But there is what could be considered an exception.

Though the Priestly Benediction is an entity, an editor has framed it by a two-verse introduction (Num 6:22–23) and by the single verse that concludes the chapter. Verse 23 ends with להם, "to them." The unknown editor strengthened coding of several Jehoiachin spellings by placing that word in front of the benediction. Inclusion of להם improved the spellings/opportunities ratio of יהויכין from ten of twelve to twelve of fourteen. Using להם as a source of letters also brought כניהו to seventeen (from fifteen) spellings in twenty-one opportunities. This is especially interest-

---

23. Though eight of the nine words that recorded an A or a B shared three common letters (נ, כ, י), there are nine other Hebrew personal names with those same letters that did not score A or B. Also, fifty-three of the 456 personal names shared ה , ו , and י but only six made the list. Common letters may have had some influence, but they were certainly not determinative.

ing because it raises כניהו from a B to an A value (table 1.2 uses B). One doubts that this reinforcement was coincidental.

Before drawing final conclusions about any code, readers may wish to verify the letter sequences in each table. Table 1.1 is self-evident, and for table 1.2 the note supplies what is needed to trace the other Jehoiachin versions.[24] This next note contains sequences for the three non-Jehoiachin words—Cushi, Shecaniah, and Jecoliah.[25] All told, *the Priestly Benediction carries within its short text eighty-seven coded spellings of Jehoiachin.*[26] The question is not whether these spellings exist but rather whether they are coincidental. Before we address the coincidence question, here is a review:

- Four hundred fifty-six Hebrew personal names contain only the thirteen letters appearing in Num 6:24–26, the Priestly Benediction
- Computer runs against a large sample of scripture, using particular rules, established A, B, and other values for frequencies of those 456 names
- Among the particular rules are that each spelling uses one letter per text word, with text words spaced at regular intervals, and with letters in any sequence
- All 456 names were tested against Num 6:24–26 to determine the presence of A or B values
- Nine Hebrew personal names, six of which are variations of Jehoiachin, recorded A or B values
- The six Jehoiachin variations made a total of eighty-seven coded spellings within the benediction's fifteen text words.

So far we have considered Jehoiachin spellings that use multiple text words. But squarely in the middle of the Priestly Benediction is a shorthand

---

24. Starting words within verses (24-2, 25-1, etc.) and intervals (1, 2, etc.) are shown for spellings 4 through 8 in table 2. For יכניה: (1) 24-2, 3; 25-1, 2, 3, 4, 5; 26-2; (2) 24-2, 3; 25-1, 3; (3) 24-2. For יכוניה: (1) 24-1, 2, 3; 25-2, 3, 4, 5; 26-1, 2; (2) 24-1, 2, 3; 25-1, 2. For כניהו: (1) 24-2, 3; 25-1, 2, 3, 4, 5; 26-1, 2; (2) 24-2, 3; 25-1, 2, 3; (3) 24-2. For יהויכין: (1) 24-1, 2; 25-2, 3, 4, 5; 26-1; (2) 24-1, 2, 3. For יוכן: (1) 24-3; 25-1, 2, 3, 4, 5; 26-1, 2, 3; (2) 24-2, 25-1, 2, 3, 4, 5; (3) 24-2; 25-2, 3; (4) 24-2, 3.

25. Intervals, verses, and starting words for כושי are: (1) 24-1; 25-3, 4, 5; 26-1, 2, 3, 4; (2) 24-1, 3; 25-2, 4; (3) 24-3; 25-1, 3; (4) 24-1, 3. For שכניה: (1) 24-1, 2, 3; 25-1, 2, 3, 4, 5; 26-1, 2; (2) 24-1, 3; 25-2. For יכליהו: (1) 24-2, 25-2, 3, 4, 5; 26-1, 2; (2) 24-1, 2, 3; 25-1, 2.

26. Jehoiachin spellings in items 3–8 of table 1.2 total 87 (14 + 13 + 14 + 15 + 10 + 21).

version of this technique. Word eight of the fifteen-word benediction is ויחנך, "and be gracious to you." That single word is an anagram containing the four letters of יוכן, which is the jar-handle spelling of Jehoiachin. (An anagram transposes letters to form a different word.) This will become important later. For now, note the anagram as a curiosity.

## ARE JEHOIACHIN SPELLINGS COINCIDENTAL?

Is the grouping of coded versions of Jehoiachin in the Priestly Benediction a coincidence? The answer is no, it is not coincidental that six of the nine high-value names in the Priestly Benediction are variations of Jehoiachin. Imagine choosing while blindfolded six red balls and three black balls in nine draws from a vat containing 456 balls, six of them red and the remaining 450 colored black. The odds against picking all six red balls (the Jehoiachin spellings) in nine pulls are 1.7 billion to one.[27] Understood in this way, the six A and B groups of Jehoiachin spellings in the Priestly Benediction cannot have occurred by chance alone. Within the benediction there is strong evidence of a code that uses one letter per text word, with letters in any sequence, from text words spaced at regular intervals.

Here is a different approach. There are eighty-seven coded Jehoiachin spellings concealed within the fifteen-word Priestly Benediction. To test whether this concentration is unusual, a random sample of five hundred fifteen-word passages was chosen to represent Hebrew Scripture as a whole.[28] Next, the six Jehoiachin versions were run against those five hundred passages.

---

27. P = a combination of (9 choose 6) (447 choose 3) / 456 choose 9 = $5.72 \times 10^{-10}$. (This is known as a hypergeometric probability since the sampling is partitioned without replacement.)

28. To obtain five hundred fifteen-word passages, chapters were randomly selected without replacement and fifteen-word verses or combinations of consecutive verses totaling fifteen words were picked. In all, 293 of scripture's 929 chapters were needed to assemble the five-hundred-passage sample. Numbers 6:24–26 and verses containing "Jehoiachin" would have been excluded from the sample, but none was picked.

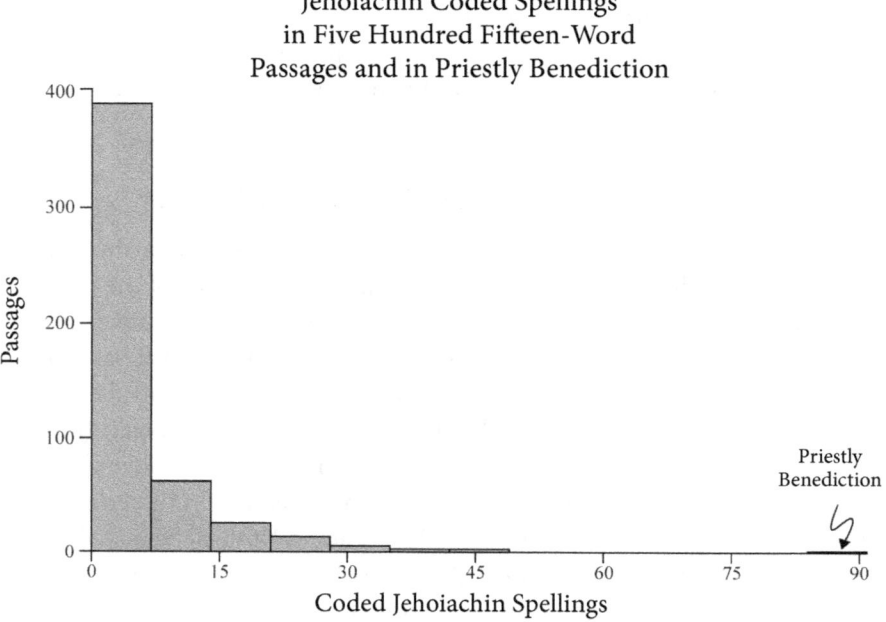

Jehoiachin Coded Spellings
in Five Hundred Fifteen-Word
Passages and in Priestly Benediction

The chart portrays the result. Nearly four hundred passages had seven or fewer coded spellings (the bar on the left), sixty-two contained eight to fourteen spellings, and totals diminished quickly thereafter. The best that the sample could do was two passages with forty-three Jehoiachin spellings each. The chart contrasts this with the Priestly Benediction passage, which conceals eighty-seven spellings, twice as many as the best from the five-hundred-passage sample. There is only one chance in ten thousand that the proportion of Jehoiachin encodings in the Priestly Benediction follows that of the five-hundred-passage sample.[29]

In summary, these tests show that the coded spellings within the Priestly Benediction differ from Hebrew Scripture as a whole in ways that are statistically significant. What brings this significance to light? The coding rules do. They produce the data, which are the eighty-seven discrete Jehoiachin spellings. To repeat, within the Priestly Benediction there is strong evidence of a code that uses one letter per text word, with letters in any sequence, from text words spaced at regular intervals.

---

29. The chi-square proportions are 87/1, 2,508/500. P = $1.01 \times 10^{-4}$, or one in ten thousand. Spellings in the sample total 2,508.

## The Jehoiachin Code in Scripture's Priestly Benediction

Replication is a way to validate (or discredit) evidence. A second batch of five hundred fifteen-word verses was randomly chosen from Hebrew scripture, a sample that by design contained none of the verses from the previous sample. Testing produced two A or B Jehoiachin values, which is the same as the first sample. In addition, sample two contained ten percent *fewer* coded spellings overall than the first sample. When outcomes of the second sample are compared with Jehoiachin values and spellings in the Priestly Benediction, results are the same as or more extreme than those obtained with the first sample. This confirms the original finding: coded Jehoiachin spellings within the Priestly Benediction differ from Hebrew scripture as a whole in ways that are statistically significant. In short, the Jehoiachin coding is not coincidental.

### WAS JEHOIACHIN A SUBSTITUTE KING?

The benediction also contains other coded spellings that help to date Num 6:24–26. That coding involves the cuneiform term for substitute king, *sarpuhi* (שרפוהי), a word not found in Hebrew Scripture). In the ancient Near East, an eclipse was an omen that the ruler had offended the gods and must die, though planet location and favorable shadowing could overcome this omen. But just as often, portents were unfavorable, so to honor the portents while avoiding the fate, the true king crowned another. That substitute then personally assumed the fate that the gods had decreed against the ruling king. The replacement's reign was never longer than one hundred days, and sometime within that period the authorities dispatched him. Then, with the omens satisfied, the king could safely return to his throne. Seventh-century BCE archives from Nineveh reveal that the Assyrian kings employed substitute kings.[30] Professor Simo Parpola, who edited the archives, has told the author that the custom originated in Babylon and probably also was practiced by the Neo-Babylonians.[31]

Was Jehoiachin a Babylonian *sarpuhi*? Quite possibly he was. The Priestly Benediction and the verses adjacent to it are filled with Jehoiachin-Sarpuhi coded spellings of the highest quality. Within the benediction itself (Num 6:24–26) there are twenty-three such spellings that combine

---

30. Parpola I and Parpola II. The excursus in Part II discusses *sarpuhi*. We suggest that scholars start with the excursus before going to the letters that mention Assyrian substitutes. The catalogue of sources in xxvi–xxxii of the second volume is most helpful.

31. April 29, 2004 email and July 16, 2006 conversation with Professor Parpola.

the Babylonian loan word with the six versions of Jehoiachin. These coded groups produce three A values and single values rated B, D, and E. The third column of table 1.3 shows this. The usual practice is to ignore values below the B level. However, this case merits an exception because the verses that frame the benediction have been artfully worded so as to greatly increase Jehoiachin-Sarpuhi spellings. These jump from twenty-three to forty-three, and the groups rated B, D, and E move up to A, which gives the Jehoiachin-Sarpuhi versions a straight-A report card. The table's two right columns show this transformation.

TABLE 1.3—COMPARING JEHOIACHIN-SARPUHI CODED SPELLINGS FOR PRIESTLY BENEDICTION ONLY AND FOR BENEDICTION WITH ADJACENT VERSES (SPELLINGS/OPPORTUNITIES AND VALUES)

|   | Message | Hebrew Spelling | Benediction Only S/O | Value | With Adjacent Verses S/O | Value |
|---|---|---|---|---|---|---|
| 1 | JehoiachinSarpuhi | יויכינשרפוהי | 4/4 | A | 8/8 | A |
| 2 | JehoiachinSarpuhi | יכוניהשרפוהי | 4/4 | A | 8/8 | A |
| 3 | JehoiachinSarpuhi | יהויכינשרפוהי | 3/3 | A | 8/8 | A |
| 4 | JehoiachinSarpuhi | יכניהשרפוהי | 4/5 | B | 8/8 | A |
| 5 | JehoiachinSarpuhi | כניהושרפוהי | 4/5 | D | 5/5 | A |
| 6 | JehoiachinSarpuhi | יוכנשרפוהי | 4/6 | E | 6/6 | A |

The Priestly Benediction's author certainly did an exceptional job in coding his twenty-three Jehoiachin-Sarpuhi spellings within just fifteen words. Also, just as certainly the editors who framed this short masterpiece between other verses outdid themselves. Compared to the grace of the Priestly Benediction, the phrases that these writers chose are choppy and repetitive—but now we know the reason why. They picked their words to encode their news. Here is that text: "The Lord spoke to Moses, saying: Speak to Aaron and his sons, saying, Thus you shall bless the Israelites: You shall say to them ... [the benediction follows] ... So they shall put my name on the Israelites, and I will bless them" (Num 6:22–23, 27). Table 1.4 within the note allows scholars to verify the Jehoiachin-Sarpuhi coding.³²

Again the question: Was Jehoiachin a *sarpuhi*? The coding evidence appears overwhelming. And what do astronomy and scripture say? The eclipse that probably triggered Jehoiachin's substitute kingship occurred over Babylon on February 19, 561 BCE.³³ Scripture records that King Evil-Marduk released Jehoiachin from prison on either March 31 or April 2 (Jer 52:13 and 2 Kgs 25:27).³⁴ Each spring during the New Year's Festival the king of Babylon was crowned anew. Therefore, any substitute reigning at the time had to perish before the festival began, lest the stand-in rather than the true king receive coronation for the coming twelve months. In the year of Jehoiachin's release, New Year's Day fell on April 6. If Jehoiachin did indeed become Babylon's king, he would have died on or before April 6, 561 BCE, less than a week after he left prison.

The substitute-king possibility could explain the three non-Jehoiachin coded names in the Priestly Benediction. Jecoliah could have been Jehoiachin's queen. If she was, she too would have died, because the practice was to kill both wife and husband.³⁵ As to the other highly rated names, Cushi and Shecaniah might have been members of Jehoiachin's retinue in Babylon, and so have been executed with the royal couple.

The 2 Kgs 25 and Jer 52 texts that cover the end of Jehoiachin's life are rich in hints about substitution. Jehoiachin is taken from prison and

32. This table 1.4 shows Jehoiachin-sarpuhi coded spellings for the Priestly Benediction and its adjacent verses (Num 6:23–27):

|   | Hebrew Coded Word | Start First Spelling | First Spelling Sequence | Start Last Spelling | End Last Spelling |
|---|---|---|---|---|---|
| 1 | יויכינשרפוהי | 8 | 23-10 | נירהיוושייפכי | 25-1 | 26-7 |
| 2 | יכוניהשרפוהי | 8 | 23-10 | ניוהישרופכי | 25-1 | 26-7 |
| 3 | יהויכינשרפוהי | 8 | 23-10 | ניוהיהירופכיש | 25-1 | 27-1 |
| 4 | יכניהשרפוהי | 8 | 23-10 | נשרהייויהפך | 25-1 | 26-6 |
| 5 | כניהושרפוהי | 5 | 23-13 | היהשרופכניו | 25-1 | 26-6 |
| 6 | יוכנשרפוהי | 6 | 23-12 | רההכושיופינ | 25-1 | 26-5 |

33. Kudlek and Mickler, *Eclipses of the Ancient Near East*, 148.

34. Parker and Dubberstein, *Babylonian Chronology*, 28 provides the basis for Julian dating.

35. Lambert, "Substitute King Ritual," 110; Parpola I, 229; Parpola II, xxvi.

given new clothes. He eats at the king's table and sits upon a throne higher than that of any other king in Babylon. Finally, King Evil-Marduk lifts up his head, perhaps by decapitating him. Most interesting is that the Second Kings account uses "day" four times and the Jeremiah one employs it five. These might signify a difference of opinion about whether Jehoiachin reigned four days rather than five before his execution. Those wanting a fuller discussion of Jehoiachin's possible substitute kingship may wish to consult the author's 2005 book.[36]

## COMPARING THE AMULETS WITH SCRIPTURE

Returning to the Ketef Hinnom plaques, the silver amulets contain fragments of other biblical texts and end with portions of the Priestly Benediction. Reconstructions by the Barkay group show differences between the plaques, as well as between them and the MT's version of the Priestly Benediction.[37] Both amulets lack the second *kaph* in the opening word of the MT's benediction, while Ketef Hinnom II omits the *waw* in the benediction's third word and also drops the *waw* from שלום at the end of the benediction. The Ketef Hinnom I text breaks off after the benediction's sixth word, while the scribe incising the other amulet either committed a copying error by omitting five words, or simply abridged the full benediction. Barkay thinks "the shortened text may be a paraphrase based on the complete version."[38]

A final matter is whether the amulets also contain significant levels of Jehoiachin coding. Ketef Hinnom I has only six of the benediction's fifteen words, so we must concentrate upon Ketef Hinnom II, which has the initial seven and the final three words of the MT's text.[39] To make the MT and the Ketef Hinnom II texts of equal fifteen-word length, let us include the five words on the amulet that preceded its partial benediction. Here are those fifteen words:

הא ליהוה העזר והגער ברע יברך יהוה ישמרך יאר יהוה פניו אליך וישם

לך שלם

36. Kavanagh, *Secrets*, 54–69.
37. Barkay et al., "Amulets," 61, 68.
38. Barkay, "Priestly Benediction," 166.
39. Barkay et al., "Amulets," 68 shows the painstaking reconstruction of Ketef Hinnom II.

## The Jehoiachin Code in Scripture's Priestly Benediction

These yield no Jehoiachin-Sarpuhi combinations and just twenty-two coded spellings of the Jehoiachin versions, compared to eighty-seven for the MT of Num 6:24–26.[40] Moreover, the amulet's spellings produced not a single A or B value for any of the names that were highly rated in the Priestly Benediction. The Ketef Hinnom scribe drastically reduced the hidden spellings by truncating the benediction and omitting three of its original letters. The best explanation is that he or she knew nothing about the Priestly Benediction's Jehoiachin coding.

What does all this mean for dating the amulets? Coding proves that Jehoiachin is the subject of the Priestly Benediction.[41] Also, the powerful Jehoiachin-Sarpuhi coding makes it likely that he was a substitute king. If so, we can establish the date of Jehoiachin's death with precision. He would have died on April 5 or 6 of 561. It follows that because Num 6:24–26 *is* a benediction, it was written after rather than before the Judean king's death. This in turn places an upper limit on the Ketef Hinnom amulets. They could not have been etched before the spring of 561, and perhaps were made well after that. Another consideration is that the scribe who carved the second amulet apparently was ignorant of the benediction's concealed spellings. This knowledge gap suggests a separation in time between composing the original benediction and etching the amulets, an interval that could even be measured in generations.

Though coding was surprisingly common in the ancient world, it is not a light thing to announce a new biblical code. Yet this chapter maintains—and supports with examples and probabilities—that a previously unrecognized code exists within Hebrew Scripture. The code described by Michael Drosnin in *Bible Code* (1997) is worth noting.[42] It uses long sequences of letters to form words that predict events. He thinks that no human hand could have fashioned such a thing, while in contrast this chapter's Jehoiachin code clearly was done by humans. Drosnin's code

---

40. Jehoiachin-coded spellings on the amulet begin at words 5 through 11. Text-word intervals are in parentheses. The initial words for יויכין and יבוניה are: (1) 6, 7, 8, 9; יכניה: (1) 7, 8, 9, 10; יהוכין: (1) 6, 7, 8; בניהו: (1) 7, 9, 10; and יובן: (1) 8, 9, 10, 11. Non-Jehoiachin spellings are כושי: (1) 6, 10, 11, 12; (2) 2, 4, 6, 8. For שכניהו: (1) 6, 7, 8, 10. For יכליהו: (1) 7, 8, 9, 10; (2) 2, 4. For שרפוהי: (1) 6, 7, 8.

41  As an aside, an editor prefaced the benediction with "sons of Israel." However, an individual is clearly the subject of Num 6:24–26 since six of its fifteen words employ the second-person singular.

42. For critiques of Drosnin see Witztum, "Genesis Letter Sequences," 429–38; and McKay et al., "Solving the Code Puzzle," 150–73.

can skip thousands of letters before adding a letter to make a word; the Jehoiachin spellings use a maximum of four words before selecting a letter, and anagrams use but one text word apiece. The Drosnin code claims to predict modern events such as the Holocaust and the Kennedy and Rabin assassinations, while this book's code confines itself to the sixth century BCE. Both codes employ probabilities.

Chapter 2 will show how Ezekiel, Jeremiah, and Second Isaiah employed a variation of this newly discovered code against King Jehoiachin.

## 2

## Extending the Bible Code

### INTRODUCING ANAGRAMS

THE OPENING CHAPTER SET forth the basics of the so-called Jehoiachin code within Hebrew Scripture: one letter from text words at regular intervals with hidden spellings made from letters in any sequence. The code could handle short words like יוכן, Jehoiachin, and longer ones like יהויכינשרפוהי, Jehoiachin-Sarpuhi. And as the Priestly Benediction proves, in expert hands it could be used with Scripture's most elevated language. Readers will appreciate the sorts of things the code can achieve. So far it has allowed us to place an upper limit on the date of the Priestly Benediction, identify Jehoiachin as the subject, and learn that the Judean exile died as a substitute king. In addition, the code has contributed to dating the Ketef Hinnom amulets.

Did the benediction's author invent the code for his sole use? That is most unlikely. The skill with which the writer (or writers) blended those fifteen perfect text words with eighty-seven concealed Jehoiachin spellings bespeaks years of experience and no little schooling. Also, the editors who added most of the Jehoiachin-Sarpuhi ciphers in framing the Priestly Benediction employed that same sophisticated craft. And of course the benediction was addressed to others in the Diaspora, experts who would well know how to search beneath the text. This chapter will show that during the Exile coding was widely used. We shall start with the Major Prophets and their anagrams. (An anagram transposes the letters of one word to spell another.)

# The Exilic Code

## EZEKIEL ASSAILS KING JEHOIACHIN

Eight hundred seventy-nine words in Scripture contain the four letters יוכן, which is the jug-handle version of Jehoiachin.[1] Ninety-five of these anagrams are within the book of Ezekiel, a figure far out of proportion to its length.[2] Ezekiel's frequent use of Jehoiachin anagrams is plausible since the prophet shared over thirty years in Babylonia with the Judean king and—assuming there is something to these anagrams—used the code to convey news about Jehoiachin. What did Ezekiel have to report?

Ezekiel 16 is remarkable because it contains more Jehoiachin anagrams than any other chapter of Scripture. The probability that this concentration is due to coincidence is zero.[3] Here are specific examples of the chapter's Jehoiachin anagrams. In v. 15 the prophet ostensibly addresses only Jerusalem: "You ... lavished your whorings [תזנותיך] on any passerby." Note the Jehoiachin anagram for יוכן within the word for whoring. Ezekiel liked this so well that he used it four times more in vv. 22, 33, 34, and 36. Warming to his theme, with another anagram Ezekiel likened Jehoiachin's conduct to "the deeds of a brazen whore; building [בבנותיך] your platform at the head of every street" (vv. 30–31). In a previous verse the prophet expanded the indictment: "You took your sons and your daughters [בנותיך] ... and these you sacrificed to them [idols] to be devoured" (v. 20). This verse's יוכן anagram seems to make the shocking accusation that Jehoiachin had sacrificed his children to Babylonian gods—though one hopes Ezekiel was exaggerating for effect.

Another passage portrayed Sodom and Samaria as sisters of Jerusalem, but even they "have not done as you and your daughters [ובנותיך] have done" (v. 48; see 55, which also uses daughters). The judg-

---

1. The twenty-four ways to spell a four-letter word (abcd, abdc, acbd . . . bacd, etc.) can be assembled with a single search using BibleWorks. After running, send results to a word-processing file, and then cull verses that contain duplicate anagrams. (I found that ninety-five of the Bible's 879 legitimate יוכן anagrams share a verse with another anagram.)

2. The probability that so many Jehoiachin anagrams occur by chance in Ezekiel is one in thirty-two million. The chi-square proportions are 95/19123 and 784/285778. P = $3.14 \times 10^{-8}$. The first proportion consists of the Jehoiachin anagrams and words in the book of Ezekiel, while the second has the anagrams and words in the remainder of scripture. To replicate this data, follow the instructions in note 1.

3. The chi-square proportions are 17/833 and 862/304,068. P = $9.75 \times 10^{-21}$. The first proportion consists of the Jehoiachin anagrams and words in Ezekiel 16, and the second has the anagrams and words in the remainder of scripture.

ment was that God would "bring [ונתתיך] blood upon you in wrath . . . They shall strip you of your clothes . . . and leave you [והניחוך] naked and bare" (vv. 38–39). And further: "Because you have not remembered the days of your youth [נעוריך] . . . I have returned your deeds upon your head . . ." (v. 43). Ezekiel 16 employs seventeen Jehoiachin (יוכן) anagrams (vv. 27, 45, and 56 have not been quoted), and all but one are hostile. The only exception is נעוריך in v. 60. That talks of covenant, and is clearly from an editor.

Jehoiachin was one of many captive kings held in the Babylonian court, where protocol must have been long-established and strictly enforced. Frequent public worship of Marduk, Shemesh, and other gods in Babylon's pantheon were surely duties of the court's puppet kings. As to Jehoiachin's children, there would have been pressure to devote them to service of one of Babylon's powerful temples, a service that might conceivably have included child sacrifice.[4] While we may feel sympathy for Jehoiachin, Ezekiel did not. To him, idol worship was the most grievous possible offense.

Ezekiel used the יוכן anagram elsewhere in his writings to continue his attacks.[5] And what was to happen to the exiled king? "I will fling you [ונטשתיך] into the wilderness . . ." (29:5); "They shall cut off your nose and your ears [ואזניך] . . ." (23:25); and "I . . . will hand you over [ונתתיך] as plunder to the nations" (25:7). Ezekiel sufficiently valued another anagram to work it into three prophecies: "You shall be no more [ואינך]" (26:21; also see 27:36 and 28:19).

When Jehoiachin's supporters protested the abuse, the prophet retorted with this: "Yet you say, 'The way of the Lord is unfair [תכן].' Hear now, O house of Israel: Is my way unfair [תכן]? It is not your ways that are unfair [יתכנו]?" (18:25). Ezekiel pairs the Jehoiachin anagram יוכן with the unusual verb, תכן "to measure," and he repeats that pairing four verses later (18:29).

In this instance, to what was the prophet responding? Probably to the opening verses of Hannah's prayer in 1 Samuel, where anagrams of יוכן flank criticism of an arrogant talker: "There is no Rock like our God [כאלהינו]. Talk no more so very proudly, let not arrogance come from

---

4. Nabonidus, the last king of Babylon, installed his own daughter as high priestess of Nanna in Ur. Clay, "Nabonidus Cylinder," 31–33.

5. See Ezek 20:39 (במתנותיכם); 22:4 (שנותיך); 23:29 זנוניך and ותזנותיך), 35 (תזנותיך), 49 (גלוליכן); 28:18 (עוניך); 33:25 (ועינכם); and 36:31 (עונתיכם).

your mouth; for the Lord is a God of knowledge, and by him actions are weighed [תכן]. The bows of the mighty are broken, but the feeble [ונכשלים] gird on strength" (1 Sam 2:2–4). Ps 75:2–4 and Prov 16:2–3 have the same verb-anagram arrangement and probably are part of the same argument. The psalm supports Jehoiachin while Proverbs sides with Ezekiel. This is exactly the sort of back-and-forth that one should expect from this system of anagram codes.

Anagrams also reveal that the debate about Jehoiachin's behavior continued within Ezekiel's own book. Either a changed Ezekiel or a more-sympathetic editor used coded anagrams to temper the prophet's harsh views of Jehoiachin: "Yet, I will remember my covenant with you in the days of your youth [נעוריך], and I will establish with you an everlasting covenant" (Ezek 16:60). This next continues the covenant language: "You shall be my people, and I [ואנכי] will be your God" (36:28). Another example is, "On the day that I cleanse you from all your iniquities [עונתיכם], I will cause the towns to be inhabited" (36:33). Finally, 39:28 promises the exiles would be gathered [וכנסתים] "into their own land." Though these are positive citations, the book of Ezekiel contains fifteen anagrams castigating Jehoiachin for every anagram defending him.

## OTHER PROPHETS USE ANAGRAM CODE

Does Second Isaiah share Ezekiel's critical attitude toward Jehoiachin? Encodings indicate that to an extent he does. "You have wearied me with your iniquities [בעונתיך]," says Isa 43:24, using the anagram for יוכן. Also, "Stand fast in your enchantments . . . with which you have labored from your youth [מנעוריך]!" (47:12); and in v. 15 the same Jehoiachin anagram is linked with traders and stargazers. Elsewhere, the prophet mocks, "'My idol did them, my carved image and my cast image [ונסכי] commanded them'" (48:5). And finally, "Because of your sins [בעונתיכם] you were sold" (50:1).

But Second Isaiah matches neither the frequency nor the ferocity of Ezekiel's attacks upon the exiled king. To the contrary, most of the Isaiah anagrams are positive. At first the prophet contrasts the awesome God to the no-gods Jehoiachin has chosen: "Who is like me [כמוני] . . . ?" asks the Lord (44:7); "I will dry up your rivers [ונהרתיך]" (44:27); and "I am God, and there is no one like me [כמוני]" (46:9). Then God makes this extraordinary pledge: "'I will give you [ונתתיך] as a light to the nations, that my salvation may reach to the end of the earth'" (49:6). A woman will forget her nursing child, "yet I [ואנכי] will not forget you." Moreover, "your daughters [ובנתיך]" will be carried on the shoulders of liberators (49:15, 22). A threat with two יוכן anagrams against unnamed enemies follows: "I will make your oppressors [מוניך] eat their own flesh, and they shall be drunk [ישכרון] with their own blood" (49:26).

Isaiah 54 continues the theme of promise: "Your habitations [משכנותיך]" shall be extended, and "the disgrace of your widowhood [אלמנותיך]" remembered no longer (54:2, 4). "In righteousness you shall be established [תכונני]," writes the prophet (54:14). Reaching beyond the corpus generally attributed to Second Isaiah, chapter 60 says, "I will appoint Peace as your overseer and Righteousness as your taskmaster [ונגשיך]" (60:17). Four other pro-Jehoiachin anagrams also grace this extraordinary chapter.[6]

Like Ezekiel, Second Isaiah uses anagrams to condemn Jehoiachin's idolatry, but unlike Ezekiel, the unknown prophet devotes far more of his material to sustaining his king. Interestingly, both prophets allot the same proportion of their words to the יוכן anagrams. Though Second Isaiah has only twenty-two of them while Ezekiel has ninety-five, the difference is due not to more frequent use but to Ezekiel's greater length.

The book of Jeremiah contains close to three dozen negative Jehoiachin anagrams. "Your whoring [בזנותיך]," "your iniquities [עונותיכם]," "provoked me [הכעסוני] . . . with their images," and "made a fatal mistake [בנפשותיכם]" are among the prophet's citations (Jer 3:2; 5:25; 8:19; and 42:20). He accused, "Under every green tree . . . you sprawled and played the whore. Yet I [ואנכי] planted you as a choice vine" (2:20–21). Jeremiah himself witnessed several deportations, and prophesied that Jehoiachin and the soon-to-be-exiled King Zedekiah were like inedible "bad figs [וכתאנים]" (24:8). And Jehoiachin would "see the king of Babylon eye to eye [ועיניך]" (34:3). Then Jeremiah made his threat about exile another way: "Chemosh shall go out into exile, with his priests [כהניו] and attendants" (48:7). The prophet repeated the יוכן anagram in "priests" five more times (2:26; 5:31; 33:18; 34:19; and 49:3)—and all but one (33:18) were pejorative.

---

6. For other pro-Jehoiachin anagrams see Isa 60:4 (ובנתיך), 7 (ישרתונך), 8 (וכיונים), and 10 (ישרתונך). Five Jehoiachin anagrams in Second Isaiah chapters have not been mentioned. They are: ואנכי in 50:5; 51:15; and 54:16; as well as כיונק in 53:2, and ומכאבינו in 53:4.

Jeremiah complained that not listening "has been your way since your youth [מנעוריך]" (22:21). These are similar: "You shall call to them, but they will not answer you [יענוכה]" and "I [ואנכי] myself have spoken to you persistently, and you have not obeyed me" (7:27; 35:14). False worship was one of Jehoiachin's offenses, for the people "have forsaken me, and have profaned [וינכרו] this place by making offerings in it to other gods" (19:4). Wives (ונשיכם) were also involved in the apostasy (44:25). Cakes [כונים] for worship of the queen of heaven was a Jehoiachin anagram that Jeremiah used twice (7:18; 44:19), and Jewish devotees in Egypt told the prophet that "our kings [מלכינו]" had worshipped the queen of heaven with no ill effects (44:17). The note lists a final group of anti-Jehoiachin anagrams.[7]

Jeremiah proclaimed that Jehoiachin would never again rule in Judah, and that none of his offspring would sit upon the throne of David (Jer 22:24–30). The prophet was correct, of course, but he does not explain the king's offense. Coded anagrams, however, explain it very well—Jehoiachin worshipped other gods.

Like Second Isaiah's chapters and the book of Ezekiel, the Jeremiah text also contains anagrams that support King Jehoiachin. Four come from chapters 31 and 32, which scholars identify as a separate unit within the book. "I am going to restore the fortunes of the tents of Jacob, and have compassion on his dwellings [ומשכנתיו]" is one example (30:18). Another is, "Keep your voice from weeping, and your eyes [ועיניך] from tears (31:16)." These others are couched in covenant language: "a covenant that they broke, though I [ואנכי] was their husband," as well as "You shall be my people, and I [ואנכי] will be your God" (31:32, 30:22; see also 11:4). Some coded words even portray Jehoiachin as a military leader vanquishing enemies (49:19, 22; 50:44; 51:12, 25), and two others (2:2; 7:7) fall in no particular category.

Ezekiel and Jeremiah use Jehoiachin anagrams in similar ways. Both Ezekiel and Jeremiah harshly condemn the exiled king for his idolatry, though their books do contain passages about compassion and forgiveness. Whether or not editors wrote these latter verses is a question for others. Second Isaiah, however, speaks far more words in support of the beleaguered king. There is a reason for citing so many passages. It is to

---

7. Thirteen anti-Jehoiachin anagrams not yet cited are: Jer 2:25 word 1, 32–7; 3:19–1; 5:17–6; 6:23–2; 7:21–5; 20:4–14; 23:32–14; 29:23–17; 48:2–10, 46–11; 49:10–15, 18–4.

offer readers sufficient material to decide if Jehoiachin anagrams constitute part of a bona fide code. These items favor that conclusion:

- There is a thirty-two-million-to-one probability that the concentration of anagrams in Ezekiel cannot be due solely to chance.
- The anagram technique is simple and easy to apply.
- Anagrams often improve understanding of the passage.
- The Priestly Benediction contains a Jehoiachin anagram.
- Other codes, including anagrams, exist within Hebrew Scriptures.

This book will return again and again to the code identified within the Priestly Benediction and to the anagram technique illustrated above. Before moving on, pause to consider what anagrams have shown us. They establish that Second Isaiah appears to have been active during Jehoiachin's lifetime, give context to over one hundred prophetic passages, and reveal the extraordinary fault lines between the sixth-century prophets and their exiled king. Now it is time to present what may be the most important development in Hebrew Scripture's code.

## THE ATHBASH CODE

Athbash is a well-established code within Scripture. The *IDB* defines athbash as "A Hebrew cryptographic scheme in which the letters of the alphabet in reverse were substituted" by using parallel rows of letters.[8] For example, the athbash of Babylon, בבל, is ששך. Jeremiah 51:41 reads, "How Sheshach is taken . . . How Babylon has become an object of horror among the nations!" For the RSV, the meaning of Jer 51:41 was so clear that it simply translated the cipher as "Babylon" and footnoted "Sheshach." The NRSV reversed that, using "Sheshach" and footnoting "Babylon."[9] Jeremiah has a second example of athbash. Two words in Jer 51:1 contain the athbash for "Chaldeans," another term for Babylonians. (The Septuagint overrode the cipher and substituted the Greek for "Chaldeans." In doing so the translator proved he knew his athbash.) A decade ago Scott B. Noegel used the

---

8. Roberts, "Athbash," 306. The newsletter of the American Cryptogram Association called athbash an "unusually-playful cipher . . . a monoalphabetic Beaufort system." Dendai, "Mezuzah Cryptogram," 88.

9. The NRSV's footnote to Jer 51:41 reads, "*Sheshach* is a cryptogram for *Babel*, "Babylon."

computer to translate the entire book of Jeremiah into athbash.[10] Then he scanned the ciphered text for meaningful Hebrew words. This ingenious approach yielded nine additional athbash possibilities, bringing likely athbash occurrences in Jeremiah to a dozen.

In the athbash cipher, the letters above and the letters below are interchangeable. For example, the athbash of יעקב, "Jacob," is מזדש. The arrows in the center row show the exchange.

ATHBASH OF יעקב = מזדש

| כ | י | ט | ח | ז | ו | ה | ד | ג | ב | א |
|---|---|---|---|---|---|---|---|---|---|---|
| ↓ |   |   |   | ↑ |   |   | ↑ |   | ↓ |   |
| ל | מ | נ | ס | ע | פ | צ | ק | ר | ש | ת |

A biblical author who wanted to encode "Jacob" could use the athbash version מזדש as an alternate for יעקב. This would give the writer a greater choice in selecting text words that supported the coded spelling. But once substitution is agreed upon there is no reason to stop at just two versions of Jacob. There are, after all, twenty-two letters in the Hebrew alphabet, and so far we have used but two of them as a first letter—*yod* and *mem*. The way to coax more spellings from the athbash array is to rotate it: raise the bottom right letter to the top right and drop the top left one to the bottom left. The rotation is like that of a tractor tread, moving counterclockwise. This supplies a third way to spell Jacob, which is כהבק. Again, the arrows show the exchange. Note that the rotation pushes two of the יעקב letters opposite each other, which is shown by the up-and-down paired arrows.

---

10. Noegel, "*Atbash* in Jeremiah," 82–89, 160–66, 247–50.

## Extending the Bible Code

### ATHBASH OF יעקב = כהבק

| ת | א | ב | ג | ד | ה | ו | ז | ח | ט | י |
|---|---|---|---|---|---|---|---|---|---|---|
|   |   | ↓↑ |   |   | ↑ |   |   |   |   | ↓ |
| ש | ר | ק | צ | פ | ע | ס | נ | מ | ל | כ |

Then nine more rotations produce nine additional athbash spellings, making eleven athbash versions plus the original true one—twelve in all. But the rotation after that yields a duplicate, which makes us look elsewhere to move the total from twelve to twenty-two. Making the first athbash word מזדש into the reference word does the trick, as this last table illustrates.

### ATHBASH OF מזדש = חנפת

| ת | א | ב | ג | ד | ה | ו | ז | ח | ט | י |
|---|---|---|---|---|---|---|---|---|---|---|
| ↑ |   |   |   | ↓ |   |   | ↓ | ↑ |   |
| ש | ר | ק | צ | פ | ע | ס | נ | מ | ל | כ |

Nine more rotations using מזדש as the reference word completes the process. The ancient writer (and the modern researcher) now has twenty-two versions of Jacob to use in encoding biblical texts. The note gives the athbash versions of Jacob, while appendix 1 shows all possible athbash letter exchanges.[11]

Here is anecdotal evidence that someone used rotating athbash to encode the name Jacob in Isa 40–55. The first example is from the ninth word of Isa 43:24 through the first word of the following verse, seven text words in all. Its translation is, "But you have burdened me with your sins; you have wearied me with your iniquities. I, I am He . . ."

```
   1      14      13      12      11    10    9
```

הרויתני אךָ העבדתני בחַטאאותיך הוגעתני בעַונתיךָ אנֹבִי

Within these seven words someone concealed spellings of four different athbash versions of Jacob. The first version is נראו. It begins at word 9 and

---

11. The athbash versions of יוקב are: אפנט, בחכע, גקעך, דימץ, השצם, ולסר, זארס, חנפת, שסלז, רדזל, קמיה, צבהי, פכחג, עתגח, סטוא, מזדש, נראו, לצשד, כהבק, טגתף, and תוטן.

ends at word 12, taking one letter each from the first four text words in the order, ר, א ג, and ו, which are in italics. The next athbash version of Jacob is בחכע. It has three rows starting at words 10, 11, and 12. The sequences are כבחע, בחעך, and חעבך with each letter underlined. Word 11 starts two fresh Jacob versions, a single row of עתגח (with a sequence of תחגע) and two consecutive rows of תוטן (with sequences of תטון and טתון). In summary, these seven text words contain a total of seven coded spellings of four Jacob athbash versions.

Turning to chapter 54, we find that the prophet packed five different athbash versions of Jacob into his final verse. As shown below, the eighth word of Isa 54:17 starts a תוטן row with a נותט sequence. Word 12 begins רדזל with a רזלד row. Word 15 starts the coding of three different athbash versions. דימץ (דיצמ sequence) and צבהי (בהצי) have but one row each, and קמיה has three: text words 15–18 with יהקם, 16–19 with הקימ, and 17–20 with קימה. Readers can plot these coded rows using this text:

14   13   12   11   10   9   8

לשון תקום אתך למשפט תרשיעי זאת נחלת

20   19   18   17   16   15

עבדי יהוה וצדקתם מאתי נאם יהוה

Isaiah 41:4–5 offers a change of approach. Here the author coded nine consecutive נראו athbash rows into two adjacent verses. The rows begin at the fourth word of v. 4 and end at the second word of v. 5. The reader can work out the sequences of these four-letter coded rows by using the underlined letters in the text below:

2   1   13   12   11   10   9   8   7   6   5   4

קרא הדרות מראש אני יהוה ראשון ואת אחרנים אני הוא ראו איים

With so many of the נראו letters in such a short span, it is not surprising there are other spellings beside single-interval rows. Athbash words using every other text word start at words 5, 6, 7, and 8, and those taking letters from every third word begin at 4, 5, and 6. The passage even contains a coding that uses every fourth word starting at text word 4. In all, the

*Extending the Bible Code*

author fashioned seventeen Jacob athbash signatures within the eighteen opportunities that a text of this length gives. Seventeen of eighteen is impressive. And the letters of word 9 even form a stand-alone anagram of נראו.

These examples of Jacob coding in the Second Isaiah chapters illustrate the freedom that rotating athbash gave the skillful biblical author. Now we return to anagrams, coding within single text words, and to their use *in athbash* by the prophets to attack Jehoiachin. The Jeremiah examples include:

- "Their apostasies [פשעיהם using פשעם, a variation of יוכן] are great" (Jer 5:6)
- "this evil family in all the places where I have driven them [הדחתים using דתהח]" (Jer 8:3)
- "He turns it into gloom and makes it deep darkness [לערפל using עלפר]" (Jer 13:16)
- "I have winnowed them with a winnowing fork in the gates [בשערי using רעשב] of the land" (Jer 15:7).

Ezekiel links "transgressions" (פשעיהם or פשעיכם) to a Jehoiachin athbash anagram (פשעם) seven times, and employs other spellings to the same effect.[12] For example, "Your altars [מזבחותיכם using ובזי] shall become desolate" (Ezek 6:4) and "With hooks they put him in a cage [בסוגר using ברגו], and brought him to the king of Babylon" (Ezek 19:9).

Still on the subject of Jehoiachin, we switch from athbash anagrams to athbash coding in order to examine a specific chapter. Is it true, as many commentators hold, that the lament in Ezek 9 concerns Jehoiachin?[13] Prompted by the hooks-cage anagram, I tested the whole chapter for Jehoiachin-Sarpuhi coding. This table shows the results.

---

12. The seven instances of "transgression" that include the Jehoiachin anagram פשעם are in Ezek 14:11; 18:30, 31, 31; 21:24; 37:23; 39:24.

13. Berridge, "Jehoiachin," 663.

# The Exilic Code

## TABLE 2.1—JEHOIACHIN-SARPUHI ATHBASH CODES IN EZEKIEL 9

| | True Word | Athbash Word | Number | First Sequence | Start Verse-Word | Search Value |
|---|---|---|---|---|---|---|
| 1 | שרפוהייכניהו | עפרטיהדאהיט | 2 | פהיעאיררהדטט | 2-9 | A |
| 2 | שרפוהייכניהו | עפרטיהדאהיט | 2 | רפהיטטדאעיה | 6-3 | A |
| 3 | שרפוהייכוניה | עפרטיההדטאהי | 1 | פההעאירהיטטד | 2-9 | A |
| 4 | שרפוהייכוניה | עפרטיההדטאהי | 1 | רפהיטטדאעיהה | 6-3 | A |
| 5 | שרפוהייוכן | עפרטיההטדא | 1 | היעארפהדטט | 2-10 | A |
| 6 | שרפוהייויכן | עפרטיההטהדהא | 1 | פההעאהרהיטטד | 2-9 | AAA[14] |

The search found six high athbash values of Jehoiachin-Sarpuhi that ran either from verses 2 to 3 or from 6 to 7 (following Hebrew Scripture's numbering). The strongest was the AAA spelling of עפרטיההטהדהא, which is an athbash of שרפוהייויכן, Jehoiachin-Sarpuhi. The cage-Jehoiachin anagram and the coding that connects *sarpuhi* and Jehoiachin lead to these conclusions:

- The first nine verses of Ezek 9 are at least in part about Jehoiachin.
- Since laments generally follow events quickly, the chapter could have been written soon after Jehoiachin's death in the spring of 561.
- Ezekiel died prior to Jehoiachin (as chapter 6 will show), so an editor inserted this into the book of Ezekiel.

We have pursued this example to illustrate the new light that coding, athbash, and anagrams can shine upon familiar passages. All told, the pro-

---

14. The computer search program calibrates coded words after searching a randomly drawn sample of 499 passages. The highest values among the 499 are saved to a database. Values equaled spellings formed divided by attempts to form them. Usually only the highest values are used. These are termed A values, but they can be artificially expanded. Suppose a word's highest value in the 499 sample was .10, but search of a text produced a .15 or a .20. To recognize these, a value 1.5 times the A level drew an AA rating, and anything at or over two times the A mark received a rating of AAA.

phetic books contain well over five hundred coded Jehoiachin anagrams. These await more detailed analysis.

## ANAGRAMS PORTRAY CYRUS

Exilic authors applied the variations of athbash extensively to anagrams and to coding. A signal example is Cyrus, who in 539 BCE conquered the Babylonian empire. Anagrams mark the great Persian king as the Melchizadek of Gen 14 and Ps 110. Here is the Genesis excerpt: "And King Melchizedek [ומלכי־צדק yields וכקץ, a Cyrus anagram] of Salem brought out bread and wine; he was priest of God Most High . . . And Abram gave him one tenth of everything. Then the king of Sodom said to Abram, 'Give me the persons, but take the goods [והרכש yields כורש, a Cyrus anagram] for yourself'" (Gen 14:18, 20–21). (To detect the anagram in "Melchizedek," we must assume a single word. Considering the nearby presence of the second anagram, this seems to be what the writer intended.) Cyrus is Melchizedek, he awards Salem (probably Jerusalem) to Abram, Abram pays him, and the king of Sodom (Edom?) proposes a split of booty with Abram.

The only other place in Hebrew Scripture that Melchizedek appears is Ps 110. Verses 1–4 contain the Cyrus anagrams: "The Lord says to my lord, 'Sit at my right hand until I make your enemies your footstool [לרגליך yields לגכי, a Cyrus anagram]'. . . From the womb of the morning [משחר gives חמשר, a Cyrus anagram], like dew, your youth will come to you. The Lord has sworn and will not change his mind, 'You are a priest forever according to the order of Melchizedek.'" Lines about corpses, battle, and victory close the psalm. "Melchizedek" in this instance lacks a *waw*, so no Cyrus anagram results. But the two other Cyrus anagrams still give the psalm one of the highest Cyrus frequencies in the Bible. Considering the two passages together, Cyrus, Abram, and Jerusalem (probably) are involved. And so are bodies and fighting. The king of Sodom (Edom?) is an ally. This sounds like a revolt against intruding neighbors, with Cyrus hired as a mercenary to lead the Israelite army.

Before going further, consider Cyrus anagrams in two other passages. The prophet Ezekiel wrote this:

> Is it not enough for you to feed on the good pasture, but you must tread down with your feet [רגליכם contains two Cyrus anagrams, גרלם and רגבי] the rest of your pasture? When you drink of clear

water, must you foul the rest with your feet [Cyrus anagrams גרלם and רגבי]? And must my sheep eat what you have trodden with your feet [Cyrus anagrams גרלם and רגבי], and drink what you have fouled with your feet [Cyrus anagrams גרלם and רגבי]? (Ezek 34:18–19)

This concentration of Cyrus anagrams has no parallel in Scripture. The association with Cyrus must have ended badly, and now the Israelites must live with what the great man has fouled. No talk of Melchizedek now. And to add force to the anagrams, Ezekiel encoded four one-interval spellings of כורשמלכפרס, "Cyrus king of Persia," and eleven spellings of כורשמלכאנשן, "Cyrus king of Anshan," so as to run beneath the text.[15] This famous passage summarizes the Judeans' opinion of Cyrus: "My companion stretched out his hand against his friends, he violated his covenant. His speech was smoother than butter [מחמאת contains the Cyrus anagram מחתא], yet war was in his heart; his words were softer than oil, yet they were drawn swords" (Ps 55:21–22, RSV).

When could these passages have been written? There is no reason to attribute Ezek 34 to anyone but the prophet, and his final dated prophecy was 573.[16] Another chapter of this book will reason that the Babylonians killed Ezekiel in 569. So sometime before 569 he was castigating Cyrus the Great for befouling Judah. Ezekiel and Second Isaiah very likely were contemporaries. Both used anagrams to criticize King Jehoiachin, and both mention Cyrus. Ezekiel did it with anagrams and coding, while Second Isaiah specifically named the Persian king in Isa 44:28 and Isa 45 (twice). In addition, in Isaiah chapter 41 the anonymous prophet employed rotating athbash to encode "Cyrus," "Cyrus king of Persia," and "Cyrus King of Anshan" some thirty-two times, as the table shows:

---

15. Starting at text word 18-14, the first of four spellings of king of Persia has a sequence of שלפרכסורכמ. מכרוסכרפלש. The value of this group of four is AAA. Starting at word 18-6, the first of eleven king-of-Anshan encodings is spelled וכרבשמששאנשן. Every subsequent text word through 19-1 begins a spelling except for 18-8.

16. Greenberg, "Ezekiel," 1081–82.

## TABLE 2.2—VALUES OF CYRUS ATHBASH SPELLINGS CONCEALED WITHIN ISAIAH 41:1-13

| Name | True Word | Athbash Word | Verse-Word Start/Finish | Text Words, Spellings | Search Value |
|---|---|---|---|---|---|
| Cyrus | כורש | אציך | 8–9/10–1 | 15, 14 | A |
| Cyrus | כורש | אציך | 11–8/13–1 | 15, 11 | A |
| Cyrus king of Persia | כורשמלכפרס | יסאתחטידאו | 7–11/8–4 | 11, 2 | A |
| Cyrus king of Anshan | כורשמלכאנשן | חמשרוזחצהרה | 1–7/2–6 | 12, 2 | AAA |
| Cyrus king of Anshan | כורשמלכאנשן | חמשרוזחצהרה | 8–5/9–7 | 12, 2 | AAA |
| Cyrus king of Anshan | כורשמלכאנשן | רגכיצקרחפיפ | 1–10/3–1 | 21, 1 | AAA |

Cyrus the Great probably was born during the first decade of the sixth century.[17] After ruling Anshan in southern Iran for a time, he ascended the Persian throne in 558 BCE, conquered the Medes (to Babylonia's north) in 550, and defeated the Lydians (in Anatolia) about five years later. In 539 Cyrus marched unopposed into Babylon. According to the first chapter of Ezra, the new king of Babylon then issued a decree allowing Jews to return to Jerusalem to rebuild their temple. Because in the book of Isaiah the Lord calls Cyrus "my shepherd" and "anointed," scholars have reasonably concluded that Second Isaiah made his prophecies close to 539, when Cyrus took Babylon. If true, this would have meant that Second Isaiah prophesied only toward the Exile's close (Cyrus captured Babylon in 539).

But evidence from coding offers additional information. First, coding in the opening chapter shows that Ezekiel, King Jehoiachin, and Second

---

17. Mallowan, "Cyrus," 7. Mallowan chooses 598 for the birth year.

Isaiah appear to have been contemporaries. Ezekiel's last dated prophecy is from 573 and Jehoiachin probably met his death in 561. Next, Ezek 34 says as clearly as text, anagrams, and coding can that Cyrus king of Anshan befouled Israel. Psalm 55 adds that the Persian harmed his ally and broke his covenant. This could have happened in the 570s or—less likely—in the 560s, if Ezekiel lived into that decade. Second Isaiah proclaimed that Cyrus would "build my city and set my exiles free" (Isa 45:13), but apparently the prophet spoke far too soon. The venture to which he seems to have referred failed.

Unfortunately, we know nothing historical about the early life of Cyrus.[18] For that matter Cyrus does not emerge on the Near Eastern scene until the middle of the 550s when, according to the dream of Babylon's King Nabonidus, "Cyrus, king of Anshan, his [Marduk's] youthful servant" would rise against and defeat the Median kingdom.[19] Cyrus was a grandson of the Median king, and one can suppose that at an early age Cyrus soldered in his grandfather's armies (at eighteen Alexander the Great commanded in battle the cavalry wing of the Macedonian army). It is credible, then, that Cyrus in his twenties led troops and abetted revolt in Judah. The Gen 14 account of Melchizedek indicates that Cyrus, the Israelites, and perhaps Edom recaptured Jerusalem. However, what came next must have been a disaster. The revolt apparently was crushed by Nebuchadnezzar, probably with enthusiastic help from Judah's neighbors. Later chapters will explore this catastrophe's consequences.[20]

Cyrus's intervention in Palestine and the ensuing revolt were years in advance of the proper time. In, say, 571 BCE the kingdom of Lydia dominated Anatolia to Palestine's north, while the undiminished power of Babylon blocked Cyrus's access to his Persian homeland to the east. Cyrus had not yet even won control over the Medes—it was to be almost twenty years before he could accomplish that. But Cyrus was young and ambitious, and perhaps Second Isaiah convinced the Persian that because God blessed their enterprise, the nearly impossible could be done.

This section introduced rotating athbash, a technique that exilic authors applied to both coding and anagrams. Applications of rotating athbash allowed us to link the Bible's Melchizedek and history's Cyrus,

---

18. Young, "Cyrus," 1231.
19. Tadmor, "Nabunaid Inscriptions," 351.
20. For more about this insurrection, see Kavanagh, *Secrets*, 369–74.

and to uncover a Cyrus-led revolt in Judah. Because Ezekiel and Second Isaiah each used Cyrus coding and anagrams, Second Isaiah presumably prophesied while Ezekiel still lived. It is also notable that these Cyrus encodings are the first mention of the great Persian by his contemporaries. They predate the dream of Nabonidus by almost twenty years.

## INTRODUCING WORD LINKS

Having established the fundamentals of coding, we now can turn to a second tool that readers should consider for OT textual analysis. It is simple in concept and produces solid results. Biblical students from the very first have noticed word connections within Scripture. Today no one disputes that the Bible's authors cited one another. Scholars have developed innerbiblical categories such as allusion, exegesis, textuality, and interpretation, and subcategories such as aggadic, legal, scribal, and mantological.[21] Professor Sheri Klouda has written, "The basic term 'intertextuality,' as broadly understood by contemporary literary theorists, embraces all the possible relations that can be established between texts. These relationships can extend from quotations and direct references to indirect echoes and common words."[22] By Klouda's definition, what this book will use is a branch—but just one branch—of intertextuality. It is not intended to rival any other approach. Indeed, it can serve those other approaches well. Its name is Word Links, and it deals only with vocabulary.[23] Biblical authors used it (or something very like it) to pack extra information into their writings. Texts connected by Word Links augmented the original passage, and could substantially change its meaning.

This example illustrates how a Word Link can reverse the surface meaning of a text. Esther 1:2 says, "In those days when King Ahasuerus sat on his royal throne..." However, five Hebrew words form a Word Link with Jer 36:30. It reads, "He shall have no one to sit upon the throne of David, and his dead body shall be cast out to the heat by day and the frost by night."[24] That disposed of Ahasuerus.

21. See, for instance, Eslinger, "Inner-Biblical Exegesis, 47–58; Day, "Inner-biblical Interpretation," 230–46; and especially Fishbane, *Biblical Interpretation*.

22. Klouda, "Psalm 97 in Isaiah 60 and 62."

23. I have encountered the term Word Links just once elsewhere. Leslie McFall used it in passing in "Logical Arrangement of the Psalter," 242.

24. Ahasuerus (Xerxes) died by assassination and received burial in a stone tomb close to his father's. Olmstead, *History of the Persian Empire*, 289.

*A Word Link connects two passages that have in their texts the same unique batch of words. That particular batch will appear nowhere else in Scripture except in those two passages.* A corollary is that *the linking words in each passage must be reasonably close.*[25] This book will allow fifteen text words as the maximum gap between linked words, though in practice batches of linked words are usually far more compact.[26] A normal Word Link contains six shared words within the length of a verse, which averages thirteen words. The median number of shared words is six, and the upper range is a dozen-plus.

Word Links are easy to use. Adverbs, pronouns, prepositions, common verbs, and well-worn nouns lend themselves admirably to linking. It is the *combination* that matters, not how common or uncommon the words within it are.[27] Those who analyze intertextuality understand that biblical writers often selected their words to accord with other scriptural passages. Word Links takes this one small step forward to emphasize that authors *grouped* those words. What matters in the matching process is solely vocabulary. Meaning at this stage counts for nothing. And it is the stress upon vocabulary that necessitates uniqueness of word batches. If every combination were permitted, a passage could have thousands of meaningless links. The example below makes that point. It shows five text words taken from 2 Kgs 25:28–29, a passage concerning King Jehoiachin. The text words are ranked by occurrence in Hebrew Scripture.

---

25. Another corollary is that identical Hebrew words, such as "serve" and "servant," are interchangeable for linking purposes. Eliminating this practice, however, would make almost no difference.

26. Gaps between shared words averaged only 2.9 text words. Decreasing maximum gaps from fifteen to ten text words would decrease total links by only about four percent. Though until now I have employed a fifteen limit, I recommend ten.

27. One can make almost four million unique combinations by picking six words from a list of forty.

## TABLE 2.3—WORD LINK EXAMPLE

|   | Hebrew Word | Strong Number | In OT Verses | Verses After Words Added |
|---|---|---|---|---|
| 1 | אשר | 834 | 3,354 | 3,354 |
| 2 | על | 5921 | 1,810 | 385 |
| 3 | בית | 1004 | 1,706 | 54 |
| 4 | דבר | 1696 | 1,048 | 9 |
| 5 | יהודה | 3063 | 754 | 1 |

אשר appears in 3,354 verses, while על is present in nearly 2,000, and the two occur together in no less than 385 verses. But note the decline that the right column shows as search words are added: 3,354 to 385 to 54 to 9 to 1. Clearly, biblical writers could easily have fashioned unique batches of words to make their Word Links. The verse that contains all five words is Jer 11:17, which is about God's anger with Judah for its Baal worship. These five linking words fall within ten text words in the Jeremiah verse. In the Jehoiachin passage, 2 Kgs 25:28–29, the matching words come within thirteen text words, split between two verses (which is why it did not register in the search). The table includes Strong numbers because it is sometimes simpler to use them. However, one should be open to considering roots rather than the hard-and-fast Strong numbers. After all, exilic writers did not parse vocabulary in such a fashion. Verse divisions, too, were later additions, so while analysts may use verses for a first cut, counted text words are what finally matter.

Another principle is that the word-link technique must ignore composition dates. If two texts share a unique set of words, regardless of when each might have been written, a Word Link is formed. Thus Word Links sidestep a common difficulty in comparing biblical texts. The analyst need make no decision as to which passage preceded the other. (He or she is of course free to draw such a conclusion, but the linking process in no way depends upon it.) However, if authors intentionally fashioned Word Links, how can one explain links between, say, a Second Kings master and a Chronicles text? How can a passage written hundreds of years later be said to throw light upon the earlier one? The answer is that later authors also used Word Links to add dimension and detail to their writing. Their situation was similar enough to benefit from a reference to the earlier author. Indeed, the more-recent author may even have been retelling that prior story. Whatever the reason, we can benefit at each end from the practice, first when we analyze the older text and then when we weigh the younger one.

Finally, Word Links handles large numbers of texts at once—hundreds rather than handfuls. In fact, the more texts linked with a master passage, the better one's chance of discovering the full meaning of the master. Isaiah 52:13–15, the preface to the Suffering Servant chapter, has some eight hundred Word Links—it took that many to identify the Servant of the Lord. The passage that ends the book of Second Kings relates the apparently laudatory release of Jehoiachin from his Babylonian prison. But 468 links from that text instead tell a tale of judicial murder. (But a single link can also be an eye-opener. See chapter 4 for the story of how a Word Link furnished the first clue to Second Isaiah's identity.)

Here is a review of Word Links:

- Word Links gives additional information about the master passage.
- A link connects two passages that contain the same unique batch of words.
- The linked words within a text must be reasonably close together.
- The sole basis for selection is vocabulary.
- No more than one satellite text may share identicle words with the master text.
- Dates of composition can be ignored.
- Expect hundreds of links.

Word Links make their own best argument. They work. They give information previously unavailable to students of the Bible, and (as we shall read) help to solve thorny questions such as the identity of the Suffering Servant. There is nothing extreme about these links. They are but another category of intertextuality, which most accept. Also, Word Links impose no modern practice upon ancient writers. To the contrary, Word Links—simple to use and easy to find—were fully within the capabilities of those who wrote Scripture. To illustrate this newly available tool for scholars, chapter 3 will be entirely devoted to a Word Link study of the final verses of the book of Second Kings. The application will, I suggest, forever change our understanding of that passage.

3

## The Word–Link King of Babylon

### WORD LINKS EXPLAINED

A WORD LINK CONNECTS *two passages that have in their texts the same unique batch of words. That particular batch will appear nowhere else in Scripture except in those two passages, and the linking words in each passage must be reasonably close together.* With this definition before us, we are ready to consider a specific application.

Appendix 2 lists 468 links for 2 Kgs 25:27–30. It divides these into twenty-four subject groups, including one labeled unassigned (which is less than one-tenth of the total). The subjects include exile, idols, prison, fasting, substitute king (with subcategories), burial, killing children, and Davidic line, among others. To present the Jehoiachin story, we shall use the most revealing of the links and follow the outline that appendix 2 provides. (In practice, assembling and classifying Word Links is the most time-consuming part of any analysis. This note offers suggestions.[1])

Readers might justifiably ask whether this author expected to find substitute-king links before starting, and thus pre-selected the subject categories. After all, the Jehoiachin-Sarpuhi coding results detailed in chapter 1 made it highly likely that the Babylonians enthroned and then killed Jehoiachin. The answer is that I did expect to find evidence of substitution in the 2 Kings Word Links. However, that expectation stemmed

---

1. Consider this technique. First, choose a limited text, say of fifteen words. Next, using one of the commercially available search programs, find and send to a word-processing file every Word Link possible. I used Strong numbers, but others may prefer to go straight to Hebrew. Be inflexible about deleting links that contain exactly the same matching words. Copy and study the linked passages. Then begin sorting into categories. As you sort, new categories will suggest themselves. Have an unassigned category. (Later, you will be able to place most of these.) After a few reviews of the passages, get into detail.

from findings about the Suffering Servant rather than prior evidence about Jehoiachin. For the record, I did these things in this sequence: (a) about 1985 found the name of Second Isaiah by using word associations; (b) several years later used that name to establish the existence of coding; (c) about 1990, directed by John Brinkman to the work of Simo Parpola, found evidence that the Suffering Servant died as a substitute; (d) the next year expanded word associations into Word Links and found the Suffering Servant's name; (e) in the late 1990s applied Word Links to 2 Kgs 25:27–30 and confirmed that Jehoiachin was also a substitute; (f) in 2006, while preparing the Priestly Benediction article for *Biblica*, discovered significant Jehoiachin-Sarpuhi coding in that text.

Given this history, were the subject categories for Word Links in Second Kings pre-selected? To a considerable extent they were. However, what matters most are the links themselves. Those links could not have been pre-selected, and they have determined subject categories. Now here is the text of 2 Kgs 25:27–30.

> In the thirty-seventh year of the exile of King Jehoiachin of Judah, in the twelfth month, on the twenty-seventh day of the month, King Evil-merodach of Babylon, in the year that he began to reign, released King Jehoiachin of Judah from prison; he spoke kindly to him, and gave him a seat above the other seats of the kings who were with him in Babylon. So Jehoiachin put aside his prison clothes. Every day of his life he dined regularly in the king's presence. For his allowance, a regular allowance was given him by the king, a portion every day, as long as he lived.

There are almost 470 Word Links with this master passage, and about a third of them also contain Jehoiachin codes or anagrams. Appendix 2 uses italics to designate anagrams and coding, a practice followed throughout this chapter. Clearly, a Word Link has more force if encoded with "Jehoiachin." We shall discuss the links by subject, arranged in rough chronological order. The period covered is from shortly before Jehoiachin's accession to Judah's throne in late 598 BCE to soon after his death in April of 561.

## LINKS SET EXILE'S CONTEXT

We begin with these word-link prophecies of exile. Isaiah tells King Hezekiah, who reigned in Judah well before Jehoiachin, that "Some of your own sons ... shall be eunuchs in the palace of the king of Babylon" (2 Kgs 20:18). Joshua 23:13 says that failure to drive out all the nations will make them "a snare and a trap for you ... until you perish from this good land that the Lord your God has given you." As italics indicate, this, too, contains Jehoiachin coding. Jeremiah attributed Judah's exile to "what King Manasseh son of Hezekiah of Judah did in Jerusalem" (*Jer 15:4*). In another linked passage, God says through the same prophet, "I am now making my words in your mouth a fire, and this people wood, and the fire shall devour them" (*5:14*). *Jeremiah 17:27* is similar, but adds that Jerusalem's palaces will also be devoured. Another link goes to Ezek 12:6, in which the Lord bids Ezekiel to carry baggage away in the dark—a prophetic enactment of Israel's exile.

After Jehoiachin's 597 surrender to Nebuchadnezzar, Jeremiah gave a pronouncement about two baskets of figs. (The links are to Jer 24:1-2, 3-8; 29:15-17.) The good figs were the exiles around Jehoiachin, and the bad ones were King Zedekiah with his officials. Two other Word Links threaten Judah and Egypt with the King of Assyria (*Isa 7:20; 20:3-4*). However, since both contain Jehoiachin coding, the passages carry sixth-century messages. The same is true of a Micah prophecy against Jerusalem that promises to make the city a desolation (*Mic 6:16*).

There are many links that recount Jehoiachin's fall. The first Word Link shares ten words with the 2 Kgs 25:27-30 master: "Jehoiachin was eighteen years old when he began to reign; he reigned three months in Jerusalem ... He did what was evil in the sight of the Lord ... the city was besieged ... King Jehoiachin of Judah gave himself up to the king of Babylon, himself, his mother, his servants, his officers, and his palace officials. The king of Babylon took him prisoner" (2 Kgs 24:8-12). A Second Chronicles link, reaching back, tells the same story (*2 Chr 36:7-10*). This next one provides additional detail: Nebuchadnezzar "carried away Jehoiachin to Babylon; the king's mother, the king's wives, his officials, and the elite of the land, he took into captivity from Jerusalem to Babylon. The king of Babylon brought captive to Babylon all the men of valor, seven thousand, the artisans and the smiths, one thousand, all of them strong and fit for war" (*2 Kgs 24:15-17*).

A number of Word Links suggest that when Nebuchadnezzar deposed Jehoiachin, he also levied a tribute upon the Judeans. Though this is new historical information, it simply follows a practice common in the ancient world. Indeed, this first link tells of the Assyrians requisitioning treasure from Hezekiah. "King Hezekiah of Judah sent to the king of Assyria at Lachish, saying, 'I have done wrong; withdraw from me; whatever you impose on me I will bear.' The king of Assyria demanded of King Hezekiah of Judah three hundred talents of silver and thirty talents of gold" (2 Kgs 18:14). In addition: "at registration all of them shall give a ransom for their lives to the Lord, so that no plague may come upon them for being registered"; "The weight of the golden earrings that he requested was one thousand seven hundred shekels of gold"; ". . . he overlaid it with six hundred talents of fine gold"; "'Why have you not required the Levites to bring in from Judah and Jerusalem the tax levied by Moses?'"; and "the king's secretary and the officer of the chief priest would come and empty the chest and take it and return it to its place. So they . . . collected money in abundance."[2] All of these support that Nebuchadnezzar levied a steep assessment upon the Judeans.

Word Links next proceeded to King Zedekiah. He held Judah's throne for eleven years after Nebuchadnezzar installed him in Jehoiachin's stead. But "Zedekiah rebelled against the king of Babylon. And . . . King Nebuchadrezzar of Babylon came with all his army against Jerusalem, and they laid siege to it" and took the city. "He put out the eyes of Zedekiah, and bound him in fetters, and the king of Babylon took him to Babylon, and put him in prison until the day of his death . . . So Judah went into exile out of its land" (*Jer 52:3–7, 11, 27*). (Italics indicate Jehoiachin coding support even though the passages are about King Zedekiah.) In the aftermath, the Babylonian commander "burned the house of the Lord, the king's house, and all the houses of Jerusalem; every great house he burned down" (*2 Kgs 25:9*). Zedekiah got no sympathy from the prophets. In this link with Ezekiel the Lord said, "I will surely return upon his head my oath that he despised, and my covenant that he broke . . . I will bring him to Babylon and enter into judgment with him there for the treason he has committed against me" (*Ezek 17:19–20*).

Like those who wrote the rest of the books of Kings, the as-yet unknown author of 2 Kgs 25:27–30 was an historian. And like a good historian he was careful to establish the context of Jehoiachin's 561 BCE release from prison. As we now know, that author did this with Word Links, links that reached back almost forty years to the calamitous events that ended Judah's national life.

2. *Exod 30:12; Judg 8:26*; 2 Chr 3:8, *24:6, 11*. Other tribute links are *Exod 30:4* and 2 Kgs 5:23. Italics mean the Word Link also contains Jehoiachin coding.

Chapter 2 described the prophetic reaction to Jehoiachin's shocking worship of Babylonian gods. Not unexpectedly, then, the 2 Kgs 25 master passage has Word Links to texts about idols. The Lord told Moses that after his death "'this people will begin to prostitute themselves to the foreign gods in their midst, the gods of the land into which they are going; they will forsake me, breaking my covenant that I have made with them'" (*Deut 31:16*). Ezekiel wrote, "Any of those of the house of Israel who take their idols into their hearts . . . I the Lord will answer those who come with the multitude of their idols" (Ezek 14:4); and Jeremiah added, "The Lord . . . has pronounced evil against you, because of the evil that the house of Israel and the house of Judah have done, provoking me to anger by making offerings to Baal" (Jer 11:17). The author of 2 Kgs 25:27–30 said through Word Links that the Exile was Judah's punishment for straying to other gods.³ All these links were aimed at Jehoiachin in Babylon, though the denunciations may also have targeted others.

During his thirty-six years of exile, Jehoiachin was a puppet king in Nebuchadnezzar's court for some of the time, and also served stretches in prison. These Word Links seem to belong to that period: "The taskmasters were urgent, saying, 'Complete your work, the same daily assignment as when you were given straw'"; "'you shall bear your iniquity, forty years, and you shall know my displeasure'"; and "'Here we are slaves to this day . . . [the land's] rich yield goes to the kings whom you have set over us because of our sins; . . . and we are in great distress'" (Exod 5:13; *Num 14:34*; Neh 9:36–37).

Word Links with the Second Kings master passage record the exiled king's reactions. The linked Ps 4:6 says, "'O that we might see some good! Let the light of your face shine on us, O Lord!'" A link from Nehemiah—written well after our master passage—expresses Jehoiachin's feelings to modern readers: "I carried the wine and gave it to the [Persian] king. Now, I had never been sad in his presence before. So the king said to me, 'Why is your face sad, since you are not sick? This can only be sadness of the heart.' Then I was very much afraid" (*Neh 2:1–2*).⁴

---

3. For other links about idols see Judg 18:19; 1 Kgs 13:3; 15:1–3; *16:29–31*; 2 Kgs 13:10–11; *15:8–9*; 23:11–12; 2 Chr 2:4–5; Jer 44:17; Ezek 16:19; 18:5–6, *14–16*; 20:31; *22:4*; 33:27; 44:12.

4. Other links about oppression and Jehoiachin's reaction to it are *Gen 6:18–19*; Deut 24:15; *Prov 10:9–14*; *14:1–3*; 17:26–28; *25:19–28*; 2 Chr 12:12; *Esth 3:7*; 9:15–16.

## The Word–Link King of Babylon

There are also hints that Jehoiachin might have been a fugitive while in Babylon. Here is one: "Cain said to the Lord, 'My punishment is greater than I can bear! Today you have driven me away from the soil, and I shall be hidden from your face; I shall be a fugitive and a wanderer on the earth, and anyone who meets me may kill me'" (*Gen 4:13–14*). Additionally, "But on the second day, the day after the new moon, David's place was empty. And Saul said to his son Jonathan . . ."; and "'Do not be afraid; for the hand of my father Saul shall not find you; you shall be king over Israel'" (1 Sam 20:27; *23:17*).[5]

As to Jehoiachin's terms in prison, this Word Link, which also conceals an A-value Jehoiachin coding, offers a fascinating possibility: "the king of Assyria found treachery in Hoshea; for he had sent messengers to King So of Egypt, and offered no tribute to the king of Assyria, as he had done year by year; therefore the king of Assyria confined him and imprisoned him" (*2 Kgs 17:2–5*). Jehoiachin could well have been imprisoned by Nebuchadnezzar for conspiring with one of Babylon's enemies. Here are prison Word Links: "'Thus says the king: Put this fellow in prison, and feed him on reduced rations of bread and water'"; "to open the eyes that are blind, to bring out the prisoners from the dungeon, from the prison those who sit in darkness"; and "The officials were enraged at Jeremiah, and they beat him and imprisoned him in the house of the secretary Jonathan, for it had been made a prison. Thus Jeremiah was put in the cistern house, in the cells, and remained there many days" (1 Kgs 22:27; Isa 42:7; *Jer 37:15–16*). In this next link the Philistines made sport of Samson: "When their hearts were merry, they said, 'Call Samson, and let him entertain us.' So they called Samson out of the prison, and he performed for them" (Judg 16:25). Did the Babylonians do this to King Jehoiachin? Scripture contains at least seven other prison-related links to the 2 Kings master.[6]

On February 19, 561, an eclipse shadowed the moon over Babylon.[7] Its duration was two hours and twenty-five minutes. Jupiter, the king's protective planet, was visible initially, but by the time the shadow darkened Babylon's lunar quadrant, the planet had dropped below the west-

---

5. Another possible fugitive link is *1 Kgs 20:32*. Those tracking Word Links in the future should consider whether 1 Sam 23:17–18 refers to a bond between Jehoiachin and Evil-Marduk formed when they were fellow courtiers or prisoners.

6. Additional prison-related links are *Gen 31:40–41; 37:24; Isa 42:7, 22; 51:13–14*; Jer 18–20; and 2 Chr 18:26.

7. Kudlek and Mickler, *Ancient Near East Eclipses*, 148.

ern horizon. This meant certain death for Evil-Marduk or his substitute king. The eclipse hit just four months after Evil-Marduk's coronation. In all, he was to reign for only twenty-two months before his brother-in-law assassinated him to seize the throne. In 2 Kgs 25, the author wrote Amel-Marduk's name as *Evil*-Marduk. "Evil" meant "foolish" in Hebrew. A contemporary tablet charged him with ignoring the welfare of Babylon's temples.[8] Another source claimed his government was "illegal and impure."[9]

A Word Link with 2 Kgs 25:27–30 said that Rehoboam "disregarded the advice that the older men had given him and spoke to them according to the advice of the young men, 'My father [Nebuchadnezzar is implied] made your yoke heavy, but I will add to your yoke; my father disciplined you with whips, but I will discipline you with scorpions'" (*1 Kgs 12:13–14*, link includes v. 12; see also *12:6–8*). The first three Hebrew words of the link's twelfth verse contained letters that spell "Evil-Marduk." And the author spelled "Evil-Marduk" twice in nearby verses, one of which also spoke of oppression.[10] Evil-Marduk seemed rash, willful, and inexperienced—the weak son of a dominant father.

The Second Kings text said that Evil-Marduk put Jehoiachin's "seat [throne] above the other seats [thrones] of the kings who were with him in Babylon." As king of Babylon, Jehoiachin would have received an elevated throne. The word "above" was מעל, meaning "higher than." But that same word could also mean "act treacherously." The author repeated the trick with בגד ("garment"), which was another version of "act treacherously."

Why these undertones of treachery? Not many years before, the Suffering Servant had agreed to be Nebuchadnezzar's substitute (more on this in chapter 6). The servant's price seems to have included an end to persecution and the release of Judean captives. Also, the servant would almost certainly have made Nebuchadnezzar pledge that Jehoiachin would never become a substitute king.

Word Links with the 2 Kings passage indicate that the bargain had been in writing. Here are some of those links: "And you shall write on the stones all the words of this law very clearly." The Lord wrote the com-

---

8. Grayson, *Babylonian Texts*, 89.

9. Berosus quoted by Josephus *Apion* 1.20, 147.

10. The opening words of 1 Kgs 12:14 are וידבר אליהם כעצת. Letters within these spell אויל מרדך, "Evil-Marduk." Words 13–15 of v. 10, דברו אליך לאמר, also yield "Evil-Marduk."

mandments "on two stone tablets, and gave them to me." "And he gave to Moses . . . the two tablets of the covenant, tablets of stone, written with the finger of God." A final link spoke of written commandments "that the Lord had spoken to you on the mountain" (*Deut 27:7–9*; *5:22*; *Exod 31:18*; *Deut 10:4*). It is no small thing that Jehoiachin coding underlies each of these Word Links. The "mountain" would have been Babylon's ziggurat, the center of priestly power.

A legend said Evil-Marduk had to disinter his father's body and drag it before he could release Jehoiachin.[11] (At issue was whether a successor could ignore a predecessor's decree.) But new kings commonly freed political prisoners, so Evil-Marduk need not have dishonored his father to free Jehoiachin.[12] The real story behind the dragging probably was this: Nebuchadnezzar had covenanted with the Suffering Servant to protect Jehoiachin. But Evil-Marduk could break that covenant only if he first dishonored Nebuchadnezzar, and so he dragged his father's body. The legend implied that the decree Evil-Marduk overruled kept Jehoiachin imprisoned. Instead that decree had previously kept Jehoiachin safe.

Nebuchadnezzar had ruled Babylon for forty-three years and must have left numerous sons. A Word Link with the master passage suggests that Evil-Marduk solved the problem by slaughtering his brothers. Zimri, "when he began to reign, as soon as he had seated himself on his throne, he killed all the house of Baasha; he did not leave him a single male of his kindred or his friends. Thus Zimri destroyed all the house of Baasha, according to the word of the Lord" (*1 Kgs 16:11–12*).[13]

## JEHOIACHIN'S HUNGER STRIKE

To protect the true king, authorities normally enthroned a substitute as quickly as they could. However, with Jehoiachin they delayed some forty days after the eclipse. Why? They waited because the Judean king would not cooperate. *Jehoiachin went on a hunger strike.* Dozens of Word Links support this. The following concern famine. God took away "all support

---

11. Saldarini, *Avot*, 117–18. Another legend said Nebuchadnezzar had barred his son from succession, and that Evil-Marduk agreed to accept the throne only if his father's corpse were dragged. Sack, "Evil-Merodach," 679.

12. Saldarini, *Avot*, 117, n 9.

13. Other Word Links that may pertain to Evil-Marduk's succession are Judg 3:19–20; *1 Kgs 1:24–25*, 21:4; 2 Kgs 19:4. Italics mean the Word Link also contains Jehoiachin coding.

of bread, and all support of water." He gave cleanness of teeth and lack of bread. After seven years of plenty, "seven years of famine began to come." "In the days when the judges ruled, there was a famine in the land . . ." Next, in David's time there was famine for three years. In another link Elisha announced, "'The Lord has called for a famine . . . for seven years.'" This grisly link finishes: "'Give up your son; we will eat him today, and we will eat my son tomorrow.'"[14]

These next links pertained to individuals. "Then food was set before him to eat; but he said, 'I will not eat until I have told my errand.'" "Therefore Hannah wept and would not eat." Though others urged David to eat, he refused food until the sun went down. Ezra spent the night mourning over the exiles, and he "did not eat bread or drink water." Nehemiah said, "'Twelve years, neither I nor my brothers ate the food allowance of the governor.'" And Daniel denied himself meat and wine for three weeks.[15]

Three Moses Word Links are especially pertinent. For forty days "'I neither ate bread nor drank water, because of all the sin which you had committed'" (Deut 9:18). This verse fitted Jehoiachin's situation so exactly that one suspects an editor at work on Deuteronomy's ninth chapter. A second link said that while with God for forty days and nights, Moses "neither ate bread nor drank water" (Exod 34:28-29). And Deuteronomy 9 again: "'I remained on the mountain forty days and forty nights'" without eating or drinking (Deut 9:9-11). "The mountain" presumably was the Tower of Babel, where Jehoiachin's captors probably kept him during his fast.

Word Links also suggested Jehoiachin ate vegetables during the period. "'Let us be given vegetables to eat and water to drink,'" said Daniel. Ezekiel lived on wheat, barley, beans, and lentils for 390 days. Proverbs added, "Better is a dinner of vegetables where love is than a fatted ox and hatred with it."[16]

According to Word Links, the exiles held vigil with their king. Consider these linked passages: Jehoshaphat "proclaimed a fast throughout all Judah"; in Jehoiakim's time "all the people . . . proclaimed a fast before the Lord"; and Esther instructed, "'Hold a fast on my behalf, and neither eat nor drink for three days, night or day. I and my maids will also

---

14. *Isa 3:1*; Amos 4:6-7; *Gen 41:53-54*; Ruth 1:1; 2 Sam 21:1-2; 2 Kgs 8:1; 6:28.

15. Quotations are within the parameters of these Word Links: Gen 24:32-33; 1 Sam 1:7; 2 Sam 3:35; Ezra 10:5-6; Neh 5:13-15; *Dan 10:2-5*.

16. Dan 1:12; *Ezek 4:9-10*; Prov 15:17.

fast as you do.'"[17] Five links showed that the exiles abstained from leavened bread during part of Jehoiachin's ordeal. This was typical: "'Seven days you shall eat unleavened bread . . . for whoever eats leavened bread . . . shall be cut off from Israel.'"[18] Even though exclusion is threatened, what courage this showed! Imagine such widespread passive resistance throughout Babylonia.

The flaw in the substitute ritual was that the victim had to accept voluntarily the eclipse's deathly omens—which Jehoiachin refused to do. Evil-Marduk waited anxiously as time passed. "For forty days the Philistine came forward and took his stand, morning and evening" (1 Sam 17:16), a link that comes from the story of David and Goliath. Knowledgeable exiles would have understood who that Philistine was. The chapter's author had previously spelled אוילמרדך, "Evil-Marduk," seventy-six times in 17:8–11, the passage that related Goliath's challenge to the Israelite army.

The use of forty days is important. Second Kings 25 and Jer 52 gave almost identical Jehoiachin accounts. But Kings said Evil-Marduk released Jehoiachin on the twenty-seventh of the month, while Jeremiah had the twenty-fifth. No scholar, ancient or modern, has satisfactorily explained the difference, but the following may do so. Based upon the date in 2 Kgs 25, Jehoiachin saw daylight forty-two days after the February 19th eclipse. Based upon the release date in Jer 52, the span was exactly forty days. Of course neither account mentioned the eclipse. This writer's opinion is that Jeremiah changed Jehoiachin's detention to forty days so as to show that Jehoiachin resisted kingship for a long time. Forty often conveyed such a meaning. Examples are Moses spending forty days atop Sinai, and the Israelites wandering forty years in the wilderness.

To force Jehoiachin to cooperate, the Babylonians slew his heirs. These Word Links testified: "'kill every male among the little ones,'" In other links, Job's sons and daughters died, Aaron's two sons died, Jeroboam's son died, and brother had to succeed brother "because Ahaziah had no son."[19] Here are more Word Links on this dismal subject. Athaliah "set about to destroy all the royal family of the house of Judah" (2 Chr 22:10) and Absalom lamented, "'I have no son to keep my name in remembrance'"

---

17. 2 Chr 20:3; Jer 36:9; Esth 4:16. See Zech 8:19.

18. Exod 12:15 is quoted. The other links are *Exod 12:18–19*; 13:3–4; 23:15; Lev 22:16–17; Deut 16:3; 1 Kgs 13:7–9, 11, 17–19, 21–22; *2 Chr 30:21–22*. See Lev 7:27–28. Leviticus 7:18 and Hos 2:12 may also belong to this category.

19. Num 31:17–20; *Job 1:17–19*; Lev 16:1–2; 1 Kgs 14:17–20; 2 Kgs 1:17.

(*2 Sam 18:18*). Also, Jeremiah prophesied about Jehoiachin, "'He shall have none to sit upon the throne of David'" (Jer 36:30). The Lord said that even if Jehoiachin were the signet ring on His right hand, yet "I would tear you off and give you into the hands . . . of King Nebuchadrezzar'" (Jer 22:24–25). These killings went far toward extinguishing David's line.[20]

A shrine to Marduk topped the Tower of Babel, which was the city of Babylon's ziggurat.[21] Herodotus wrote that it contained a golden table and a great couch where a woman awaited the god's pleasure.[22] During the annual New Year's Festival the king played Marduk's role and, probably in this very room, bedded a priestess.

Every substitute king had a substitute queen appointed by the authorities.[23] Certainly it would be consistent if substitute kings and queens also consummated their unions atop the ziggurat.[24] In seeming confirmation, a Word Link suggests a woman persuaded Jehoiachin to eat—in that very room. According to scripture, a woman built for Elisha "'a small roof chamber with walls'" with "'a bed, a table, a chair, and a lamp'" (2 Kgs 4:10), which sounds like Marduk's chamber. Moreover, she "urged him to eat some food" (2 Kgs 4:8). Any female that the Babylonians set in Jehoiachin's way would have worked to get the Judean king to break his fast. Another Word Link is especially apropos: "Saul thought, 'Let me give her to him that she may be a snare for him and that the hand of the Philistines may be against him'" (1 Sam 18:21).

Of particular interest are no less than five Word Links from the story of Adam and Eve in Gen 3 (Gen 3:1, 5–6, *14*, 17, 22–23). At the urging of the serpent, the woman entices the man to eat from the tree of knowledge. As a result, the Lord expels them from the garden and in effect sentences them to death. Experts are urged to consider whether the Genesis story was written with a substitute king in view—either Jehoiachin or another.

---

20. Jehoiachin's grandson Zerubbabel appeared briefly in Judah forty years afterward. Other passages about children's (or sacrificial animals') deaths linked to 2 Kgs 25:27–30 are Num 28:1–3; 29:17; *Judg 11:33–35*; 2 Sam 12:17–18, *20–21*; 13:36; 1 Kgs 3:18–19, 22, 25; *2 Chr 21:13*; Isa 56:5–6; *Lam 2:19–20*. Italics mean the Word Link also contains Jehoiachin coding.

21. Langdon, "Nebuchadnezzar XVII," 151.

22. Herodotus *Histories* I.181–82.

23. Parpola II, xxiv. Recall that a woman's name, Jecoliah, was highly coded in the Priestly Benediction. It is not unlikely that she was Jehoiachin's Hebrew wife and died with him. The substitute queen would have been a different person.

24. Parpola I, 111 (letter 139).

Word Links with the Second Kings master include passages about attractive females—the Levite's concubine, David's sighting of Bathsheba, and the crowning of Esther as queen of Persia.²⁵ Others are: "May the Lord make the woman who is coming into your house like Rachel and Leah," "gather all the beautiful young virgins to the harem in the citadel," and "He who finds a wife finds a good thing."²⁶

Here are links that say Jehoiachin finally broke his fast. "They gave him also a piece of fig cake and two clusters of raisins. When he had eaten, his spirit revived," "So I, Daniel . . . lay sick for some days; then I arose and went about the king's business," and "'You shall eat in the presence of the Lord . . . you and your households.'"²⁷ Also, Abraham "took curds, and milk and the calf that he had prepared, and set it before them" (Gen 18:8). This from Exodus: "'You shall set the bread of the Presence on the table before me always'" (Exod 25:30). And from Chronicles: "'We have had enough to eat and have plenty to spare'" (2 Chr 31:10). Numerous other linked passages made the same point, that Jehoiachin had decided to eat.²⁸ Evil-Marduk might even have attended Jehoiachin's first meal: "So Saul ate with Samuel that day" (1 Sam 9:24).

## JEHOIACHIN'S ELEVATION

When Jehoiachin relented and took nourishment, he agreed to assume Babylon's kingship and die in Evil-Marduk's stead. The Judean was released from confinement either four or six days prior to New Year's Day, the date that marked commencement of the festival featuring the king's annual enthronement. The immanence of New Year's Day meant that authorities had to kill Jehoiachin quickly to prevent him from becoming Babylon's king for the whole ensuing year.

These links with our master Second Kings passage refer to Jehoiachin's temporary elevation: "'The Lord will . . . give strength to his king, and exalt the power of his anointed'"; "'It is you who shall be shepherd of my people Israel' . . . and they anointed David king over Israel"; "'I anoint

---

25. Judg 19:29–30; 2 Sam 11:2; Esth 2:17.

26. *Ruth 4:11*; Esth 2:3; Prov 18:22. Other links in this category are: *Lev 15:26–28*; Judg 19:8; *Ezra 10:16–17*; Esth 1:19; 2:9; 7:8–9; 8:1.

27. 1 Sam 30:12; Dan 8:27; 12:7.

28. Gen 27:9–10; 45:18; Exod 23:10–12; *Lev 11:2*; 24:7–9; 26:10–12; *Num 11:17–21*; 28:23–25; *Deut 8:10–13*; 15:20–21; *26:11–12*; Josh 5:12–13; 1 Sam 9:24; 1 Kgs 17:14–16; 2 Kgs 4:8–11, *43–44*; *Eccl 3:12–14*; 8:15; Ezek 2:8.

you king over the people of the Lord, over Israel'"; "'Your sons shall sit on the throne of Israel to the fourth generation'"; and "God, your God, has anointed you with the oil of gladness beyond your companions."[29] Every substitute was in effect a second king, which explained why several links mentioned two kings. The first has the king of Israel and the king of Judah sitting side-by-side on their thrones (*1 Kgs 22:8-10*). A link from Isaiah speaks of two evil kings, and so does this one from Daniel: "The two kings, their minds bent on evil, shall sit at one table and exchange lies" (Isa 7:16; Dan 11:27). The Daniel 11 link certainly reaches back to the Second Kings master from a later time, and so does an Esther Word Link that hints strongly at substitution: "So Haman took the robes and the horse and robed Mordecai and led him riding through the open square of the city, proclaiming, 'Thus shall it be done for the man whom the king wishes to honor'" (Esth 6:11).[30]

Numerous Word Links connected the Jehoiachin passage to ones about kings. For example, "his king shall be higher than Agag, and his kingdom shall be exalted"; "'have dominion ... over every living thing that moves upon the earth'"; "'you may reign over all that your heart desires'"; and "'Are you indeed to reign over us?'"[31] Put "a beautiful crown upon your head," said an Ezekiel link (*16:12-13*); and Nathan asked David, "'who should sit on the throne of my lord the king after him?'" (*1 Kgs 1:27*).

The raison d'être for substitute kingship was to shift an eclipse's evil omens from the reigning monarch to the substitute. But the deadly transfer was valid only if the substitute swore to accept it. A letter to the king of Assyria illustrates this: "The substitute king ... entered the [Babylonian] city of Akkad safely on the night of the 20th and sat upon the throne. I made him recite the scribal recitations before the Sun-god, *he took all the celestial and terrestrial omens on himself,* and ruled all the countries."[32] The "celestial and terrestrial omens" without doubt included curses.

---

29. 1 Sam 2:10; 2 Sam 5:2-3; 2 Kgs 9:6; 15:12-13; *Ps 45:7*.

30. Other passages that can be viewed as substitute-king Word Links are: Exod 29:29-30; *Judg 9:15-16; 11:11*; 1 Sam 29:5-6; 2 Sam 2:10-11, 19:11-12; 1 Kgs 9:10; 2 Kgs 3:13-14; Esth 6:11-13; *Eccl 5:17-19; Prov 1:5-9, 20:1-3; Isa 6:1-2*.

31. Word Links within which these quotations occur are: Num 24:7-8; *Gen 1:28-29; 2 Sam 3:19-20; Gen 37:8-9*. Other king links are 1 Kgs 2:11-12 and Prov 30:21-23.

32. Parpola I, 227, my italics.

## The Word-Link King of Babylon

Word Links trace Jehoiachin's ordeal as king of Babylon. Probably he had to lead a procession, which this link (also quoted above) could have described: "So Haman took the robes and the horse and robed Mordecai and led him riding through the open square of the city, proclaiming, 'Thus shall it be done for the man whom the king wishes to honor'" (Esth 6:11). For Jews, the most offensive part of enthronement would have been kneeling before a pagan idol. For Jehoiachin, however, it should be said that he had worshiped Babylon's gods for years.

It must have been especially repugnant for Jehoiachin to accept the transfer of curses that the eclipse had brought upon Babylon's king. The foremost Word Link that referred to it is from Ps 109. Verses 19–21 form the actual link with the master passage, but I have included v. 18 because of its importance: "He clothed himself with cursing as his coat, may it soak into his body like water, like oil into his bones. May it be like a garment that he wraps around himself, like a belt that he wears every day" (*Ps 109:18–19*). Coding shows that Jehoiachin is the subject of these lines.) A letter from 671 BCE to the Assyrian king from his agent in Babylon said that curses had not only been read to the substitute king before the sun god, but that they had then been attached to the seam of his garment "to make sure that he was constantly 'afflicted' by them."[33] The psalm's Word Link also suggests that the authorities compelled Jehoiachin (whose name is coded beneath the text) to drink ground curse tablets. Assyrians forced a similar thing.[34] So did Moses. He ground the golden calf to powder, mixed the powder with water, and then made the Israelites drink the mixture (Exod 32:20). In a different link Satan said to God, "'But stretch out your hand now, and touch all that he has, and he will curse you to your face.'" And in this final link the Genesis author turns the curse against the snake, i.e., Babylon. "God said to the serpent, 'Because you have done this, cursed are you among all animals and among all wild creatures; upon your belly you shall go, and dust you shall eat all the days of your life.'"[35]

Second Kings 25:29–30 emphasized that Jehoiachin drew rations daily. "And his allowance, a continual allowance, was given to him from the king, a daily rate for every day, all the days of his life (Interlinear)." This daily issuance was a departure. Thirty years earlier, Jehoiachin's household

---

33. Parpola I, 19; Parpola II, 30.
34. Parpola I, 21.
35. Job 1:11–13; *Gen 3:14*. Curse links not quoted are Deut 28:31; 1 Kgs 8:31–32; *Job 5:2–5*; and *Prov 11:26–30*.

had drawn fourteen quarts of oil at once, certainly far more than a single day's needs.[36] As Evil-Marduk's guest, Jehoiachin would not have drawn his personal allowance. Instead, the king's kitchen would have requisitioned food for the whole royal table. But the words about a daily ration would fit if Jehoiachin was a substitute king. Then the palace commissary would have made daily issues to Jehoiachin for his entire court. Notably, Assyrian records showed wine was issued to the substitute king himself for an entourage of three hundred people.[37] In reality, the king's table at which Jehoiachin dined was his own. Also, he ate from his soon-to-be executioner's hand, for a link said, "The captain of the guard gave him an allowance of food" (Jer 40:5).

The subjects of food and drink were closely associated with substitutes, for the replacement king hosted daily banquets.[38] Word Links illustrate this. King Ahasuerus "gave a banquet for all his officials and ministers. The army of Persia and Media and the nobles and governors of the provinces were present" (*Esth 1:1–3*). According to this next link, Nabal "was holding a feast in his house, *like the feast of a king*. Nabal's heart was merry within him, for he was very drunk" (1 Sam 25:36, italics added). In another Word Link (*2 Sam 11:13*), King David got Uriah drunk. Separately, the Nineveh letters indicate authorities intoxicated a substitute before leading him through his enthronement ceremony.[39] Heavy drinking in such circumstances should not surprise us. Some of that is still done at wakes.

What did the Jews think of such carousing? A Word Link from Ps 23 said, "You prepare a table before me in the presence of my enemies" (*Ps 23:5*). Despite guards aplenty, Jehoiachin's table in Nebuchadnezzar's palace had become the Lord's Table. Again, "He said to me, 'This is the table that stands before the Lord'" (*Ezek 41:22*). As to the revelry, "'Your new moons and your appointed festivals my soul hates; they have become a burden to me'" (Isa 1:14). Two links from Ecclesiastes reached back to Second Kings: "I searched with my mind how to cheer my body with wine—my mind still guiding me with wisdom—and how to lay hold on

---

36. *ANET*, 308. Jehoiachin received ten *silas* of oil, equivalent to fourteen quarts.

37. Parpola II, xxviii, item 6a.

38. A "sumptuous banquet" was a regular feature of the substitute's day. Parpola II, xxv.

39. Parpola I, 21; Parpola II, xxiv. The candidate king and queen were "treated with wine."

## The Word-Link King of Babylon

folly" and "It is better to go to the house of mourning than to go to the house of feasting; for this is the end of everyone" (*Eccl 2:3, 7:2*).[40]

As Evil-Marduk's substitute, Jehoiachin briefly oversaw enormous wealth. Word Links said, "Then she gave the king one hundred twenty talents of gold, a great quantity of spices, and precious stones"; "The king also made a great ivory throne, and overlaid it with the finest gold"; Job "had fourteen thousand sheep, six thousand camels, a thousand yoke of oxen, and a thousand donkeys"; and "the weight of gold that came to Solomon in one year was six hundred sixty-six talents of gold."[41] A score of other links are similar.[42]

Some Word Links put wealth in perspective. A diviner said, "'If Balak [Moab's king] should give me his house full of silver and gold, I would not be able to go beyond the word of the Lord." Proverbs weighed in with, "How much better to get wisdom than gold!" And Ecclesiastes, thinking of substitute kings, wrote, "Those to whom God gives wealth, possessions, and honor, so that they lack nothing . . . yet God does not enable them to enjoy these things, but a stranger enjoys them."[43] Jehoiachin's name is coded beneath the last two of these Word Links.

"Jehoiachin put aside his prison clothes" (2 Kgs 25:29) for good reason. This seventh-century Nineveh letter shows that the Assyrians lavishly outfitted their substitutes. "As regards the substitute king of Akkad [Babylon], order should be given to enthrone him. As regards the clothes of the king, my lord, and the garments for the statue of the substitute king, as regards the necklace of gold, the sceptre and the throne . . ."[44] Word Links with the master passage reinforce Nineveh's archaeological evidence. "'God . . . will give me bread to eat and clothing to wear'" (Gen 28:20). And "'For the man whom the king delights to honor, let royal robes be brought, which the king has worn'" (Esth 6:7-8). In a third link, one

---

40. Other Word Links that belong with feasting are: *1 Kgs 17:14-16*; Eccl 9:7-9; 10:16-19.

41. Quotations are within these Word Links: 1 Kgs 10:8-10, 17-20; Job 42:11-12; *2 Chr 9:11-13*.

42. Links not quoted that speak of wealth are Gen 28:18-20; *Exod 38:24*; Num 31:38-41; *Deut 14:26*; 2 Sam 9:9-11; 19:17-19; 1 Kgs 4:7, 21-25; 5:9-11; 8:61-63; 14:28-29; 22:30-31; *1 Chr 27:1*; *Ezra 1:9-11*; *2:65-67*; *Neh 7:67-71*; Esth 6:8; Job 1:3-4, 11-12; Prov 27:21-23.

43. Num 24:13; *Prov 16:16*; *Eccl 6:2*.

44. Parpola I, 109.

king got another to wear his clothes (1 Kgs 22:30–31), a fitting description of what actually occurred: Jehoiachin literally stepped into Evil-Marduk's shoes. Often with regard to Word Links, biblical authors believed in repetition. To make the point, there are fifteen other connected passages about wealth or clothing.[45]

## DEAD BY NEW YEAR'S DAY

After his coronation, Jehoiachin had but five days to live. These Word Links could have come from his mouth: "'My days are swifter than a weaver's shuttle, and come to their end without hope. Remember that my life is a breath . . .'"; and "'Thou hast made my days a few handbreadths, and my lifetime is as nothing in thy sight. Surely everyone stands as a mere breath!'" A different link, however, was less sympathetic: "Who knows what is good for mortals while they live the few days of their vain lives, which they pass like a shadow?" And another Word Link made a similar point while broadly hinting at substitution: "Though sinners do evil a hundred times and prolong their lives, yet . . . neither will they prolong their days."[46]

In Word Links, repetition serves to clarify. For example, here are some of the nearly three dozen links about death and burial: "'in the day that you eat of it you shall die'"; "he breathed his last and died, and was gathered to his people"; "those who touch the dead body of any human being shall be unclean seven days"; "'you deserve to die'"; "today Adonijah shall be put to death'"; "in the end it is the way to death"; "both great and small shall die in this land"; "Those who stay in this city shall die by the sword, by famine, and by pestilence"; "Ishmael son of Nethaniah . . . struck down Gedaliah son of Ahikam . . . with the sword and killed him"; and Jonah said, "'It is better for me to die than to live.'"[47] Remember that all these links are bound by common vocabulary to the Second Kings master.

---

45. Wealth or clothing Word Links not cited are: *Exod 38:24*; Deut 14:26; 2 Sam 9:9–11; 19:17–19; 1 Kgs 4:7, 21–25; *5:9–11*; 8:61–63; *1 Chr 27:1*; Ezra 1:9–11; *2:65–67*; Neh 7:67–70; Job 1:3–4, 11–12; Prov 27:21–23.

46. *Job 7:6–7*; Ps 39:5; Eccl 6:12; 8:12–13.

47. Quotations are from these Word Links: *Gen 2:16–19*; 25:16–17; Num 19:10–11; 1 Sam 26:16; 1 Kgs 2:23–24; Prov 16:22–25; *Jer 16:4–6*; 38:2–5; *41:1–2*; Jonah 4:8. Unmentioned links about death are: Gen 43:25–27; Num 20:28–29; 28:9–11; Deut 30:15; Josh 23:14–15; Esth 2:23; Jer 4:22–23. Italics indicate passage contains Jehoiachin coding.

With irony the passage relates Evil-Marduk's kindness toward Jehoiachin. But what seemed was not what was. Word Links offer scholars the opportunity to present to others the reality that lies behind appearance.

How did Jehoiachin die? A half-dozen links describe how the Babylonians executed Jehoiachin. Here are actual links to 2 Kgs 25: "'within three days Pharaoh will lift up your head'"; "'within three days Pharaoh will lift up your head—from you!'"; "'His head shall be thrown over the wall to you'"; they "brought the head of Ishbaal to David"; "they lifted up their heads no more"; and "'I will strike you down and cut off your head.'" A seventh connection talked of hair weighing four-and-one-half pounds when cut from the head. The note shows the linked passages.[48] Singly, the linked verses indicate little. But taken together, they announce that the Babylonians had decapitated the Judean king.

At death Jehoiachin would have received a king's full honors. Here is a description of a Neo-Babylonian royal funeral.[49] King Nabonidus "laid her body to rest wrapped in fine wool garments and shining white linen. He deposited her body in a hidden tomb with splendid ornaments of gold set with beautiful stone beads, containers of scented oil . . ." Kings and governors came from across the empire to grieve, and a period of mourning was announced for the Babylonian people. Though surely not as grand, a substitute king's funeral would have been similar. The following describes a seventh-century substitute's funeral in Babylonia. "We prepared the burial chamber. He and his queen have been decorated, treated, displayed, buried and wailed over. The burnt-offering has been burnt, all omens have been canceled, and numerous . . . rituals . . . and scribal recitations have been performed in perfect manner."[50] It sounds like a magnificent sendoff.

As these links indicate, Jehoiachin apparently wanted interment at Jerusalem: "'I asked of the Lord . . . that I may dwell in the house of the Lord all the days of my life,'" said one Word Link. Another was, "They buried him in the city of David among the kings." This famous verse, which coding tells us is about Jehoiachin, is especially poignant: "For a day in your courts is better than a thousand elsewhere. I would rather be a

---

48. *Gen 40:13*, 19; 2 Sam 20:21; 4:8; *Judg 8:28*; 1 Sam 17:46; and 2 Sam 14:26 talks of hair upon a head.

49. *ANET*, 561–62; translator's marks omitted.

50. Parpola I, 229.

doorkeeper in the house of my God than live in the tents of wickedness."[51] According to two other linked passages, Evil-Marduk may have allowed Jehoiachin burial in Israel.[52]

Word Links with the master Second Kings passage interpreted Jehoiachin's death as an offering to "remove the guilt of the congregation, to make atonement for their behalf before the Lord" (*Lev 10:17*). Jehoiachin the scapegoat carried "all the iniquities of the people of Israel, and all their transgressions, all their sins" (Lev 16:21). A number of other links made similar connections.[53] This Word Link was less theoretical. God instructed Ezekiel, "Lie on your left side, and I will place the punishment of the house of Israel upon it." Next he told the prophet to lie on his right side "and bear the punishment of the house of Judah; forty days I assign you" (Ezek 4:4–6). Note that through Word Links the author of 2 Kgs 25 interpreted Jehoiachin's death as atoning for the whole people of Israel. On the other hand, for Assyrians (and very likely for Babylonians also) atonement centered upon the true king. In Parpola's words, the ancients thought the substitute king's "principal role was to act as a substitute sufferer who took it upon himself to bear the sins of the king and atone for them with his own blood."[54]

By the late 560s, when Jehoiachin languished in prison, the Judeans had lost Jerusalem, the Promised Land, Solomon's temple, and the monarchy. Word Links with the master passage offered hope in face of this dire situation. God said to Abraham, "'My covenant I will establish with Isaac, whom Sarah shall bear to you at this season next year'"; and "'To your offspring I will give this land.'" Another link reminded that when the Conquest was completed, "Not one of all the good promises that the Lord had made to the house of Israel had failed; all came to pass."[55] As to the monarchy, David prayed that "'with your blessing shall the house of your servant be blessed forever'" and Solomon quoted what God had promised David: "'Your son, whom I will set on your throne in your place, shall build the house for my name'" (2 Sam 7:29; 1 Kgs 5:5).

51. *Ps 27:4*, 2 Chr 24:15–16, *Ps 84:10–11*.

52. Judg 16:30–31, and especially *Gen 50:3–5*, indicate that Jehoiachin was laid to rest in Israel.

53. Exod 12:5–8; *Lev 15:13–15; 16:27–29*; 17:10; *23:18; 25:29; Num 29:11–12, 19–20*; 1 Sam 2:24–25; *Ezra 3:4–6*; Neh 10:31–33.

54. Parpola, "Substitute King Ritual and Jesus."

55. Gen 17:21–23; 24:7; Josh 21:44–45.

## The Word–Link King of Babylon

But accompanying these hopeful Word Links were others that described the dynasty's pathology: "Concerning King Jehoiakim of Judah: He shall have no one to sit upon the throne of David" and "As I live, says the Lord, even if King Coniah [Jehoiachin] son of Jehoiakim of Judah were the signet ring on my right hand, even from there I would tear you off and give you into the hands of those who seek your life" (Jer 36:30; 22:24–25). Then the author of our master passage by Word Link added, "If you will not heed these words, I swear by myself, says the Lord, that this house [of the king of Judah] shall become a desolation" (Jer 22:5). In this next, the Lord damned nation, city, and temple: "'I will remove Judah also out of my sight, as I have removed Israel; and I will reject this city that I have chosen, Jerusalem, and the house of which I said, My name shall be there'" (2 Kgs 23:27). And these things came to pass.

Our master Second Kings passage could have been written in the year 561, the nadir of the Exile. Jerusalem and its temple lay in ruins, the Babylonians had slain every royal family member they could catch, and voracious neighbors were devouring what remained of Judah. In face of this, exilic writers still hung their hopes on God's faithfulness. Using Word Links, the author of 2 Kgs 25:27–30 cited these passages: "The surviving remnant of the house of Judah shall again take root downward, and bear fruit upward"; "the ransomed of the Lord shall return, and come to Zion with singing; everlasting joy shall be upon their heads ... and sorrow and sighing shall flee away"; and "In days to come the mountain of the Lord's house shall be established as the highest of the mountains, and shall be raised above the hills; all the nations shall stream to it."[56] It could be said that the bleaker the outlook, the grander the vision.[57]

Jehoiachin, the last King of Judah, though weak, died heroically. Second Kings 25:27–30, which relates his final days, has been a fitting passage to illustrate this new scholarly tool of Word Links. With both coding and Word Links established, we are ready to address in chapter 4 one of the foremost mysteries of scripture—the identity of Second Isaiah.

---

56. Quotes are from these links: 2 Kgs 19:29–30; Isa 35:8–10, 2:2. Others in this vein are Jer 33:14; Ezek 37:19; Hos 1:11; Mic 4:1; Hag 2:19–22; Zech 12:6–7.

57. Even authors of post-exilic books took care to link writings about the temple's restoration to the exilic Jehoiachin-release passage: *Ezra 1:5–7*; 7:8–10; 8:35–36; 9:9; Neh 2:3; and also see 2 Chr 23:2–3. Word Links that have not been cited in the Davidic Line category are: 1 Sam 2:28; 3:11–12; *17:14–15*; 2 Kgs 1:17; *Jer 22:1–2*; *33:14*. Italics mean the passage contains Jehoiachin coding or anagrams.

# 4

# Second Isaiah's Identity

## GENESIS-ISAIAH CONNECTION

THIS CHAPTER WILL IDENTIFY the most excellent writer in all of Scripture. Called Second Isaiah, he or she is an unknown prophet who many think lived in the sixth century BCE, during the Babylonian Exile of the Jews. Second Isaiah makes the short list of history's greatest religious thinkers. The prophet's portrayals of God make the spirit sing; they still astound. New Testament writers quoted him frequently, and his Shakespearian language remains in current use in liturgies and hymnbooks.

The book of Isaiah contains Second Isaiah's work, along with that of others, including the prophet named Isaiah who lived in the eighth century. Second Isaiah mentions Cyrus the Persian who liberated the Judeans from Babylon rule. Until modern times, everyone thought eighth-century Isaiah had foretold sixth-century Cyrus. Today most agree that a later hand wrote Isa 40–55.[1] Once commentators had concluded that there was a Second Isaiah, the next step was to identify him or her. But no one has yet succeeded in doing so, and in recent years scarcely anyone has ventured a new guess. A generation ago, a noted scholar concluded that Second Isaiah was "a man whose name we shall never know."[2]

The prophet wrote Isa 49:1–6, which analysts agree is autobiographical. Did those verses disclose Second Isaiah's identity? Shown below is a side-by-side comparison of Isa 49:1–3, 5 and Gen 25:21–26, which relates the story of Jacob's birth. The passages share fifteen common words, including six of seven words in this key phrase from Isa 49:1: "The Lord

1. Friedman, "Isaiah," 46.
2. Thomas, "Creative Epoch," 41.

## Second Isaiah's Identity

[יהוה] called [קרא] me before I was born [בטן], while I was in my mother's [אם] womb [מעה] he named [שם] me."

### TABLE 4.1—SHARED WORDS IN ISAIAH 49:1-3, 5 AND GENESIS 25:21-26

| Isa 49:1-3, 5 | Gen 25:21-26 |
|---|---|
| Listen to me, O coastlands, pay attention, you peoples [לאם] from far away! The Lord [יהוה] called [קרא] me before I was born [בטן], while I was in my mother's [אם] womb [מעה] he named [שם] me. He made my mouth like a sharp sword, in the shadow of his hand [יד] he hid me; he made me a polished arrow, in his quiver he hid me away. And he said [אמר] to me, "You are my servant [עבד], Israel, in whom I will be glorified." . . . And now the Lord [יהוה] says [אמר], who formed me in the womb [בטן] to be his [לו] servant [עבד], to bring Jacob [יעקב] back to him . . . | . . . the Lord [יהוה] granted his [לו] prayer, and his wife Rebekah conceived. The children struggled together within her; and she said [אמר], "If it is to be this way [אם], why do I live?" So she went to inquire of the Lord [יהוה]. And the Lord [יהוה] said [אמר] to her, "Two nations are in your womb [בטן], and two peoples [לאם] born of you [מעה] shall be divided; the one [לאם] shall be stronger than the other [לאם], the elder shall serve [עבד] the younger." When her time to give birth was at hand, there were twins in her womb [בטן]. The first came out red, all his body like a hairy mantle; so they named [קרא] him Esau. Afterward his brother came out, with his hand [יד] gripping Esau's heel; so he was named [שם] [קרא] Jacob [יעקב]. |

Second Isaiah chose his vocabulary with a view to the birth story of Jacob. Why? Genesis 25 says Rebekah had twins in her womb, and Esau came out first. "Afterward his brother came out," the text reads, "with his hand gripping Esau's heel; so he was named Jacob." The New Oxford Annotated Bible notes, "*Jacob* is interpreted by a play on the Hebrew word for 'heel,' i.e. 'he takes by the heel'" (Oxford's italics). Genesis says that while still within his mother's womb, Jacob grabbed his twin by the heel and so acquired his name. And Isa 49:1 says, "While I was in my mother's womb he named me."³

In Gen 25, the patriarch Jacob earns his name before his birth. In Isa 49, Second Isaiah says God named him before birth. The passages are a match in meaning, and are strongly connected by common words. Second Isaiah's name appears to be Jacob. In the Isaiah autobiographical passage the anonymous prophet of the Exile seems to announce his name. Each birth produced a child named Jacob. And remember that six of the seven words clustered in the Isaiah 49 birth announcement also appear in the Gen 25 passage. These words appear together only in the Gen and Isaiah passages. It is an extraordinary Word Link, with a word combination that is unique to Gen 25 and Isa 49.

By comparison, the prophet Jeremiah's birth account supports the Jacob finding in an interesting way. While Jeremiah was still in the womb, God "formed," "knew," "consecrated," and "appointed" him (Jer 1:5). Second Isaiah, writing afterward of his own birth, surely had the great Jeremiah in mind. According to Second Isaiah, "The Lord called me" and then "he named me." Using "called," the prophet presents his credentials to be a prophet. With "named me" he goes Jeremiah one better. Jeremiah might have been formed and known within the womb, but Second Isaiah, while still inside his mother, receives at God's hand that most intimate of things, his very name. In Hebrew Scripture, the name is "the essence of personality, the expression of innermost being."⁴

Furthermore, Isa 49:3 reads, "And he said to me, 'You are my servant, Israel, in whom I will be glorified.'" After speaking to the prophet ("he said to me"), God called him "Israel." Prior verses clearly addressed an individual. How could the prophet suddenly have become the nation Israel? This paradox has ever stumped commentators. However, once one assumes the author's name is Jacob, the problem disappears. The patriarch had been both Jacob and Israel, and likewise so was the prophet. Isaiah 49:3 could have read, "You are my servant, Jacob-Israel."

Moreover, it is a scholarly commonplace that Second Isaiah frequently used "Jacob." This, too, argues that Jacob was the prophet's own name. In the first ten chapters of his corpus, Second Isaiah uses Jacob no less than twenty-two times. Phrases like "God of Jacob," "Jacob my ser-

---

3. In Isa 49:1, the Tanakh translates the causative of "remember" as "named." One could also render it "he caused my name to be famous."

4. Abba, "Name," 501.

vant," and "seed of Jacob" abound. Also, the prophet loved to use Jacob and Israel in parallel, as in "Israel, my servant, Jacob, whom I have chosen" (Isa 41:8). In 44:1 he playfully reversed the order: "O Jacob my servant, Israel whom I have chosen!" The prophet, a master of ambiguity, rings the changes on Jacob and Israel by pairing them with God, servant, name, seed, glory, and house. The patriarch carried the names of both Jacob and Israel, so the prophet's interchangeable use of the two names also tells us that Second Isaiah's name is Jacob.

## RABBIS BEND SCRIPTURE TO GLORIFY JACOB

Scholars estimate that the patriarchs Abraham, Isaac, and Jacob lived between 2000 and 1500 BCE—at least a millennium before Second Isaiah.[5] The patriarch Jacob ranks with David as the most clearly drawn character in Hebrew Scripture, and the patriarch's character is consistent throughout. He is greedy, duplicitous, and fearful. While still in the womb, Jacob fights with his brother. As an adult, he takes advantage of a heedless Esau to trade lentils and bread for the older twin's birthright. Later, with the connivance of his mother, Jacob disguises himself as Esau and steals the firstborn's blessing from their blind father.

To escape retribution, Jacob goes to Haran, where he meets his cousin Rachel, whom he eventually marries. Jacob becomes the chief herdsman of Laban, his father-in-law, and uses the position to enlarge his own flocks at Laban's expense. At length, Jacob flees to Haran with wives, children, servants, and flocks. Laban pursues, and overtakes the fearful patriarch in Canaan. There, to Jacob's surprise and relief, the two men talk, swear an oath, and part amicably.

Jacob's confrontation with his brother Esau, however, is still to be faced. The patriarch divides his entourage into several parts. He sends herds, servants, and even wives and children ahead to soften his brother's anger. That night, as Scripture says, "Jacob was left alone; and a man wrestled with him until daybreak" (Gen 32:24). Though the wrestling put Jacob's thigh out of joint, he refused to release the "man" until he had his blessing. His adversary responded, "You shall no longer be called Jacob, but Israel [one who strives with God], for you have striven with God and with humans, and have prevailed" (Gen 32:28).

---

5. Hicks, "Patriarchs," 677; and Sarna, "Patriarchs," 181.

Thus renamed, a frightened and limping Jacob-Israel meets Esau the following day—and his twin forgives him! Jacob then reneges on a promise to follow Esau to Edom, and instead takes the road to Canaan. After a bloody run-in with the Canaanites, Jacob flees once more, this time to Bethel. There God promises that he would father a nation. Eventually, Jacob brings his family to Egypt, where Pharaoh welcomes and honors the old man. Jacob dies in Egypt after blessing each of his sons, the founders of the twelve tribes of Israel.

Scripture's unsparing portrait of Jacob pictures a man on the run. But Jacob is also a man blessed of God, the third link in the Abraham-Isaac-Jacob chain that is to secure the Promised Land for the tribes of Israel. What has Jacob the patriarch to do with Jacob the prophet? The prophet was a genius with words, an inspired and inspiring leader of his people. His voice has reverberated down the centuries, and those reverberations about the prophet can still be felt in rabbinic literature. The rabbis wrote that neither Abraham nor Isaac equaled Jacob, "who was regarded as a model of virtue and righteousness."[6] Jacob was "the greatest of the patriarchs," and Abraham himself once escaped death just so that Jacob might descend from him.[7] After Jacob's demise, it was his merit, not that of the other patriarchs, that sustained Israel. God's throne had Jacob's image carved upon it, and God gave the patriarch a position little lower than the angels.[8] "The glorification of Jacob is of very high antiquity," said an expert on rabbinic literature.[9] That glorification is extraordinary in view of what the Bible says about Jacob's character.

To put Jacob's glaring moral lapses in better light, the rabbis used imagination. Jacob agreed to be born after his brother because otherwise Esau would kill Rebekah, their mother. The reason Jacob wanted Esau's birthright was so that he could offer sacrifices, the prerogative of the firstborn. Moreover, Esau was unsuitable for so spiritual a task. Jacob did not steal his brother's blessing, but took only his due. Though Jacob kissed his cousin Rachel at the well in Haran, the rabbis pardoned him because she was a blood relation. Jacob himself was not subject to evil impulse, and so

---

6. Aberbach, "Jacob in Aggadah," 1198. Aberbach cites *b. Pesaḥ* 56a; *Gen. Rab.* 68:11; *Song Rab.* 3:6 n. 2; and *b. Mak.* 24a.

7. Aberbach, citing *Gen. Rab.* 76:1; 63:2; *Lev. Rab.* 36:4; and *b. Sanh.* 19b.

8. Aberbach, 1199, citing *Song Rab.* 3:6; *Lev. Rab.* 36:4; *Mid. Ps.* 8:7; and *Gen. Rab.* 82:2.

9. Ginzberg, *Legends*, 1:276.

forth.[10] While some rabbis occasionally criticized Jacob, most were apologetic. They sought to excuse the patriarch by explaining away Scripture.

Jacob's preeminence among the sages is especially strange considering the towering figure of Abraham. Of the three patriarchs, Jacob was a rogue, Isaac a nonentity, and Abraham a giant. Both testaments give Abraham his due. Chapter 11 of the New Testament's book of Hebrews contains a classic chapter on faith, a roll call of the heroes of Scripture. Hebrews 11 allots to Isaac and Jacob a grudging verse apiece while giving Abraham line after inspirational line.

Rabbinic literature should have glorified Abraham rather than Jacob, but surprisingly it does not. Instead, the rabbis chose to exalt the patriarch, almost certainly because of the enduring reputation of the prophet Jacob. Other rabbinic material sustains this view. A Talmud tractate said Jacob the patriarch missed the servitude of the Diaspora, though it was the prophet rather than the patriarch who lived during the Exile.[11] Rabbinic literature contains many references to Jacob's great learning and to his study of the law. Isaiah 49:3 reads, "'You are my servant, Israel, in whom I will be glorified.'" Just before quoting that passage, the Talmud discussed teachers of the Torah.[12] The Talmud writers knew that the author of the quoted verse had taught Torah, and at the same time implied Israel was the servant's name. Scripture offers no basis for associating the patriarch Jacob with Torah studies. But there was every basis for assuming the prophet Jacob excelled in the Torah, and that he taught it. Another example is that when a pregnant Rebekah passed a synagogue or an academy, Jacob would attempt to break out of the womb.[13] The Jacob of rabbinic literature was the exilic prophet, not the patriarch. The rabbis invented stories about the patriarch to glorify the prophet.

At thirteen Jacob entered the House of Study of Shem and Eber.[14] *Genesis Rabbah*, the earliest Midrash, states, "Our father Jacob spent another fourteen years secluded in the Land and studying under Eber."[15] This brings us to academies. The opening book of the Talmud says Scripture

---

10. Aberbach, 1199–1200. This note does not list the numerous rabbinic sources that Aberbach cites.

11. *b. Shabb.* 118b.

12. *b. Yoma* 86a.

13. *Gen. Rab.* 63:6, cited by Aberbach, 1197.

14. *Tar. Yer.* Gen 25:27; *Yash. Tol.* 53b; and others, cited by Ginzberg, 316.

15. *Gen. Rab.* 618.

sometimes used "tent" as a metaphor for academy, and the great medieval scholar Rashi agreed.[16] Thus "tents of Shem" in Gen 9:27 referred to an academy. Another candidate for the metaphor was Gen 25:27, which concludes Jacob's birth story. The verse says, "Jacob was a quiet man, living in tents." Elsewhere in the narrative, Jacob pitched his tent before at Shechem (Gen 33:19) and beyond Migdal-eder (Gen 35:21). Quite possibly the prophet himself was announcing his academy's current whereabouts.

Here are the reasons that Second Isaiah's name is Jacob:

- A strong Word Link ties Second Isaiah's birth account in Isaiah to the Jacob birth story in Genesis.
- Second Isaiah's description in Isa 49 of his own naming while within the womb exactly fits the Genesis account of Jacob's birth.
- The frequent use of Jacob in the Second Isaiah chapters support that the prophet uses this name as a signature.
- To assume that the prophet bears the same names as the patriarch— Jacob and Israel—resolves textual problems.
- When rabbinic authors turned scriptural warts into dimples, they were exalting the exilic prophet, not the ancient patriarch.
- The learned Jacob whom the rabbis describe fits the prophet, not the patriarch.
- Finally, there is one chance in three thousand that the number of Jacob coding rows in Isa 40–55 is coincidental (see below).

For a century, scholars have titled the prophet Second Isaiah. Perhaps the time has come to call him Second Jacob.

## ANOTHER TEST OF CODING

The opening chapter found that the Priestly Benediction contains a code that spells Jehoiachin numerous times. Then chapter 2 traced Jehoiachin anagrams to the writings of Second Isaiah, Jeremiah, and Ezekiel, and extended coding to include Cyrus the Persian. Strong evidence that Jacob is Second Isaiah's name makes Isa 40–55 a good place to test coding again, this time with Jacob. For convenience, we shall consider only rows, that is, coded spellings taking letters from consecutive text words.

---

16. *b. Ber.* 16a; Rosenbaum and Silbermann, trans., *Pentateuch with Rashi*, 116.

## Second Isaiah's Identity

The Bible contains 4,114 יעקב rows, with eighty-six of them located within Isa 40–55. Here is just one instance. The initial Jacob row is in the seventh through the tenth words of Isa 40: עַל לֵב יְרוּשָׁלַם וְקִרְאוּ. The Jacob letters are in italicized underline, and the sequence is עביק.

The ratio of Jacob rows per text word in Isa 40–55 is almost fifty percent higher than in the rest of Scripture, and the probability of this occurring by chance is about one in three thousand.[17] What can explain this high number of Jacob rows? Part of the answer could be the frequency of the word "Jacob" in Second Isaiah chapters. Subtracting the effects of Jacob text words from both Isa 40–55 and from the rest of Scripture moves the probability of coincidence from one in three thousand to one in eighty-one.[18] However, one in eighty-one is still statistically significant (at .012 percent), so the difference remains even after excluding Jacob text words. The conclusion is that *the same code used in the Priestly Benediction to form Jehoiachin spellings was used by Second Isaiah in Isa 40–55 to form Jacob spellings.*

And did the prophet also use anagrams to spell יעקב within single text words? The answer, at least in Isa 40–55, must be no since only ויבקע in Isa 48:21 qualifies. Instead of using anagrams, the prophet frequently worked his own names—Jacob and Israel—into his text.

## SCHOLARLY OPPORTUNITY

Since we now know that Second Isaiah used Jacob and Israel interchangeably, perhaps a look at Isa 40–55 will reveal how the prophet signed his work. Such opportunities are rare.

The prophet Jacob often used Jacob and Israel in parallel to introduce himself, and not infrequently he included servant. To illustrate, "But now hear, O Jacob My servant, Israel whom I have chosen! Thus says the Lord, who made you, who formed you in the womb" (Isa 44:1–2). Womb, very likely, alludes to the Jacob birth story. Here is a second example: The Lord "formed me in the womb to be his servant, to bring back Jacob back to him, and that Israel might be gathered to him" (Isa 49:5). This next

---

17. The chi-square proportions are 86/4,287, 4,028/297,827. The numerators are Jacob rows in Isa 40–55 and in the rest of scripture, and the denominators are opportunities to make a row in the same categories. P = $3.31 \times 10^{-4}$, or 1 in 3,200.

18. The chi-square proportions are 74/4,240, 3,839/295,515. The numerators and denominators are the same as in the previous note. However, totals reflect subtraction of words surrounding "Jacob" appearances.

verse has the same elements. Jacob and Israel could be the nation, or the prophet, or both, though this verse's birth elements point to Jacob the prophet. "Listen to me, O house of Jacob, all the remnant of the house of Israel, who have been borne by me from your birth, carried from the womb . . ." (Isa 46:3). This is similar: "For the Lord has redeemed Jacob, and will be glorified in Israel. Thus says the Lord, your Redeemer, who formed you from the womb . . ." (Isa 44:23–24). "Formed" and "womb" reminded readers of the birth story in Gen 25.

In Jacob-Israel parallels, Second Isaiah skillfully mixed the corporate and the individual. For example, in Isa 49:6 God said, "'It is too light a thing that you should be my servant to raise up the tribes of Jacob and to restore the survivors of Israel.'" Another Jacob-Israel parallel does the same thing: "Do not fear, you worm Jacob, you insect Israel! I will help you, says the Lord; your Redeemer is the Holy One of Israel" (Isa 41:14). In the following, Jacob and Israel are both individuals. "Remember these things, O Jacob, and Israel, for you are my servant; I formed you, you are my servant; O Israel, you will not be forgotten by me" (Isa 44:21). And yet another example: "For the sake of my servant Jacob, and Israel my chosen, I call you by your name, I surname you, though you do not know me" (Isa 45:4).

This mixing of personal and corporate with Jacob and Israel has perplexed scholars. But difficulties dissolve once one understands that the prophet bore the names of both Israel and Jacob. Second Jacob probably relished the apparent confusion. He understood that those he addressed knew the secret.[19] Whatever else Jacob meant in these passages, he certainly intended them as signatures. The term "Jacob IDs" will stand for these and other plays upon Jacob and Israel. IDs have a more neutral meaning than signatures, which is important because Jacob IDs were used not only by the prophet but also by those assailing him. In either case they identified Second Jacob.

In addition to the Jacob-Israel pairings, the prophet also used Jacob itself, usually with a modifier. For example, "Bring your proofs, says the King of Jacob"; "Do not fear, O Jacob my servant"; "the offspring of Jacob"; "'The Lord has redeemed his servant Jacob!'"; and "Your Redeemer, the Mighty One of Jacob" (Isa 41:21; 44:2; 45:19; 48:20; 49:26).

---

19. The seventeen Jacob-Israel parallels in Isa 40–55 are 40:27; 41:8, 14; 42:24; 43:1, 22, 28; 44:1, 5, 21, 23; 45:4; 46:3; 48:1, 12; 49:5, 6.

## Second Isaiah's Identity

Since the prophet used Jacob with modifiers, it is not surprising that he employed Israel in the same manner. Begin with "That you may know that it is I, the Lord, the God of Israel, who call you by name" and "invoke the God of Israel" (Isa 45:3; 48:1). In another variation Second Jacob may be addressing his disciples: "In the Lord all the offspring of Israel shall triumph and glory" (Isa 45:25). The prophet also used "Israel my glory" and "my servant, Israel" (Isa 46:13, 49:3). But his favorite seems to have been "Holy One of Israel," which is a hallmark of his writings. He works it three times into Isaiah chapter 41: "your Redeemer is the Holy One of Israel," "the Holy One of Israel has created it," and "in the Holy One of Israel you shall glory" (41:14, 20, 16). Interestingly, Jacob IDs disappear from work attributed to the prophet after Isaiah chapter 49, except for Holy One of Israel inclusions in chapters 54 and 55 (and a single God of Israel reference in Isa 52). In all, the exilic prophet employed Holy One of Israel eleven times in Isa 40–55.[20]

Here is an inventory of Second Jacob's use of Jacob and Israel in Isa 40–55 and the extent to which they occur in the balance of Scripture.

TABLE 4.2—JACOB-ISRAEL IDS IN HEBREW SCRIPTURE

| Type of ID | Isa 40–55 | Balance of Scripture |
|---|---|---|
| Jacob with Mighty One, God, seed, name, servant, or house | 22 | 353 |
| Jacob-Israel Parallels | 17 | 56 |
| Holy One of Israel | 11 | 21 |
| Israel alone (excluding parallels) | 1 | 1,000+ |
| Israel with God, seed, name, servant, house, or glory | 15 | 360 |
| Israel with sons (or Israelites) | 0 | 502 info only |
| Israel with people | 0 | 78 info only |
| Israel with King (meaning Lord) | 2 | 1 |
| Total Unduplicated IDs | 45 | 787 |

20. Holy One of Israel appears in Isa 41:14, 16, 20; 43:3, 14; 45:11; 47:4; 48:17; 49:7; 54:5; 55:5.

In identifying Jacob IDs in the rest of Scripture, all the Jacob and Israel variations found in Isa 40–55 count, except for one. That exception is Israel used alone. It appears just once in the Second Isaiah chapters (Isa 45:17), but over one thousand times elsewhere. Inclusion of solitary Israel occurrences would swamp the analysis, and to little purpose. While further work could identify some of these (for example, Ezek 13:4 and Amos 4:12), the table excludes them. Separately, though "people of Israel," "sons of Israel," "Israelites," and the like do not appear in Isa 40–55, the term occurs often in the balance of Scripture alongside other IDs. Because of this, it seems appropriate to list it with Jacob IDs, but not to include it in Total Unduplicated IDs. After excluding overlaps, there are forty-five Jacob IDs in the Isaiah chapters and close to eight hundred in the remainder of Scripture.

Now to what exilic Jacob wrote or may have written. The best starting place is the prophet's home ground, Isaiah chapters 40–55. Chapters 42 through 49 are filled with IDs, important ones. Jacob-Israel parallels are numerous, and so are instances of Holy One of Israel. Two chapters contain five of these, one has four, and two other chapters have three apiece. Isaiah 41, 43, 44, and 48 win mention for their high ID frequencies (IDs divided by text words), and chapter 45 almost makes it. Chapters 40, 42, 46, and 47 each contain only one Jacob-Israel parallel or Holy One of Israel, but one is enough to assign authorship to Second Isaiah, especially considering the strength of neighboring writings. After chapter 49, major IDs take a holiday until chapters 54 and 55. Isaiah 54:5 says, "The Holy One of Israel is your Redeemer, the God of the whole earth he is called." And the next chapter contains, ". . . because of the Lord your God, the Holy One of Israel, for he has glorified you" (Isa 55:5). Almost a score of Jacob IDs within Isa 40–55 remain to be quoted, but the lesson should be clear. Jacob the prophet, also called Israel, wrote and signed most of those chapters.

Isaiah 52 contains one ID, "God of Israel" (Isa 52:12), so it might also be from the pen of Second Jacob. But based solely upon Jacob IDs, chapters 50 and 51 are not by him. Neither is Isa 53, which is regrettable. It concerns the Suffering Servant and may be the most important chapter in Hebrew Scripture. In summary, Jacob IDs strongly support that a half dozen of the so-called Second Isaiah chapters were written by Jacob the prophet, an equal number probably were by him, and—based solely on Jacob-Israel IDs—three were not.

*Second Isaiah's Identity*

## JACOB IDS IN SCRIPTURE

The book of Isaiah traditionally has been divided into three sections. The third section, chapters 56–66, has been attributed to someone known only as Third Isaiah. Chapter 60 begins "Arise, shine; for your light has come," and goes on to describe the future glory of Zion. If any part of Third Isaiah is by Jacob, it is chapter 60, for it contains Mighty One of Jacob and refers twice to the Holy One of Israel (Isa 60:16, 9, 14). Four other Third-Isaiah chapters have IDs, but nothing as distinctive as this. Next, the jewel in the Third Isaiah collection is Isa 61, which sounds like Second Jacob even though it contains no IDs. If Jacob wrote Isa 61, he did not apply his signature in the usual way.

Chapters 1–39 constitute the first section of the book of Isaiah. Almost half contain Jacob IDs, indicating that the exilic prophet wrote, edited, or was the subject of at least some of these chapters. The best candidate is chapter 17, which has three IDs. It begins with an oracle against Damascus that includes an anti-Jacob parallel: "The remnant of Aram will be like the glory of the children of Israel, says the Lord of hosts. On that day the glory of Jacob will be brought low, and the fat of his flesh will grow lean" (Isa 17:3–4). Though Israel and Jacob are in parallel, it appears that the second line has been added to discredit Second Jacob. In any event, Jacob's signature is being used against him. A few verses later two solid Jacob IDs appear: God of Israel and Holy One of Israel.

Isaiah chapter 10 also features Jacob IDs. It reads, "On that day the remnant of Israel and the survivors of the house of Jacob [parallel ID] will no more lean on the one who struck them, but will lean on the Lord, the Holy One of Israel [ID], in truth. A remnant will return, the remnant of Jacob, to the mighty God. For though your people Israel [parallel ID] were like the sand of the sea, only a remnant of them will return" (Isa 10:20–22). Such a concentration may be an insert—and a hostile one at that. Isaiah 29:19, 22–23 has a similar cluster of IDs. (They include Holy One of Israel, house of Jacob, Jacob, and the parallel Holy One of Jacob and God of Israel.)

Here is another example of the doors that Jacob IDs can open. Isaiah chapter 2 is attributed to the eighth-century prophet Isaiah. It contains the famous lines, "they shall beat their swords into plowshares, and their spears into pruning hooks; nation shall not lift up sword against nation, neither shall they learn war any more" (Isa 2:4). Standing like quotation

73

## The Exilic Code

marks in the two flanking verses are "God of Jacob" and "house of Jacob." These give us solid reason to think that Jacob, the previously unknown prophet of the Exile, wrote those swords-into-plowshares phrases, which signifies that some First Isaiah chapters have an exilic context.

Since the prophet used variations of Jacob as a signature, one should go where the Jacobs are to find his writings. Nowhere is use of that name more plentiful than in the Jacob Cycle in Genesis. This could mean that Second Jacob wrote those Genesis chapters, or that he edited older material. It could also be that that some of the saga of the patriarch Jacob is autobiographical. One thinks of his stops at Bethel, Shechem, and Eder, and his visits to Egypt. However, while chapters 25, 27–32, 34, 35, 46, and 47 are awash with Jacobs, the lack of Jacob-Israel parallels raises doubts about whether the prophet wrote them. The single exception is chapter 49, which contains three parallel IDs (vv. 2, 7, and 24). If the exilic prophet wrote any part of the Jacob Cycle, it was Genesis 49.

Turning elsewhere, Jacob evidently wrote and signed the Balaam story in the book of Numbers. Balaam was a seer whom the king of Moab summoned to curse the people of Israel. But instead of cursing them, Balaam could only bless. (The context is very likely substitute kingship.) Here are parallel IDs from chapter 23: "'Come, curse Jacob for me; Come, denounce Israel!'"; "'Who can count the dust of Jacob, or number the dust-cloud of Israel?'"; "'He has not beheld misfortune in Jacob; nor has he seen trouble in Israel.'"; "'Surely there is no enchantment against Jacob, no divination against Israel; now it shall be said of Jacob and Israel, "See what God has done!"'" (Num 23:7, 10, 21, 23). Moreover, the next chapter contains three other Jacob-Israel parallel IDs (Num 24:5, 17, 18–19). Jacob the prophet surely wrote the Balaam chapters, Num 23 and 24.

Similarly, Second Jacob used signature parallels to good effect in Deut 33, the lyrical blessing by Moses of the tribes of Israel: ". . . as a possession for the assembly of Jacob . . . the united tribes of Israel"; "They teach Jacob your ordinances, and Israel your law"; and "So Israel lives in safety, untroubled is Jacob's abode" (Deut 33:4–5, 10, 28). Another text is 1 Sam 5:7–6:3. If it is not by Jacob, he is at least one of its subjects. Within nine verses someone used the phrase "Ark of the God of Israel" a half-dozen times. "God of Israel" is a recognized ID for Jacob, and nowhere else is the ark linked with that phrase. The more common terms are "Ark," "Ark of the Lord," and "Ark of the Covenant of the Lord." The Second Samuel narrative told about damage that the captured ark caused among the Philistines, who may have served as stand-ins for the Babylonians.

If IDs were always signatures, then Second Jacob wrote the long prayer Solomon gave when he dedicated the Jerusalem temple (1 Kgs 8:14–53). No fewer than seven IDs dot the opening third of the prayer, all of them "God of Israel" (1 Kgs 8:15, 16, 17, 20, 23, 25, 26). The remainder of the prayer repeats the phrase, "my [or his or your] people Israel" seventeen times. Thus that single chapter contains twenty-four Jacob IDs. But would a master like Jacob have used such repetitive language? Martin Noth attributed this chapter to Dtr, which is his shorthand for Deuteronomistic Historian.[21] Frank Cross states that an exilic editor retouched Dtr's work, including part of Solomon's prayer.[22] Cross calls this editor $Dtr^2$. Assuming that either Dtr or $Dtr^2$ wrote 1 Kgs 8, this still-unknown author seems to have chosen Jacob as a subject of the chapter.

## JACOB THE PSALMIST

Scholars have known for some time that many psalms have characteristics similar to Isaiah chapters 40–55. Let us see if Jacob IDs confirm this connection, beginning with IDs in opening verses. Psalm 81:1 starts "Sing aloud to God our strength; shout for joy to the God of Jacob." Psalm 85:1 has "you restored the fortunes of Jacob." Another begins, "When Israel went out from Egypt, the house of Jacob from a people of strange language" (Ps 114:1). And also, "May the Lord answer you in the day of trouble! The name of the God of Jacob protect you!" (Ps 20:1). However, Second Jacob IDs are more frequently found at the end of psalms: "Jacob will rejoice; Israel will be glad" (twice); "Blessed be the Lord, the God of Israel" (twice); "The God of Jacob is our refuge"; and "The God of Israel ... he gives power and strength to his people" (Pss 14:7 and 53:6; 41:13 and 106:48; 46:11; 68:35).

Jacob the prophet never had a bad writing day, but in Ps 78 he outdid himself. It is a pleasure to read, a masterpiece. The psalm is a long recounting of God's glorious deeds and Israel's unfaithfulness. For IDs, it contains no less than three Jacob-Israel parallels and a Holy One of Israel (Ps 78:5, 21, 41, 71). Psalm 105 is another example of Second Isaiah's authorship. Here is its first Jacob-Israel ID: "O offspring of his servant Israel, children

---

21. Noth, *History*, 96, 138.
22. Cross, *Myth and Epic*, 287. Cross thinks $Dtr^2$ added vv. 46–53 to the prayer.

of Jacob, his chosen ones" (105:6).²³ A second ID is also a parallel: "Then Israel came to Egypt; Jacob lived as an alien in the land of Ham" (105:23). A third instance is "confirmed to Jacob as a statute, to Israel as an everlasting covenant" (105:10).

Of the 150 psalms, no less than one quarter of them contain Jacob IDs. The note lists them.²⁴ This is not to claim with certainty that Jacob the prophet wrote fully a quarter of the psaltery. Probably other factors also had influence, including the efforts of collaborators and disciples, the effects of imitation, and perhaps even coincidence. But the one-quarter finding is surprising considering that not a person on the planet is prepared to certify the author or historical context of even one psalm. Later chapters will use coding to test for dating and authorship of individual psalms. In the meantime, readers should know that heavy Jacob coding in the book of Psalms cannot be coincidental.²⁵ Odds of billions to one assure that Jacob was an important author and/or subject of the book of Psalms.

## OTHER JACOB IDS

Perhaps the most sacred passage in Scripture tells of Moses hearing God's call from a burning bush. The Lord said, "'I am the God of your father, the God of Abraham, the God of Isaac, and the God of Jacob'" (Exod 3:6). "God of Jacob," of course, is an ID. When in 3:13 Moses asks God's name, the reply is, "'I am who I am.' He said further, 'Thus you shall say to the Israelites [possible ID], "I am has sent me to you."'" God then instructs Moses, "'Thus you shall say to the Israelites [possible ID], "The Lord, the God of your ancestors, the God of Abraham, the God of Isaac, and the God of Jacob [ID] has sent me to you"'" (Exod 3:14–15). For good mea-

---

23. The NRSV offers "Israel" as an alternate reading based upon 1 Chr 16:13. It replaces "Abraham."

24. In addition to those cited, psalms that contain Jacob IDs are: *22:23*; 24:6; 25:22; 44:4; 46:8; 47:4; 59:5, 13; 68:8; 69:6; *71:22*; 72:18; 75:9; 76:6; 77:15; 79:7; *81:4*; 83:4; 84:8; 87:2; *89:18*; 94:7; 98:3; 99:4; 114:7; 115:12; 132:2, 5; *135:4*, 12, 19; 136:22; 146:5; *147:19*. Italics indicate Holy One of Israel or a Jacob-Israel parallel ID.

25. A coding row is formed from letters taken from consecutive text words. Psalms has 370 Jacob coding rows in 19,029 opportunities to make a row. The rest of Hebrew scripture contains 3,744 Jacob coding rows in 283,085 opportunities. The chi-square test yields a P of $1.8 \times 10^{-12}$, or one chance in 550 billion of coincidence. (Subtracting coding rows formed around the text word Jacob has no practical effect. The new chi-square probability of coincidence would still be one in 3.9 billion.)

## Second Isaiah's Identity

sure in the next verse the author adds, "the God of Abraham, of Isaac, and of Jacob" (3:16). Three Jacob IDs indicate that the prophet of the Exile wrote this passage, a text central to the faith of Jew and Christian alike.

There is even more evidence than these three God-of-Jacob IDs. Earlier, this writer showed for information only some five hundred occurrences of Israelites in a list of possible Jacob IDs. (The problem was that the term Israelites, בני ישראל, did not appear in Isa 40–55.) But in the burning bush chapter, Second Jacob works six of these into his text (Exod 3:9, 10, 11, 13, 14, 15). Two of these are shown above as possible IDs. Here are the other four: "'The cry of the Israelites [possible ID] has now come to me . . . I will send you to Pharaoh to bring my people, the Israelites [possible ID], out of Egypt.' . . . But Moses said to God, 'Who am I that I should go to Pharaoh, and bring the Israelites [possible ID] out of Egypt?'" Then Moses said further, "'If I come to the Israelites [possible ID] and say to them . . .'" (Exod 3:9–13). Probably these "Israelites" phrases should be added to the three Jacob IDs and the figure for Jacob-Israel IDs in the burning-bush chapter should be nine rather than three. Three is a lot; nine would be a torrent.

Chapters 30 and 31 comprise an insert into the book of Jeremiah. Because the chapters feature themes of restoration and comfort, they are commonly called the Book of Consolation or the Little Book of Comfort. These appear to be a collection of originally separate passages, most of which are poetic. According to at least one expert they bear similarities to the work of Second Isaiah.[26] The Book of Consolation is filled with Jacob IDs, making it almost certain that at least part of it came from Jacob's hand. Consider these parallel IDs: "Have no fear, my servant Jacob, says the Lord, and do not be dismayed, O Israel"; "Sing aloud with gladness for Jacob . . . and say, 'Save, O Lord, your people, the remnant of Israel'"; and "He who scattered Israel will gather him . . . For the Lord has ransomed Jacob" (Jer 30:10; 31:7, 10–11).

The prophet may have preferred parallels, but he also used Jacob by itself in the Book of Consolation. For instance, "It is a time of distress for Jacob; yet he shall be rescued from it"; "Have no fear, my servant Jacob . . . Jacob shall return and have quiet and ease"; and "I am going to restore the fortunes of the tents [academies] of Jacob" (Jer 30:7, 10, 18).

---

26. Lipinski, "Jeremiah," 1354.

If Jeremiah preached God's judgment, then the prophet Jacob spoke of God's grace. It may be that Jacob's use of "Israel" reached furthest to express that grace. In the preface to Jeremiah chapter 30 God instructed, "Thus says the Lord, the God of Israel [ID]: Write in a book all the words that I have spoken to you. For the days are surely coming, says the Lord, when I will restore the fortunes of my people, Israel [ID] (Jer 30:2-3). Jeremiah 31 says, "I will sow the house of Israel [ID] and the house of Judah with the seed of humans and the seed of animals" (31:27).

Continuing in the Book of Consolation, we find someone—Jacob or a follower—speaking in the prophetic future. He announces, "The days are surely coming, says the Lord, when I will make a new covenant with the house of Israel [ID] and the house of Judah" (Jer 31:31). However, this was not to be like the previous Mosaic covenant their fathers broke. "But this is the covenant that I will make with the house of Israel [ID] after those days, says the Lord: I will put my law within them, and I will write it on their hearts; and I will be their God, and they shall be my people" (31:33). Experts have called this new covenant "remarkable" and "astonishing" in its "abrogation of the entire paraphernalia of religious indoctrination."[27] This passage might even represent the apogee of Hebrew Scripture, and Jacob could well be its author.

Jacob's influence in the Book of Consolation may extend beyond Jeremiah 30 and 31, because the next two chapters contain nine other Jacob IDs.[28] Jeremiah 32:26-35 is about destruction, apostasy, and defilement. Then there is a dramatic change in tone. What follows is a prophecy from "the God of Israel," a Jacob ID. The rebuttal looks beyond Jeremiah's promised destruction to a time when the scattered would be gathered. "I am going to gather them from all the lands to which I drove them . . . I will bring them back to this place, and I will settle them in safety. They shall be my people, and I will be their God" (Jer 32:37-38)—vintage Second Jacob. Jack R. Lundbom describes a complex editing and layering process that may have formed the Book of Consolation.[29] Jacob IDs should shed further light on how that Scripture evolved.

---

27. Mendenhall and Herion, "Covenant," 1192-93.

28. Other Jacob IDs in Jer 31 and also in 32 are: 31:14, 15, 21, 36; 32:4, 14, 17, 26, 26. Two (32:21 and 33:4) may be hostile to Jacob.

29. Lundbom, "Jeremiah," 714-15.

## Second Isaiah's Identity

Scripture contains several hundred other Jacob and Israel IDs that if discussed would exceed both readers' patience and author's space. The note lists those of highest quality that this chapter does not cover.[30]

Now let us glance over our shoulder. Second Isaiah's name is Jacob. Vocabulary from a strong Word Link connects the Isa 49 description of Jacob's naming with his birth story in Genesis, and the two accounts fit remarkably together. Rabbinic tradition and significant Jacob coding in Second Isaiah chapters also support the Jacob finding. Finally, the prophet's frequent use in Isa 40–55 of Jacob and Israel marks these as signatures (termed IDs). All of which leads us to this summary of what we know about Jacob IDs:

- Isaiah 40–55 is full of Jacob and Israel forms, with Holy One of Israel and Jacob-Israel parallels being the most significant.

- IDs mark Second Jacob as the author of most Second Isaiah chapters and portions of the First and Third Isaiah writings.

- IDs and coding establish a significant Jacob presence in Psalms.

- IDs indicate the prophet probably wrote, among other things, the Balaam and burning bush stories, the plowshares passages, and the Book of Consolation.

Still to come is how others used IDs to criticize the exilic prophet.

### OTHER PROPHETS ATTACK JACOB

If biblical prophets were known for their enemies, Jacob was well known. Consider prophecies by Jeremiah. In chapter 2 Jeremiah uses a parallel Jacob ID against Jacob's supporters. "Hear the word of the Lord, O house of Jacob, and all the families of the house of Israel [ID]!" (Jer 2:4). Then comes a poetic outburst against Israel's apostasy featuring several more anti-Jacob IDs: "As a thief is shamed when caught, so the house of Israel [ID] shall be shamed" (Jer 2:26, see 2:14). The next chapter continues in the same vein: "As a faithless wife leaves her husband, so you have been faithless to me, O house of Israel [ID]" (Jer 3:20). However, two scant

---

30. Jacob-Israel parallel IDs and Holy One of Israel IDs that have not been or will not be discussed are: Gen 32:28; 35:10; 46:2; 48:2; 49:2, 7, 24; Exod 19:3; 2 Kgs 17:34; 19:22; 1 Chr 16:13, 17; Isa 1:4; 5:19, 24; 9:8; 12:6; 14:1; 27:6; 30:11, 12, 15; 31:1; 37:23; Jer 10:16; 46:27; 50:29; 51:5, 19; Lam 2:3; Ezek 20:5; Nah 2:2.

verses before came an editor's insert that belied Jeremiah's message: "In those days the house of Judah shall join the house of Israel [ID], and together they shall come . . . to the land that I gave your ancestors" (Jer 3:18).

Here are more attacks by Jeremiah: "all the house of Israel [ID] is uncircumcised in heart"; "the house of Israel [ID] and the house of Judah have broken the covenant that I made"; "Can I not do with you, O house of Israel [ID], just as this potter has done? says the Lord. Just like the clay in the potter's hand, so are you in my hand, O house of Israel [ID]"; and "'Thus says the Lord of hosts, the God of Israel [ID]: Drink, get drunk and vomit, fall and rise no more, because of the sword that I am sending among you'" (Jer 9:26, 11:10, 18:6, 25:27). And so forth. There are over fifty negative IDs within the book of Jeremiah, almost all of them "God of Israel." Perhaps 80 percent of those IDs seemed aimed at Second Jacob or others in his camp.[31]

As to the pro-Jacob passages in the Book of Jeremiah, surely these were not inserted during the older prophet's lifetime.[32] One explanation is that Jacob himself placed the material. Another possibility is Baruch, who some think was Jeremiah's biographer.[33] However, this book's appendix 4 shows there is no significant Baruch coding in the book of Jeremiah, so the editor could have been Jacob himself or a talented follower other than Baruch.

Like the book of Jeremiah, the Ezekiel text also has inserts that sound like Jacob. Take Ezek 28:25. God says, "When I gather the house of Israel [ID] from the peoples among whom they are scattered . . . then they shall settle on their own soil that I gave to my servant Jacob [ID]." Another is similar. Speaking of the Israelites (an ID), the Ezekiel text says, "My servant David shall be king over them . . . They shall live in the land that I gave to my servant Jacob [ID]" (Ezek 37:24–25). A third passage

---

31. Some of the fifty-three negative Jacob IDs in the Book of Jeremiah are aimed at people other than Jacob and his likely allies. Five are addressed to false prophets (Jer 28:2, 14; 29:8, 21, 25) who might also have shared Second Jacob's views. Zedekiah accounts for five (Jer 21:4; 34:2, 13; 37:7; 38:17), and others for six (Jer 12:14; 25:15; 27:4; 33:4; 39:16; 48:1). That leaves thirty-seven anti-Jacob IDs for Jacob himself or for those around him. The figure becomes forty-two if false prophets are included.

32. Pro-Jacob passages in the book of Jeremiah include chapters 10, 30, 31, and 33; much of 51; and sections 3:15–18; 23:7–8; 32:36–44 (and perhaps 14–15); 35:18–19; 46:27–28; and 50:18–20.

33. Lundbom, "Baruch," 617. Lundbom mentions H. Gevaryahu and J. Muilenburg.

certainly has the ring of Second Jacob. It begins with a parallel ID: "Now I will restore the fortunes of Jacob, and have mercy on the whole house of Israel [parallel ID] ... and I will never again hide my face from them, when I pour out my spirit upon the house of Israel [ID]" (Ezek 39:25, 29). Earlier in the same chapter is: "My holy name I will make known among my people Israel [ID] ... and the nations shall know that I am the Lord, *the Holy One in Israel* [ID] (39:7, italics added).

Ezekiel sandwiches this next parallel ID between talk of idols and rebellions: "On the day when I chose Israel," says the prophecy, "I swore to the offspring of the house of Jacob" (Ezek 20:5). Like Jeremiah, Ezekiel frequently uses Jacob IDs, but while Jeremiah relies upon "God of Israel," Ezekiel employs "house of Israel."[34] Ezekiel appears to apply the term to numerous groups in Palestine, though this next passage could target Jacob himself: "Say to the house of Israel [ID] ... When you ... make your children pass through the fire, you defile yourselves with all your idols to this day. And shall I be consulted by you, O house of Israel [ID]?" (Ezek 20:30–31).

Jacob IDs make clear that Second Jacob was at odds with Jeremiah and Ezekiel, two giants of prophecy. Moreover, IDs also indicate that Jacob (or perhaps his descendants) had opponents among those who wrote the Minor Prophets. Hosea contains eight anti-Jacob IDs, Amos fourteen, Micah seven, and Malachi three. Here are some of the Hosea barbs: "In the House of Israel [ID] I have seen a horrible thing; Ephraim's whoredom is there, Israel is defiled"; "I will make Ephraim break the ground; Judah must plow; Jacob [ID] must harrow for himself"; and "Ephraim has surrounded me with lies, and the house of Israel [ID] with deceit" (Hos 6:10; 10:11; 11:12). Add this disdainful parallel ID: "Jacob fled to the land of Aram, there Israel served for a wife, and for a wife he guarded sheep" (Hos 12:12). A final Hosea ID deserves several lines: "The Lord has an indictment against Judah, and will punish Jacob [parallel ID] according to his ways ... In the womb he tried to supplant [עקב, a play upon Jacob] his brother, and in his manhood he strove with God" (Hos 12:2–3). Second Jacob probably was in Palestine, for his opponents repeatedly linked him with Judah and Ephraim. The Hosea author was a formidable enemy, if only because he wrote so well. And we must hold open the possibility that

---

34. "House of Israel" IDs in the Book of Ezekiel that appear to target Second Jacob are: Ezek 6:11; 9:9; 12:24, 27; 13:9; 14:4–7, 11; 18:6, 15, 25, 29, 29–31; 20:5, 13, 27, 30, 31, 39; 24:21; 33:7, 10, 11, 20.

these could even be post-exilic compositions written by those still debating deeply held grievances.

The Amos material is of equal caliber, which suggests that the same hand could have written parts of both prophecies. The book of Amos is somewhat perplexing. On the one hand its IDs against Jacob are apt and powerfully stated. On the other, most come from chapters 3 through 6, and "the vast majority of scholars consider this section of the book to contain the actual words of Amos."[35] But it seems that sixth-century (or later) critics bent the eighth-century book of Amos to throw it at Jacob. Amos has so many Jacob IDs that two of its chapters rank among Scripture's highest in ID frequency.[36]

Here is a parallel ID from Amos: "Hear, and testify against the house of Jacob [ID] ... on the day I will punish Israel for its transgressions, I will punish the altars of Bethel" (Amos 3:13–14). Other IDs are: "Alas for those who are at ease in Zion, and for those who feel secure on Mount Samaria, the notables ... to whom the house of Israel [ID] resorts!"; "I abhor the pride of Jacob [ID]"; and "The Lord has sworn by the pride of Jacob [ID]" (Amos 6:1, 8; 8:7). In these final IDs a note of pity (or editing) emerges: "The eyes of the Lord God are upon the sinful kingdom, and I will destroy it from the face of the earth—except that I will not utterly destroy the house of Jacob [ID], says the Lord. For lo, I will command, and shake the house of Israel [ID] ..." (Amos 9:8–9).

Micah's text is a battleground. As in the book of Jeremiah, IDs both for and against Second Jacob are plentiful. Micah's opening verses predict a cataclysmic judgment of melting mountains and cleft valleys: "All this is for the transgression of Jacob, and for the sins of the House of Israel [parallel ID]. What is the transgression of Jacob [ID]? Is it not Samaria?" (Mic 1:5). And again, "Listen, you heads of Jacob and rulers of the house of Israel [parallel ID] ... you who hate the good and love the evil, who tear the skin off my people, and the flesh off their bones" (Mic 3:1–2). To which a defender may have replied: "I will surely gather all of you, O Jacob, I will gather the survivors of Israel [parallel ID]; I will set them together like sheep in a fold, like a flock in its pasture; it will resound with people" (Mic 2:12). Beyond that, the whole of Mic 4 sounds like a Second Jacob insert. It repeats the transcendent swords-to-plowshares passage from Isa 2, and

---

35. Willoughby, "Amos," 208.

36. Amos 5 ranks twelfth and Amos 7 ranks seventeenth in frequency of Jacob IDs among the 929 chapters in Scripture.

also contains this summons: "'Come, let us go up to the mountain of the Lord, to the house of the God of Jacob [ID]'" (Mic 4:2).

Another denunciation of Second Jacob in Micah contains two sets of parallel IDs: "I am filled with power, with the spirit of the Lord, and with justice and might, to declare to Jacob his transgression and to Israel [parallel ID] his sin. Hear this, you rulers of the house of Jacob and chiefs of the house of Israel [parallel ID], who abhor justice and pervert all equity" (Mic 3:8-9). And the more tranquil voice of a pro-Jacob writer responds, "The remnant of Jacob, surrounded by many peoples, shall be like dew from the Lord" (Mic 5:7). Second Jacob's supporters or descendents had the final say, for the book closed with this ID: "You will show faithfulness to Jacob and unswerving loyalty to Abraham" (Mic 7:20).

The book of Malachi is also a mixture. It starts with: "Is not Esau Jacob's brother? says the Lord. Yet I have loved Jacob but I have hated Esau" (Mal 1:2-3). However, in something aimed at Jacob's followers or descendants, the short book says, "May the Lord cut off from the tents [academies] of Jacob" any who profane the sanctuary (Mal 2:12). Another anti-Jacob ID follows toward the end of Malachi's book: "For I the Lord do not change; therefore you, O children of Jacob, have not perished" (Mal 3:6). This may sound mild, but the prophet sharpens his indictment by including anagrams of Jacob's name in four nearby words, using the roots "extort" and "rob." The anagrams of יעקב are ובעשקי in 3:5; היקבע and קבעים in 3:8; and קבעים in 3:9. Such spellings are unusual, and four within a passage is unparalleled.

The prophet Obadiah voices only pro-Jacob IDs. The prophet warns Edom that, "For the slaughter and violence done to your brother Jacob, shame shall cover you" (Obad 10). A few verses later he says sympathetically, "the house of Jacob shall take possession of those who dispossessed them" (Obad 17). And in the next line Jacob becomes an avenger: "The House of Jacob shall be a fire . . . and the House of Esau stubble" (Obad 18). Jacob IDs in the books of other minor prophets—Nahum, Zephaniah, and Zechariah—are also positive.[37]

IDs within the prophetic books suggest bitter disagreements during and perhaps after the Exile. Apparently these centered upon Second Jacob, his followers, and the causes he or they represented. Listed by books, Jeremiah, Ezekiel, Hosea, Amos, Micah, and Malachi are fiercely

---

37. Positive Jacob IDs in other books of the Minor Prophets are: Nah 2:2; Zeph 2:9, 3:15; Zech 8:13.

hostile; though Jeremiah, Ezekiel, Micah, and Malachi also contain positive Jacob IDs. On the plus side are ID passages in Isaiah, Zephaniah, Nahum, Obadiah, and Zechariah. When we understand the nature of these disputes, we shall better understand the Exile and the years that followed it.

This book opened by revealing the code that underlies the Priestly Benediction, and detailing how Ezekiel, Jeremiah, and Second Isaiah used coded anagrams against the exiled King Jehoiachin. This current chapter first identifies Second Isaiah as Jacob, discusses Jacob IDs, and then shows how opponents used IDs against him. Chapter 5 will lead us to another discovery, one that pairs Second Jacob with a man who has been called the father of Judaism.

# 5

# Coding Revelations of Psalm Fifty-One

## THE PSALM'S INTENSE CODING

PSALM FIFTY-ONE IS AT once a lament for sins committed, a public yet very private request that God excuse the sinner, and an appeal that He create in the psalmist a clean heart and restore him to useful service. Here are some of the psalm's lines:

> Have mercy on me, O God, in your kindness, in your immense compassion delete my rebellious acts.
> Again and again, wash me of my guilt, and of my sin clean me.
> My rebellious acts that face me I know too well, and my sin is ever before me.
> Against you alone have I sinned, and before your eyes committed the crime;
> And so you are just when you sentence, and blameless when you judge...
> Wash me, and I'll be much whiter than snow.
> Let me hear songs of joy and gladness, the bones you crushed rejoice.
> Turn your face from my sins, and delete all my crimes.
> A clean heart, O God, create in me...
> That I may teach rebels your ways, and sinners to return to you (Ps 51:3–6, 9–12, 15).[1]

Psalm 51 is both immediate and deeply personal. In this, the psalm could be compared to Michelangelo's Pieta or to Hamlet's to-be-or-not-to-be soliloquy. And the psalm is exceptional in another way, a way not recognized until this writing. Not one of the other 928 chapters in Hebrew

---

1. Dahood, *Psalms II*, 1–2. The verses in the NRSV are 1–4, 7–10, and 13.

Scripture has such intensity of coding.[2] The psalm is short as OT chapters go. At 153 words it is less than half the average length of Hebrew chapters. But what marks Psalm 51 as exceptional is coding frequency. The measure of this is coding points divided by chapter words. This allows comparison of the coding strength of all chapters, regardless of length. I took about thirty names like "Ezekiel," "Jehoiachin," and "Nebuchadnezzar" and tested them for coding against every chapter in the OT. I then used coding points and chapter lengths to rank each name between one and 929. Three-quarters of the chosen coding groups were either in first or second place among Scripture's chapters, and all but two of the others were in the top ten. The probability of getting results like this by coincidence is zero. Here are the frequency rankings of those words coded within the psalm:

## TABLE 5.1—CODING FREQUENCIES IN PSALM 51 RANKED BY PLACE AMONG 929 CHAPTERS

*Rank*      *Persons*

| Rank | Persons |
| --- | --- |
| First | Ahihud son of Shelomi, Amariah son of Hezekiah, Azariah son of Amaziah, Azariah son of Zephaniah, Azrikam son of Azel, Chimham, Cyrus, Daniel-Sarpuhi, Ezra, Gemariah son of Shaphan, Jacob-Israel, Jehizkiah son of Shallum, Shecaniah son of Jahaziel, Shelemiah son of Abdeel, Shenazzar son of Jehoiachin, Solomon son of David, Zedekiah |
| Second | Ahaziah son of Jehoram, Ezekiel, Ezekiel-Sarpuhi, Nabonidus-Belshazzar, Zedekiah-Sarpuhi |
| Third | Jehoiachin-Sarpuhi |
| Fourth | Zephaniah |
| Sixth | Jeremiah |
| Tenth | Nebuchadnezzar |
| Fourteenth | Baruch |
| Sixteenth | Jehoiachin |

---

2. Psalm 51 has the most intense coding of any chapter of Hebrew Scripture for the group of names submitted to it. These names tended to be exilic in nature. Names more common to the Persian or the Greek period might produce different results.

The table makes it clear that the psalm's authors intentionally worked these code groups into their text. "Groups" is used because most of the names have multiple spellings and versions. In fact the average of the psalm's coding groups is three spellings per group. This is to say that those who wrote this masterpiece used repetition for emphasis. Along with repetition they also employed rarity, using athbash to make single unusual letter combinations. (As chapter 2 explained, athbash is a well-established code within Scripture that substituted letters for other letters.) The coding pattern, of course, was the familiar one letter per text word, from words at regular intervals, with spellings in any sequence. The two groups shown below illustrate both rarity and repetition. They involve Jehizkiah son of Shallum, and are excerpted from appendix 3.

### TABLE 5.2—CODED PSALM 51 SPELLINGS SUITABLE FOR REPLICATION (EXAMPLE OF APPENDIX 3, PART B, ITEMS 173, 174)

| Hebrew of Jehizkiah Son of Shallum | Hebrew Athbash | Value/ Spellings | First Sequence, Span (Interval) | Other Spellings Verse-Word (Interval) |
|---|---|---|---|---|
| יחזקיהובנשלם | מסעדמצשטבכי | A/one | בסמעכטישצדם 14-6–16-3(1) | |
| יחזקיהובנשלם | כמנבבעקזתטח | AAA/five | כבחענתממקבכזט 6-1–11(1) | 6-2, 5–7(1) |

The next-to-last column of the first item has בסמעכטישצדם, which is a letter sequence of an athbash spelling of Jehizkiah son of Shallum. The coding in Ps 51 runs from the sixth word of v. 14 to the third word of v. 16. It is not difficult to trace the coding. Here is the text, using underline for emphasis:

נדיבה תסמכני אלמדה פשעים דרביך וחטאים אליך ישובו הצילני מדמים אלהים

The interval is one, which is also true of the second item in table 5.2 above. That item encodes a different athbash of Jehizkiah son of Shallum five times—at text words 6-1, 6-2, 6-5, 6-6, and 6-7. The chart gives sequence for 6-1, which makes the other four easier to find. Using the MT, readers might wish to work out those spellings also. The footnote gives one set of answers (a coding sometimes has several correct sequences).[3]

At this point, some might still be skeptical that this code exists in Hebrew Scripture. Part B illustrated above has been designed for scholars who wish to satisfy themselves about this. In total, there are *811 spellings* in part B of appendix 3 with clearly indicated letter sequences. One-third (274) of the coded spellings are displayed in the exact sequence that appears in the text, as in the Jehizkiah example above. With these it is simply a matter of proofing the spellings in appendix 3 against Ps 51 in the MT. All 811 coded spellings employ one letter per text word, from words at regular intervals, with spellings in any sequence.

Table 5.3 shows a portion of the opening section of appendix 3, which is a close companion to this chapter. Part A contains the 132 highest-rated groups found in Ps 51. The groups run from "Abidan the Scribe" to "Zephaniah son of Tahath." The floor for inclusion is 24 points, the equivalent of three AAA codes—and three is a lot.

## TABLE 5.3—NAMES WITH HIGHER CODING IN PSALM 51 (EXAMPLE OF APPENDIX 3, PART A, ITEMS 65-68)

| Rank in 929 | Name | Groups by Values (Point Total) | Description from Scripture and Other Sources |
|---|---|---|---|
| 1 | Jacob-Israel, etc. יעקבבנשלמות | AAA-16, AA-2, A-18 (172) | Prophet Second Isaiah, second highest point total |
| 1 | Jehizkiah S Shallum יחזקיהובנשלם | AAA-7, A-5 (66) | A chief of Ephraim, 66 points |
| 16 | Jehoiachin, etc. כניהובנאליקים | AAA-4, A-4 (40) | King of Judah, exiled in Babylon |
| 3 | Jehoiachin-Sarpuhi יכנישרפוהי | AAA-5, A-3 (46) | Died a substitute king in 562 |

3. Possible sequences of the Jehizkiah coded spellings are: כחעכתמקבזטן for word 6-2, כתמקבזנבתטח for 6-5, עמקבזכנבתטח for 6-6, and עקבזכנבתטחם for 6-7.

The four individuals named in the table are already familiar to us. Jacob-Israel is Second Isaiah. His 172 coding points place him second among Ps 51's encodings, which consist of thirty-six coding groups (sixteen AAAs + two AAs + eighteen As). This is more than sufficient to place Jacob coding in the psalm at the head of all 929 chapters, as the 1 in the first column indicates. We also have seen Jehizkiah son of Shallum previously. He served as an example of coding in the table before this. The psalm's authors gave the name Jehizkiah sixty-six points and a number-one ranking in coding frequency. These mark him as special—though we do not yet know how he was special. As to Jehoiachin and Jehoiachin-Sarpuhi, we already have devoted a full chapter to this exiled king of Judah.

The biggest news is that this smaller-sized chapter of Scripture can produce a great deal of new grist for scholars to mill. And for every ancient identified in appendix 3 there is an additional person's name encoded in the psalm that missed the twenty-four-point cutoff, though let it be said that the smaller the point total the greater the chance of coincidental occurrence. Undoubtedly, the psalmists did not intentionally encode some of those names that accumulated fewer than twenty-four points. Still, the figure of 260-plus names that recorded codes at some level considerably understates what Ps 51 actually contains. Those names come from testing about twenty-five thousand possibilities against the chapter. However, perhaps four or five times that number have yet to be calibrated for the master data file, let alone run against this psalm and the rest of Scripture. If all were run, the names in Ps 51 might total a thousand or more. It may take a generation of scholarly work to map all the coding combinations that experts can think of against every line of the Hebrew Bible. Despite its limited scope, this book takes a first step toward fulfilling that goal.

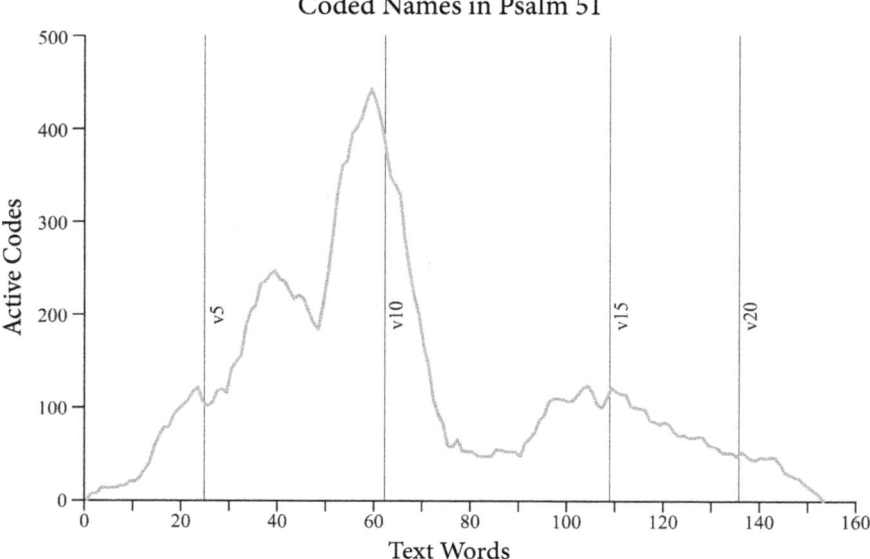

The figure above graphs Ps 51's coded words. The horizontal axis tracks the psalm's 153 text words. To help orient readers, the graph also shows some verse locations. The vertical axis measures the codes active at any word. Active codes are those brought forward from the previous word, plus new codes begun at the word, minus codes completed at that word. The graph's shape is surprising. It shows that the authors concentrated their spellings in the psalm's first half. The fifty-ninth text word (of 153) is most heavily coded, with 441 active ciphers. After reaching that peak, the total plummets to a tenth that number. The writers have hidden three-quarters of the psalm's codes in the first half of the text. I have worked with several other texts, and the patterns are similar—dramatic peaks followed by deep troughs. Elsewhere, the longest spans of heavy coding concentrations have run up to seventy words (along the horizontal axis), and Ps 51's concentration is about the same length.

Imagine controlling over four hundred ongoing spellings at once! This graph makes one thing certain: Ps 51 had far more than one author. No matter what his or her genius, no person working alone could have controlled such a complex process. Perhaps the composers used writing boards like those unearthed at Nimrod.[4] Certainly coding would re-

---

4. Fales and Postgate, *Imperial Records*, 161; Millard, "Israelite Literacy," 28.

quire some such device. Without it, who could simultaneously track four hundred (or maybe one thousand) coded spellings? One could envision several boards with many knotted threads of different hues. Due to the complexity that coding adds to composition, there might have been several people working each board.

No matter how many labored on this complex work, it could not have been completed in a few days or even within a week. Did the scribes work in shifts? Surely there would have been divisions of labor, not only of groups around different composing boards, but also people developing lists of the names to be included, someone working on athbash variants, scribes, copyists, apprentices, couriers, a reference librarian, and other specialists as well. Could twenty skillful people produce such a thing? Perhaps, and if they could they would still need to live within a community of families, shepherds, farmers, laborers, soldiers, artisans, weavers, and so forth.

Were parts of Ps 51 composed at different times? As the graph shows, the first eighty words are an entity. That mass of codes could not be amended without disruption. The psalm's second half, however, may be a different matter. It could have been edited or even added later—except for a single run of spellings. The name Azariah the son of Zephaniah has twelve coded spellings that commence at the very first word of Ps 51 and run through the tenth word of v. 19.[5] This covers nearly ninety percent of the psalm, and strongly suggests that it was written as an entity—or at minimum, that Azariah participated in every section of the psalm.

Now we move to the specifics of Ps 51's coded names. Starting with some of the strongest coding, the 172 Jacob-Israel points are second to Daniel in all the names tested. Numerous different coded spellings of Jacob-Israel combinations crowd beneath the Hebrew text. They include "Jacob," "Israel," "Jacob the prophet," "house of Jacob," "sons of Jacob," and "seed of Jacob" as well as both "Jacob son of Shelomoth" and "Israel son of Shelomoth."[6] This variety helps account for the numerous points. Asking

---

5. See items 26 and 27 of Part B of appendix 3. The two series for Azariah son of Zephaniah overlap. The first group of ten encodings starts at word 1-1 and ends at word 16-8, while the second group of two starts at 10-4 and ends at 19-10.

6. Scripture's text does not name the father of Jacob the prophet. Word associations narrowed the field to three possibilities, and full athbash spellings were run against an eighty-chapter OT sample. Ezekiel 22 contained eye-catching AAA values of the א and ט athbash versions of יעקבבנשלמות. These could not have been coincidental. Experience confirms the choice in that Jacob-son-of-Shelomoth consistently furnishes higher coding

many questions of a text tends to generate more coded answers. Knowing about Second Jacob for some years, I have had more time to develop alternatives for Jacob than for most others—hence the variety. However, all those coded spellings certainly put Second Jacob in the running for authorship of Ps 51.

Over forty of the Jacob points come from "Jacob son of Isaac." Isaac of course was one of the patriarchs and ostensibly lived a millennium before Jacob the prophet. It is not unlikely that the prophet coded the son-of-Isaac signature as an additional layer of concealment. This seems to have been the case, since Ps 51 ranks first among all 929 OT chapters in coding frequency of other Jacob variations and of Jacob son of Isaac. The odds against both occurring by coincidence in any chapter of Scripture are slightly below one million to one.[7]

## AN EXILIC EZRA?

The examination that discovered the Jacob codes was part of a general inspection of Ps 51 for Hebrew personal names. During the inspection, "Ezra" codes kept turning up. In fact, eventually I found fifty-five different spellings concentrated in over a dozen groups (see items 116–132 of appendix 3, part B). They include "Ezra," "Ezra son of Seraiah," "Ezra the priest the scribe," "Ezra the priest," and "Ezra the scribe." Indeed, with over one hundred points Ezra ranks fourth in coding strength. As Second Isaiah, Jacob seems to have prophesied during the sixth century BCE. Scripture placed Ezra the son of Seraiah about 150 years later, so it was surprising to find such Jacob and Ezra coding concentrations in the same psalm. Moreover, the coding of both Ezra-related words and Jacob-related words in Ps 51 ranked first among all 929 chapters in Scripture. The odds against both occurring first by coincidence in any chapter of Scripture are tiny.[8]

But this does not necessarily make Ezra and Jacob contemporaries. Ezra in the fourth century might possibly have edited words that Second Jacob wrote in the sixth century. That would have been possible, except that within the psalm at least one Ezra group overlapped each of the Second

---

values than any other Jacob combination. Shelomoth appears to have been an official in the temple treasury during the later monarchy.

7. The odds against Ps 51 containing higher Jacob-related and Jacob-son-of-Isaac coding than any other chapter in Scripture are 863,000 to one (1 / 929 x 929 = .000001159).

8. The odds against Ps 51 containing higher Jacob and Ezra coding than any other chapter in Scripture are the same as those shown in the note above.

Jacob groups. Seventeen significant Jacob-coded groups stretched from v. 2 through the first word in v. 12, and Ezra codes in vv. 4 through 10 used the same text words as the Jacob coding rows. The intermixture of Jacob and Ezra codes is such that later insertion of Ezra codes is impossible. The authors worked both sets of codes into Ps 51 as they composed it.

Another way to deal with this Jacob-Ezra problem is to move Second Jacob from the Exile to the Persian period. However, the great majority of scholars for good reason hold that the setting of Isaiah chapters 40–55 was the Babylonian Exile.[9] The Exile was underway and Babylon ruled. Moreover, Second Isaiah (that is, Jacob) called Cyrus by name (Isa 44:28; 45:1), and it is well established that Cyrus the Great lived in the sixth century BCE. Additionally, moving Jacob to the fifth century would sunder that prophet's ties to Ezekiel, Jeremiah, and King Jehoiachin, including all the coding ties that the opening chapters of this book revealed. Pushing sixth-century Jacob later in time so as to join him with a fifth-century Ezra would be an error, plain and simple.

Some advocate that the Ezra who was a supposed hero of the postexilic period never existed. The *ABD*, whose task is to summarize such matters, stated that after G. Garbini's 1986 book, "there appeared a strong scholarly revival of the opinion that Ezra never existed at all, and was invented in 159 b.c. to be the emblem of a religious reform."[10] Also, material in Scripture about Restoration Ezra is disordered. For example, experts cannot establish with certainty when Ezra might have arrived in Jerusalem from Babylon. Working with the year 458, the traditional choice, conservative scholar Peter Ackroyd noted a gap of thirteen years between Ezra's arrival and when he carried out his central task, which was implementing the law. And once started, Ezra took only about twelve months to accomplish his mission. Ackroyd, like others, also questioned the lack of interplay between Nehemiah and Ezra, the two stalwarts of the Restoration.[11]

There could be another explanation for Ezra the son of Seraiah being alive in two different time periods. Coding in Ps 51 was what it was, but whoever wrote the book of Ezra could have erred in making Ezra the son of Seraiah. Perhaps a different Ezra made the trek from Babylon, and the

---

9. C. North, "Isaiah," 737; Clifford, "Second Isaiah," 490.
10. R. North, "Ezra," 727. North cited Garbini, *Storia e ideologia*, 1986.
11. Ackroyd, *Exile and Restoration*, 191–92.

author, writing many years after that event, confused the father of that Ezra with the parent of the exilic Ezra. Working against this, however, is the returnees' scrupulous examination of lineage, even to the extent of separating those of foreign descent from Israel (Neh 13:1–3).

There are other possibilities. Could two Ezras—from the Exile and from the Restoration—have had the same father's name? Ezra 7:1 identifies the Ezra of the Restoration as "Ezra son of Seraiah" who lived "in the reign of King Artaxerxes of Persia." But Ps 51 contains five AAA code sets that spell out "Ezra son of Seraiah." And one can quickly find that exilic Ezra by working through the genealogy in Ezra chapter 7. It reads, "Ezra son of Seraiah, son of Azariah, son of Hilkiah, son of Shallum . . ." (Ezra 7:1–2). Seraiah, Azariah, Hilkiah, and Shallum were chief priests. A comparable list in First Chronicles moves in the other direction with the same result. It reads, "Shallum begot Hilkiah, Hilkiah begot Azariah, Azariah begot Seraiah." Then it continues, "Seraiah begot Jehozadak; and Jehozadak went into exile . . ." (1 Chr 5:39–41). So before Nebuchadnezzar put Seraiah to death in 586 (2 Kgs 25:18–21), the chief priest fathered both Ezra and Jehozadak. The chief priesthood at this time probably was hereditary, so after Seraiah's execution Jehozadak would have assumed that office, even in Babylon.

Jehozadak was the son of the chief priest Seraiah, and so was Ezra, who presumably joined his brother in the march to Babylon. The *IDB* noted, "Ezra also claims descent from Seraiah . . . and thus it can be assumed that Ezra went into exile with his brother Jehozadak. However, Jehozadak was evidently Seraiah's first-born son."[12] But Scripture also says that same Ezra returned to Palestine either 130 or 190 years later (depending upon which Artaxerxes one favors).

For more on the two-Ezra question, let us turn to an apocryphal book sometimes known as Second Esdras. Written in the second or third century CE, it begins, "The book of the prophet Ezra son of Seraiah . . ." After giving seventeen more generations, it concludes, "Who was a captive in the country of the Medes in the reign of Artaxerxes, king of the Persians" (2 Esd 1:1–3). That covered restoration Ezra. But alternate versions begin with: "The word of the Lord that came to Ezra son of Chusi *in the days of King Nebuchadnezzar*" (italics added). Enter the Ezra of

---

12. Achtemeier, "Seraiah," 279.

Nebuchadnezzar's time. "Chusi," incidentally, was probably a town some twenty-five miles north of Jerusalem.

Other chapters of Second Esdras came from the pen of a first-century Jew. That portion began, "In the thirtieth year [557 or 556 BCE] after the destruction of the city [of Jerusalem], I was in Babylon—I, Salathiel, who am also called Ezra" (2 Esd 3:1).[13] The author of Second Esdras adopted the pseudonym of Ezra and placed himself in Babylon during the time of the Exile. Interestingly, the Second Esdras author also used three Jacob-Israel parallels, just as Second Jacob might have. For example, "'Take courage, O Israel; and do not be sorrowful, O house of Jacob'" (2 Esd 12:46, see also 5:35 and 9:30). In conclusion, well into the Common Era some believers honored Ezra by writing under his name and identified him as living during the Exile.

The rabbis recognized Ezra's greatness. For instance the Talmud credited him with introducing square Assyrian letters for Hebrew Scripture. Perhaps the highest praise was: "Had Moses not preceded him, Ezra would have been worthy of receiving Torah for Israel."[14] According to the Talmud, Ezra led in governance as well as in scholarship. He set up regulations for schools and "ordained" ten enactments to regulate weekly life (washing, baking, public Torah reading, etc.).[15] Other traditions said that when the Babylonians destroyed the temple, they burned the Scriptures as well. God then charged Ezra to write them anew. To do so he worked from a copy of the Torah, dictating to five expert scribes.[16] Doubtless great amounts of Scripture did burn with the temple, but surely the Judeans would not have delayed a century and a half to replace the writings. Instead, they would have commenced work as soon as they could. Legend closely links Ezra with that work and with introducing Assyrian-style block letters. If the legends have a basis in fact, Ezra lived and worked during the Exile.

But we have more than just legend to connect Ezra to the Exile. Jacob probably was exilic and Baruch, the scribe who originally served Jeremiah, certainly was. Coded Words frequently connect the two with Ezra. The fourth chapter of the book of Ruth contains three unusual Coded Words. Verse 11 had a word meaning "and the elders" and v. 17 included two

---

13. Louis Ginzberg made a sensible suggestion about Salathiel. "A slight curving of the letter ח made of שלחאל 'the messenger of God' שלתאֵל Salathiel." *Legends*, 6:446.

14. *b. Sanh.* 21b.

15. *b. B. Bat.* 21b, *B. Qam.* 82a–82b.

16. Ginzberg, *Legends* 6: 446 n. 50.

occurrences of "and they called." Each had an Ezra CW, and each also contained CWs for Baruch and for Jacob.[17] That is, within those three text words, clever authors wrote words that linked the three men together. In all of Scripture there are only twenty-four such triple Baruch-Ezra-Jacob CWs.[18] Two chapters have two of the rarity (1 Chr 15 and Esth 2), and the final chapter of Ruth contains three.

One Baruch-Ezra-Jacob Coded Word offers an amusing yet most informative use of triple CWs. In Judg 6:5 a critic compared the three to Midianites: "For they and their livestock [Baruch, Ezra, and Jacob CWs] would come up, and they would even bring their tents [read academies], as thick as locusts ... so that they wasted the land as they came in." Stating the obvious, the three worked together and had critics. Next, they founded academies ("tents") to teach others and presumably to write. That makes sense since Jacob was legendary for his learning, Ezra was the archetype of scribes, and Baruch was a known teacher. Finally, note the locale. The three were opening those academies in Israel rather than in Egypt, Babylonia, or elsewhere. Since Nebuchadnezzar maintained few if any garrisons there after he ravaged Judah, the three companions would have enjoyed considerable freedom in founding new institutions.[19]

Disregarding these connections, there may be another way to explain how the coded names of Ezra and Jacob could have been interwoven under Ps 51's text. Suppose that whoever wrote the psalm was composing, say, an honor roll of Israel's heroes—regardless of when they might have lived. Perhaps future coding work will be able to test such a possibility. Pending that, however, the evidence suggests that Jacob and Ezra were exilic contemporaries.

In addition to the Ezra finding, Ps 51's coding offers another startling discovery. The names of virtually all of King David's numerous sons are encoded in the psalm, and half of them possess sufficient coding points

---

17. "And the elders" in Ruth 4:11 is והזקנים. That word supplies the letters needed for anagrams of Baruch, Ezra, and Jacob, which are יונק, וקים, and קמיה. "And they called," which appears twice in v. 17, is spelled ותקראנה. The CWs derived from it for Baruch, Ezra, and Jacob are אהקן, הנאר, and נראו.

18. Verses that contain within a single text word CWs of Baruch, Ezra, and Jacob are: Lev 10:19; Judg 6:5; Ruth 4:11, 17, 17; 2 Kgs 6:32, 10:5; 1 Chr 15:18, 21, 21:16; 2 Chr 35:25; Ezra 10:8; Esth 2:3, 14, 9:3; Pss 41:11, 78:48; Isa 54:10; Jer 52:19; Ezek 10:19, 11:1; Dan 6:21, 8:3; Zech 8:3.

19. Though archaeologists have found evidence of Assyrian occupation in Israel, they have discovered almost no trace of Babylon's presence.

to make the appendix 3 listing.[20] Shephatiah with eighty-four leads, and Absalom, Solomon, and Ithream are close behind. Others with at least twenty-four points include Adonijah, Eliphelet, Elishama, Elishua, Shammua, and Shimea. The test for each of the princes included "son of David" with the person's name, and a majority also have spellings naming the mother ("Shephatiah son of Abital," "Solomon son of Bathsheba"). How should scholars grasp this nettle?

It is out of the question that Ps 51 comes from the Davidic era. Names like Baruch, Ezekiel, Jeremiah, and Nebuchadnezzar are coded at significant levels, which mean this writing can be no earlier than the sixth century. Are we free to conclude, then, that these sons of David are sixth-century personages? David is, after all, a generic name that can apply to any monarch in the Davidic line. Until 562 Israel had such a king, but Jehoiachin's death ended the line. Shephatiah, Absalom, and the rest may be pseudonyms, for the names of Jehoiachin's children listed in 1 Chr 3:17–18 are Shealtiel, Malchiram, Pedaiah, Shenazzar, Jekamiah, Hoshama, and Nedabiah. The term David could have covered fathers who were other recent kings of Judah, like Jehoiakim and Zedekiah. If this speculation is well grounded, then scholars might next consider whether accounts about David's children in the books of Samuel and Kings speak of sixth-century Babylon rather than tenth-century Israel.

Another likely son of a Judean king is Chimham. Like Ezra, Cyrus, Jacob, and others, Chimham's frequency of coding within Ps 51 is higher than that of any other chapter. "Chimham" came to our attention because the word לדוד, "to David," contains an athbash CW of Chimham.[21] And "to David" prefaces half the psalms. The name Chimham appears twice in Scripture. One marks the location of an inn at or very near Bethlehem (Jer 41:17). The other occurrence is in Second Samuel. King David, after regaining his throne following a revolt, asks wealthy Barzillai to cross the Jordan and accompany him to Jerusalem. Barzillai protests that he is too aged to leave Gilead, and offers someone named Chimham instead. The old man says, "'But here is your servant Chimham; let him go over with my lord the king; and do for him whatever it seems good to you.'" David then replies, "'Chimham shall go over with me, and I will do for him what-

---

20. 2 Sam 3:2–5; 5:14–16; and 1 Chr 3:1–8 list the sons born to David in Hebron and Jerusalem.

21. An athbash of "Chimham," כמהם, is ודלד, which has the same letters as לדוד, "of David."

ever seems good to you; and all that you desire of me I will do for you'" (2 Sam 19:37–38).

Exceptional results came from testing Psalms for Chimham Coded Words. The frequency of Chimham CWs in the book of Psalms is triple that of a large sample of Scripture, so it seemed reasonable to include Chimham among the names to test for coding in Ps 51.[22] The first-place result justifies that inclusion.

## SUBSTITUTE KINGS IN PSALM 51

Previous chapters offered evidence that King Jehoiachin of Judah died at the hands of the Babylonians as a *sarpuhi*, a substitute king. Guided by this, we tested Ps 51 for coding evidence that others had met the same end. The results were positive. Measured against the coding frequencies of all 929 OT chapters, Daniel-Sarpuhi ranked first, Ezekiel-Sarpuhi and Zedekiah-Sarpuhi ranked second, and Jehoiachin-Sarpuhi ranked third. Ezekiel and Daniel we shall deal with in a future chapter, and Jehoiachin has already had full exposure. Now, what of Zedekiah?

Psalm 51's authors laid heavy coding stress upon the name of Zedekiah, who was Judah's last king. Including the five Zedekiah-Sarpuhi groups, the writers encoded over sixty spellings of his name, each of which can be replicated using part B of appendix 3. One Zedekiah athbash, אסתטנם, even has eleven consecutive repetitions.[23]

The words of Scripture also indicate that Zedekiah died as a substitute. During Nebuchadnezzar's final siege of Jerusalem, God through Jeremiah prophesied to Zedekiah, "I am going to give this city into the hand of the king of Babylon, and he shall burn it with fire. And . . . you shall see the king of Babylon eye to eye and speak with him face to face; and you shall go to Babylon" (Jer 34:2–3). After these hard words, Jeremiah then appeared to soften. The prophet continued, "You shall not die by the sword; you shall die in peace. And as spices were burned for your ancestors, the earlier kings who preceded you, so they shall burn spices for you

---

22. Kavanagh, *Secrets*, 340–59 has a fuller discussion of "Chimham."

23. Eleven consecutive Zedekiah spellings in Ps 51 start at text words 7-6, 8-1 to 8-7, and 9-1 to 9-3. The authors also spelled in athbash the letters of his name within a single text word, which is highly unusual for a word containing six Hebrew letters. The CW is in תחטאני, which is the opening text word of the ninth verse. The athbash version of Zedekiah is תחאנטי.

and lament for you, saying, 'Alas, lord!'" (Jer 34:4–5).[24] This passage seems to promise a peaceful death and a royal funeral, while the former ones prophesied trial, blinding, and exile. Though scholars struggle with this contradiction, most agree that 34:2–5 is by Jeremiah himself.

Years before, when Zedekiah swore allegiance to Babylon, he probably heard his name inserted in this ancient formula: "Just as this man of wax is blinded so will __ be blinded" should he break his oath.[25] Zedekiah knew that the penalty for oath breaking was blinding, and Jeremiah's prophecy reminded him of this. In the event, he did see Nebuchadnezzar "eye to eye." And in his last sighted minutes Zedekiah also saw his nobles and his sons executed. Then his captors put out his eyes. Afterward, Zedekiah trekked in chains to Babylon, and to prison (2 Kgs 25:7, Jer 52:11). The Greek version of Jer 52:11 adds that Zedekiah was confined in the "house of the mill."[26] Like the blinded Samson, Zedekiah had to push millstones in the dark.

How then could Jeremiah have prophesied a peaceful death? He did not. The prophet used Word Links to convey the reverse—that Zedekiah would die violently. Citing himself with a Word Link, Jeremiah said, "They shall become as dung on the surface of the ground. They shall perish by the sword . . . Both great and small shall die in this land; they shall not be buried, and no one shall lament for them" (Jer 16:4–6). Another Jeremiah link said, "On that day, says the Lord, courage shall fail the king and the officials . . . the sword is at the throat!" (Jer 4:9–10).

Though his death was to be violent, Zedekiah would have a royal interment, the funeral of a substitute king (Josephus wrote of Zedekiah that Nebuchadnezzar "buried him magnificently").[27] Though the burial was good, the death was not. The Babylonians probably beheaded Zedekiah. The Talmud seems to confirm this. It inserted a few lines about funeral pyres into a discussion of decapitation.[28] That insert quoted Jeremiah's prophecy about Zedekiah's funeral. By associating Zedekiah's rites with

---

24. Laments, pyres, and spices were features of a king's funeral (Jer 22:18–19; 2 Chr 16:14, 21:19).

25. Deist, "Punishment of Zedekiah," 72. The curse was adapted from an Aramaic stela so as to fit Zedekiah.

26. Althann, "Zedekiah," 1070, which cited van der Toorn, "Judges xvi 21 and Akkadian Sources," 248–53.

27. Josephus, *Ant.* 10:154.

28. *b. Sanh.* 52b.

## The Exilic Code

decapitation, the Talmud implied that this was the manner of the Judean king's death.

Here is the weightiest evidence that Zedekiah was a substitute king. Words three, four, and five of Jer 34:5 said, "and as spices were burned for your ancestors, the earlier kings." Words three and four contained letters that spelled "substitute," תמורת, and word five supplied "king."[29] Nearby, the second and third words of v. 5 have the letters for substitute, as do the last two words of v. 4. Significantly, v. 4 had the words "die by the sword," lending added support to substitute kingship. For extra measure, someone else worked the eight letters spelling "substitute king" into the fourteenth through the sixteenth words of the first verse of that same chapter (Jer 34:1). That made four such spellings within a few verses, verses that predicted how Zedekiah would end his life. All this is beyond coincidence. Understanding that Zedekiah was a substitute explains why Nebuchadnezzar gave a traitor a king's funeral.

The editor took double pains to establish just when Jeremiah made his prophecy in chapter 34 about Zedekiah. Jeremiah 34:1 said that the prophet spoke when Nebuchadnezzar was "fighting against Jerusalem and all its cities." Jeremiah 34:6–7 gave more detail. It said the prophet had made his pronouncement while Jerusalem, Lachish, and Azekah still resisted—that is, before the Babylonians captured King Zedekiah. Jeremiah's editor wanted careful readers to know this prophecy about substitute kingship was foresight, not hindsight.

### DANIEL COMES ALIVE

Psalm 51 has four AAA and two A groups of "Daniel-Sarpuhi" code, which is sufficient to give it a first in frequency among 929 chapters. But the exiles also used an additional designation for substitute king. It was התמורתמלך, which formed "Daniel the substitute king," דנאלהתמורתמלך. The infrequently used word תמורה means exchange or recompense, and a תמורתמלך would be an exchange king. In the psalm's usage, sometimes the author substituted דניאל for דנאל and the article ה might or might not be inserted. The result within Ps 51 was spectacular. The Daniel-the-substitute-king codes added eight AAA and ten A groups to the six original Daniel-Sarpuhi groups. This produced 120 coding points, third highest

---

29. Jer 34:5 contains ובמשרפות אבותיך המלכים, which produces תמורת מלך, "substitute king."

among all names (Jacob was second). And what exilic personage had the greatest number of coding points? It was a combined Daniel-Belteshazzar, with 184 points (Daniel used the Babylonian name of Belteshazzar). Interestingly, excluding substitute-king codes, "Belteshazzar son of David" and "Belteshazzar the prisoner" outscored the Daniel combinations, which included "Daniel son of Abigail," "Daniel son of David," "Daniel the prisoner," "Daniel son of Eliakim," and "Daniel son of Jehoiakim" (Jehoiakim was Eliakim's throne name).

The book of Daniel reached its final form in the second century, and so far scholars have been unable to pierce the book's wall of legend to establish that Daniel was a real person. But this coding constitutes hard, verifiable evidence; and it possesses a strength that gives it first place among all OT chapters. Daniel, it seems, was a real person, one that died as a substitute king.

To share with readers some examples of this new Daniel reality, we resort again to Coded Words (abbreviated CW). These contain within a single text word the letters of "Daniel" or of its athbash variant. Jacob, Jeremiah, and Ezekiel had the same objections to Daniel's worship of Babylon's gods that they had with King Jehoiachin's. Indeed, many of these denunciations contain side-by-side Jehoiachin and Daniel CWs. Starting with Second Jacob: "You have burdened me with your sins; you have wearied me [Daniel CW] with your iniquities" (Isa 43:24); "The carpenter ... makes it in human form [Daniel CW], with human beauty, to be set up in a shrine" (Isa 44:13); "it is I, the Lord, the God of Israel, who call you by your name [Daniel CW]. For the sake of my servant Jacob, and Israel my chosen, I call you by your name [Daniel CW] ... though you do not know me" (Isa 45:3–4); and "because of your sins [Daniel CW] you were sold, and for your transgressions [Daniel and two Jehoiachin CWs] your mother was put away" (Isa 50:1).

Jeremiah also took umbrage with both Jehoiachin and Daniel: "You have polluted the land with your whoring [Daniel and two Jehoiachin CWs] and wickedness" (Jer 3:2). This next phrase has no less than three counterparts: "they have gone after other gods to serve them [Daniel CW]" (Jer 11:10; see 13:10; 25:6; 35:15). Ezekiel, who was also an exile in Babylonia, added: "you gave your gifts to all your lovers, bribing them to come to you from all around for your whorings [Daniel and two Jehoiachin CWs]" (Ezek 16:33, also 16:34 and 16:36); "my holy name you shall no more profane with your gifts [Daniel and Jehoiachin CWs] and

## The Exilic Code

your idols" (Ezek 20:39); and "you played the whore [Daniel CW] with the nations, and polluted yourself with their idols" (Ezek 23:30). That was how the Major Prophets reacted to Daniel.

And here are the views of the Minor Prophets. Judging by their coded reactions, Daniel achieved wealth and high position in Nebuchadnezzar's court. The sixth-century editor of Hosea said, "By their wickedness they make the king glad, and the officials by their treachery [Daniel CW]" (Hos 7:3). Perhaps this same hand, working in Amos, denounces Daniel for his injustice: "Alas for those who lie [Daniel CW] on beds of ivory, and lounge on their couches, and eat lambs from the flock" and "You that trample on the needy, and bring to ruin [Daniel CW] the poor of the land" (Amos 6:4, 8:4).

From Micah comes: "For you have kept the statutes of Omri [Ahab's father] and all the works of the house of Ahab, and you have followed their counsels. Therefore ... you shall bear the scorn [Daniel CW] of my people" (Mic 6:16). And Malachi added Ezra and Jehoiachin to Daniel's indictment: "I will draw near to you for judgment [Jehoiachin CW]; I will be swift to bear witness against the sorcerers [Daniel CW], against the adulterers [Ezra CW], against those who swear falsely, against those who oppress the hired workers in their wages, the widow and the orphan, against those who thrust aside the alien, and do not fear me" (Mal 3:5).

Scholars will appreciate that the coding process raises many, many new questions. A major one regards the Ps 51 coding results. Who are all these people that according to Scripture lived in different centuries? Appendix 3 briefly describes for us those with significant coding. Characterizations of the first dozen names are typical: "Scribe, helped Moses with census"; "Pre-monarchy judge, son of Samuel"; "King David's son, revolted against father"; "King David's son"; "Mother of King Hezekiah"; "King of Judah 842"; "Asherite leader from time of Joshua"; "Probably son of King Hezekiah"; "King of Judah 800–783"; "Son of Saul, hanged under David"; "Daughter of Ahab and Jezebel"; and "Father of Shapan, Josiah's secretary." If the names seem to favor kings, it probably is because these were calibrated to the database ahead of most others, and then tested against Ps 51. In addition, exilic standouts like Jacob, Ezra, and Daniel also made the list. What was tested, then, produced this variety of names. It is well to remember, though, that no more than a quarter of Scripture's father-son and father-daughter combinations have been tried against the psalm.

About a fifth of the highly coded names in Ps 51 are clearly exilic. These include Jacob, Daniel, Ezra, Baruch, Nebuchadnezzar, Nabonidus-Belshazzar, Cyrus, Ezekiel, Jeremiah, Zedekiah, and Zephaniah, as well as lesser known individuals such as Zephaniah's son Azariah, Hilkiah's son Gemariah, and Tobshillem's son Jaazaniah (from the Lachish letters). But unresolved is the question of why the psalm has so many highly coded names from different periods of Israel's history.

## CODING DATES PSALM 51

What can coded names tell us about when Ps 51 was written? First, the strength of the four *sarpuhi* codes is impressive. Daniel-Sarpuhi was the best among 929 chapters, Ezekiel- and Zedekiah-Sarpuhi rated number two, and Jehoiachin-Sarpuhi was third-best. The odds against obtaining this outcome by coincidence are over six hundred billion to one. Also, these substitutions are dateable events, based as they are upon eclipses. Of the four, we can be certain only about when Jehoiachin died, which was in the spring of 561 BCE. As the next chapter will show, the best estimate for Ezekiel's death is 569. And what are the death dates for Zedekiah and Daniel? The rebel Zedekiah fell into Nebuchadnezzar's hands in about 587, and Daniel had been taken to the Babylonian court twenty years before as a sort of hostage in training. Given that Babylon installed substitutes at the rate of about one every two years, common historical sense would say that Zedekiah, at least, would have perished well before the 560s. This means that Ps 51 could not have been written before the second half of 561, after Jehoiachin's execution. The Daniel and Daniel-Sarpuhi categories have extremely high coding totals. However, it is possible that Daniel escaped substitution under the Neo-Babylonians, and instead served as a substitute in the early Persian period.

Two other code groups also bear upon the psalm's dating. The Nabonidus-Belshazzar combination has a strong fifty-eight points. Nabonidus reigned as Babylon's last king between 556 and 539. Inexplicably, he decamped from the capital about 552 and spent some ten years in Arabia. Then he returned to Babylon in late 543 for the final years of his reign.[30] During Nabonidus' absence, his son Belshazzar exercised many of his father's royal duties, and for this reason I combined the two names in a single category. The conclusion is that Ps 51 could not have

---

30. Beaulieu, "Reign of Nabonidus," 259.

been written before Nabonidus came to the throne and, given the prominence of Belshazzar coding, probably not before his son had been regent for some time—perhaps in the middle 540s.

The final category that concerns the psalm's date is Cyrus coding. "Cyrus," "Cyrus king of Anshan," and "Cyrus king of Persia" have twenty-four spellings between them totaling forty-six points. (Scholars who wish to replicate these spellings should check appendix 3B.) Cyrus the Great probably led a revolt in Israel sometime in the 570s and conquered Babylon in 539. A question is whether the Cyrus coding in Psalm 51 refers not just to the abortive revolt, but to his conquest of Babylon as well. To probe this I tested the psalm for "Cyrus king of Babylon," a combination not previously employed. Surprisingly, this produced four AAA code groups, the ones shown below:

TABLE 5.4—"CYRUS KING OF BABYLON" CODED IN PSALM 51 (EXCERPT FROM APPENDIX 3, PART B, ITEMS 82–85)

| English | Hebrew | Hebrew Athbash | Value/ Spellings | First Sequence, Span, (Interval) | Other Spellings Verse-Word (Interval) |
|---|---|---|---|---|---|
| Cyrus K Babylon | כורסהמלכבבל | בזסנחתאבככא | AAA/one | נאבחכסכאבהתז 1-1–6-10(4) | |
| Cyrus K Babylon | כורסהמלכבבל | התנסשזוהצצו | AAA/one | שצההותנצסוז 6-6–9-2(2) | |
| Cyrus K Babylon | כורסהמלכבבל | תהמלורשתטטש | AAA/six | שוטממתהתתרלש 6-11–10-1(2) | 7-2, 4, 6, 8-2(2); 8-4(1) |
| Cyrus K Babylon | כורסהמלכבבל | שעחטסאתשללת | AAA/ three | תחעתאטסלללשש 8-5–10-2(1) | 8-7, 9-1(1) |

These code groups show that Psalm 51 was written after Cyrus the Great had conquered Babylon and assumed kingship. He entered the capital on October 12, 539 BCE and took the throne quickly thereafter. The first concealed spelling in the table begins on 1-1, the psalm's opening word, and this may even be the first biblical announcement of the Cyrus enthronement. He reigned for a decade before dying in battle on a frontier of his empire, so Ps 51 could have been written anytime during the 530s. However, this analysis does not test for coding of names of the kings who followed Cyrus—Darius I, Xerxes (called Ahasuerus), Artaxerxes I, and the rest, let alone Alexander and his Greek successors. Later coding may show that Psalm is more a history of days gone by than a newspaper-like report of recent events. But if we were to assign a tentative date to the psalm based only upon coding we now know to be within it, a time not long after Cyrus ascended Babylon's throne seems appropriate. However, future research might prove that to be too early.

And what is the underlying theme of Ps 51? There may be writings in Scripture that rejoice at the Persian king's victory over Babylon, but this is not one of them. Instead the psalm is a somber review of the terrible costs to Israel of its continued rebellions against authority. I use Michael Dahood's Anchor Bible translation because it captures this mood: "O God, in your kindness, in your immense compassion delete my rebellious acts. Again and again, wash me of my guilt, and of my sin clean me. My rebellious acts that face me I know too well, and my sin is ever before me. Against you alone have I sinned, and before your eyes committed the crime..." (Ps 51: 2-4).[31] The coding beneath the text told knowing readers of Zedekiah's revolt, his punishment as a substitute king, the Cyrus uprising, the sacrifice of Ezekiel, Daniel's execution, and the likely murder by Babylon of Davidic descendents— Shephatiah, Absalom, Solomon, Ithream, and the rest. The heirs could have been Jehoiachin's children; they might also have been those of Jehoiakim (as coding says Daniel was) or of Zedekiah. Moreover, Ps 51's coding seems to include a roll call of revolt victims, the previously unknown heroes who perished in Babylonian pogroms and prisons because of uprisings in Israel. And finally, the encodings may name Jews who died in battles with neighboring states, with the armies of Nebuchadnezzar, and perhaps with the troops of King Nabonidus.

Criticism of Jacob, Ezra, Jehoiachin, Daniel and others indicates deep divisions among the exiles. The differences certainly included the worship and allegiance due the Lord, matters of justice, and how to survive under foreign rulers. The psalm said, "Give me again your saving joy, and by your generous spirit sustain me, that I may teach rebels your ways, and sin-

---

31. Dahood, *Psalms II*, 1–2.

ners to return to you" (Ps 51:12–13). This could be an appeal to reconcile factions. Unthinkable though it is, these words might even be an entreaty not to revolt against Cyrus, the new king of Babylon. The tragic outcome of the uprising that the Persian led seems still to have rankled thirty years later. (If subsequent work proves that Ps 51 has a date well into the Persian period, the coding may also indicate other revolts of which we as yet know nothing.)

As to authorship, many people must have contributed to this complex and powerful psalm. If Ezra or Jacob survived the Exile, they surely had a part. A lead scribe appears to have been Azariah, the son of Zephaniah the prophet. Shelemiah son of Kore and Jehizkiah son of Shallum also have high points and may have been leading spirits in the psalm's creation. It is also possible, however, that coding suitable for identifying Ps 51's author or authors has yet to be applied to this text.

Finally, it is time to address two of Scripture's greatest mysteries. The first is the identity of the Suffering Servant of the Lord, and the second is how he met his end. Chapter 6 will do this and also offer an opinion on how these findings shaped Jesus's views of his own death.

# 6

# The Suffering Servant and the Son of Man

## THE SERVANT AS A SUBSTITUTE

ISAIAH 53 DESCRIBES AN innocent sufferer who died mysteriously, and whose death somehow redeemed others. That unknown person has been termed the Suffering Servant. Christopher North has found over one hundred different candidates for the servant.[1] Five decades ago H. H. Rowley wrote, "No subject connected with the Old Testament has been more discussed than . . . the identity of the Suffering Servant."[2] Rowley in turn quoted a scholar writing in 1908 who lamented, "The literature of the subject has grown to such an extent that no one can boast of having fathomed all the recesses of this sea."

The University of Chicago's John Brinkman is an expert in Neo-Babylonian history. Some years ago he suggested to me that the Suffering Servant might have died as a substitute king. Professor Brinkman directed me to Simo Parpola, whose work shows that in the seventh century BCE Assyrian kings enthroned substitutes at Nineveh and in neighboring Babylonia.[3] This book's earlier chapters discussed Jehoiachin's substitute kingship and the prevalence of *sarpuhi* coding in the Priestly Benediction and in Ps 51. Also coding has enabled us to add Daniel, Ezekiel, and Zedekiah to the list of victims of this ancient practice. Certainly this evidence must be kept in mind as we examine Isa 53 for the possibility that the Suffering Servant also died as a substitute king.

1. C. North, *Suffering Servant*.
2. Rowley, *Servant of the Lord*, 3.
3. Parpola I and Parpola II. In 1993, Helsinki Press published the similarly titled *Letters from Assyrian and Babylonian Scholars*, which omitted the Excursus on substitute kings in Parpola II, xxii–xxxii. Those interested in the Suffering Servant should consult this 1983 out-of-print source.

## The Exilic Code

Before proceeding to the Isaiah text we need to lay the foundation for the practice of substitution in Babylon itself. To Mesopotamians, history's weight was heavy. According to Paul-Alain Beaulieu, "All notions of progress, evolution, or even change, were alien to their world view."[4] The Babylonians and Assyrians worshipped the same gods and used the same rites. In addition, though the king of Assyria reigned from Nineveh, he simultaneously wore the crown of Babylon. Therefore, whenever an eclipse's portents threatened both Assyria and Babylon, the same substitute king ascended each throne. In fact, the Assyrians were enthroning substitute kings in Babylon a scant forty years prior to the Neo-Babylonian dynasty's founding. Moreover, Babylon's priestly bureaucracy remained in place after that nation had ousted the Assyrians.

Simo Parpola, the recognized expert on substitute kings, has concluded that the substitute-king practice originated with the Babylonians and spread from there across the ancient Near East. Still later, "as the Roman Empire spread into the Near East, the ritual also gained a foothold in the West."[5] He also says that details of Hittite substitute-king rituals prove that they came from Babylonian originals.

Such ceremonies were not simple, as this letter from the Assyrian king's chief exorcist attests. "As regards the ritual about which the king said yesterday: 'Perform it before the 24th day,' we cannot make it; the tablets are too numerous, god knows when they can write them. It took us five to six days even to get ready with the preparation of the figurines..."[6] Too much work, too few hands. Only a large priestly bureaucracy could perform such rituals, and the Assyrians maintained such a bureaucracy in Babylon. After the Babylonians gained their independence, they very likely continued to appoint substitutes—and frequently, too. Eighty-one eclipses occurred over Babylon during the exile of the Jews (597–539 BCE), and I estimate at least forty required substitutes. This squares with the testimony of the Nineveh letters, where eight of sixteen eclipses (in just thirteen years) brought Assyrian substitutes to the throne.

---

4. Beaulieu, "Antiquarianism in Neo-Babylonian Period," 37.

5. Parpola, "Substitute King Ritual and Jesus."

6. Parpola I, 129. Parpola II, 163–67, has the commentary. This ceremony, which followed an eclipse, was performed to protect the king against witchcraft rather than to seat a substitute in Nineveh. However, the eclipse's shadowing would still have required a substitute in Babylonia.

## The Suffering Servant and the Son of Man

Was the Suffering Servant a substitute king? Let us test Isa 52:13 through 53:12. "See, my servant shall prosper; he shall be exalted and lifted up, and shall be very high" (Isa 52:13). If the servant became king of Babylon he was indeed exalted. He would also have prospered, for he would have replaced a king of vast wealth. Further, the servant literally would have been very high. As king of Babylon his throne would have been higher than those of the court's puppet kings. Consider Judah's King Jehoiachin, whom we now know to have been a substitute. When he left prison, he received "a seat [throne] above the other seats of the kings who were with him in Babylon" (2 Kgs 25:28). Continuing, Isa 52:15 says, "Kings shall shut their mouths because of him." These would have been puppet kings, Nebuchadnezzar's trophies and hostages. Any substitute for him became a king of kings.

"By a perversion of justice he was taken away . . ." (Isa 53:8). The substitute-king process was unjust. It certainly would have been "a perversion of justice" if the Babylonians used substitution to kill the servant. In addition, some exegetes say authorities took the servant from prison,[7] while the Nineveh letters show the Assyrians stockpiled candidates in confinement pending the next eclipse.[8]

Isaiah 53:10 and 11 say, "When you make his life an offering for sin," and "The righteous one, my servant, shall make many righteous, and he shall bear their iniquities." This would fit the substitute model. Here are reports to Assyrian monarchs.[9] "The substitute king of the land of Akkad [Babylon] took the signs on himself." The signs, of course, were evil portents. And, "I made him recite the scribal recitations before the Sun-god, he took all the celestial and terrestrial omens on himself . . ." This ritual transferred the eclipse's evil to the substitute. To paraphrase Isaiah 53, the substitute became an offering for sin, made many righteous, and bore their iniquities. The Nineveh letters show these matters were vital to the true king. This was life, not theater. The king was a dead man unless the eclipse's evils could be shifted to his substitute.

Quoting scripture again, "so shall he startle [sprinkle] many nations . . ." (Isa 52:15). Every substitute king presided over the "many nations" of Babylon's polyglot empire. The NRSV has "startle," others "sprinkle."

---

7. Thomas, "Recent Isaiah 53 Study," 84; Driver, "Servant of Lord," 94.

8. Parpola I, 229. The Persians also kept prisoners for future substitute kings, or at least took substitutes from prisons. See Parpola II, xxx–xxxi (items 15, 16).

9. Parpola I, 21, 227.

Either serves, though sprinkle better expresses the atoning effect of the servant's blood. Isaiah 53:9 said, "They made his grave with the wicked and his tomb with the rich." At last this puzzle has a solution. After conducting a king's funeral, the executioners buried the servant with other Babylonian royalty. To the exiles from Judah, of course, royal Babylonians were both rich and wicked. We have previously quoted this description of a Babylonian royal funeral during the Exile period.[10] King Nabonidus "laid her body to rest wrapped in fine wool garments and shining white linen. He deposited her body in a hidden tomb with splendid ornaments of gold set with beautiful stone beads, containers of scented oil . . ." Kings and governors came from across the empire to grieve, and the Babylonian people had a period of mourning. A substitute king's funeral might have been something like this.

Conclusion: the Suffering Servant died as a substitute king. This affirmation builds upon previous coding evidence, brings unity to the text, and makes sense of previously unexplainable passages. This is not the first publication of the servant-substitute news. Professor John H. Walton of Wheaton College has written, "the imagery, background, and obscurities of the Fourth Servant Song can be adequately resolved when the passage is read in the light of the substitute king ritual."[11]

## SUFFERING SERVANT'S IDENTITY

Who was the Suffering Servant? As we shall see, word linkages point toward Ezekiel, one of the four candidates that coding would support. A century ago R. Kraetzschmar footnoted the "extraordinary similarity" between Ezekiel and the Suffering Servant. Kraetzschmar "thought it strange that no one had so far conjectured that Ezekiel was the 'historical original' of the Servant."[12] Sixth-century timing permits the choice. Scholars generally place the servant's death within the Exile, and Ezekiel was an exilic prophet. The latest date Ezekiel himself gave for a prophecy was April of 571 BCE.[13]

10. Pritchard, "Mother of Nabonidus," 561–2. Translator's marks omitted.

11. Walton, "Substitute King Ritual in Isaiah 53," 734.

12. Kraetzschmar, *Ezechiel*, 46, n 3, cited by C. North, 56. According to North's note on page 98, by 1900 Kraetzschmar had completed a monograph on Isaiah 53 that connected Ezekiel and the Suffering Servant. However, Kraetzschmar died soon afterward, and the monograph never appeared.

13. Greenberg, "Ezekiel," 1081–82.

## The Suffering Servant and the Son of Man

On January 5, 569, an eclipse darkened Babylon's sun. The planets and shadowing were such that Nebuchadnezzar had to name a substitute. The 571 prophecy and the 569 solar eclipse point to Ezekiel. Also, God repeatedly called Ezekiel "son of man." As discussed later, the book of Sirach connects son of man and solar eclipse. Does Scripture support the choice of Ezekiel?

According to Isa 53:2, "He grew up before him like a young plant, and like a root [Cyrus CW] out of dry ground." This might fit Ezekiel. He was a youth when he reached Babylon, and grew to maturity in exile. The Cyrus CW could have supplied the reason he was being sacrificed, and "dry ground" could have been a euphemism for Babylonia. Next, Isa 52:14 said, "So marred was his appearance, beyond human semblance, and his form beyond that of mortals [sons of men]." Ezekiel suffered paralysis and muteness, and may also have been disfigured.[14] Most importantly, "sons of men," which the NRSV translated "mortals," probably alerted the initiated that the victim was to be Ezekiel, the son of man.

"He had no form or majesty that we should look at him, nothing in his appearance that we should desire him . . . as one from whom others hide their faces he was despised, and we held him of no account" (Isa 53:2–3). (The term majesty צדר, is not infrequently used with kings.) Ezekiel's visions, odd ways, and harsh prophecies would have estranged him from his fellows. And the prophet shunned others. "For the most part Ezekiel lives in a separate world," wrote D. N. Freedman. "Other people drift in and out of the book, but there is little direct contact."[15] "He was despised, and we held him of no account," fits what we know of Ezekiel.

Isaiah 53:7 said, "Like a sheep that before its shearers is silent, so he did not open his mouth." This, too, was in character. Ezekiel was mute for considerable periods. More importantly, this verse's vocabulary points directly at Ezekiel. "Silent," "open," "not," and "mouth" occurred elsewhere together only in three places, each of which is an Ezekiel prophecy.[16] Exiles knowing Word Links would immediately have understood that Ezekiel was the Suffering Servant.

"A man of suffering [or sorrows], and acquainted with infirmity" (Isa 53:3) also described the prophet. The Lord told Ezekiel, "Moan therefore,

---

14. For Ezekiel's physical problems see Ezek 3:14–27; 4:4–8; 12:18; 24:22–27; and 33:22.

15. Freedman, "Ezekiel," 453. Greenberg, 1082, quoted Freedman.

16. Ezekiel 3:26–27, 24:27, and 33:22. Each had "son of man" nearby.

mortal [son of man]; moan with breaking heart and bitter grief before their eyes" (Ezek 21:6). Next, consider this poignant passage in which God addressed the son of man and said, "I am about to take away from you the delight of your eyes; yet you shall not mourn or weep … Sigh, but not aloud; make no mourning for the dead." "So I spoke to the people in the morning," Ezekiel said, "and at evening my wife died" (Ezek. 24:16–18). A dead wife, yet God prohibited mourning! Ezekiel was indeed a man of sorrows.

In the sixth century, Judah was in revolt. In response, Nebuchadnezzar removed two Jewish kings, razed Judah's cities, and brought three groups of exiles to Babylonia. Even there, false prophets continued to preach rebellion. Jeremiah and Ezekiel opposed the rebels, but to little effect. Nebuchadnezzar, sick of the sedition, had good reason to think the exiles were a fifth column. Very likely, persecution followed.

There are seven Second Jacob passages about persecution. Here is one: "But this is a people robbed and plundered, all of them are trapped in holes and hidden in prisons" (Isa 42:22).[17] Whatever "all" meant, the authorities had a major persecution underway. They had filled their prisons, and then pushed the overflow into pits. Assuming an exilic setting, the Babylonians must have believed that every prominent exile carried the taint of Judah's rebellion. Did they think the Suffering Servant also carried it?

"But he was wounded for our transgressions [Jehoiachin and Daniel CWs] … stricken for the transgression [Jehoiachin CW] of my people … was numbered with the transgressors [Jehoiachin CW]; yet he bore the sin of many, and made intercession for the transgressors [Jehoiachin and Daniel CWs]" (Isa 53:5, 8, 12).[18] Although innocent, the Suffering Servant had been "wounded" and "stricken" for rebellions in Judah. Ezekiel, too, was innocent, but as a leading citizen of the Exile he also would have suffered. The CWs indicate the taint of rebellion also threatened the lives of Daniel and Jehoiachin, two other prominent exiles, and that Ezekiel's intercession prevented their executions. (Quite possibly Daniel and

---

17. Other persecution passages by Second Jacob are Isa 42:7; 47:6; 49:9, 24; 51:13–14, 23.

18. The NRSV has "transgression." Others use variations of "rebellion." See McKensie, *Second Isaiah,* 130; and Hollenberg, "Nations in Isaiah 40–55," 35–36. The CWs identified as "Daniel" are actually "Koheleth," which means preacher. Work done elsewhere indicates Daniel also used this name.

Jehoiachin were involved in plotting the Cyrus-led uprising.) One could conclude that the innocent Ezekiel and the innocent Suffering Servant were one and the same. Moreover, God Himself previously had symbolically punished Ezekiel for Israel's iniquity (see Ezek 4:4). This prefigured Isa 53:6, which said, "The Lord has laid on him the iniquity of us all."

The servant's silence was striking. The author made this point three times within sixteen Hebrew words. "He was oppressed, and he was afflicted, yet he opened not his mouth [once] . . . like a sheep that before its shearers is silent [twice], so he did not open his mouth [thrice]" (Isa 53:7). The Suffering Servant said absolutely nothing. Why not?

The servant refused to participate, to accept the eclipse's evil omens by swearing to them. This letter from the Assyrian archive illustrates the victim's role. "The substitute king, who on the 14th sat on the [Assyrian] throne in Nineveh . . . entered the city of Akkad [in Babylonia] safely on the night of the 20th and sat upon the throne. I made him recite the scribal recitations before the Sun-god, he took all the celestial and terrestrial omens on himself, and ruled all the countries."[19] From Nineveh to Akkad, three hundred miles in fewer than six days! There was good reason to hurry. The eclipse had doomed the king. In Parpola's words, death "was the fate decreed by the gods to the ruling king *personally* as a punishment for his conduct as king."[20] That certainly applied to Nebuchadnezzar. The gods would kill either him or his substitute within one hundred days. But still, the Suffering Servant remained silent—painfully so.

This is what they did to Ezekiel. "Surely he has . . . carried our *sorrows*; yet we esteemed him *stricken*, *smitten* by God, and *afflicted*. But he was *wounded* for our transgressions, he was *bruised* for our iniquities; upon him was the *chastisement* that made us whole, and with his *stripes* we are healed" (Isa 53:4–5, RSV, italics added). This language is full of violence. Consider these synonyms for the italicized words: "physical pains," "beaten," "humbled," "pierced," "struck," "crushed," "discipline," and "blows that cut." The Suffering Servant earned his title.

But as happens often, weakness became strength. Ezekiel, the one whom God had previously stricken mute, held out until Nebuchadnezzar freed his Jewish prisoners and halted the persecution. Scripture said, "Upon him was the punishment that made us whole, and by his bruises

---

19. Parpola I, 227.
20. Parpola II, xxiv, his italics.

we are healed . . . The righteous one, my servant, shall make many righteous, and he shall bear their iniquities . . . he bore the sin of many, and made intercession for the transgressors [rebels]" (Isa 53:5, 11, 12). The tortures Ezekiel endured "healed" the rebels, making them "whole." He "shall make many righteous," i.e., not guilty. Ezekiel must finally have assented to become king of Babylon. In exchange, Nebuchadnezzar pardoned the rebels, agreed to protect Daniel and King Jehoiachin, and ended the persecution.

The agreement was in writing—perhaps on stone tablets—as these Word Links with the Jehoiachin substitute-king verses in 2 Kgs 25:27–30 attest: "These words the LORD spoke with a loud voice to your whole assembly at the mountain, out of the . . . thick darkness [Daniel and Jehoiachin CWs] . . . He wrote them on two stone tablets, and gave them to me." And, "Then Moses and the levitical priests [Jehoiachin CW] spoke to all Israel, saying: Keep silence and hear [Daniel CW], O Israel! This very day you have become the people of the LORD your God. Therefore [Daniel CW] obey . . ." (Deut 5:22 and 27:9–10).[21]

There is more. "I will allot him a portion with the great [rabs], and he shall divide the spoil with the strong [numerous ones]," said Isa 53:12. This has two clever wordplays. *Rab*, the singular of "the great," prefaced Babylonian titles like Rab-Mag and Rab-Saris, and the author uses the plural here. Apparently the Suffering Servant struck a bargain to recover from the rabs—the king's ruling elite—a portion of the plunder seized from the exiles. Then, once Ezekiel had retrieved what spoil he could, he divided it, though not with "the strong" as translations commonly read. Like "great," "strong" is a plural adjective. Usually it means "numerous ones," strong in numbers, rather than strong in power.[22] Ezekiel distributed the recovered loot to the "numerous ones," his fellow exiles. Here is a paraphrase: "I will apportion spoil to him from the chiefs, and he shall divide it among the numerous ones."

It may take scholars years to reach consensus about whether (1) the Suffering Servant died as a substitute king and (2) Ezekiel was that person. In advance of the debate, Simo Parpola, the foremost authority on substitute kingship, has rendered opinions. He answers the two questions with "probably" and "maybe." In an April 29, 2004, email he wrote,

---

21. The Daniel CWs are spellings of Koheleth.
22. Brown, BDB, 783.

Your idea that Isaiah's suffering servant in fact was a Jewish substitute king enthroned in Babylon is fascinating, and I believe it has a good chance of even being correct; it fits the facts and makes sense. The suggested identification of the suffering servant with Ezekiel is also fascinating. The scenario reconstructed by you admittedly involves a great deal of speculation, but it is not implausible.

## RECONSIDERING ATONEMENT

In the ancient world, the substitute was a stand-in for the king. But eclipses did more than threaten the king. Eclipses laid curses on the whole nation. Esarhaddon's agent in Babylonia wrote the Assyrian king, "This eclipse ... *afflicted the Westland*; the king of the Westland will die *and his country decrease or, according to another tradition, be lost.*"[23] The country as well as the king was to suffer. *Ritual for a Substitute King* showed that priests buried the ashes of the substitute's goods with the dead king and queen. It went on to state, "*Then the purification of the land will be achieved*, ditto the purification of the king."[24] The substitute's death cleansed both land and king. In another document, Assyria's regent in Babylonia prayed, "At the time of evil, the eclipse of the Moon-god ... At the time of the menace of evil omens and signs that are unfavorable, *which are upon my palace and my land.*"[25]

Though we might distinguish between king and kingdom, residents of Babylonia probably saw them as more of a unity, particularly when thinking of Nebuchadnezzar, a monarch who had reigned for the lifetime of most Babylonians. In Parpola's words, the ancients thought the substitute king's "principal role was to act as a substitute sufferer who took it upon himself to bear the sins of the king and atone for them with his own blood."[26] But Hebrew Scripture gave a somewhat different emphasis to the Suffering Servant's death. The author of Isa 53 personalized the matter. The servant cared nothing about purifying a king or kingdom. Instead, Ezekiel shall "make many righteous." The shift was to people, many of them, and also toward covering specific offenses, which in all likelihood were those of his rebellious countrymen.

23. Parpola I, 227, italics added.
24. Lambert, "Substitute King Ritual," 110, italics added.
25. Langdon, "Accadian Prayer," 83, italics added.
26. Parpola, "Substitute King Ritual and Jesus."

Isaiah 53's interpretation of the pagan ritual differs in another way. The Lord prized the servant. Ezekiel was especially precious in God's eyes because he accepted torment in order to cover his people's offenses. In contrast, we know that the Assyrians viewed and treated substitutes contemptuously. The king-to-be could be a prisoner or a political enemy "whose life did not matter much or who would have deserved death anyway."[27] But before authorities could kill their substitute, the victim had to accept that he was accursed. The Babylonians sought to damn the Suffering Servant; Isa 53 honored him.

An eclipse rendered a death sentence on the king. Either he or a surrogate had to die within one hundred days. Though one hundred was a maximum for a substitute's reign, the term was often shorter, so that the replacement lived from day to day. A Nineveh letter said, "As regards the substitute king about whom the king, my lord, wrote to me: 'How many days should he sit?' . . . he could go to his fate on the 16th. Or if it suits the king, my lord, better, he could as well sit the full 100 days."[28]

Isaiah 53:10 said, "When you make his life an offering for sin, he shall see his offspring, and shall prolong his days." In the substitute-king context, "When you make his life an offering for sin" meant God had led Ezekiel to agree to become Nebuchadnezzar's substitute. In exchange, the Babylonian king may have consented to spare the prophet's children. According to the great British scholar Sidney Smith, a man's existence was prolonged while his name abided through progeny.[29] The RSV noted that since a man's name was "the bearer of his person, the father lived on in the son."[30] So "he shall see his offspring" perhaps related to saving Ezekiel's children.

As to "prolong his days," one explanation is that Nebuchadnezzar promised Ezekiel the full hundred days of kingship. However, that would have carried Ezekiel's reign into the New Year's Festival, and denied the true king his annual enthronement as king of Babylon. Alternately, the king could have allowed Ezekiel to stay alive well beyond his allotted time. But neither of these would have been acceptable to Nebuchadnezzar. Ezekiel

---

27. Parpola II, xxiv.
28. Parpola I, 109.
29. Smith, *Isaiah Chapters*, 102.
30. *The New Oxford Annotated Bible with the Apocrypha*, RSV, note on Deut 25:6. See also note on Gen 48:16.

had to die quickly, and the Babylonian king had to regain the throne by New Year's Day.

Here is the third possibility. By "prolong his days" Isa 53's author also could have meant that the servant experienced earthly death and then (a) was restored to life or (b) lived on through his descendants. To some, these possibilities might seem strange, but there was biblical precedent for it. Elisha, the man of God, brought the Shunammite woman's son back from the dead (2 Kgs 4:32–37); Elijah revived a dead child (1 Kgs 17:17–24); and at the collective level God breathed life into the dried bones of Israel (Ezek 37:1–14). (This omits discussion of Dan 12:1–3, a far later text that speaks directly about resurrection of the righteous and judgment of the unrighteous.) Jon D. Levenson has written that "the inevitability and irreversibility of death in the Hebrew Bible is only part of the story. The other part is the ubiquitous promise of life . . . offered by a God who enjoins his people . . . to 'choose life.'"[31] Promises made to others can be realized by their descendents, as with Abraham and David. And, "Even though the subject's death is irreversible . . . his or her fulfillment may yet occur, for identity survives death."[32] Biblical writers thought that, though death was very real, restoration after death was fully within God's power.[33] This combination of fulfillment through progeny and identity surviving death can describe the Suffering Servant's situation. Though he died as a substitute king, "he shall see his offspring, and shall prolong his days" (Isa 53:10).

In due time we shall follow a clandestine debate within scripture about whether the son of man lived, a debate that would overflow into the New Testament. Now, however, we should examine coding and Word Links for further evidence about whether Ezekiel was the Suffering Servant.

## CODING AND WORD LINKS SUPPORT SERVANT CHOICE

The last three verses of Isa 52 serve as a preface to the chapter that follows. For our purpose it matters little whether or not those verses were originally an integral part of Isa 53. The important thing is to check coding regarding Ezekiel's possible substitute kingship. Table 6.1 displays fifteen coding groups that address the question. The first three groups occur in Isa 52:13–15 and the other twelve are encoded within Isaiah

---

31. Levenson, *Resurrection and Restoration*, 179.
32. Ibid., 113.
33. Levenson, "World Repaired," 78.

chapter 53. The table has the same format as appendix 3 (studied in the chapter on Ps 51) so that anyone with a smattering of Hebrew may replicate the fifty spellings in the table's fifteen groups.

To summarize the table, the coding evidence that Ezekiel was the Suffering Servant is exceptional. The five Hebrew words that begin the Isa 52:13–15 passage start five coded spellings of "Ezekiel," and each of those spellings employs consecutive text words. The English translation of those five words is, "See, my servant shall prosper; he shall be exalted and lifted up." On the second word of this three-verse announcement starts a long athbash spelling of "Ezekiel the substitute king," יחזקאלהתמורתמלך. Using a letter from every second text word, the spelling stretches almost all the way through chapter 52's final verses.[34]

Isaiah 53 contains four groups of fifteen-letter spellings of "Ezekiel the substitute king," several of which have AAA values. Other codes include "son of man," "Ezekiel," "Ezekiel-Sarpuhi," "substitute," "substitute king," and שויסקאל, a nickname for Ezekiel in the Talmud.[35] In addition, an athbash for the biblical version of "Ezekiel" has two codes that complete their spellings on Isa 53's final text word. Thus scripture's Suffering Servant passage, Isa 52:13—53:12, starts and ends with Ezekiel's encoded name. The Ezekiel-related coding in the whole passage amounts to forty-eight points, which compares well with point totals of names encoded in Ps 51.

---

34. The presence of fifteen-letter codes raises questions about the practice of coding in Hebrew Scripture. There is no good reason to stop at fifteen encoded letters or at an interval of five, which at present is the maximum distance between text words that supply a letter. My own program cannot handle searches for words longer than fifteen letters, but those designing future programs should consider extending this limit.

35. *b. Qidd.* 70a.

## TABLE 6.1—EZEKIEL CODING IN ISAIAH 52:13—53:12

| English | Hebrew | Hebrew Athbash | Value/ Spellings | First Sequence, Span, (Interval) | Spellings Verse-Word (Interval) |
|---|---|---|---|---|---|
| Ezekiel | יחזקאל | אגדניש | A/five | נשדיאג 52:13-1–6(1) | 13-2–5(1), 3(3) |
| E the Sub King | יחזקאלהתמורתמלך | אגדנישוכרהמכרשת | AAA/ one | כמגשכנשתדהרוויאר 52:13-2–15-12(2) | |
| Son of Man | בנאדם | גמדאן | A/five | דמנגא 52:13-3–7(1) | 13-4, 5(1), 3, 6(3) |
| E the Sub King | יחזקאלהתמורתמלך | אגדנישוכרהמכרשת | AAA/ one | רגרתונכממשאשהדיך 53:1-4–6-1(4) | |
| E the Sub King | יחזקאלהתמורתמלך | אגדנישוכרהמכרשת | AAA/ one | דרמאכהכנגיושתשר 53:3-6–5-9(2) | |
| Son of Man | בנאדם | לבכנא | A/ten | באנכל 53:3-11–4-2(1) | 3-12(1, 2, 3), 13(1); 4-1, 2, 4(1); 2, 4(2) |
| Substitute King | תמורתמלך | הנשזהנסע | A/one | זהנשסנהע 53:3-11–4-12(2) | |
| Substitute | תמורת | שחסאש | A/one | שחאסש 53:3-13–4-8(2) | |
| Ezekiel Pseudo | שויסקאל | ושפלחדס | AA/ three | חפדוסשל 53:5-2–8(1) | 5-3, 4(1) |
| E the Sub King | יחזקאלהתמורתמלך | אגדנישוכרהמכרשת | A/three | תיהחלכלזמאתורמק 53:7-5–8-3(1) | 7-6, 7(1) |
| Ezekiel-Sarpuhi | יחזקאלשרפוהי | יחזקאלשרפוהי | A/five | חולפזהאיירשק 53:7-8–3(1) | 7-9–12(1) |
| E the Sub King | יחזקאלהתמורתמלך | יחזקאלהתמורתמלך | A/one | לכלזהאתמוקתרמח 53:7-9–8-7(1) | |
| Son of Man | בנאדם | ריקתט | A/three | תירטק 53:7-15–8-3(1) | 7-16, 8-2(1) |
| Ezekiel | יחזקאל | חוהפשי | A/four | חויפשה 53:9-10–10-6(2) | 9-10, 11(1), 12(2) |
| Ezekiel | יחזקאל | חוהפשי | A/six | חשוהיף 53:12-7–22(3) | 12-7, 9(2), 15-17(1) |

## The Exilic Code

The second major reason for suspecting that Ezekiel was the Servant of the Lord is Word Links. A prior chapter defined a Word Link as two passages that have in their texts the same unique batch of words. That particular batch would appear nowhere else in scripture except in those two places. Isaiah 52:13–15 contains just thirty-six Hebrew words, yet it produces at least 1,249 Word Links, an extraordinary total. About two hundred of these include "son of man" or "sons of men," which were linked with the words בני אדם in Isa 52:14. Indeed, this flood of son-of-man links first suggested to me that Ezekiel might be the Suffering Servant.

Here are four son-of-man links—the merest sample from two hundred. These involve prison, where Ezekiel spent time.[36] "I lie in the midst of lions that greedily devour the sons of men; their teeth are spears and arrows, their tongues sharp swords" (Ps 57:4). (Possibly "lions" referred to the friezes that lined Babylon's Processional Way.) Were their captors feeding sons of men to the lions? It was a known Babylonian practice. The word translated as "greedily devour" means "are aflame." Perhaps, too, the Babylonians were burning Ezekiel's followers, the sons of men, alive. The Babylonians also practiced that. The book of Daniel's fiery furnace and den of lions illustrated both barbarities. Another link said the Lord "does not willingly afflict or grieve the sons of men. To crush under foot all the prisoners of the earth . . . to subvert a man [אדם] in his cause, the Lord does not approve" (Lam 3:33–35). Psalm 107 contained multiple Word Links to Isa 52:13–15, with several including the refrain, "for his wonderful works to the sons of men!" Here is one, without its refrain. "Some sat in darkness and in gloom, prisoners in misery and in irons, for they had rebelled against the words of God . . ." (Ps 107:10–11 NRSV). And this one is more hopeful: "Let them thank the Lord . . . for his wonderful works to the sons of men! For he shatters the doors of bronze, and cuts in two the bars of iron" (Ps 107:14–16).

Both coding and Word Links offer evidence that Ezekiel, the son of man, was the Suffering Servant. But readers should know of another possibility. Daniel has eight coding groups within Isaiah 53 (but none in 52:13–15). Coded spellings include "Belteshazzar son of David," "Daniel," "Daniel son of Abigail," "Daniel son of Eliakim," and "Daniel son of Jehoiakim," as well as "Daniel the prisoner." In addition, the chapter also contains two groups of "Daniel the substitute king." In points, Daniel

---

36. The translations employ the RSV.

coding slightly exceeds that for Ezekiel. Should we say that Daniel could have been the Suffering Servant? From the description of him in the book of Daniel, the answer is no. According to scripture, young Daniel was a prodigy—admired, intelligent, attractive, and wise beyond his years, a star in Nebuchadnezzar's court. These impressions are at variance with Isaiah 53's view of the servant. That text said, "He had no form or majesty that we should look at him, nothing in his appearance that we should desire him. He was despised and rejected by others" (Isa 53:2–3). While Ezekiel meets these qualifications, Daniel certainly does not.

Additionally, the CWs in Isa 53 strongly suggest that Ezekiel's resistance saved the lives of Daniel and of King Jehoiachin, who may have been co-conspirators in the Cyrus plot. Here are those verses again: "But he was wounded for our transgressions [Jehoiachin and Daniel CWs] ... stricken for the transgression [Jehoiachin CW] of my people ... was numbered with the transgressors [Jehoiachin CW]; yet he bore the sin of many, and made intercession for the transgressors [Jehoiachin and Daniel CWs]" (Isa 53:5, 8, 12).

## THE MORTAL SON OF MAN

Isaiah chapter 53 had to be clear enough to describe Ezekiel's judicial murder, while sufficiently obscure to avoid provoking Babylon. Moderns think obscurity triumphed. But at least through New Testament times, some always knew that Ezekiel, the son of man, had been the Suffering Servant.

The book of Ecclesiastes (225 BCE) probably followed the servant's death by some three hundred years. Ecclesiastes used "son of man" and "sons of men" often. Frequently "sun" was close at hand. For example, "This is an evil in all that is done under the sun, that one fate comes to every one. Moreover the hearts of all [sons of men] are full of evil ..." (Eccl 9:3). Again, "The sons of men are snared at an evil time ... I have also seen this example of wisdom under the sun" (Eccl 9:12–13).[37] These "sun"–"sons of men" pairings hint that Ezekiel died after a solar eclipse.

The following adds a Suffering Servant connection: "under the sun ... the heart of the sons of men is fully set to do evil. Though a sinner does evil a hundred times and prolongs his life ... neither will he prolong his days" (Eccl 8:9, 11–13). The term "hundred times" probably refers to the

---

37. Unless otherwise noted, the rest of this section uses the RSV for translation.

substitute's hundred-day reign. Notably, this Ecclesiastes passage shares "prolong his days" with Isa 53:10: "He shall see his offspring, and shall prolong his days." Proverbs 28:16 and Deut 17:20 also have the equivalent of "prolong his days."[38] Proverbs said, "A ruler who lacks understanding is a cruel oppressor; but one who hates unjust gain will prolong his days." Deuteronomy admonished a king to copy out and then study a law prohibiting multiplication of horses, wives, and treasure. Proverbs was friendly and Deuteronomy hostile to the newly wealthy Ezekiel, king of Babylon. Another text, Ps 89, disputed that the son of man still lived. "Remember how short my time is—for what vanity you have created all mortals [sons of men]! Who can live and never see death? Who can deliver his soul from the power of Sheol?" (Ps 89:47–48). The psalmist did not agree that the son of man was immortal.

Nor did Ecclesiastes hold the son of man in high regard. Sons of men did evil and had evil hearts. Also, sons of men shared with beasts the fate of death (Eccl 3:19). Madness was in the hearts of sons of men "while they live, and after that they go to the dead" (Eccl 9:3).

The book of Sirach (early second century BCE) said, "Human beings [son of man] are not immortal. What is brighter than the sun? Yet it can be eclipsed" (Sir 17:30–31). *This connects son of man with a solar eclipse,* and it supports that it was a solar eclipse that triggered Ezekiel's enthronement. Significantly, Sirach agreed with Ecclesiastes that the son of man was mortal. Presumably others were arguing that the son of man was *im*mortal.

The book of Daniel followed Sirach by a few decades. Daniel 7:13 has "one like a son of man" (RSV) who became immortal. He received everlasting dominion over "all peoples, nations, and languages." It sounds like Ezekiel, the son of man, who briefly ruled Babylon's diverse empire. Elsewhere, in chapter 10, "one like the son of man" came to strengthen Daniel. Daniel 10:15–17 has four of the words from Isa 53:7: "Like a sheep that before its shearers is dumb, so he opened not his mouth." If that were not sufficient, the Daniel author added "sons of men" and "servant"![39] The Suffering Servant came to strengthen Daniel in chapter 10, and the kingly

---

38. In Deut 17:20 the more literal Strong translation has "prolong his days" (יאריך ימים).

39. This uses the RSV translation for "sons of men." Isaiah 53:7 and Dan 10:15–17 have strong connections with Ezek 3:26–27, 24:27, and 33:22. The linked passages all referred to one who was mute.

## The Suffering Servant and the Son of Man

son of man in Daniel chapter 7 was also the Suffering Servant, or one very like him.

Tobit (200 BCE) passed along the son-of-man secret. The angel Raphael twice said, "'It is good to guard the secret of a king, but to acknowledge and reveal the works of God, and with fitting honor to acknowledge him'" (12:7, 11). Presumably, the angel implied the *substitute* king. A century later, Wisdom of Solomon connected within a few lines "throne," "servants," "sons of men" (RSV), and "king" (Wis 9:4–7). About the same time 1 Esdras wrote, "The king is unrighteous . . . all human beings [sons of men] are unrighteous . . . There is no truth in them and in their unrighteousness they will perish" (1 Esd 4:37).

The Dead Sea Scrolls (100 BCE and later) argued that the son of man had been mortal and imperfect. The Community Rule said, "What is the son of man in the midst of Thy wonderful deeds? . . . Kneaded from the dust, his abode is the nourishment of worms."[40] And the Scrolls' Hymn 12 says, "Righteousness, I know, is not of man, nor is perfection the way of the son of man."[41] First Enoch (175 BCE—75 CE) wrote, "From the beginning the Son of Man was hidden, And the Most High preserved him in the presence of his (heavenly) host, And revealed him to the elect."[42] Only now can we understand what this meant. Isaiah 53 had concealed the son of man "from the beginning." Subsequently, God had kept him hidden from all but the elect, those who knew the secret of the Suffering Servant.

In summary, Ecclesiastes and Sirach used "sun" and "son of man" together. In those books, as in First Esdras and the Dead Sea Scrolls, the son of man was mortal. But to the authors of Daniel and First Enoch, the son of man was immortal. Ecclesiastes and Wisdom paired "servant" with "son of man." These also matched him with "king," as did Tobit, First Esdras, and Daniel. Ecclesiastes, Sirach, First Esdras, and the Scrolls offered scathing (though veiled) criticism. When Jesus chose the title "son of man," he thrust himself into an ongoing controversy.

The New Testament's book of Hebrews continued the secret tradition. Hebrews quoted Ps 8: "'What is . . . the son of man that thou carest for him? Thou didst make him *for a little while* lower than the angels, thou

---

40. Vermes, *Scrolls in English*, 117.
41. Ibid., 265–66.
42. Black, *Books of Enoch*, parables 62.6–7.

hast crowned him with glory and honor, putting everything in subjection under his feet'" (Heb 2:6–8 RSV, italics added). Psalm 8 quite possibly described Ezekiel, the substitute king. God crowned the son of man with glory and honor, and gave him the dominion of the king of Babylon. "For a little while" was also apt, for Ezekiel's reign was brief. (That phrase came from the Septuagint, not from the original Hebrew. When the Septuagint's author translated Ps 8 from Hebrew to Greek, he inserted "for a little while," proving he knew the son of man secret.) Hebrews 2:9 says that Jesus had been "crowned with glory and honor because of the suffering of death, so that by the grace of God he might taste death for every one." That, too, sounded like the Suffering Servant–substitute king.

A passage in Mark's gospel set a terminus to the sub rosa debate over whether the son of man was immortal. In Mark 9:9, Jesus instructed his disciples to remain silent about the transfiguration "until the Son of Man had risen from the dead."[43] They obeyed, "questioning what this rising from the dead could mean" (Mark 9:10). As Mark wrote it, Jesus understood the son of man to be immortal, while his followers had no inkling of the issue. As a matter of interest, the Matthew parallel omitted the disciples' puzzlement (Matt 17:9). It could be said that the New Testament closed a five-century debate about whether the first son of man was immortal. Henceforth the issue would become the second son of man's immortality. But the New built upon the Old. This parallel was at the heart of the matter: Ezekiel, the first son of man, was to "prolong his days" (Isa 53:10). Jesus, the second son of man, was to rise from the dead (Mark 8:31).

In the lengthy controversy about the son of man's mortality, the writers seem to have been debating about an individual, the prophet Ezekiel. Still, there is much to suggest that "son of man" could also be understood as a collective term for "everyman" or, drawing on other Near Eastern belief systems, it could signify "perfect man."[44]

The following may help. The term "son of man" appears in the book of Ezekiel scores of times, frequently in this form: "And the word of the Lord came to me: 'Son of man . . .'" This stilted phrase might well have originated with editors, who could have added most of the ninety-three

---

43. This and subsequent translations are from the NRSV.

44. Funk et al., *Five Gospels*, 183. Funk comments on the "mankind" interpretation. Parpola notes the parallels in the ancient world (as well as in Jewish mysticism) among "son of man," "perfect man," and ideal king: *Assyrian Prophecies*, nn. 124, 193, 211 on XCIII, CI, CII.

## The Suffering Servant and the Son of Man

son-of-man phrases to the book of Ezekiel. They would have had Isa 53 fresh in mind and been familiar with Mesopotamian myths. The lavish use of "son of man" could have implied that Ezekiel was God's perfect man, the prototype of humankind. This prototype would have been in addition to being the Suffering Servant who died as a substitute king.

### SUBSTITUTE-KING MOTIF IN THE SYNOPTIC GOSPELS

Mark and Matthew certainly knew that the OT's son of man had died as a substitute king, and probably Luke did too. The synoptic writers drew heavily on the substitute-king motif, particularly for accounts of the passion. Mark provided the bulk of the items, but Q, Luke, and Matthew also contributed. Many strands of the substitute-king tradition braid together in the New Testament. Assyrian, Babylonian, and Persian substitution practices must have differed somewhat. In addition, Zedekiah, Daniel, Jehoiakim, Jehoiachin, and Ezekiel died as substitutes, and we can assume that their deaths inspired different scriptures. Though the substitute-king motif within the gospels has more sources than one can now identify, here is a start.

These are kingly parallels. The devil took Jesus to "a very high mountain" to tempt him with the world's kingdoms (Matt 4:8). Ezekiel received a similar offer, to rule Babylon's splendid empire. And as icing, by using "a very high mountain" Matthew pointed to the Tower of Babel, a ziggurat that was termed "The Mountain" in a drama performed during Babylon's New Year's Festival.[45] In another parallel, Jesus asked how it benefited a man to gain the world and forfeit his life (Mark 8:36). Ezekiel paid his life after gaining the world's most magnificent kingdom. Again, authorities forced kingship on Ezekiel, while Pilate tried to do the same to Jesus (Mark 15:2, 18). Further, Ezekiel's crime was that he was king of Babylon, while the criminal charge on the cross of Jesus read, "The King of the Jews" (Mark 15:26). Next, a battalion of soldiers attended Jesus (Mark 15:16), and Ezekiel had scores of soldiers watching him.

Here is another example. Jesus asked, "'The wedding guests cannot mourn as long as the bridegroom is with them, can they?'" (Matt 9:15). Matthew's use of "mourn" emphasized the short time between the marriage and death. Ezekiel became a bridegroom when authorities com-

---

45. Pallis, *Akitu Festival*, 221–22.

pelled him to marry a substitute queen, and then they put him to death a few days later.

The substitute-king motif continued. Ezekiel and Jesus each bore the title son of man. Authorities anointed Ezekiel as a king, and Peter declared Jesus to be the anointed one, the Christ (Mark 8:29). Ezekiel would have led a coronation parade through Babylon, and disabled by torture, might well have ridden an ass.[46] The parallel is that Jesus rode a colt during his regal Palm Sunday entrance into Jerusalem (Mark 11:7, 9). Moreover, Luke's version inserted "King" into a line from Psalms. The crowd shouted, "Blessed is the *King* who comes in the name of the Lord!" (Luke 19:38, italics added; compare Ps 118:26). Very likely the gospel writers were evoking the coronation traditions of Judah (see 1 Kgs 1:32–40 and 2 Kgs 11) to present Jesus as a potential king.[47] If anything, however, these served as further camouflage for the deeper substitute-king secret.

The Babylonians put royal robes on the first son of man, and gave him a crown and a scepter. Soldiers attired Jesus in a purple cloak and crown of thorns (Mark 15:17), to which Matthew's account added a mock scepter (Matt 27:29). Then the soldiers "began saluting him, 'Hail, King of the Jews!'" (Mark 15:18). Another parallel is that as king, Ezekiel had to host sumptuous banquets,[48] while Jesus hosted the Last Supper (Mark 14:17–26) and at other times was accused of being a glutton and a drunkard (Matt 11:19). Moreover, the first son of man Ezekiel sat upon a throne; and it was said of Jesus that when the second "'Son of Man comes in his glory . . . he will sit on the throne of his glory'" (Matt 25:31).

Chapter 2 touched upon Ezekiel's disgust with Cyrus and the mess that Judah's rebellions against Babylon had made. Despite the prophet's innocence, the Babylonians apparently thought him a rebel, for Isa 53 mentioned rebellion frequently. The Suffering Servant was wounded for rebellions, stricken for rebellions, and numbered with rebels. The synoptic gospel writers took pains to picture Jesus the same way. Buy swords, Jesus directed his followers, so that he himself might be "'counted among the lawless [rebels]'" (Luke 22:36–37). Authorities used weapons to seize

---

46. See also Zech 9:9. Ecclesiastes wrote of servants on horses (Eccl 10:7). The Preacher may have had in mind the Suffering Servant, since previous verses mentioned sun and folly seated on high.

47. For Judean coronation traditions, see von Rad, "The Royal Ritual in Judah."

48. See Parpola II, xxv.

## The Suffering Servant and the Son of Man

Jesus as though taking "a bandit" (Mark 14:48).[49] Also, a supporter of Jesus struck the high priest's slave (Mark 14:47). Jesus freed the rebel Barabbas (Mark 15:15), just as Ezekiel freed the rebel captives. Likewise, Jesus' mission included proclaiming release to captives (Luke 4:18), and Ezekiel freed the imprisoned Judeans. At the end, Jesus hung between two outlaws (Mark 15:27).

As a substitute king, Ezekiel had to endure a lengthy cursing ceremony. Jesus faced numerous charges, and was as silent in face of them (Mark 15:4–5) as Ezekiel had been (Isa 53:7). Jesus questioned whether his disciples were able to drink the cup he was to drink (Mark 10:38), and later asked God to "'remove this cup from me'" (Mark 14:36). According to a Nineveh letter, substitute kings were "treated" with wine before their cursing and enthronement ceremonies. In addition, the ancients may have dispatched their substitute kings with poison (though the Babylonians probably beheaded Ezekiel).[50] Both Jesus (Mark 15:15) and Ezekiel (Isa 53:5) endured flogging. Like Ezekiel, Jesus was handed to foreigners to die (Mark 10:33). On the cross, the chief priests mocked Jesus, "'He saved others; he cannot save himself'" (Mark 15:31), while Ezekiel gave himself up to save others. When Jesus died, tombs were opened (Matt 27:52); the Suffering Servant agreed to die so that prisons could be opened. The substitute king took sins to the nether world, and Jesus had authority to forgive sins (Mark 2:10).

And this is especially interesting. Disciples asked Jesus why the scribes said that Elijah's coming would precede the messiah (Mark 9:11). The scribes seemed to know that a solar eclipse preceded the Suffering Servant's coming. The words "Elijah" and "sun" in Greek have almost identical spellings, and the book of Malachi has the two words close together. In the Greek OT Mal 4:2 has "sun [*helios*] of righteousness," and verse 4:5 says, "I will send you the prophet Elijah [*Helias*] before the great and terrible day of the Lord comes." Closely related to this, a midday eclipse found Jesus on the cross (Mark 15:33), and an eclipse at the very same hour led to Ezekiel's death.

In Assyria (and surely in Babylon) officials burned a dead substitute's regal symbols of office, but not his clothes.[51] Probably Ezekiel's guards split

---

49. Funk, *Five Gospels*, used "rebels."
50. Parpola I, 21; Parpola II, xxvi, 271.
51. Lambert, "Substitute King Ritual," 110.

his royal wardrobe among themselves, and they well may have thrown dice for it. Psalm 22:18 said, "They divide my clothes among themselves, and for my clothing they cast lots." As for Jesus, soldiers gambled for his garments (Mark 15:24).

Substitute kings had royal burials. "We prepared the burial chamber," an official wrote the King of Assyria, and went on to describe the ceremony, which included spices and embalming.[52] Thus Ezekiel was buried with royalty. Isaiah 53:9 described it this way: "They made his grave with the wicked and his tomb with the rich." According to Mark's gospel, Joseph of Arimathea donated his new tomb for burial (Mark 15:43). Since Joseph was a follower of Jesus, wickedness was not at issue, and Mark did not mention Joseph's financial status. Matthew's gospel solved half the problem by calling Joseph rich (Matt 27:57).

Other burial practices in the gospels might have substitute traditions as their source. Three women brought embalming spices to treat Jesus (Mark 16:1). The parallel was that Ezekiel's body was treated with spices. Jesus' body was laid in a new tomb (Matt 27:60), while Mesopotamian substitutes went to a royal "burial chamber."[53] In the Gospel of Matthew, Jesus spoke of "the coming of the Son of Man." Then he continued, "Wherever the corpse is, there the vultures will gather" (Matt 24:27–28). But what can the son of man have to do with vultures around a body? A lot, if Jesus referred to the funeral of the other son of man. For burial of a family member, one Babylonian king assembled "people from far off provinces, he summoned even kings, princes and governors."[54] When kings and governors flocked to bury Ezekiel, they came like vultures to a corpse. Moreover, in Greek scripture "son," "and," "man," and "vulture" occurred together only twice. Matthew 24:28, which is the vulture passage, and Ezek 17:2–3 each contained these very words, making a Word Link. The Ezekiel passage even includes the prophet's title, "son of man" (RSV). The author of Matthew was making a parallel for knowing readers between Jesus and Ezekiel the substitute, whose body had drawn the dignitary-vultures.

---

52. Parpola I, 229.

53. Ibid. The symbol for burial chamber was E KI.MAH. The E added "house" to the word for tomb or grave. The term frequently occurred with royalty, such as King Assurbanipal or the wife of Esarhaddon. Reiner, *Assyrian Dictionary*, 8:370–71.

54. Gadd, "Nabonidus Inscriptions," 53.

Ezekiel's death voided curses upon king and people. An Assyrian reported that Damqi died "as a substitute for the king, my lord, and for the sake of the life of the prince Samas-sumu-ukin. *He went to his destiny for their ransom.*"[55] Compare it to Mark 10:45: "'For the Son of Man came not to be served but to serve, and *to give his life a ransom for many*'" (italics added). The table displays the substitute-king motif in the synoptic gospels.

## TABLE 6.2—SUBSTITUTE-KING MOTIF IN THE SYNOPTIC GOSPELS

### A. Kingly Rule

| *Ezekiel* | *Jesus* | *Text* |
|---|---|---|
| Son-of-man (SOM) title | SOM title | Mark 8:31 + |
| Offered Babylon | Satan offers all kingdoms | Matt 4:8–10 |
| Got world, paid life | Why get world, pay life? | Mark 8:36 |
| A bridegroom | A bridegroom | Mark 2:19 |
| Hosts sumptuous banquets | Hosts Last Supper | Mark 4:14 |
| Anointed as king | "You are the Christ" | Mark 8:29 |
| Babylon coronation parade | Psalm Sunday entrance | Mark 11:9 |
| Riding horse | Riding colt | Mark 11:7 |
| Large bodyguard | Battalion of soldiers | Mark 15:16 |
| King of Babylon | Pilate: King of the Jews? | Mark 15:2 + |
| King of Babylon | Soldiers: King of the Jews? | Mark 15:18 |
| King of Babylon | Blessed is king who comes | Luke 19:38 |
| Crime: King of Babylon | Crime: King of Jews | Mark 15:26 |
| Royal robes and crown | King's cloak, thorn crown | Mark 15:17 |
| Throne for SOM | Throne for SOM | Matt 25:31 |
| Royal scepter | Reed scepter | Matt 27:29 |

---

55. Parpola I, 229, italics added. Note 12 on page 271 of Parpola II changed "rescue" to "ransom."

# The Exilic Code

## B. Rebellion and Trials

| Ezekiel | Jesus | Text |
|---|---|---|
| Branded rebel | Two swords make rebel | Luke 22:38 |
| Branded rebel | Captured with swords | Mark 14:48 |
| Branded rebel | Priest's slave wounded | Mark 14:47 |
| Died as rebel | Crucified between rebels | Mark 15:27 |
| Freed rebel captives | Freed rebel Barabbas | Mark 15:15 |
| Freed rebel captives | Proclaim captive release | Luke 4:18 |
| Handed to foreigners | Handed to foreigners | Mark 10:33 |
| Cursing ceremony | Trials | Mark 14–15 |
| Many curses, silent | Many charges, silent | Mark 15:4–5 |
| Whipped | Whipped | Mark 15:15 |
| Solar eclipse | Three hours of darkness | Mark 15:33 |
| Solar eclipse first | Elijah precedes messiah | Mark 9:11 |

## C. Death

| Ezekiel | Jesus | Text |
|---|---|---|
| SOM died | SOM had to die | Mark 8:31 + |
| Wine began ordeal | Can you drink same cup? | Mark 10:38 |
| Wine began ordeal | Prayed to remove cup | Mark 14:36 |
| Soldiers divided garments | Soldiers divided garments | Mark 15:24 |
| Prisons opened | Tombs opened | Matt 27:52 |
| Buried with rich man | Joseph of Arimathea rich | Matt 27:57 |
| Body in royal tomb | Body in new tomb | Matt 27:60 |
| Spices for body | Spices for body | Mark 16:1 |
| Corpse drew dignitaries | Corpse drew vultures | Matt 24:28 |
| Took sins to nether world | Authority to forgive sins | Mark 2:10 |
| Saved others, not self | Saved others, not self | Mark 15:31 |
| Body disappeared | No body in tomb | Mark 16:6 |
| Shall prolong his days | Eternal life | Matt 28:20 |
| Death ransomed others | Death ransomed others | Mark 10:45 |

*The Suffering Servant and the Son of Man*

## FRESH EVIDENCE FOR JESUS SCHOLARS

For two millennia scholars have striven to define the nature of Jesus and his mission. Of late, discussion has centered on the extent to which the synoptic gospels understood Jesus to be the son of man and/or the Suffering Servant. This book has something to contribute to such a discussion—fresh evidence bearing upon that set of problems. In brief, this chapter presents five evidentiary findings:

1. Ezekiel, the son of man, died as a substitute king.
2. The Suffering Servant died as a substitute king.
3. The son of man was the Suffering Servant.
4. Authors of the synoptic gospels employed a substitute-king motif.
5. Isaiah 53's claim that the Suffering Servant–substitute king lived after death led to a long dispute about whether the son of man had eternal life.

These new findings can allow different approaches to old problems, and may even help to resolve them. Gospel sources attributed numerous son-of-man statements to Jesus. To simplify, in the synoptic gospels most sayings fall into two groups. The first concerns the earthly Jesus, often focusing on suffering to come. For instance, "'For the Son of Man goes as it is written of him, but woe to that one by whom the Son of Man is betrayed!'" (Mark 14:21). In the second group, the son of man is an otherworldly figure who would ring down history. Jesus said, "'You will see the Son of Man seated at the right hand of the Power,' and 'coming with the clouds of heaven'" (Mark 14:62).

Let us repeat the first three points: Ezekiel, the son of man, died as a substitute king; the Suffering Servant also died this way; and this same son of man was the Suffering Servant. These discoveries open a previously unrecognized triangulation, which is son of man–substitute king–Suffering Servant. New Testament experts now can consider a son of man who is kin to the Suffering Servant. In the past, scholars have had to choose either an apocalyptic figure or an everyman. In most of the earthly sayings, neither works. But Suffering Servant does work, and very well. This illustrates: "'The Son of Man is to be betrayed into human hands, and they will kill him, and three days after being killed, he will rise again'" (Mark 9:31). Now substitute this: "'The apocalyptic figure is to be betrayed into human hands, and they will kill him . . .'" Or this: "'Everyman is to be betrayed into human hands, and they will kill him . . .'" Both are nonsense. But try Suffering Servant: "'The Suffering Servant is to be betrayed into human hands, and they will kill him . . .'" "Suffering Servant" makes sense, and rising after being killed confirms the connection. Isaiah 53:10 says the servant "shall prolong his days." Only by rising again could this come to pass, since a substitute king's reign was never, never ever prolonged past one hundred days. (Ezekiel's reign was even less. It was ten or eleven days shorter because Nebuchadnezzar needed to regain the throne by the start of Babylon's New Year's Festival.[56])

On the question of atonement, does it make a difference if Jesus knew that the first son of man's death actually set prisoners free? (According to Scot McKnight, perhaps a majority of scholars today hold that Jesus did not undertake his own death "consciously and deliberately . . . as an atonement."[57]) But the substitute-king motif in Mark, Matthew, and Luke casts the NT atonement problem in a different light. The motif strongly suggests that the gospel writers saw Jesus's death as modeled on the Suffering Servant's—preordained, voluntary, and atoning.

The fifth evidentiary finding involves the argument within scripture about whether or not the son of man could live again after being executed as a Babylonian substitute. Among other things, it places Daniel chapters 7 ("one like the son of man" RSV) and 10 within a succession of advocates for or against whether the son of man was alive, advocates that include the authors of Ecclesiastes, Proverbs, Sirach, Tobit, the Dead Sea Scrolls, First Enoch, and Hebrews. Knowing this, analysts may be freer to examine the book of Ezekiel as the source from which Jesus chose the title for his earthly son-of-man sayings.

However, the son of man-substitute king-Suffering Servant triangulation may not apply to Jesus' apocalyptic son-of-man statements. It adds no clarity to insert Suffering Servant here: "'You will see the Suffering Servant seated at the right hand of the Power' and 'coming with the clouds of heaven'" (Mark 14:62). The book of Daniel might be the source of the thought or perhaps, as Robert Funk suggested to me years ago, none of

---

56. A solar eclipse on January 5, 569, eventually brought Ezekiel to Babylon's throne. He would have been killed on or just before New Year's Day, which fell on April 4 that year.

57. McKnight, *Jesus and His Death*, 71.

the apocalyptic son-of-man sayings in the synoptic gospels originated with Jesus.

The closing chapter of this book will use coding in a global way. The purpose is to determine, to the extent possible, which of Hebrew scripture's 929 chapters were written before, during, and after the Exile, and also the influence of exilic coding upon later OT authors.

# 7

# The Breadth of Exilic Coding

## CHARACTERISTICS OF CODING

IN THE OPENING CHAPTER we found that the Priestly Benediction concealed numerous Jehoiachin codes, which employed one letter per word taken from text words at regular intervals. Chapter 2 expanded this coding discovery to include anagrams that the Major Prophets used against Jehoiachin for his worship of Babylonian gods. Then we introduced athbash that could produce twenty-two different spellings for each encoded word. These newly discovered coding techniques supported that the true name of Second Isaiah was Jacob and that the Suffering Servant was Ezekiel. In chapter 5, we showed that Ps 51 brimmed with coded names, and that no other chapter in scripture matched it for coding intensity. Finally, probability tests and hundreds of examples confirmed that this code existed and was used during the sixth-century Exile of the Judeans.

But discovery and description of the Bible's code is one thing. Attempting to define the extent of its influence is quite another. Still, this final chapter will attempt to do just that—use coding to detect chapters that were written before, during, and after the Exile, and while doing so measure the extent to which exilic coding influenced post-exilic authors. But there are several caveats. The first is that because exilic writers did not invariably use coding, a study of this sort will miss some sixth-century work. For example, Second Jacob IDs are prominent in the burning bush and Balaam stories (Exod 3 and Num 23 and 24), the Book of Consolation (Jer 30), and in a number of psalms including Pss 14, 24, 25, 47, 87, 99, 132, and 146. The evidence is that Jacob wrote these chapters, yet detectable coding within them is minimal. Moreover, some chapters that obviously are by Jeremiah or Ezekiel also lack significant coding.

## The Breadth of Exilic Coding

A second caveat is that the coding used in this chapter is mainly exilic. The names are not from the period of the monarchy, the Persian era, or the Hellenistic era. Different coding sets would certainly produce different results (or possibly no results at all). About two-thirds of the names to be tested, including several that this book has uncovered (Ezra, Jacob, and Chimham, as well as "substitute king"), come directly from the Exile. Other names already known as exilic include Daniel, Ezekiel, Zedekiah, Jeremiah, Jehoiachin, Shenazzar, Seraiah, Shelemiah, Baruch, Gemariah, Ezekiel, Cyrus alone, Nabonidus, and Nebuchadnezzar. One of the thirty-six codings is a title: "Cyrus king of Babylon." His reign is beyond the far edge of the Exile if one draws the line at 539 BCE, the year that Cyrus conquered Babylon. At the Exile's other boundary stands Jeremiah, whose career began well before King Jehoiachin's deportation in 597 BCE. Other names among the thirty-six, while not directly associated with the Exile, had high coding-point totals in Ps 51, a work that may have originated soon after the Exile.

Here is the approach. Coded spellings for the thirty-six names were run against the text of each of Hebrew Scripture's 929 chapters. Then name-by-name and chapter-by-chapter probabilities were calculated using chi-square tests. In this way we determined the statistical significance of each name within each chapter. In doing so we applied a one-percent threshold. That is, if the name's frequency in the chapter had a probable coincidence of one percent or less, it was significant. In total this process turned up *over six thousand entries* in Scripture's 929 chapters. Large though that number seems coding of these thirty-six names (let alone others) is far more extensive. Speaking only of the thirty-six, the statistically significant coding by itself surely is far less than half of scripture's total. Coding of those same thirty-six words within so-called non-significant chapters awaits detailed scholarly examination. It should prove rewarding since biblical writers often used coding to emphasize specific textual points.

Five of this study's thirty-six names carry with them specific dates or periods. "Nebuchadnezzar" coding by implication refers to the years 605 to 562, when that king reigned in Babylon. "Ezekiel-Sarpuhi" in effect was an event that probably occurred in 569, and "Jehoiachin-Sarpuhi" must be associated with the year 561. "Nabonidus"-"Belshazzar" refers to the 556–539 BCE period when King Nabonidus ruled Babylon or when his son Belshazzar acted as regent. And "Cyrus king of Babylon" covers the years 539, when the great man conquered Babylon, through 530, when he met his death. These five encodings can offer clues as to the date of a chapter's composition. It is important to note, however, that no specific coding covers the centuries of Persian rule after the death of Cyrus.

Appendix 4 shows every significant coding of the thirty-six names in scripture, and we are about to view several of its pages. The symbol # stands for probabilities of coincidence that begin at .01 (one percent) and tail off to .0000001. About half the encodings fall in this category. The other half indicates probabilities of coincidence lower than .0000001, and these are shown by a + sign. The short of this is that few of the findings can be due to coincidence alone and readers may approach them with confidence. The data are what they claim to be, though their literary significance of course rests upon how one interprets them.

Table 7.1 is an excerpt from Appendix 4 that displays encodings in 1 Kings 1–15. It covers the names "Jehoiakim-Sarpuhi" to "Zephaniah." Shaded areas indicate the five names with chronological significance. The right column gives the total coding hits (out of thirty-six) in each chapter and the modest percentage of hits (nine percent) in 1 Kings.

## The Breadth of Exilic Coding

### TABLE 7.1—CODING IN FIRST KINGS 1–16

| Book, Chapter | Jehoiakim-Sarpuhi | Jeremiah | Seraiah son of Tanhumeth | Shecaniah son of Jahaziel | Shelemiah son of Abdeel | Shelemiah son of Kore | Shenazzar son of Jehoiachin | Shephatiah son of David | Solomon son of David | Substitute King | Zedekiah | Zedekiah-Sarpuhi | Zephaniah | Nebuchadnezzar: (605-562) | Ezekiel-Sarpuhi: (569) | Jehoiachin-Sarpuhi: (561) | Nabonid-Belshzr: (556-539) | Cyrus K Babylon: (539-30) | Chapter Hits, Book Percent |
|---|---|---|---|---|---|---|---|---|---|---|---|---|---|---|---|---|---|---|---|
| 1 Kings | | | | | | | | | | | | | | | | | | | 9% |
| 1 | | | | | | | | | | | | | | | | | | | |
| 2 | | | | | | | | | | | | | | | | | | | |
| 3 | | | | | | | | | | | | | | | | | | | 1 |
| 4 | | | | | | | | | | | | | | | | | | | |
| 5 | | | | | | | | | | | | | | | | | | | |
| 6 | | + | + | + | # | # | # | + | + | | + | # | + | # | # | # | # | + | 27 |
| 7 | | # | # | | # | # | # | # | # | # | # | # | # | + | # | # | # | # | 28 |
| 8 | | | | | | | | | | | | | | | | | | | |
| 9 | | | | | | | | | | | | | | | | | | | |
| 10 | | | | | | | | | | | | | | | | | | # | 1 |
| 11 | | # | | | | | | | | | | | | | | | | | 1 |
| 12 | | | | | | | | | | | | | | | | | | | |
| 13 | | | | | | | | | | | | | | | | | | | 1 |
| 14 | | | | | | | | | | | | | | | | | | | |
| 15 | | | | | | | | | | | | | | | | | | | 1 |
| 16 | | | | | | | | | | | | | | | | | | | |

Two things catch the eye. The first is the lack of hits. All but two chapters are almost devoid of exilic coding. And this is as it should be since most scholars hold that this historical material was written prior to the Exile. The other remarkable thing is the coding concentrations in 1 Kgs 6–7. These chapters describe the features of Solomon's temple and palace. Twenty-seven and twenty-eight of our thirty-six names, respectively, have significant coding, including nine out of ten shadings in the chronological category. Conveniently, each chapter heavily codes "Cyrus King of Babylon," which tells us that they were added to scripture sometime after 539 BCE. This table presents something like an x-ray of exilic coding within the body of First Kings. Probably one could say that the authors fashioned chapters 6–7 to provide a rack upon which to hang coding.

Table 7.2 shows far more coding activity. It covers Prov 7–21. The right-hand column lists the hits in each chapter.

## The Breadth of Exilic Coding

### TABLE 7.2—CODING IN PROVERBS 7-21

| Book, Chapter | Jehoiakim-Sarpuhi | Jeremiah | Seraiah son of Tanhumeth | Shecaniah son of Jahaziel | Shelemiah son of Abdeel | Shelemiah son of Kore | Shenazzar son of Jehoiachin | Shephatiah son of David | Solomon son of David | Substitute King | Zedekiah | Zedekiah-Sarpuhi | Zephaniah | Nebuchadnezzar: (605-562) | Ezekiel-Sarpuhi: (569) | Jehoiachin-Sarpuhi: (561) | Nabonid-Belshzr: (556-539) | Cyrus K Babylon: (539-530) | Chapter Hits, Book Percent |
|---|---|---|---|---|---|---|---|---|---|---|---|---|---|---|---|---|---|---|---|
| Prov 7 |  |  |  |  | + |  | # |  |  |  |  | # | # |  | + |  | # |  | 41% |
| 8 |  | + | + | + | # | + |  | + |  |  |  | + |  | # | # |  | # |  | 14 |
| 9 |  | + | # | + |  | # |  |  |  |  |  |  | # |  |  |  |  |  | 21 |
| 10 | + | + | + | + |  | + | + |  | # | + | + | + | + | + | + |  | + | # | 8 |
| 11 | + | + | + | + | + | + | # | # | + |  | + | + | + |  | # | + | + | # | 30 |
| 12 | + |  | + | + |  | + | # | # | + |  |  |  | # | + | + |  | + | # | 24 |
| 13 |  | + | # |  |  | + | # |  |  |  |  |  |  |  |  |  |  |  | 18 |
| 14 | + | # | + | + |  | + | + |  |  |  |  | + | # |  | + |  | + |  | 14 |
| 15 |  |  | # |  |  | + | + |  |  | # | # |  |  |  | + | # | # | # | 21 |
| 16 | # | + | # | + | # | + | # | + |  | # |  | + | # | # | + | # | + |  | 13 |
| 17 | # | # | + |  |  | + | + | # | # |  | + | + | + |  | + |  | + | + | 25 |
| 18 | # | + | + | + |  | + | # |  |  |  |  | # | + |  | + |  | + |  | 23 |
| 19 |  |  | # | # |  | # |  |  |  |  |  |  | # |  | + |  |  | # | 19 |
| 20 |  |  | # |  |  | + | + |  |  |  |  |  | # | + | + |  | + |  | 6 |
| 21 |  | + | + |  | + | + | + |  |  |  | + |  | + | + |  | + | # |  | 14 |
|  |  |  |  |  |  |  |  |  |  |  |  |  |  |  |  |  |  |  | 23 |

## The Exilic Code

As the right column shows, all but two of the chapters are in double digits, which is impressive. Also, Proverbs as a whole has a forty-one percent coding density, which is fourth highest among OT books. The shaded cells at the right are time-sensitive codings, and it appears that much of the work on these books was done during the years when Nabonidus and then Cyrus ruled Babylon—between 556 and 530 BCE. It is well to keep in mind, however, that no coding work has been done for later rulers: Cambyses, Darius, Xerxes, and the rest.

I hope these two tables encourage students of the Bible to browse in an unhurried way through the pages of this book's appendix 4. It has important things to say to novice and expert alike. In the meantime, please consider the observations below on coding densities in the Bible.

## HOW EXTENSIVE IS SIXTH-CENTURY CODING?

(If readers choose, they can put a marker at the start of appendix 4 and follow along.) Most of Genesis is free of the coding of exilic names, though ten chapters include date-sensitive codes that suggest composition in the Exile or during or after the reign of Cyrus. The genealogy in Gen 10 has too many significant exilic encodings to date from an early period. Likewise, chapter 19 contains a dozen such codings, including a + rating for "Cyrus," which might place it in the 560s. An early lesson for us is the lack of coding in Gen 14, which marks the appearance of Melchizedek to Abram. This book's second chapter maintains that "Melchizedek" contains a Ciphered Word for "Cyrus" (Gen 14:18). If it does, then those who wrote about the Exile's events also used methods other than coding to tell their stories.

The initial twenty-two chapters of the Bible's second book have but modest traces of coding, with the exception of Exod 12, which is full of it. Interestingly, that chapter relates that, "At midnight the LORD struck down all the firstborn in the land of Egypt, from the firstborn of Pharaoh who sat on his throne to the firstborn of the prisoner who was in the dungeon" (Exod 12:29). This sounds like a payback to the Egyptians (read Babylonians) for slaughtering the heirs of former Judean monarchs who had become substitute kings. Except for chapters 29 and 31–34, the book of Exodus from chapter 23 on contains plenty of time-related exilic coding.

## The Breadth of Exilic Coding

Glancing at appendix 4's portrayal of Leviticus, one can easily identify the Holiness Code (chapters 17–27) because of its lack of exilic coding. Some say the Holiness Code is an appendage to the prior Leviticus chapters, and it could be.[1] However, the lack of exilic coding leads one to think it was composed before the Exile and predates the first sixteen chapters. Most of the Leviticus chapters preceding the Code contain scattered coding, though chapters 4, 9, 15, and 16 have larger concentrations.

Moving to the book of Numbers, the exilic/post-exilic portions are easy to select. The first two chapters constitute a census of the Israelites—and each has twenty-five significant coding groups. It appears that the coding and not the census must have been central to the authors. Other chapters with high counts are 7, 10, 19, 26, and many of chapters 28–36. The most entertaining section of Numbers is the Balaam story (21–24), and judging by the Jacob IDs, most of it comes from Second Isaiah. These are devoid of coding, so in this case the prophet chose not to employ the technique.

The books of Deuteronomy, Joshua, Judges, First and Second Samuel, and First and Second Kings were structured and edited from older materials by a single editor (or group of editors), whom Noth called the Deuteronomistic Historian (Dtr). Scholars have reached a consensus that these seven books are a unit, though views differ on when Dtr may have worked. Noth places Dtr in the sixth century at the middle of the Exile, while Frank Cross thinks a pre-exilic version from Josiah's reign underlies the DH.[2] Lack of coding in the DH argues strongly that Cross has the best of the argument. However, the important thing for us is that whenever he or she may have written, *Dtr used coding sparingly*. By contrast, chapters inserted into the DH text become visual standouts. Table 7.3 shows this well.

---

1. Levine, "Leviticus," 316.
2. Noth, *History*, 27; Cross, *Canaanite Myth and Hebrew Epic*, 287.

## TABLE 7.3—CODING IN JOSHUA 9-23

| Book, Chapter | Jehoiakim-Sarpuhi | Jeremiah | Seraiah son of Tanhumeth | Shecaniah son of Jahaziel | Shelemiah son of Abdeel | Shelemiah son of Kore | Shenazzar son of Jehoiachin | Shephatiah son of David | Solomon son of David | Substitute King | Zedekiah | Zedekiah-Sarpuhi | Zephaniah | Nebuchadnezzar (605-562) | Ezekiel-Sarpuhi (569) | Jehoiachin-Sarpuhi (561) | Nabonid-Belshzr (556-539) | Cyrus K Babylon (539-530) | Chapter Hits, Book Percent |
|---|---|---|---|---|---|---|---|---|---|---|---|---|---|---|---|---|---|---|---|
| Josh |   |   |   |   |   |   |   |   |   |   |   |   |   |   |   |   |   |   | 21% |
| 9 |   |   |   |   |   |   |   |   |   |   |   |   |   |   |   |   |   |   | 1 |
| 10 |   |   |   |   |   |   |   |   |   |   |   |   |   |   |   |   |   |   |   |
| 11 |   |   |   |   |   |   |   |   |   |   |   |   |   |   |   |   |   |   |   |
| 12 | # | # | # | # |   |   | + |   |   |   | # |   | # | # |   | + | # |   | 19 |
| 13 |   | + | + | # | # | + |   | + | + | # |   | + | + | + | + | # | + | # | 32 |
| 14 |   | # |   |   |   |   |   |   |   |   |   |   |   |   |   |   |   |   | 2 |
| 15 | # | + | + | # | + | + | + | + | + | + | + | + | + | + | + | + | + | + | 35 |
| 16 |   | + | # | + |   | + | + | + | + |   |   | # | # | + | # | + | + | # | 23 |
| 17 |   |   |   |   |   |   |   |   |   |   |   |   |   | # |   |   |   |   | 2 |
| 18 |   |   |   |   |   |   |   | # |   |   |   |   |   |   |   |   |   |   | 4 |
| 19 | + | + | + | + | + | + | + | + |   |   | + | + | + | + | + | + | + |   | 33 |
| 20 |   |   | # |   |   |   |   |   |   |   |   |   |   |   |   |   |   |   | 1 |
| 21 |   | + |   |   |   |   | # |   |   | # |   |   | # | # |   | + | # | + | 13 |
| 22 |   |   |   |   |   |   |   |   |   |   |   |   |   |   |   |   |   |   |   |
| 23 | # |   |   |   |   |   |   |   |   |   |   |   |   |   |   |   |   |   | 1 |

## The Breadth of Exilic Coding

Joshua 12, 13, 15, 16, 19, and 21 all share heavy coding. Indeed, Josh 15 is one of only two chapters in scripture to possess significant coding for thirty-five of thirty-six exilic names. "Cyrus king of Babylon" is encoded in four of the Joshua chapters, and the other two take the dating as far as the Nabonidus-Belshazzar era. Noth himself states that Josh 13–21 "was probably added to Dtr's work later."[3] Ignoring content and acting only upon the excerpt above, we conclude that Josh 12 is also a later addition, and recommend that scholars take a second look at chapters 14, 17, 18, and 20. Lack of coding suggests that these were part of the DH original.

Assuming that heavier coding indicates additions to Dtr's work, one can easily identify some twenty chapters that are not a part of the DH.[4] About half of these same chapters have also been excluded by Noth. One chapter on the excluded list is Judg 5, the lyrical Song of Deborah. Until now it has been identified as archaic Hebrew poetry. The RSV calls it "the oldest remaining considerable fragment of Hebrew literature."[5] The Song, however, originated during the Exile and very likely is by Jacob the prophet. Nineteen different sets of codings ("Jacob," Jacob the Levite," and "Jacob son of Shelomoth," each with athbash variants) extend to all but two of the verses in Judg 5. Though only a simple "+" in appendix 4 under "Jacob-Israel" covers the matter, the probability that the coding is coincidental is very small.[6] This same chapter also contains three significant date-sensitive codings: Ezekiel-Sarpuhi (569 BCE), Jehoiachin-Sarpuhi (561) and Nabonidus-Belshazzar (between 556 and 539).[7] Perhaps Jacob was one of the redactors of the DH. The purpose of this excursion is to establish that in the Song of Deborah Jacob the prophet used coding, for there have been other texts in which he did not. The prophet's on-again,

---

3. Noth, *History*, 41 n. 1.

4. The chapters in Deuteronomy through Second Kings with heavier coding are Deut 32, 33; Josh 7, 12, 13, 15, 16, 19, 21; Judg 5, 8, 12, 16; 1 Sam 6, 8; 2 Sam 17, 22; 1 Kgs 6, 7; and 2 Kgs 5, 19. This list contains only full chapters; partial chapters that later writers may have added to the DH have not been considered.

5. Note to Judg 5 in *New Oxford Bible*, RSV. See also Boling, "Judges," 1109.

6. The probability that the Jacob coding in Judg 5 is coincidental is $1.4 \times 10^{-15}$. Though the text is said to be corrupt, the computer easily produced the nineteen Jacob coding groups from the MT.

7. In Judg 5, Jehoiachin-sarpuhi has five coding groups, four of which are of AAA quality. Its P value in a chi-square test is $2.0 \times 10^{-10}$. Nabonidus-Belshazzar has sixteen groups (six for Nabonidus, ten for Belshazzar) with a P value for coding of $6.6 \times 10^{-16}$. Judges 5 also contains significant coding of eight other exilic names.

off-again approach to coding will become more significant when we try to determine when coding entered Hebrew literature.

We turn now to the Writings, beginning with Song of Songs. Commentators have been unable to agree on its purpose or provenance, except to say that it is a collection of love poems that did not originate with Solomon.[8] However, coding brings new light to Songs. First, it ranks third in coding density among Hebrew Scripture's thirty-nine books, and that coding, of course, is heavy with exilic names. The first seven of the chapters of Songs contain significant codings ranging from seven to twenty-five names, while the eighth and final chapter has but one, which is "Jehizkiah son of Shallum."

Chapters 1–7 contain time-sensitive names. The earliest chapter may be the first, which has a + for "Jehoiachin-Sarpuhi" (561 BCE). "Nabonidus-Belshazzar" (556–539) is the latest coding in chapters 2, 4, and 6, while two others conceal "Cyrus king of Babylon." Song of Songs could be a remembrance of exilic events written far after the period—including well into the Persian period. However, considering the book's dense coding, one must also consider the late Exile or during Cyrus's early years as king of Babylon. As to authorship, "Amariah son of Hezekiah" is significantly coded in all but the last chapter, and "Daniel" and "Shelemiah son of Kore" have six codings apiece.[9] The absence of coding in the final chapter (except for "Jehizkiah") implies that it could date from a far later time. Eighteen coded groups involve substitute kings. These include *sarpuhi* combined with Jehoiakim, Jehoiachin, Ezekiel, and Zedekiah, as well as "substitute king" itself. Substitute kingship, then, may be the overall theme for the book of Songs.

## THE STRUGGLE IN PROVERBS

Coding in the book of Proverbs is heavy throughout. The average chapter contains fifteen significant coding groups with a range of two to thirty groups. Scholarly dating for the book runs from the end of the monarchy (late seventh century) to the fifth or fourth century BCE.[10] Authorities also

---

8. Schoville, "Songs," 150; Murphy, "Book of Songs," 150.

9. Readers should remember that running a thousand or more additional coded names against the Songs chapters may at some future date turn up better candidates for authorship.

10. Scott, "Proverbs," 1273; Blank, "Proverbs," 940.

## The Breadth of Exilic Coding

understand Proverbs to have been collected over time with the purpose of instructing young men. But the book's robust coding is exilic, though "Cyrus king of Babylon" adds a touch of the Persian period. A dozen of the thirty-one chapters include Cyrus coding and eight others lead with combinations of "Nabonidus-Belshazzar."[11] Though this new information on composition of Proverbs is better than that available to any modern scholar, it is still far from perfect. What it lacks is encodings of all other possible rulers of the Jews after 530 BCE, the year when Cyrus died. Such a thing, however, will take time, and for the present we must do our best with what we have.

Were the Proverbs chapters composed over a longer period of time? It does not appear so. All but a few chapters are heavily coded with exilic names. These may have been incorporated into a book at a time well beyond the Exile, but their sub rosa subject matter suggests they were produced during a few decades. Were the proverbs written to instruct young men? Undoubtedly they were used that way, but the underlying (literally) purpose of Proverbs seems to have been to convey information—and argumentation—on exilic topics.

Here are concrete examples of how the authors of Proverbs used coded scripture to contest with one another. On the one hand is Jacob the prophet; on the other are unidentified critics. The attack upon Jacob begins, You "who rejoice in doing evil and delight in the perverseness of evil; those whose paths are crooked, and who are devious in their ways. You will be saved from the loose woman, from the adulteress with her smooth words . . ." (Prov 2:14–16). Under these words is an AAA "Jacob the Levite" coding plus an A-rated cipher of "Jacob the prophet." In this next one, coding of "Jacob son of Shelomoth" makes the addressee clear because it begins at chapter 4's opening word: "Listen, children, to a father's instruction, and be attentive, that you may gain insight . . ." (Prov 4:1). Later the author-sage counsels, "Put away from you crooked speech, and put devious talk far from you" (Prov 4:24). For emphasis an AAA "Jacob son of Shelomoth" runs below that text.

---

11. There are five date-sensitive names. "Nebuchadnezzar" (605–562) is the earliest and "Cyrus king of Babylon" (539–30) the latest. "Ezekiel-sarpuhi" (569) and "Jehoiachin-sarpuhi" (561) are events tied to specific years. "Nabonidus-Belshazzar" (556–539) occupies the place nearest to Cyrus. Eleven of the twelve Proverbs chapters with Cyrus coding also contain earlier date-sensitive names. The same is true of the "Nabonidus-Belshazzar" spellings—seven of those eight chapters also have earlier names.

## The Exilic Code

The whole of chapter 8 could have been by Second Jacob (or at least by a defender, during or even well after the Exile). Twelve Jacob-Israel coding groups undergird this text. The probability that this concentration is coincidental is .000000000007.[12] Here are some of his words: "Riches and honor are with me, enduring wealth and prosperity . . . I walk in the way of righteousness, along the paths of justice, endowing with wealth those who love me, and filling their treasuries. The Lord created me at the beginning of his work, the first of his acts of long ago" (Prov 8:18, 20–22).

Unconvinced, Jacob's critics continued their attacks, emphasizing their words through coding: "Whoever heeds instruction is on the path to life, but one who rejects a rebuke goes astray. Lying lips conceal hatred, and whoever utters slander is a fool" (Prov 10:17). This Proverbs chapter has stronger Jacob coding than any other. The next one, chapter 11, once again struck at Jacob's wife: "Be assured, the wicked will not go unpunished, but those who are righteous will escape. Like a gold ring in a pig's snout is a beautiful woman without good sense" (Prov 11:21–22). The text contains AAA codings of "Jacob the Levite" and "Jacob son of Shelomoth." And Prov 12:4 repeats the slander: "A good wife is the crown of her husband, but she who brings shame is like rottenness in his bones." Lest exilic readers miss the target of the insult, verses 3 and 5 contain identical Ciphered Words for "Jacob." The text word צדיקים is a CW for דימץ, an athbash spelling of יעקב.

But the prophet turns this device against his critics. Proverbs 28:1 uses the same word, צדיקים, but adds a waw to achieve וצדיקים. This converts the CW for Jacob alone into a CW for both Jacob and Ezra. (The Ezra CW is וקים). The English text runs: "The wicked flee when no one pursues, but the righteous [וצדיקים] are as bold as a lion. When a land rebels it has many rulers; but with an intelligent ruler there is lasting order." Indeed, the whole of chapter 28 seems to be a defense of Jacob. Verse 12 says, "When the righteous [צדיקים, a Jacob CW] triumph, there is great glory, but when the wicked prevail, people go into hiding." And Jacob or his defenders have arranged to have the chapter's very last word, which not surprisingly is צדיקים. That final verse reads, "When the wicked pre-

---

12. The chi-square proportions are 56/258 and 24,986/304,643. $P = 7.0 \times 10^{-12}$. The first proportion consists of the Jacob coding points and text words in Proverbs 8, while the second has the coding points and words in the remainder of Scripture.

## The Breadth of Exilic Coding

vail, people go into hiding; but when they perish, the righteous increase" (Prov 28:28).

Proverbs 28 does not rate either a # or a + in appendix 4 because coding is less frequent. But when Jacob's defenders used it, they encoded to good effect. The chapter begins with five coded spellings of בחכעעומדההרן, which is an athbash of "Jacob son of Shelomoth." That is, words 1, 2, 3, 4, and 5 of the first verse use consecutive text words to launch encodings. They end upon words 4, 5, 6, 7, and 8 of the second verse. Pairing this with the צדיקים cited above, it can be truly said that Jacob had both the first and the last word of this chapter.

Proverbs 20 is from the hands of Jacob's opponents. They use mass coding of Jacob and his titles, as these hostile verses show. "Bread gained by deceit is sweet, but afterward the mouth will be full of gravel. Plans are established by taking advice; wage war by following wise guidance. A gossip reveals secrets; therefore do not associate with a babbler" (Prov 20:17–19). Crossing these verses are three AAA groups coding "Jacob the Levite" (twice) and "Jacob son of Shelomoth."[13] As Jacob supporters themselves were to do in Prov 28, the authors employed consecutive spellings to underline their message. Four straight coded spellings of the Jacob athbash בצכע begin at word 17-8, and כצלעעתגח, an AAA athbash of "Jacob the Levite," is stitched from 17-8 through 19-1.

At the end of the book, Jacob rises strongly to the defense of his wife. Verses 10–31 of Prov 31 are a hymn to the woman of worth. That section is crammed with Jacob coding. If these verses were considered by themselves they would stand near the top in coding strength among all Proverbs chapters. The passage begins, "A capable wife who can find? She is far more precious than jewels. The heart of her husband trusts in her, and he will have no lack of gain. She does him good, and not harm, all the days of her life . . ." (Prov 31:1–3). The coding suggests Jacob wrote this. If so, it shows his versatility. Imagine one author penning this justly famous description of a good woman, the Song of Deborah, and the burning bush account.

The quotations above deal mostly with the argument between Second Jacob and his critics. While the attacks sound deeply personal, they probably are based upon differences in policy—and, at a guess, differences

---

13. Proverbs 20 has thirteen statistically significant code groups of "Jacob," "Israel," "seed of Jacob," "Jacob the Levite," and "Jacob son of Shelomoth." The probability of this being due to coincidence is $1.5 \times 10^{-13}$.

between leaders in Israel and in Babylonia. Who might those leaders in Babylonia have been? Four of our thirty-six names lead in significant coding within Proverbs. "Daniel" has such coding in twenty-one of the book's thirty-one chapters, while "Seraiah son of Tanhumeth," "Azariah son of Amaziah," and "Shelemiah son of Kore" have twenty each. Azariah was a ninth-century king of Judah (which does not fit this context), Seraiah was a troop commander in Judah with Gedaliah (Jer 40:8), and Shelemiah was with King Jehoiachin in Babylon.[14]

Those who approach the book of Proverbs as an account of the late Exile rather than as a collection of maxims may be able to add much to our knowledge both of scripture and of biblical history. For instance, what does it mean that two AAA codings of Nabonidus bridge the following: "A wise king winnows the wicked, and drives the wheel over them. The human spirit is the lamp of the Lord, searching every inmost part. Loyalty and faithfulness preserve the king, and his throne is upheld by righteousness" (Prov 20:26–28). In addition, Appendix 4 shows that Proverbs 20 as a whole rates a + symbol for Nabonidus-Belshazzar coding. For now these findings incline us toward an earlier date for Proverbs than is generally thought. But all of the evidence is not yet in.

Job is another book that has its share of exilic coding. Although it has a lower coding frequency than Proverbs or Songs, about half of the Job chapters contain eight or more significantly coded names. To the extent that the thirty-six names tested thus far offer clues, the time-weighting of the book of Job is equally split between the reigns of Nebuchadnezzar and Nabonidus-Belshazzar. Only chapters 8, 12, and 39 contain significant "Cyrus king of Babylon" spellings. (Let it be said that this evidence seems too frail to support firm dating conclusions.)

When we examine the names prominently coded in Proverbs, Songs, and Job we find similarities. Table 7.4 below uses the same format as that of Appendix 4, but shows only half as many names. The table takes the half-dozen names in each book having the most significantly coded chapters and compares them. Shading shows the leaders.

---

14. Weidner, "Jojachin," 923–35; cited by Albright, "King Jehoiachin," 51–52.

## TABLE 7.4—CANDIDATES FOR SUBJECT OR AUTHORSHIP OF JOB, PROVERBS, AND SONGS (SHADED CELLS GIVE BEST CANDIDATES, MEASURED BY SIGNIFICANTLY CODED CHAPTERS)

| Book | Chapters in Book | Ahaziah son of Jehoram | Ahihud son of Shelomi | Amariah son of Hezekiah | Azariah son of Amaziah | Azariah son of Zephaniah | Azrikam son of Azel | Baruch | Daniel | Ezekiel | Jacob-Israel | Seraiah son of Tanhumeth | Shelemiah son of Kore | Shephatiah son of David | Substitute King | Zephaniah | Ezekiel-Sarpuhi (569) |
|---|---|---|---|---|---|---|---|---|---|---|---|---|---|---|---|---|---|
| Job | 42 | 11 | 17 | 16 | 8 | 12 | 12 | 8 | 20 | 11 | 11 | 15 | 21 | 15 | 6 | 13 | 9 |
| Prov | 31 | 8 | 12 | 17 | 20 | 14 | 15 | 10 | 21 | 16 | 16 | 20 | 20 | 10 | 5 | 16 | 18 |
| Song | 8 | 5 | 1 | 7 | 4 | 4 | 3 | 5 | 6 | 4 | 3 | 3 | 6 | 4 | 5 | 3 | 3 |
| All | 81 | 24 | 30 | 40 | 32 | 30 | 30 | 23 | 47 | 31 | 30 | 38 | 47 | 29 | 16 | 32 | 30 |

Begin by looking at the "All" row. The three books have a combined total of eighty-one chapters. Daniel and Shelemiah son of Kore each have significant coding in forty-seven of them, which is well above Amariah son of Hezekiah, who has forty. Seraiah is fourth with thirty-eight highly coded chapters, and Azariah and Zephaniah the prophet round out the top six. Shelemiah's name is not in scripture, but he was listed in ration tablets unearthed in Babylon that also bore King Jehoiachin's name. Daniel, of course, is the Daniel of the Bible.

Looking at the whole Bible, "Daniel" and his associated encodings have more than twice as many coding points as "Jacob," the name that holds second place.[15] This extraordinary difference marks Daniel as the Exile's most influential person, little though we know about him. Jacob—Second Isaiah—was both an extraordinary writer and a leader of Israel. It appears that Daniel also held this dual role, though judging by the book of Daniel, his career was in Babylonia rather than in Judah. In the war of words in Proverbs between Jacob and his critics, it could be that Daniel was one of the authors who used those sayings against the Judean.

Daniel and Shelemiah are either best or second-best in coding for Job, Songs, and Proverbs. One or both of them had a hand in writing (or perhaps were the subject of) almost three-quarters of these books. The proportion is somewhat higher for Songs and Proverbs than for Job. We have learned that writing scripture was not a one-person job, and the table shows that Daniel and Shelemiah had company. For the book of Job it was Ahihud son of Shelomi, Amariah son of Hezekiah, Seraiah son of Tanhumeth, and Shephatiah son of David. For the book of Proverbs, Azariah son of Amaziah joined the same Amariah and Seraiah who worked on Job. Finally, for Songs Ahaziah son of Jehoram could have helped Daniel and Shelemiah write much of that book. Baruch, who had significant coding in five of the Songs chapters, might have been a subject rather than an author. The final highly coded words in Songs were "substitute king," which tends to confirm our opinion about the subject matter of those chapters. I myself lean toward the view that these people were the authors rather than the subjects of Job, Proverbs, and Songs. And of course one or more of them could have played both roles.

Nehemiah 3 is part of the personal memoirs of Nehemiah, who was the principal leader of the Jews during the Restoration. The third chap-

---

15. Daniel's coding points for all 929 OT chapters totaled 53,726. Jacob, in second place, had 25,042.

## The Breadth of Exilic Coding

ter gives the names of those who labored to rebuild Jerusalem's walls. At the earliest, the chapter might have been written one hundred years after the close of the Exile in 539 BCE, and the text could prove to be 400 or later. Why, then, would this otherwise dull report from the Restoration conceal significant coding of thirty *exilic* names? Thirty is sufficient to place Nehemiah 3 in the pantheon of the dozen most heavily coded chapters.[16] The answer must be that the author, possibly Nehemiah himself, wanted to recall for his contemporaries and for posterity the Exile's dramatic events. One might think that Nehemiah would have encoded in his writings only confidential information from his own time. Quite possibly he did this, too, though confirmation of Restoration coding must await another occasion.

But Nehemiah 3 is not the only chapter in the later biblical books to conceal heavy exilic coding. The Chronicles-Ezra-Nehemiah group has twenty-four chapters with double-digit numbers of significantly coded names. Twenty-four! First and Second Chronicles have eight apiece, and Ezra and Nehemiah each have four.[17] Of the other Writings, Ecclesiastes has two double-digit chapters, and Esther and Ruth one apiece.[18] Three of Lamentations' five chapters also contain high coding.

This chapter gives an overview of exilic coding in Hebrew Scripture. Beneath the summaries set out in appendix 4 are some 75,000 coding groups—and this is but the yield from thirty-six names. That is a lot of detail, but it is the very sort of detail that scholars seem to relish. A related subject is that when dealing with post-exilic books we have a substantial advantage. We no longer have to choose between subject and author as we consider a coded name. When the Chronicler encoded exilic names, he or she did so to convey information about the coded subject. The purpose may have been to report some past event that a previous writer failed to mention or to encode. And of course these post-exilic writers were 2,500 years closer to the Exile's events than are we.

---

16. Chapters with the highest number of significantly coded exilic names are: (thirty names) Neh 3, Prov 10, Isa 5, 59, Nah 3; (31) Ps 80, Isa 58; (32) Josh 13, Ps 119; (33) Josh 19, Isa 3; (34) Pss 17, 51, Isa 28; and (35) Josh 15, Dan 3.

17. The twenty-four chapters with ten or more significantly coded exilic names are: 1 Chr 1, 3, 5, 6, 12, 26–28; 2 Chr 2–4, 17, 26, 29, 34, 35; Ezra 1, 4, 7, 9; and Neh 3, 7, 10, 12. Appendix 4 has details.

18. The other Writings chapters having double-digit coding are Eccl 9, 12; Esth 8; Ruth 2; and Lam 3–5.

# The Exilic Code

## CODING REVEALS JEREMIAH'S SECRET

Here is an example of what coding in one of the later books can tell us. To begin, appendix 4 shows that "Jeremiah" leads in significantly coded chapters within the Chronicles-Ezra-Nehemiah group. Second Chronicles 34 relates the reforms of King Josiah who reigned prior to the Exile. Four AAA and two A codings of "Jeremiah son of Hilkiah" traverse this passage:

> [King Josiah] began to purge Judah and Jerusalem of the high places, the sacred poles, and the carved and the cast images. In his presence they pulled down the altars of the Baals; he demolished the incense altars that stood above them. He broke down the sacred poles and the carved and the cast images; he made dust of them and scattered it over the graves of those who had sacrificed to them. He also burned the bones of the priests on their altars, and purged Judah and Jerusalem. In the towns ... he broke down the altars, beat the sacred poles and the images into powder, and demolished all the incense altars throughout all the land of Israel. (2 Chr 34:2–7)

Heavy coding makes it clear that Jeremiah participated enthusiastically in Josiah's cleansing work. One can almost see the fire-eating, twenty-year-old prophet breaking up those pagan sanctuaries. In addition, two other spellings also associate Jeremiah with refurbishment work and other kinds of service. A final AAA "Jeremiah son of Hilkiah" lies underneath "the words of the book that has been found" (2 Chr 34:21). That encoding closes on the chapter's very last word.

Discovery of the "book of the law" led Josiah to purify the Israelites' worship, and coding connects Jeremiah to the book. The origin of this book has until now been uncertain but the accounts in both Second Chronicles and Second Kings link its discovery to repairing Jerusalem's temple. The opinion of many is that the book forms part of the present book of Deuteronomy.[19] Heavy coding in Chronicles of a compound word makes it almost certain that young Jeremiah was the source of this book of the law. The compound word, ספרהתורהלירמיהו, "Jeremiah's book of the law," is encoded *ninety-nine times* in 2 Chron 34.[20] (But note that this is not one of the thirty-six words we have used in our survey.) I count

---

19. Althann, "Josiah," 1016.

20. The ninety-nine spellings of "Jeremiah's book of the law" in this large chapter are more than four times what one would expect to find. A majority of the spellings use letters taken from every fourth or fifth text word.

## The Breadth of Exilic Coding

twenty-nine spellings of "Jeremiah's book of the law" that cross this important passage: "The priest Hilkiah found the book of the law of the Lord given through Moses. Hilkiah said to the secretary Shaphan, 'I have found the book of the law in the house of the Lord'; and Hilkiah gave the book to Shaphan" (2 Chr 34:14–15).[21]

Second Kings 22 includes the parallel account of the book's discovery. Though its Jeremiah coding is less dense than that in the Chronicles passage, the key book-of-the-law verses in Kings also have underneath them AAA codes of "Jeremiah son of Hilkiah." The author was Dtr, and he used long, difficult-to-trace spellings of rare athbash words to identify the prophet.[22] Earlier in this chapter on a tour of Samuel and Kings we found that the coding was sparse enough to have been inserted by a later editor. These long encodings, however, are clearly part of the original history. They prove Dtr understood athbash coding and employed it skillfully. He also would have known young Jeremiah personally, so what he coded about the prophet bears special weight.

Unusually long "Jeremiah son of Hilkiah" encodings span this Second Kings passage: "'I have found the book of the law in the house of the Lord [said the high priest].' When Hilkiah gave the book to Shaphan, he read it . . . [Next] the secretary informed the king, 'The priest Hilkiah has given me a book.' Shaphan then read it aloud to the king. When the king heard the words of the book of the law, he tore his clothes." Then King Josiah commanded, "'Go, inquire of the Lord for me . . . concerning the words of this book that has been found . . . for great is the wrath of the Lord . . . because our ancestors did not obey the words of this book'" (2 Kgs 22:8, 10, 11, 13). These passages contain "Jeremiah son of Hilkiah" codings.

But coding of the compound word, ספרהתורהלירמיהו, "Jeremiah's book of the law," within the Second Kings account is even more important, and certainly served as a model for the Chronicler. A dozen such spellings run beneath: "The high priest Hilkiah said to Shaphan the secretary, 'I

---

21. Six spellings that are easiest for scholars to check against the MT take letters from consecutive text words. The starting words are 14-8, 9, 13, 14, 15; and 15-1.

22. Taking its letters from every third text word, the athbash סהלסרקאבכפמוסרק starts at word 8-16 and runs forty words to 10-12. The other "Jeremiah son of Hilkiah" spelling is דדנזשצחבומדשת. It extends sixty-one text words from 12-18 to 14-21, and uses every fifth text word.

have found the book of the law in the house of the Lord.' When Hilkiah gave the book to Shaphan, he read it" (2 Kgs 22:8).[23]

Coding proves that the book of the law "discovered" was by Jeremiah, and that its appearance was no accident. Others have wondered why the king's ministers consulted Huldah the prophetess instead of Jeremiah about the book, but the younger prophet's complicity may explain the choice. Perhaps officials in on the secret wanted supporting confirmation from a third party. The high priest Hilkiah and very likely Shaphan, the king's scribe, knew the book was Jeremiah's. Given that it was "Jeremiah's book of the law," it seems most likely that the young prophet himself wrote it. It was "found" in 622 BCE, which is five years after Jeremiah's call. God called him when he was "a boy," so by the time of the discovery he might have been eighteen to twenty years of age, old enough to write such a document.[24] A less likely possibility is that Jeremiah had been schooled by the person who did write this law book, or that it was one of the texts used by his tutor (assuming there was such a person). H. B. MacLean suggests that the book might have been written early in Manasseh's reign as a plan of reform to be put into effect when a suitable occasion arose.[25] However, this discussion grows speculative, and leads us from our stated purpose, which is to provide an overview of coding in the OT.

## CODING IN THE PSALTER

Coding might establish dates for much of the Psalter. The new technique provides evidence that most psalms were written no earlier than the late Exile. Seventy-nine of the 150 psalms, including almost all of the longer psalms, contain date-sensitive coding groups that are statistically significant. Thirty-four of those psalms contain "Cyrus king of Babylon" groups, which means they could have been written between 539 and 530 BCE. (Remember, however, that coding of the names of monarchs coming after Cyrus has not been tested.) Twenty-one psalms could have been finished during the reign of Nabonidus, the last Neo-Babylonian king (556–539). Two dozen other psalms contain significant coding of "Jehoiachin-

---

23. Three of the ספרהתורהלירמיהו spellings use letters from consecutive words, and are not difficult to verify. These begin at words 7-8, 10, and 12 of 2 Kgs 22. Each, of course, extends fifteen letters.

24. See Lundbom, "Jeremiah," 686.

25. MacLean, "Josiah," 997.

## The Breadth of Exilic Coding

Sarpuhi" (561), "Ezekiel-Sarpuhi" (569), or "Nebuchadnezzar" (605–562). In addition, many of the psalms that lack date-sensitive groups have one and usually several significant codings with other names that were from the exilic period, names like Jeremiah, Zedekiah, Jehoiachin, and Daniel. In summary, coding presents evidence that some three-quarters of the psalms contain exilic material, (though they could still have originated well after the sixth century). Still, at minimum this means most psalms were not composed prior to the Exile.

Four psalms contain at least thirty-one of thirty-six possible codings. Psalms 17 and 51 have an almost incredible thirty-four significant code groups. Both are among the smaller psalms, so size has little to do with relative coding results. Probably as time wore on the technicians of coding became masters of their trade, and were able to pack more and more coded information into their messages. Three of the four most highly coded psalms had significant "Cyrus king of Babylon" encodings, and the other one (the gigantic acrostic, Ps 119) contained significant "Nabonidus-Belshazzar" groups. And what was true of the psalms was more than matched by scripture's other top chapters—six had coding that placed their composition sometime after Cyrus conquered Babylon.[26]

Does coding tell us who wrote Psalms? Not exactly, but applying simple arithmetic to appendix 4 allows us to make some informed guesses. Measured by number of psalms that contain significant codings of individual names, Ezra is the leader by far. Eighty psalms have hidden within their texts significant variations of his name. Support comes from Song of Songs Rabbah, a sixth-century-CE commentary on Songs, which says that Ezra had a hand in writing the book of Psalms.[27] Table 7.5 below shows individuals ranked by significantly coding psalms.

---

26. Considering only the eleven most highly coded chapters, the latest date-sensitive coding in Ps 119 and Josh 19 is "Nabonidus-Belshazzar," while "Cyrus king of Babylon" appears in Pss 17, 51, 80; Isa 3, 28, 58; Josh 13, 15; and Dan 3.

27. *Songs Rab.* 4:19.

## TABLE 7.5—CANDIDATES FOR AUTHORSHIP OF INDIVIDUAL PSALMS (NUMERALS SHOW THE NUMBER OF PSALMS WITH SIGNIFICANT CODING)

| Ezra | 80 | Amariah/Hezekiah | 43 | Solomon/David | 37 |
|---|---|---|---|---|---|
| Jacob-Israel | 59 | Jeremiah | 42 | Shenazzar/Jehoiachin | 33 |
| Shelemiah/Kore | 59 | Ezekiel | 42 | Ahaziah/Jehoram | 33 |
| Azariah/Amaziah | 54 | Shephatiah/David | 40 | Azrikam/Azel | 32 |
| Chimham/Jehoiachin | 54 | Baruch | 40 | Azariah/Zephaniah | 29 |
| Daniel | 54 | Jehoiachin | 39 | Shelemiah/Abdeel | 25 |
| Jehizkiah/Shallum | 47 | Zedekiah | 38 | Ahihud/Shelomi | 22 |
| Shecaniah/Jahaziel | 46 | Seraiah/Tanhumeth | 34 | Gemariah/Shaphan | 18 |
| Zephaniah | 46 | | | | |

Second place in highly coded names within Psalms is a tie. Both Shelemiah son of Kore and Jacob-Israel have fifty-nine. Archaeology documents that Shelemiah for a time was with King Jehoiachin in Babylon.[28] Jacob-Israel, of course, is Second Isaiah. Recall that Jacob IDs are phrases that work "Jacob" and "Israel" into biblical texts. Examples are "Holy One of Israel" and Jacob and Israel used in parallel. The Psalter is full of Jacob IDs, many of which are not accompanied by high Jacob coding. Adding highly coded psalms to those with IDs but without such coding gives a truer picture of Jacob's influence. That combined total is eighty-one psalms, which moves Second Jacob to parity with Ezra. Chimham, Daniel, and Azariah son of Amaziah rank close behind Ezra and Jacob in contributing to Psalms.

Since no scholar on earth knows who wrote even one psalm, exilic characters with lesser total codings are also worth pointing out. Kings Jehoiachin and Zedekiah, with respective listings of thirty-nine and thirty-eight psalms, are more likely to have been a psalm's subject than its author. But one can never tell.

The whole book of 150 psalms has five subdivisions that were established by the book's original editors. The subdivisions range from seven-

---

28. Weidner, "Jojachin," 923–35; cited by Albright, "King Jehoiachin," 51–52.

## The Breadth of Exilic Coding

teen to forty-four psalms. Naturally enough, scholars speculate that these might represent differing sources for the batches. And of course differing sources might mean differences in coding levels. To test these levels I applied the chi-square method to the five psalm groups. However, the only group with a statistically significant difference in coding level was the final one, Pss 107–150. It had a probability of coincidence of .006, which is slightly below one percent, and not at all exciting. That final group won the .006 because its psalms on average had somewhat lower coding than the rest.

James Limburg has classified a majority of the psalms into seven categories: laments and prayers, liturgical, royal, wisdom, Zion, praise, and thanksgiving.[29] It makes sense that diverse groups might specialize in different types of psalms, and that one group would be more proficient than another in coding. However, this did not prove to be the case. No psalm type had coding that was significantly different from any other. The same was true of the thirty-six names coded within types. Each type had psalms with twenty-plus significant names and each type had psalms with only one encoding or with none at all. In this, Limburg's types matched the ranges of the five subdivisions in Psalms itself. Those highs are 34, 34, 31, 27, and 32 names; while the lows are 0, 0, 2, 0, and 0 names.

Measured by the coding applied, the five subsections of Psalms and the various psalm types within the Psalter possess roughly the same levels and ranges of coding differences. What can this mean? It fits well with evidence that three-quarters of the psalms contain material from the same general period, and that some psalms (by Jacob) seem to be exilic even though they lack coding. It is beginning to appear that one center or a very few centers produced a wide variety of psalm types, some of which were coded and some of which were not.

### CODED PROPHECY

Now we turn to coding in the prophets, beginning with the book of Isaiah. Isaiah traditionally is broken into three sections: First Isaiah, chapters 1–39; Second Isaiah 40–55; and Third Isaiah 56–66. The important news is that all three sections contain coding at virtually the same overall level—a lofty one—which ranks the whole of Isaiah sixth highest among scripture's thirty-nine books. Isaiah 1–39 has 32.7 percent coding density,

---

29. Limburg, "Psalms," 531–34.

## The Exilic Code

Isa 40–55 33.5 percent, and Isa 56–66 32.8 percent. The puzzling closeness of the three figures suggests that common hands made a final redaction of all three at about the same time, that the rewrite was extensive, and that these editors valued coding.[30]

The figures are interesting for another reason. Many scholars think that traces of the prophecies of eighth-century Isaiah are to be found in Isa 1–39, and that some of the Third Isaiah material reflects restoration of the temple (about 515 BCE). The heavy coding, much of which seems to be exilic, in both sections of the book offers additional data to be considered. Of course the thirty-three percent overall figure for Isaiah takes no account of coding gaps or silences. Four chapters lack coding entirely (chapters 7, 12, 50, and 56), and three others code only one or two names (19, 38, and 39). On the other side of the scale are four chapters with massive coding. Isaiah 28 ranks third among all OT chapters in names coded, and three other chapters have thirty or more.[31]

Table 7.6 simply tallies the number of significant codings in the three sections of the book of Isaiah. The familiar problem of subject or author is still with us, so I offer my opinion as to which of the names are likely to have been subjects. They include Baruch, Chimham, Ezekiel, Jehoiachin, Jeremiah, and Zedekiah. As to possible authors, we may be dealing with two sets: exilic authors and redactors.

---

30. Coding density is measured by taking total encodings in part or all of a book and dividing by number of chapters × 36, which gives maximum possible codings.

31. Isaiah 28 contains thirty-four significantly coded names. Isaiah 3, 5, and 58 each have thirty or more.

## The Breadth of Exilic Coding

TABLE 7.6—CANDIDATES FOR SUBJECT OR AUTHORSHIP OF SECTIONS OF THE BOOK OF ISAIAH

| Isaiah Sections | Ahaziah son of | Ahihud son of | Amariah son of | Azariah son of | Azrikam son of Azel | Baruch: (subject) | Chimham: (subject) | Daniel | Ezekiel: (subject) | Gemariah son of | Jehizkiah son of | Jehoiachin: (subject) | Jeremiah: (subject) | Seraiah son of | Shelemiah son of Kore | Shephatiah son of | Solomon son of David | Zedekiah: (subject) | Zephaniah: (subject) |
|---|---|---|---|---|---|---|---|---|---|---|---|---|---|---|---|---|---|---|---|
| 1st | 17 | 15 | 11 | 15 | 13 | 15 | 15 | 18 | 13 | 15 | 15 | 17 | 12 | 8 | 16 | 15 | 13 | 13 | 15 |
| 2nd | 7 | 4 | 7 | 10 | 6 | 5 | 7 | 12 | 6 | 5 | 8 | 3 | 5 | 8 | 8 | 5 | 7 | 6 | 5 |
| 3rd | 4 | 5 | 5 | 5 | 3 | 3 | 1 | 4 | 4 | 3 | 2 | 5 | 4 | 5 | 6 | 3 | 5 | 5 | 3 |
| All | 28 | 24 | 23 | 30 | 22 | 23 | 23 | 34 | 23 | 23 | 25 | 25 | 21 | 21 | 30 | 23 | 25 | 24 | 23 |

159

## The Exilic Code

Our old acquaintances Daniel, Azariah son of Amaziah, and Shelemiah son of Kore stand out as possible authors or subjects of the whole. Daniel and Shelemiah also had top scores in the Job-Proverbs-Songs group, as did Azariah. The scoring indicates that no single person had a hand in anything more than about half the Isaiah chapters. Daniel's significantly coded name appears in thirty-four of the book's sixty-six chapters, and no one else has more than thirty. For Second Isaiah, neither Ezra nor Jacob rated inclusion, while Daniel, Azariah, and three others led. This suggests either that the redactors rather than the original authors did a considerable amount of the encoding or that the Second Isaiah chapters did not originate during the Exile.

Did those redactors include Daniel and Shelemiah? They probably did not if the editing and compilation were done after the Exile's end. Recovered ration tablets prove that Shelemiah was in Babylon about 592, which is about the same time that scripture places young Daniel in Nebuchadnezzar's court. Each of them would have been in their sixties by 539, when the Persians defeated Nabonidus and Cyrus ascended Babylon's throne. And sixty-five or so would have been an advanced age for any Jewish leader during those tumultuous times. "Cyrus king of Babylon" has significant coding in eighteen chapters, with First, Second, and Third Isaiah about equally represented. Close to two-thirds of those Cyrus chapters also have "Shelemiah son of Kore" and "Daniel" codings. Ergo these chapters were finalized sometime after 539, and if high Shelemiah and Daniel codes meant author rather than subject, then both men would have been well along in years. Finally, "Daniel-Sarpuhi" drew its share of coded Isaiah chapters, twenty in all. Since it had high coding points in Ps 51, I added it to the names studied in this chapter, though I had no previous knowledge that Daniel died as a Babylonian substitute. But if he did, he could not have done any redacting during the reign of Cyrus.

It is time to speculate about dates for the Isaiah chapters. Eighteen of them contain significant codings of "Cyrus king of Babylon" and nine more lack Cyrus but have "Nabonidus-Belshazzar" (556–539). In seven others the earliest date-sensitive coding is "Jehoiachin-Sarpuhi" (561). "Ezekiel-Sarpuhi" (569) with two chapters and "Nebuchadnezzar" (605–562) with six round out the forty-two Isaiah chapters with such codes. This would suggest that the final editors incorporated lots of exilic material without retouching. However, as usual we can draw no final conclusions until we explore coding of Darius, Xerxes, and the rest.

## The Breadth of Exilic Coding

Before leaving Isaiah we must note that Isa 53 has statistically significant coding of "Cyrus king of Babylon," כורשהמלכבבל. Two AAA athbash spellings begin at words 2-14 and 3-1 and end at 3-9 and 3-11.[32] This means that the account of the Suffering Servant was written at least thirty years after Ezekiel died as Babylon's substitute king. It would then be the reflections of those who had known him well. Remembering, they wrote, "He had no form or majesty that we should look at him, nothing in his appearance that we should desire him" (Isa 53:2). They also testified that, "He shall see his offspring, and shall prolong his days (Isa 53:10). That is, even though the Babylonians had beheaded him, after three decades the authors maintained that Ezekiel still lived. This was not a hasty judgment, but rather a seasoned reflection, the result of years of discussion and debate.

This also could explain the relationship between Isa 52:13–15 and Isa 53. The prior passage could have announced Ezekiel's selection as a Babylonian substitute, quite possibly in 569 BCE. (Notably, Isa 52 contains no datable coding.) Then over thirty years later another hand wrote Isa 53, with its "Cyrus king of Babylon" spellings, and inserted that text into the book of Isaiah immediately after chapter 52.

Now we address coding in the other two Major Prophets, Jeremiah and Ezekiel. Jeremiah used the technique sparingly, but he did use it. Appendix 4 shows but a single significant coding group in Jer 25. Zedekiah, the last king of Judah, is the name featured. The chapter's final half-dozen verses are an attack against unnamed shepherds, a term that indicates rulers. Here is part of the passage: "Wail, you shepherds, and cry out; roll in ashes, you lords of the flock, for the days of your slaughter have come ... Flight shall fail the shepherds, and there shall be no escape for the lords of the flock. Hark! the cry of the shepherds, and the wail of the lords of the flock! For the Lord is despoiling their pasture, and the peaceful folds are devastated ..." (Jer 25:34–37). Running beneath this text are fifty-six spellings of "Zedekiah," "Zedekiah the king," and "Zedekiah king of Judah."

It is significant that this is the only piece of exilic coding in the chapter (though there may be coding of *pre*-exilic names, which remain unsearched). Jeremiah knew and used athbash coding, but he employed it

---

32. The athbash is מחתאזסנמדדן and the sequence from word 2-14 is מנזדמאתדחסן, ending on word 3-9. The second sequence starting at word 3-1 and ending with 3-11 is זדמאתדחסנמן. The probability that this coding is coincidental is $2.0 \times 10^{-5}$.

## The Exilic Code

lightly. Measured by coding density, the book of Jeremiah as a whole falls in the bottom quartile of OT books.

Ezekiel used coding about twice as frequently as Jeremiah. This example connects the two prophets. From Babylon Ezekiel sketched grievous acts being committed in the Jerusalem temple. The prophet's ghastly solution was slaughter, slaughter without quarter, starting at the temple's inner sanctuary. Ezekiel addressed chapter 9, which describes this, to Jeremiah in distant Jerusalem. The chapter's first, second, third, fourth, fifth, and sixth words begin spellings of "Jeremiah the son of Hilkiah," ירמיהובנחלקיהו. Using one letter from fourteen consecutive text words, Ezekiel fashioned six such spellings, not even bothering to substitute an athbash version of Jeremiah's name. Consulting appendix 4, a quarter of Ezekiel's chapters contain ten or more significant groups of exilic codings, and chapters 22 and 23, which recount the infidelities of Jerusalem and Samaria, have codings in the middle to high twenties. At least seven of the Ezekiel chapters reached their final form after the Exile ended (chapters with "Cyrus king of Babylon" encoding are 7, 16, 18, 27, 34, 41, and 46), and the others were completed earlier or contain no date-sensitive coding.

In this book's chapter 4, we saw the battles fought in the Minor Prophets by Jacob and his opponents. Remembering the heavy use of Jacob IDs, it should not surprise us to find coding concentrations in the twelve books. Table 7.7 confirms this. It shows the coding density of all thirty-nine books.

## The Breadth of Exilic Coding

### TABLE 7.7—DENSITY OF EXILIC CODING IN HEBREW SCRIPTURE (DENSITY = SIGNIFICANT CODINGS / CHAPTERS × 36)

| | | | | | |
|---|---|---|---|---|---|
| Nahum | .64 | Nehemiah | .24 | Malachi | .13 |
| Daniel | .44 | Hosea | .21 | Leviticus | .13 |
| Songs | .42 | Joshua | .21 | Zechariah | .09 |
| Proverbs | .41 | 1 Chronicles | .19 | Jeremiah | .09 |
| Habakkuk | .37 | Ezekiel | .19 | 1 Kings | .09 |
| Isaiah | .33 | Numbers | .18 | Judges | .07 |
| Micah | .32 | Jonah | .17 | Genesis | .07 |
| Lamentations | .32 | Zephaniah | .16 | 2 Kings | .05 |
| Joel | .28 | Exodus | .15 | Deuteronomy | .05 |
| Amos | .26 | Ruth | .15 | 2 Samuel | .05 |
| Psalms | .25 | Ecclesiastes | .15 | 1 Samuel | .04 |
| Job | .25 | 2 Chronicles | .14 | Haggai | .02 |
| Ezra | .24 | Esther | .14 | Obadiah | .00 |

Measured by exilic coding density, Nahum, Habakkuk, Micah, Joel, and Amos are in the top third, Hosea is above average, while Haggai and Obadiah contain little or no coding. The other four books of the Minor Prophets are toward the middle of the spread. Before doing more on the prophets, look at the right column of the table. Six of the seven books that Dtr wrote—Deuteronomy, Judges, First and Second Samuel, and First and Second Kings—all have scores with low densities. As to Joshua, the chapters done by hands other than Dtr have a clear effect. And Jeremiah, who certainly would have been influenced by Dtr, is close to the coding densities of that author's work. We should also observe that even though the Chronicler came perhaps 150 years after the Exile, he took a lively interest in exilic people and events. He receives above-average scores for the books of Ezra and Nehemiah as well as average ratings for the two books of Chronicles.

Returning to the Minor Prophets, table 7.8 shows that there are similarities in coding scores between the twelve prophets and the Job-Proverbs-Songs group. Daniel is high with twenty-three chapters, and Shelemiah has significant coding in twenty. In the Writings group Daniel and Shelemiah have a first-place tie. Here are the names from the Minor Prophets combined with the Writings group we examined earlier:

## The Breadth of Exilic Coding

### TABLE 7.8—CANDIDATES FOR SUBJECT OR AUTHORSHIP OF JOB, PROVERBS, SONGS, AND MINOR PROPHETS

| Books | Chapters in Books | Ahaziah son of Jehoram | Ahihud son of Shelomi | Amariah son of Hezekiah | Azariah son of Amaziah | Azariah son of Zephaniah | Azrikam son of Azel | Baruch | Daniel | Ezekiel | Jacob-Israel | Seraiah son of | Shelemiah son of Kore | Shephatiah son of David | Zephaniah |
|---|---|---|---|---|---|---|---|---|---|---|---|---|---|---|---|
| Job | 42 | 11 | 17 | 16 | 8 | 12 | 12 | 8 | 20 | 11 | 11 | 15 | 21 | 15 | 13 |
| Prov | 31 | 8 | 12 | 17 | 20 | 14 | 15 | 10 | 21 | 16 | 16 | 20 | 20 | 10 | 16 |
| Song | 8 | 5 | 1 | 7 | 4 | 4 | 3 | 5 | 6 | 4 | 3 | 3 | 6 | 4 | 3 |
| 12 | 67 | 16 | 17 | 18 | 16 | 13 | 19 | 16 | 23 | 13 | 10 | 19 | 20 | 16 | 10 |
| All | 148 | 40 | 47 | 48 | 48 | 43 | 49 | 39 | 70 | 44 | 40 | 57 | 67 | 45 | 42 |

## The Exilic Code

Daniel and Shelemiah are easily the leaders. Seraiah son of Tanhumeth is in third place with significant coding in fifty-seven chapters. He is especially strong in Proverbs and the Minor Prophets. This Seraiah is mentioned in scripture (2 Kgs 25:23; Jer 40:8) as one of the troop commanders who supported Gedaliah at Mizpah after the fall of Jerusalem. Turning from the three leaders, observe also how even the other totals are. Ten of these principals were either subjects or authors of at least forty chapters of scripture, and Baruch with thirty-nine was close. In ending this section we remind readers that in the future the coding strength of numerous other names is likely to be tested against scripture. Perhaps we shall find another Daniel.

## DANIEL SCHOOL IS SCRIPTURE FACTORY

Daniel had twice as many encodings in the OT as the second-best candidate, Jacob-Israel, making the book of Daniel particularly appropriate to examine. Chapters 2 through 7 are in Aramaic and the balance is in Hebrew. The Aramaic portion is the most heavily coded, but four of the six Hebrew chapters also have a fair share of encoded names. This supports that "the two languages reflect the history of composition."[33] The only exception to that would be the opening chapter, where light coding suggests that it is a Hebrew translation of an Aramaic original.[34] In chapter 1 the only significantly coded name that the translator carried over was "Daniel." Given this, the name of the author of the collection may have been Daniel, though a different Daniel than the one featured in scripture. Overall, the book of Daniel ranks second among OT books in coding density. The most heavily coded names are clearly exilic—"Baruch," "Daniel," "Jacob," and "Jeremiah"—so this appears to be an attempt to recount in coding part of the Exile's history.

Daniel chapter 3 is an account of Nebuchadnezzar's image of gold and of Shadrach, Meshach, and Abednego in the fiery furnace. The Aramaic text supports massive coding. Thirty-five of thirty-six names are coded significantly, a feat matched only by Joshua 15 out of all Scripture's chapters. And the most extraordinary encoding is for the combination "Belteshazzar-Daniel." (Belteshazzar is the name given young Daniel by the palace master. See Dan 1:7.) Various combinations of the two names

---

33. Collins, "Daniel," 31.
34. Collins and others think Dan 1 is a translation from Aramaic.

yielded four computer pages of A, AA, and AAA hits.[35] After I deleted overlaps and duplicates, 124 values remained, averaging four spellings each. And this was just for "Belteshazzar-Daniel." Including the other encoded names, the authors must have packed ten thousand coded spellings into Daniel 3. This is extraordinary, and it cannot be coincidental. The probability is zero that the "Daniel" coding was due to chance.

Only masters of coding technique could have produced such a chapter. Clearly Daniel 3 and the other chapters surrounding it had to originate from a group with superb and special skills. What other OT chapters that have similar characteristics? There are fifty-seven that have similar floods of "Daniel" coding. Six of them register a zero probability of coincidence in chi-square tests, and another fifty-two have P values with between twenty-two and ninety-nine zeroes to the right of the decimal point. These are very small numbers, and for practical purposes they all are zero—that is, there is no probability of coincidence. Possibly this work was done at just one center, peopled by talented scribes and writers, who over generations and even centuries produced scripture with such masses of Daniel coding. It would have become the signature of a group that had a large part in shaping the Hebrew Bible.

As a test, I first ranked OT chapters by their "Daniel" chi-square results, and then compared them with a list of chapters ranked by numbers of significantly coded exilic names. There was an almost perfect correlation between the two lists. The "Daniel" chi-square coding list contained two 35-hit chapters, and so did the exhaustive chapter list. "Daniel" had three 34-hit chapters, ditto the exhaustive list; and so on down to the 23-hit chapters, where the "Daniel" list contained six of seven in the category. In total, fifty-seven of the fifty-eight best "Daniel" chapters were also the top thirty-six-name chapters.[36] Conclusion: *the best "Daniel" coding drove the rest of the coding*. With an exception we shall discuss shortly, that Daniel coding is the distinctive hallmark of a single group, possibly founded or inspired by Daniel himself, and very likely continuing over many years.

---

35. I applied to Daniel 3 the same range of Daniel-related athbash spellings used with every other chapter in Scripture. The words included "Belteshazzar son of David," "Belteshazzar the prisoner," "Daniel son of Abigail," "Daniel son of Eliakim," "Daniel son of Jehoiakim," "Daniel the substitute king," and "Daniel the prisoner." Codings of "Daniel sarpuhi" were treated as a separate category.

36. Ninety-eight percent of OT chapters with twenty-two to thirty-five hits also contained the top "Daniel" chi-square scores. In the stretch between fifteen and twenty-one hits the share of chapters with high "Daniel" coding falls to fifty percent.

## TABLE 7.9—TWENTY-EIGHT CHAPTERS CONTAINING HIGHEST DANIEL CODING

| Book, Chapter | Ahaziah/Jehoram: 22 Hits | Amariah/Hezekiah: 23 | Azrikam/Azel: 20 | Baruch: 26 | Daniel: 28 | Jacob–Israel: 26 | Jehizkiah/Shallum: 24 | Seraiah/Tanhumeth: 26 | Shecaniah/Jahaziel: 21 | Shelemiah/Kore: 25 | Shenazzar/Jehoiachin: 21 | Shephatiah/David: 26 | Zephaniah: 22 | Nebuchadnezzar: 24 | Nabonidus–Belshazzar: 22 | Cyrus King of Babylon: 18 | Chapter Hits (36 Names) |
|---|---|---|---|---|---|---|---|---|---|---|---|---|---|---|---|---|---|
| Exod 25 | + | # |   | + | + | + | + | + |   | + |   | # | + |   | + | + | 26 |
| 37 | + | + |   | + | + | + | + | + |   |   | # | + | + | + | + | # | 26 |
| Num 29 | # |   | + | + | + | + | + |   |   | + | + | + |   | + |   | + | 20 |
| Josh 13 | + | + | + | # | + | + | + | + | # | + | + | + | + | + | + | # | 32 |
| 15 | + | # |   | + | + | + | + | + | # | + | + | + | + | + | + | + | 35 |
| 16 |   | + | + | # | + | + | + | # |   | + | + | + | # | + | + | # | 23 |
| 19 | + | # | + | + | + | + | + | + | + | # | + | + | + | + | + |   | 33 |
| 1 Kgs 6 | + | + | + | + | + |   | + | + |   | + | # | + | + | + | # | + | 27 |
| Job 41 | + | # | + | + | + | + | + | # | # | + | + | + | + | # | + | # | 28 |
| Ps 17 | + | + | + |   | + | + | + | + | + | + | + | # | + | + | + | + | 34 |
| 48 | + | + | + | # | + | + | + | + | # | + |   | + | + | + | + | + | 27 |
| 51 |   | + | # | # | + | + | # | + | # | # |   |   | # | + | + | + | 34 |
| 65 | + | + | # | # | + | + | # | + | # | # |   | + | # | + | + | + | 27 |
| 78 |   | # | # | + | + | + | # | # | + | + |   | + | # | + | # |   | 28 |

168

## The Breadth of Exilic Coding

| Book, Chapter | Ahaziah/Jehoram: 22 Hits | Amariah/Hezekiah: 23 | Azrikam/Azel: 20 | Baruch: 26 | Daniel: 28 | Jacob-Israel: 26 | Jehizkiah/Shallum: 24 | Seraiah/Tanhumeth: 26 | Shecaniah/Jahaziel: 21 | Shelemiah/Kore: 25 | Shenazzar/Jehoiachin: 21 | Shephatiah/David: 26 | Zephaniah: 22 | Nebuchadnezzar: 24 | Nabonidus-Belshazzar: 22 | Cyrus King of Babylon: 18 | Chapter Hits (36 Names) |
|---|---|---|---|---|---|---|---|---|---|---|---|---|---|---|---|---|---|
| Ps 106 | + |   |   | + | + | + | # | # |   | + | + | # | # | + | # |   | 27 |
| 119   | + | + |   | + | + | + | + | + | + | + | + | + | + | + | + |   | 32 |
| Prov 8 |   | + |   | # | + | + |   | + | + | + |   | + |   | # | # |   | 21 |
| 10    | + |   | # | + | + | + | + | + | + | + | + |   | + | + | + | # | 30 |
| Eccl 12 | + | + | + | # | + | # | # | + | # | + |   | + |   | + | # | # | 25 |
| Song 7 | + | + | + |   | + | # |   | + | # | + | + | + |   | + | + | # | 25 |
| Isa 3 | + | + | + | + | + | + |   | + | + | + | + | + | + | + |   | + | 33 |
| 28    | + | + |   | + | + | + | + | + | # | + | + | # | + | + | + | + | 34 |
| 58    | + | + | + | + | + | + | # | # |   | + | + | + | + | # |   | # | 31 |
| 59    | + | + | + | # | + |   | + | + | + | + | # | + | + | + | + |   | 29 |
| Ezek 23 | + | + | + | + | + |   |   | + | + | + | # | # |   | + | + |   | 28 |
| Dan 3 | + | + | # | + | + | + |   | + | + | + | + | + | + | + | + | + | 35 |
| Joel 2 | # | + | # | + | + | # | # | # | + |   | # | # |   |   | # |   | 21 |
| Nah 3 |   | + |   | + | + | + |   | + | + |   | # | + | + | + | + |   | 30 |

169

Table 7.9 shows the twenty-eight chapters in scripture with the very highest "Daniel" coding. First, look at the right-hand column, "Chapter Hits." Though the OT average is seven hits, the range for this group is twenty-one to thirty-five. This is an extraordinary showing. Next, consider the shaded boxes under "Nabonidus-Belshazzar" and "Cyrus king of Babylon." Eight of the twenty-eight chapters have significant Nabonidus coding without Cyrus marks, and "Cyrus king of Babylon" has all but two of the rest. Nabonidus and his regent Belshazzar governed from 556 to late 539 BCE, when Cyrus succeeded him. The Persian reigned until 530.

We might conclude that the Daniel School did its work in the quarter century that started about 556 BCE. However, if we did so we would stand a good chance of being incorrect. In most of those Daniel School chapters the authors encoded Nebuchadnezzar, Nabonidus, and Cyrus, and half the chapters heavily coded all three rulers. Why encode several when one would serve to date the work? Something other than simple dating was intended. Future work may show encodings of Darius followed perhaps by Ahasuerus and then Artaxerxes and so on.

Glance at the names at the top of the table. As expected, "Daniel" has + for every chapter since his coding is the organizing principle for the table. The Nebuchadnezzar, Nabonidus, and Cyrus entries are date-sensitive. The others either helped to write scripture at the Daniel School or had been part of Israel's recent history. Baruch and Jacob-Israel are prominent on the list. Baruch is a known exilic figure, and it is likely that Jacob was, too. We have found Jacob dueling with critics in the book of Proverbs. Does a high score from the Daniel School mean that Jacob-Second Isaiah was in residence with the group? And if so, what if subsequent coding research establishes that the School operated under, say, Artaxerxes (circa 450 BCE)? Would we move Jacob from an exilic to a restoration category?

The other names—Ahaziah, Amariah, Azrikam, Jehizkiah, Seraiah, Shecaniah, Shenazzar, Shephatiah, and especially Shelemiah son of Kore—are familiar. Chances are that at least some of these wrote not only these chapters but a great many others. Where might they have worked? The three best choices seem to be Babylonia, Egypt, and Israel. Given that Babylonia was a center of Jewish learning in the post-exilic period, Babylon seems the likeliest location for the Daniel School. This, however, remains speculative.

## The Breadth of Exilic Coding

Look at the left column of table 7.9 and note the variety of books represented. There are fourteen, with Psalms, Joshua, and Isaiah leading. But remember that the chapters shown are only half of the chapters probably written in the Daniel School. Appendix 4 uses shading to show fifty-seven of them, and for convenience this note enumerates them.[37] Since this study deals only with coding within whole chapters, it will not detect editing or insertion by the School of even large blocks of text (unless coding in the block is extreme enough to push the whole chapter into significance). The way the marked chapters in appendix 4 are grouped reveal areas of the School's influence. They include the later chapters of Exodus and Joshua, almost all of Proverbs and Songs, and Daniel 2–6. These suggest that the Daniel writers inserted more into scripture than this book has been able to specify.[38] It is, however, a start.

A number of the chapters consist of lists of tabernacle or ark furnishings, feast offerings, tribal censuses, boundaries, and land allotments—material that would have been easier to arrange so as to maximize coding. The poetic and narrative chapters often have a sharper edge to them like the Proverbs chapters and Isa 58 and 59. And some, like the Job and Songs texts and the dozen psalms, are of high literary order.

The primary characteristic of these fifty-seven chapters is that they contain extremely high Daniel coding, and so far I have attributed these to a single group of scholars, the Daniel School. However, Jacob IDs ("Holy One of Israel," "Jacob," Jacob-Israel parallels) and/or lines of argument suggest nine of these chapters originated with Jacob or his follow-

---

37. The chapters that probably originated in the Daniel School are: Exod 25, 27, 37, 38; Num 2, 29; Josh 13, 15, 16, 19; 1 Kgs 6; Job 10, 18, 19, 41; Pss 17, 31, 48, 51, 65, 77, 78, 80, 88, 104, 106, 119; Prov 2, 7, 8, 10–12, 14, 16, 24, 27, 31; Eccl 12; Song 2, 7; Isa 3, 5, 10, 28, 54, 58, 59; Ezek 22, 23; Dan 3, 5; Joel 2; Amos 6; Mic 6; and Nah 2, 3. All of these have + signs under "Daniel" in appendix 5. However, a + is not an indicator of Daniel School origin. Instead it simply represents the extreme half of the range of statistically significant "Daniel" coding that runs from .01 to 0. (The symbol # is the sign for the less-extreme half.) The fifty-seven chapters listed above share probabilities of coincidence for "Daniel" coding that have at least twenty-two zeros to the right of the decimal point, combined with significant coding of a large number of other exilic names.

38. Late books have been excluded from consideration. These include Dan 7–12, Ezra, Nehemiah, Esther, and Chronicles. Chapters in those books that would have met Daniel School criteria are Dan 11; Neh 3; and 2 Chr 3, 26, and 35. Note that I have not excluded Ecclesiastes. Chapter 12 of that book contains massive Daniel coding. Other chapters that have about a 50/50 chance of being from the Daniel (or Jacob) School are Num 4; Deut 33; Josh 7, 12; 1 Sam 8; Job 12, 21, 40; Pss 2, 11, 18, 37, 89; Prov 5, 21, 26, 28; Song 4; Isa 1, 26; Jer 49; Lam 4; Ezek 5, 26; Dan 4; and Zech 9.

ers. These include Isa 5 and 54; Nah 2; Pss 65, 78, 106; Job 19; and Prov 8 and 31. In these cases Jacob, his followers, or his descendents might have multiplied coding to condemn Daniel or others, and it may not be proper to attribute them to any Daniel School.

## THE HISTORY OF CODING

Finally, what have we learned about the history of encoding of our thirty-six names and titles? To begin, the Dtr historian knew coding and he or she used it. Dtr's skillful insertion of "Jeremiah's book of the law" and of other "Jeremiah" coding into the Josiah reform account proves this. The books constituting the DH may be low in exilic coding, but since Dtr clearly employed it, coding was understood and applied in the late seventh century.

Jeremiah also knew coding, though he too used it sparingly. His prophecy against shepherds with "Zedekiah" coding underneath (Jer 25:34–37) shows he practiced the art. Ezekiel employed coding about twice as frequently as Jeremiah, while Jacob-Second Isaiah was a master of it, as he was of so much else. In the Daniel School after the Exile coding reached its peak as members packed torrents of encodings into the books of Daniel, Songs, and Proverbs while adding chapters to Exodus, Numbers, Kings, Joshua, Psalms, Job, Isaiah, Ezekiel, and the Minor Prophets. Nehemiah and the Chronicler continued to practice this secret technique (Neh 3; 2 Chr 3, 26, 36) with *exilic* names, and if they devoted their attentions to names from the past it is a good bet that they also encoded names from their own times.

Daniel 11 contains very powerful "Daniel" encoding and significant codings of twenty-two other exilic names. Experts agree that the chapter's author wrote during the reign of Antiochus IV Epiphanes (175–164 BCE).[39] This brings a working knowledge of coding forward to the second century. In summary we can track coding within scripture from the end of the seventh to the first half of the second century BCE. In the future, scholars may wish to test both ends of this period (and especially the Septuagint and New Testament) to see what more coding can teach us about scripture.

---

39. Collins, "Daniel," 33.

## Appendix One—Athbash Letter Exchanges

*After selecting the letters of the true word on line 1, go to another line and substitute column-by-column to form the true word's athbash equivalent.*

# Appendix Two—2 Kings 25:27–30: 468 Word Links

Word Links with Jehoiachin coding or anagrams are shown in italics.

|   | Subject | Word Link's Chapter and Verse |
|---|---|---|
| 1 | Jehoiachin's Life | *1 Sam 1:11*; 2 Sam 19:34–35, 40–42; 1 Kgs 22:41–43; 2 Kgs 24:6–13; *1 Chr 3:4*; *2 Chr 36:7–10*; Jer 28:3–4; Ezek 18:7. |
| 2 | Judgment and Exile | Exod 23:29; *Josh 23:13*; 2 Kgs 20:18–19, 24:15–17, 25:1–4, 8–9; 2 Chr 36:4–6; *Isa 4:1, 7:20–21, 20:3–4*; *Jer 5:13–15, 15:3–4, 17:27, 24:1–2,* 3–8, 29:15–17, *39:1–2, 40:1–2,* 3–5, 44:27, *52:3–7, 11–12, 26–30*; Lam 4:1; Ezek 12:6, 24–25, 15:6–7, *17:19–20, 33:21–24*; *Dan 9:7*; *Mic 6:16*; Obad 1:20–21; Zech 2:4. |
| 3 | Tribute | *Exod 30:4, 12–13*; *Judg 8:25–26*; 2 Kgs 5:23, 18:14; 2 Chr 3:8, *24:6, 11*. |
| 4 | Pagan Idols | Judg 18:19; *Deut 31:16–17*; 1 Kgs 13:3, 15:1–3, *16:29–31*; 2 Kgs 13:10–11, *15:8–9*, 23:11–12; 2 Chr 2:4–5; Jer 11:17, 43:10–12, 44:17; Ezek 14:4, 15:3–4, 16:19, 18:5–6, *14–16*, 20:31, *22:4*, 33:27, 44:12. |
| 5 | Oppression and Prison | *Gen 4:13–14, 6:18–19,* 7:4, *31:40–41, 37:24–26, 37:28–29*; Exod 5:13; *Num 14:34*; Deut 24:15; Judg 16:24–25; 1 Sam 20:27–28, *23:17–18*; 2 Sam 18:7–8; *1 Kgs 20:32*, 22:27; 2 Chr 12:12, *18:25–26*; *Neh 2:1–2*, 9:36–37; *Esth 3:7, 9:1–4*, 15–16; *Ps 4:6*; *Prov 10:9–14, 14:1–3,* 17:26–28, *25:19–28*; Isa 42:6–7, 22, 45:12–13, *51:13–14*; Jer 18:20, *37:15–18*. |
| 6 | Evil-Marduk | Judg 3:19–20; *1 Sam 17:15–17*; *1 Kgs 1:24–25*, 12:6–8, *12–14, 16:8–12*, 21:4; 2 Kgs 19:4. |
| 7 | Plots, Broken Covenants | Exod 31:18; Deut 5:22, 10:4, 19:17, *27:7–9*; *1 Sam 20:23–24*, 23:17–18; 2 Sam 3:8, 9:7, 12–13, 14:19, *16:2*, 19:27–28; 1 Kgs 21:2; *2 Kgs 17:2–5*, Ps 41:6–9; Prov 6:14–16, *24:7–10*, 27:1–5; Jer 12:6–8. |

## 2 Kings 25:27–30: 468 Word Links

| 8 | Hunger, Fasting | Gen 3:1, 5–6, 17, 22–23, 24:32–33, *41:53–54;* Exod 12:14–15, *18–19,* 13:3–4, 23:15, 34:28–29; Lev 7:18, 27–28, *10:19–20,* 22:16–17; Deut 9:9–10, 18, 16:3; Ruth 1:1; 1 Sam 1:7, 9:19; 2 Sam 3:35, 21:1–2; 1 Kgs 13:7–9, 11, 17–19, 21–22; 2 Kgs 6:28, 8:1; 2 Chr 20:3, *30:21–22;* Ezra 10:5–6; Neh 5:13–15; Esth 4:16; Prov 15:15–17; *Isa 3:1;* Jer 36:9; *Ezek 4:9–10;* Dan 1:12–14, *10:2–5;* Hos 2:12; Amos 4:6–7; Zech 8:19. |
|---|---|---|
| 9 | Substitute Wife | *Lev 15:26–28;* Judg 19:8, 29–30; *Ruth 4:11;* 1 Sam 18:21; 2 Sam 11:2; *Ezra 10:16;* Esth 1:19, 2:3, 9, *17,* 7:8–9, 8:1; Prov 18:21–23. |
| 10 | Fast Broken | Gen 18:8–9, 27:9–10, 45:18; Exod 23:10–12, 25:30; *Lev 11:2, 24:7–9, 26:10–12; Num 11:17–21,* 28:23–25; *Deut 8:10–13,* 12:7, 15:20–21, *26:11–12;* Josh 5:12–13; 1 Sam 9:24, 30:12; 2 Kgs 4:8–11, *43–44;* 2 Chr 31:10; *Eccl 3:12–14,* 8:15; Ezek 2:8; Dan 8:27. |
| 11 | Substitute King Reign | *Gen 1:28–29,* 37:8–9; Exod 29:29–30; Num 24:7–8; *Judg 9:15–16, 11:11;* 1 Sam 2:24–25, 29:5–6; 2 Sam 2:10–11, *3:19–20,* 5:2–5, 19:11–12; *1 Kgs 1:27,* 2:11–12, 9:10, *22:8–10;* 2 Kgs 3:13–14, 9:5–6, 15:12–13; Esth 6:11–13; *Eccl 5:17–19,* 8:1–4; *Ps 45:6–10;* Prov 1:5–9, 20:1–3, 30:21–23; *Isa 6:1–2,* 7:16–17; *Ezek 16:12–13;* Dan 11:26–27; *Hag 2:10–12.* |
| 12 | S. K. Curse | *Gen 3:14;* Deut 28:31; 1 Kgs 8:31–32; Job 1:11–13, *5:2–5; Ps 109:19–21;* Prov 11:26–30. |
| 13 | S. K. Feasting | 1 Sam 25:35–36; *2 Sam 11:13; 1 Kgs 17:14–16;* Esth 1:1–3; *Ps 23:5–6; Eccl 2:3–5,* 7:2, *9:7–9, 10:16–19;* Isa 1:14; *Ezek 41:22.* |
| 14 | S. K. Riches | Gen 28:18–20; *Exod 38:24;* Num 24:13, 31:38–41; Deut 14:26; 2 Sam 9:9–11, 19:17–19; 1 Kgs 4:7, 21–25, *5:9–11, 8:61–63,* 10:8–10, 17–20, 14:28–29, 22:30–31; *1 Chr 27:1; 2 Chr 9:11–13;* Ezra 1:9–11, 2:65–67; Neh 7:67–71; Esth 6:8; Job 1:3–4, 11–12; *Prov 16:15–16,* 27:21–23; *Eccl 6:2–3.* |
| 15 | S. K. Ark | Num 17:6–7; 1 Sam 5:4, 7:2; 2 Sam 6:4, 11:11. |

# Appendix Two

| 16 | S. K. Death | Gen 2:16–19, 25:16–17, 40:13, 19, 43:25–27; Num 19:10–11, 20:28–29, 28:9–11; Deut 30:15; Josh 23:14–15; Judg 8:28; 1 Sam 17:46, 26:16; 2 Sam 4:8, 14:26, 20:21; 1 Kgs 2:23–24, 16:23; Esth 2:23; Eccl 6:12, 8:12–13; Job 7:6–7; Ps 39:5; Prov 16:22–25; Jer 4:8–10, 22–23, 16:4–6, 38:2–5, 41:1–2; Jonah 4:8. |
|---|---|---|
| 17 | S. K. Burial | Gen 50:3–5, Judg 16:30–31, 1 Kgs 2:31–32, 2 Chr 24:15–16, Ps 27:4, 84:10–11, Ezek 29:5–6. |
| 18 | S. K. Atonement | Exod 12:5–8; Lev 10:17–18, 15:13–15, 16:21, 27–29, 17:10, 23:18, 25:29; Num 29:11–12, 19–20; 1 Sam 2:10–11; Ezra 3:4–6; Neh 10:31–33; Ezek 4:4–6. |
| 19 | Killing Children | Lev 16:1–2; Num 28:1–3, 29:17, 31:17–20; Judg 11:33–35; 1 Sam 20:27, 2 Sam 12:17–18, 20–21, 13:26, 18:18; 1 Kgs 3:18–19, 22, 25, 14:17–20, 22–23; 2 Chr 21:13, 22:10; Job 1:17–19; Isa 56:5–6; Lam 2:19–20. |
| 20 | Davidic Line | Gen 17:21–23, 24:7; Josh 21:44–45; 1 Sam 2:28, 3:11–12, 17:14–15; 2 Sam 7:29; 1 Kgs 5:5; 2 Kgs 1:17, 19:29–30, 23:27–28; 2 Chr 23:2–3; Ezra 1:5–7, 7:8–10, 8:35–36, 9:9; Neh 2:3; Isa 2:1–2, 35:8–10; Jer 22:1–2, 5–6, 24–25, 33:14, 24, 36:29–30; Ezek 37:19; Hos 1:11; Mic 4:1; Hag 2:19–22; Zech 12:6–7. |
| 21 | Against Babylon | Deut 9:3, 18; 1 Sam 30:16; Josh 6:4; Isa 21:8–10; Jer 32:1–4, 39:16, 50:1–3; Ezek 29:17–18; Joel 2:2–3. |
| 22 | Against Nations | Gen 19:21; Exod 12:23; Judg 16:3; 1 Kgs 18:42; Job 40:20; Ezek 26:16–17, 32:17–18, 39:13–16; Obad 1:17–18. |
| 23 | Prophets and Priests | 1 Kgs 2:26; 2 Kgs 1:9–10; 9:14–16; 1 Chr 23:31–32; Ezra 8:17–18; Jer 25:1–3, 26:2, 19, 29:21–23, 36:1–2, 38:8–10, 45:1; Ezek 1:1–3, 19–20, 8:1, 40:1; Amos 1:1, 7:12–13; Hag 1:1. |
| 24 | Unassigned | Gen 30:33, 47:23–24, 49:26–28; Exod 6:16, 20, 26:7–8, 28:12; Lev 13:49–50, 53–54, 14:7–9, 52–53, 19:24–27; Num 1:1–3, 4:7, 10:10, 17:2, 26:2; Deut 20:19; Josh 4:8, 14:10; 1 Kgs 2:38–39, 6:2–3, 7:16, 9:25, 17:1, 18:1; 2 Chr 3:15–16, 13:15–16, 16:1, 19:11, 31:20–21; Ezra 9:12, 10:9; Neh 2:8, 13:6–8; Ps 11:4–5; Prov 15:1–5, 29:9; Isa 38:20–21; Dan 2:1–2. |

# APPENDIX THREE—Coding in Psalm 51

## PART A: NAMES WITH HIGHER CODING

Each of the 132 items listed has at least 24 points (8 for AAA, 4 for AA, and 2 for A). The second column shows the frequency ranking among the 929 OT chapters, though only about a quarter of the items have been measured. In the third column some Hebrew names have variations that are not shown.

| Item | Rank in 929 | Name | Groups by Values and (Points) | Description from Scripture and other sources |
|---|---|---|---|---|
| 1 | | Abidan, Scribe<br>אבידנהספר | AAA-2,<br>AA-2,<br>A-1 (26) | Scribe, helped Moses with census |
| 2 | | Abijah S Samuel<br>אביהובנשמואל | AAA-4,<br>AA-2, A-2<br>(44) | Pre-monarchy judge, son of Samuel |
| 3 | | Abijah Dtr Zechariah<br>אביהבתזכריהו | AAA-3, A-1<br>(26) | Mother of King Hezekiah |
| 4 | | Absolum S David & Maacah אבשלומבנדוד,<br>אבשלומבנמעכה | AAA-7,<br>AA-1, A-8<br>(76) | King David's son, revolted against father, note high points |
| 5 | | Adonijah S David & Haggith<br>אדניהבנדוד,<br>אדניהבנחגית | AAA-4, A-2<br>(36) | King David's son |
| 6 | 2 | Ahaziah S Jehoram<br>אחזיהבניהורם | AAA-4, A-1<br>(34) | King of Judah 842 |

# Appendix Three

| Item | Rank in 929 | Name | Groups by Values and (Points) | Description from Scripture and other sources |
|---|---|---|---|---|
| 7 | 1 | Ahihud S Shelomi<br>אהיהודבנשלמי | AAA-3, A-5<br>(34) | Asherite leader from time of Joshua |
| 8 | 1 | Amariah S Hezekiah<br>אמריהובנחזקיה | AAA-7<br>(56) | Probably son of King Hezekiah |
| 9 | | Amaziah S Jehoaddin<br>אמציהובניהועדן | AAA-3, A-1<br>(26) | King of Judah 800–783 |
| 10 | | Armoni S Saul & Rizpah<br>ארמניבנרצפה, ארמניבנשׁול | AAA-7, A-2<br>(60) | Son of Saul, hanged under David, note 60 points |
| 11 | | Athaliah Dtr Ahab<br>עתליהבנאחאב | AAA-3, A-1<br>(26) | Daughter of Ahab and Jezebel, proponent of Baal |
| 12 | | Azaliah S Meshullam<br>אצליהובנמשלם | AAA-5, A-2<br>(44) | Father of Shapan, Josiah's secretary |
| 13 | | Azariah Chief Priest<br>עזריהוכהנהראש | AAA-5, A-1<br>(42) | Three chief priests by that name |
| 14 | | Azariah S Ahimaaz<br>עזריהבנאחימעץ | AAA-4, AA-1, A-2<br>(40) | Grandson of Zadok, probably ninth century |
| 15 | 1 | Azariah S Amaziah<br>עזריהובנאמציהו | AAA-9<br>(72) | Chronicles high priest list (1 Chr 6:4–15), high points |
| 16 | | Azariah S Ethan<br>עזריהובנאיתן | AAA-3, A-2<br>(28) | A descendent of Judah, (1 Chr 2:8) |
| 17 | | Azariah S Hilkiah<br>עזריהבנחלקיה | AAA-5, AA-1, A-2 (48) | On Chronicles high priest list (1 Chr 6:4–15) |
| 18 | | Azariah S Jehu<br>עזריהובניהוא | AAA-6<br>(48) | A descendent of Judah (1 Chr 2:38–39) |

## Coding in Psalm 51

| Item | Rank in 929 | Name | Groups by Values and (Points) | Description from Scripture and other sources |
|---|---|---|---|---|
| 19 | | Azariah S Johanan<br>עזריהובניוחן | AAA-3, AA-1 (28) | On Chronicles high priest list (1 Chr 6:4–15) |
| 20 | | Azariah S Maaseia<br>עזריהובנמעשי | AAA-4, A-1 (34) | Repaired walls under Nehemiah |
| 21 | | Azariah S Obed<br>עזריהובנעובד | AAA-5, AA-1 (44) | Reformer, ninth-century Judahite army officer |
| 22 | | Azariah S Oded<br>עזריהובנעודד | AAA-4, AA-1, A-2 (40) | Ninth-century prophet |
| 23 | | Azariah S Zadok<br>עזריהובנצדוק | AAA-4, AA-1, A-5 (46) | High official under Solomon |
| 24 | 1 | Azariah S Zephaniah, Scribe,<br>עזריהבנצפניהו<br>עזריההספר | AAA-9, AA-1 A-4 (82) | Probable son of prophet, scribe during Exile, 82 points |
| 25 | 1 | Azrikam S Azel<br>עזריקמבנאצל | AAA-6 A-8 (64) | Descendent of Saul (1 Chr 8:38) |
| 26 | | Azrikam S Hashabiah<br>עזריקמבנחשביה | AAA-3, A-1 (26) | A Levite who returned from Babylon |
| 27 | 14 | Baruch, etc.<br>ברוכבננריהו | AAA-6, A-2 (52) | Exilic leader in Judah, author and scribe |
| 28 | | Benzoheth S Ishi<br>בנזוחתבנישעי | AAA-3 (24) | In genealogy of Judah (1 Chr 4:20) |
| 29 | 1 | Chimham, etc.<br>כמהמבניכניהו | AAA-10, AA-1, A-6 (96) | In Davidic line, led in exilic Judah (2 Sam 19:37–40) |

## Appendix Three

| Item | Rank in 929 | Name | Groups by Values and (Points) | Description from Scripture and other sources |
|---|---|---|---|---|
| 30 | 1 | Cyrus K of Persia & Babylon כורשהמלכבבל, כורשמלכפרס | AAA-8, AA-2, A-3 (78) | King of Persia, led uprising in Judah in 570s, also coded as king of Babylon |
| 31 | 1 | Daniel-Belteshazzar, etc. S Abigail & David דנאלבנדוד, דנאלבנאביגיל בלטשאצר | AAA-19, AA-2, A-12 (184) | Belteshazzar Babylonian name for exilic Daniel, son of Abigail and Jehoiakim, highest score |
| 32 | 1 | Daniel Sarpuhi, דנאלשרפוהי דנאלהתמורתמלך | AAA-12, A-12 (120) | Probable son of Jehoiakim and substitute king, note 120 points, alternate forms |
| 33 | | Delaiah S Shemaiah דליהובנשמעיהו | AAA-2, AA-2 (24) | High official in Jehoiakim's court |
| 34 | | Elihu S Barachel אליהובנברכאל | AAA-4 (32) | Speaker in Job chapter 32 |
| 35 | | Elihu S Shemaiah אליהובנשמעיה | AAA-4, A-1 (34) | Korahite gatekeeper (1 Chr 26:7) |
| 36 | | Elijah S Harim אליהובנחרם | AAA-2, AA-1, A-4 (28) | Returned from Babylon after Exile |
| 37 | | Elijah S Hilkiah אליהובנחלקיה | AAA-3 (24) | Ancestor of Judith |
| 38 | | Elioneai S Neariah אליועניבננעריה | AAA-3, A-2 (28) | Descendent of Jehoiachin (1 Chr 3:23) |
| 39 | | Eliphelet S David אליפלטבנדוד | AAA-3 (24) | King David's son |

## Coding in Psalm 51

| Item | Rank in 929 | Name | Groups by Values and (Points) | Description from Scripture and other sources |
|---|---|---|---|---|
| 40 | | Elishama S David אלישמצבנדויד | AAA-3, A-5 (34) | King David's son |
| 41 | | Elishama S Jekamiah, Scribe אלישמעבניקמיה | AAA-4, A-3 (38) | Descendent in the tribe of Judah (1 Chr 2:41) |
| 42 | | Elishua S David אלישועבנדויד | AAA-2, AA-3 (28) | King David's son |
| 43 | | Elizaphan S Parnach אליצפנבנפרנך | AAA-3, A-2 (28) | Time of Moses, leader of Ephraim (Num 34:25) |
| 44 | 2 | Ezekiel, etc. יחזקאלבנבוזי | AAA-4, A-11 (54) | Exilic prophet |
| 45 | 2 | Ezekiel Sarpuhi יחזקלשרפוהי | AAA-4, A-5 (42) | E was Suffering Servant of Isa 53, died about 559 |
| 46 | 1 | Ezra, etc. עזראבנשריה | AAA-11, AA-2, A-4 (104) | Exilic contemporary of Jacob, 104 points |
| 47 | | Gemariah S Hilkiah גמריהובנחלקיהו | AAA-4 (32) | Emissary to Babylon, friend to Jeremiah |
| 48 | 1 | Gemariah S Shaphan גמריהובנשפן | AAA-6, A-1 (50) | Official of Jehoiakim friendly to Jeremiah |
| 49 | | Gershom S Levi גרשומבנלוי | AAA-3, A-2 (28) | Head of early Levitical family |
| 50 | | Gershom S Moses גרשמבנמשה | AAA-3 (24) | One of three sons of Moses |
| 51 | | Hashabiah S Amazi חשביהבנאמציה | AAA-4, AA-2 (36) | Levite, ancestor of a musician in sanctuary |

## Appendix Three

| Item | Rank in 929 | Name | Groups by Values and (Points) | Description from Scripture and other sources |
|---|---|---|---|---|
| 52 |  | Hashabiah S Kemuel<br>חשביהבנקמואל | AAA-4, A-5 (42) | Chief of Levites under David |
| 53 |  | Hezekiah S Ahaz<br>חזקיהובנאחז | AAA-5, AA-1, A-1 (46) | King of Judah 715–687 |
| 54 |  | Hilkiah S Amzi<br>חלקיהובנאמצי | AAA-4, A-3 (38) | Levite predating David |
| 55 |  | Hilkiah S Shallum<br>חלקיהובנשלום | AAA-7, AA-1 (60) | High priest under Josiah, ancestor of Ezra |
| 56 |  | Huldah, etc.<br>חלדהאשתשלם | AAA-2, AA-1, A-2 (24) | Prophetess who advised King Josiah |
| 57 |  | Isaiah S Amoz<br>ישעיהובנאמוץ | AAA-4, AA-1, A-2 (40) | Eighth-century prophet |
| 58 |  | Isaiah S Athaliah<br>ישעיהובנעתליה | AAA-3, AA-1, A-1 (30) | Head of family that returned from Babylon |
| 59 |  | Isaiah S Eliezer<br>ישעיהובנאליעזר | AAA-5, A-2 (42) | Family in charge of dedicated gifts in temple |
| 60 |  | Isaiah S Jeduthun<br>ישעיהבנידותון | AAA-7 (56) | Head of a division of temple singers |
| 61 |  | Ishmerai S Elpaal<br>ישמריבנאלפעל | AAA-4, AA-1, A-1 (38) | A Benjaminite (1 Chr 8:18) |
| 62 |  | Ishvi S Saul<br>ישיובנשאול | AAA-3 (24) | Son of King Saul |

## Coding in Psalm 51

| Item | Rank in 929 | Name | Groups by Values and (Points) | Description from Scripture and other sources |
|---|---|---|---|---|
| 63 | | Ithream S David & Eglah<br>יתרעמבנעגלה,<br>יתרעמבבנדוד | AAA-6,<br>AA-2,<br>A-3 (62) | King David's son |
| 64 | | Jaazaniah S Tobshillem<br>יאזניהבנטבשלם | AAA-4, A-1 (34) | (T. from Lachish letter) |
| 65 | 1 | Jacob-Israel, etc.<br>יעקבבנשלמות | AAA-16,<br>AA-2, A-18 (172) | Prophet Second Isaiah, second highest point total |
| 66 | 1 | Jehizkiah S Shallum<br>יחזקיהובנשלם | AAA-7, A-5 (66) | A chief of Ephraim, 66 points |
| 67 | 16 | Jehoiachin, etc.<br>כניהובנאליקים | AAA-4, A-4 (40) | King of Judah exiled in Babylon |
| 68 | 3 | Jehoiachin Sarpuhi<br>יכניהשרפוהי | AAA-5, A-3 (46) | Died a substitute king in 562 |
| 69 | | Jehosaphat S Asa<br>יהושפטבנאסא | AAA-3, A-4 (32) | Ninth-century king of Judah |
| 70 | | Jehucal S Shelemiah<br>יהוכלבנשלמיהו | AAA-4 (32) | Courtier of King Zedekiah |
| 71 | 6 | Jeremiah, etc.<br>ירמיהבנחלקיהו | AAA-5, A-3 (46) | Exilic prophet |
| 72 | | Jeremoth S Becher<br>ירימותבנבכר | AAA-3 (24) | In Benjaminite genealogy (1 Chr 7:8) |
| 73 | | Jeremoth S Elpaal<br>ירמותבנאלפעל | AAA-4, A-3 (38) | Tribe of Benjamin (1 Chr 8:14) |
| 74 | | Jeremoth S Heman<br>ירמותבנהֵמן | AAA-5 (40) | Levite of "sons of Heman" |
| 75 | | Jeremoth S Zattu<br>ירמותבנזתוא | AAA-6, A-1 (50) | Had foreign wife at Restoration (Ezra 10:27) |

## Appendix Three

| Item | Rank in 929 | Name | Groups by Values and (Points) | Description from Scripture and other sources |
|---|---|---|---|---|
| 76 |  | Jonadab S Shimeah<br>יהונדבבנשמעא | AAA-4, A-5<br>(42) | Nephew of David, court intrigues |
| 77 |  | Jonathan S Abiathar<br>יונתנבנאביתר | AAA-3<br>(24) | Priest to King David, helps thwart Absalom's rebellion |
| 78 |  | Jonathan S Malluchi<br>יונתנבנמלוכי | AAA-5<br>(40) | Early fifth-century priest |
| 79 |  | Jonathan S Obed, Scribe<br>יונתנבנעבד,<br>יהונתנהספר | AAA-6,<br>AA-2, A-1<br>(54) | Uncle of King David, scribe in court |
| 80 |  | Jonathan S Saul<br>יונתנבנשאול | AAA-6<br>(48) | Saul's oldest son, close friend of David |
| 81 |  | Malchishua S Saul<br>מלכישועבנשאול | AAA-4<br>(32) | Youngest son of King Saul |
| 82 |  | Mattaniah S Pahatmoab<br>מתניהבנפחתמואב | AAA-4, A-1<br>(34) | Returning exile who married a foreign wife |
| 83 |  | Melchizadek<br>מלכיצדק | AAA-4,<br>AA-1, A-2<br>(40) | Represents Cyrus |
| 84 |  | Micaiah S Jehoshaphat<br>מיכיהובניהושפט | AAA-3, A-1<br>(26) | Ninth-century prince of Judah |
| 85 |  | Micaiah S Zaccur<br>מיכיהבנזכור | AAA-3<br>(24) | Prophet in northern kingdom under Ahab |
| 86 |  | Micaiah Father Achbor<br>מיכיהואביעכבור | AAA-3<br>(24) | Consults Huldah the prophetess for King Josiah |

## Coding in Psalm 51

| Item | Rank in 929 | Name | Groups by Values and (Points) | Description from Scripture and other sources |
|---|---|---|---|---|
| 87 | 2 | Nabonidus-Belshazzar בלשׁצר נבונאיד | AAA-5, AA-1, A-7 (58) | N was last king of Babylon 556–539, son B was regent |
| 88 | 10 | Nebuchadnezzar נבוכדנאצר | AAA-2, AA-1, A-3 (26) | King of Babylon 605–562 |
| 89 | | Nethaniah S Elishama נתניהובנאלישמע | AAA-5 (40) | Father of Ishmael who assassinated Gedeliah |
| 90 | | Obadiah S Azel עבדיהובנאצל | AAA-2, AA-1, A-3 (26) | A Benjaminite (1 Chr 9:44) |
| 91 | | Obadiah S Shemaiah עבדיהובנשמעיהו | AAA-3, A-2 (28) | Early returnee to Israel after Exile |
| 92 | | Pelaliah S Amzi פלליהבנאמצי | AAA-3, A-1 (26) | Priest of Ezra's time |
| 93 | 1 | Seraiah S Tanhumeth שריהבנתנחמת | AAA-8, A-2 (68) | A leader of Israel's forces during early Exile, 68 points |
| 94 | | Shammah S Agee the Hararite שמהבנאגאהררי | AAA-5 (40) | A top commander of David's forces |
| 95 | | Shammah S Jesse שמהבנישי | AAA-3 (24) | Brother of David |
| 96 | | Shammua S David & Bathsheba, שמועבנדוד שמועבנבתשוע | AAA-6, A-2 (52) | King David's son |
| 97 | | Shecaniah S Arah שכניהובנארח | AAA-3, A-3 (30) | Relative of enemy of Nehemiah |

## Appendix Three

| Item | Rank in 929 | Name | Groups by Values and (Points) | Description from Scripture and other sources |
|---|---|---|---|---|
| 98 | 1 | Shecaniah S Jahaziel<br>שכניהובניחזיאל | AAA-4 (32) | Returnee from the Exile |
| 99 | 1 | Shelemiah S Abdeel<br>שלמיהבנעבדאל | AAA-5, AA-1, A-3 (50) | Noble opposed to Jeremiah (Jer 36:26) |
| 100 | | Shelemiah S Cushi<br>שלמיהבנכושי | AAA-6, AA-1 (52) | Late seventh-century person |
| 101 | 1 | Shelemiah S Kore<br>שלמיהבנקורא | AAA-11, AA-1, A-2 (96) | Shelemiah comes from Jehoiachin tablet, 96 pts |
| 102 | | Shemaiah S Adonikam<br>שמעיהבנאדמיקם | AAA-4, A-1 (34) | To Israel from Babylon with Ezra |
| 103 | | Shemaiah S Elizaphan<br>שמיהובנאליצפן | AAA-4, A-2 (36) | Head of Levite clan in David's time |
| 104 | | Shemaiah S Harim<br>שמעיהבנחרם | AAA-2, AA-1, A-4 (28) | Priest who put away foreign wife after Exile |
| 105 | | Shemaiah S Jeduthun<br>שמעיהבנידותון | AAA-4, AA-1, A-1 (38) | Levite reformer in reign of Hezekiah |
| 106 | | Shemaiah S Joel<br>שמעיהבניואל | AAA-3, A-2 (28) | Person of Reubenite family |
| 107 | | Shemaiah S Nethanel, Scribe שמעיההספר, שמעיהבננתנאל | AAA-6, A-2 (52) | Levitical scribe for David |
| 108 | | Shemaiah S Shecaniah<br>שמעיהבנשכניה | AAA-3 (24) | Descendent of Jehoichin (1 Chr 3:22) |
| 109 | | Shemariah S Harim<br>שמריהובנחרם | AAA-5, A-2 (44) | Puts away foreign wife after Exile |

## Coding in Psalm 51

| Item | Rank in 929 | Name | Groups by Values and (Points) | Description from Scripture and other sources |
|---|---|---|---|---|
| 110 | | ShemariahS Rehoboam שמריהבנרחבעם | AAA-3 (24) | Son of tenth-century king of Judah |
| 111 | 1 | Shenazzar S Jehoiachin שנאצרבנכניהו | AAA-5, AA-1, A-4 (52) | In Babylon with his father Jehoiachin |
| 112 | 1 | Shephatiah S David & Abital, שפטיהבנדויד שפטיהבנאביטל | AAA-8, AA-1, A-8 (84) | King David's son, high point total |
| 113 | | Shephatiah S Jehoshaphat שפטיהובניהושפט | AAA-3 (24) | Son of ninth-century king of Judah |
| 114 | | Shephatiah S Maachah שפטיהבנמעכה | AAA-4, AA-1, A-1 (38) | Led tribe of Simeon in David's time |
| 115 | | Shephatiah S Mahalalel שפטיהבנמהללאל | AAA-3 (24) | Postexilic Judahite (Neh 11:4) |
| 116 | | Shephatiah S Mattan שפטיהובנמתן | AAA-3, AA-1, A-3 (34) | Tried to kill Jeremiah under King Zedekiah |
| 117 | | Shephatiah S Reul שפטיהובנרעואל | AAA-3, A-2 (28) | Ancestor of post-exilic Benjaminite family |
| 118 | | Shimea S David & Bathsheba שמעבנדויד, שמעאבנברשבע | AAA-4, AA-2, A-4 (48) | King David's son |
| 119 | 1 | Solomon S David & Bathsheba סלמהבנבתשוע, שלמהבנדוד | AAA-7, AA-1, A-3 (66) | King David's son, 66 points |

# Appendix Three

| Item | Rank in 929 | Name | Groups by Values and (Points) | Description from Scripture and other sources |
|---|---|---|---|---|
| 120 | | Uzziah S Amaziah<br>עזיהובנאמציהו | AAA-7<br>(56) | Eighth-century king of Judah |
| 121 | | Uzziah S Uriel<br>עזיהובנאוריאל | AAA-4, AA-4<br>(48) | A Levite of the sons of Kohath (1 Chr 6:24) |
| 122 | | Uzziah S Zechariah<br>עזיהובנזכריה | AAA-3<br>(24) | Jerusalemite at time of Nehemiah |
| 123 | | Zebadiah S Asahel<br>זבדיהבנעשהאל | AAA-4, A-1<br>(34) | Army officer in David's time |
| 124 | | Zebadiah S Elpaal<br>זבדיהובנאלפעל | AAA-3, AA-1, A-4 (36) | A Benjaminite (1 Chr 8:17) |
| 125 | | Zebadiah S Immer<br>זבדיהובנאמר | AAA-2, A-4<br>(24) | Put away foreign wife in Ezra's time |
| 126 | | Zebadiah S Ishmael<br>זבדיהבנישמעאל | AAA-7<br>(56) | Ninth-century judge under King Jehoshaphat |
| 127 | | Zebadiah S Meshelemiah<br>זבדיהובנמשלמיה | AAA-5, A-1<br>(42) | Levitical gatekeeper for David |
| 128 | | Zebadiah S Michael<br>זבדיהבנמיכאל | AAA-6, A-1<br>(50) | Head of family that returned with Ezra |
| 129 | 1 | Zedekiah K of Judah<br>צדקיהומלכיהודה | AAA-11, AA-1<br>(92) | Last king of Judah, exiled about 588, 92 points |
| 130 | 2 | Zedekiah Sarpuhi<br>צדקיהושרפוהי | AAA-4, A-1<br>(34) | Executed as substitute king |
| 131 | 4 | Zephaniah S Cushi<br>צפניהובנכושי | AAA-4, AA-1, A-6<br>(48) | Prophet who worked in Judah during Exile |

## Coding in Psalm 51

| Item | Rank in 929 | Name | Groups by Values and (Points) | Description from Scripture and other sources |
|---|---|---|---|---|
| 132 | | Zephaniah S Tahath שפטיהובנתחת | AAA-4, AA-1, A-1 (38) | On Levitical list of temple singers (1 Chr 6:36–37) |

## PART B: SELECTED CODED SPELLINGS FROM PSALM 51

These 808 spellings are grouped within 274 items. These are variations of twenty-two biblical names. Column four contains the athbash of column three. Use column six to trace the actual coding. It gives the coded sequence and text-word interval of the letters in column four. Picking item 1 for an example, word 6 of verse 8 has the first letter ב, and word 7 has ו, while word 4 of verse 10 contains the final letter ג. Item 1's other spelling begins at word 9-1, uses an interval of 1, and employs a slightly different sequence.

## Appendix Three

| Item | English | Hebrew | Hebrew Athbash | Value/ Spellings | First Sequence, Span, (Interval) | Other Spellings Verse-Word (Interval) |
|---|---|---|---|---|---|---|
| 1 | Ahaziah S Jehoram | אחזיהבנירם | להוניבחזהא | AAA/two | והוניבחזהא 8-6-10-4(1) | 9-1(1) |
| 2 | Ahaziah S Jehoram | אחזיהבנירם | זהבעיבהליד | AAA/three | זהבעיבהליד 5-6-6-10(1) | 5-7, 6-1(1) |
| 3 | Ahaziah S Jehoram | אחזיהבנירם | אתהבגהריוח | A/three | אתהבגהריוח 8-6-10-4(1) | 8-7, 9-1(1) |
| 4 | Ahaziah S Jehoram | אחזיהבנירם | עטבעגאנהחש | AAA/two | עטבעגאנהחש 3-7-10-2(4) | 5-7(4) |
| 5 | Ahaziah S Jehoram | אחזיהבנירם | בגרחאשתיחו | AAA/two | בגרחאשתיחו 5-6-10-2(3) | 6-2(3) |
| 6 | Ahihud S Shelomi | אחיהודבנישלמי | סהמפבצאהנבב | AAA/one | סהמפבצאהנבב 6-2-10-5(3) | |
| 7 | Ahihud S Shelomi | אחיהודבנישלמי | כאנמבואהרפק | A/two | כאנמבואהרפק 19-10-21-4(1) | 20-1(1) |
| 8 | Ahihud S Shelomi | אחיהודבנישלמי | אחיהודבלי | A/two | אחיהודבלי 8-4-10-2(1) | 8-5(1) |
| 9 | Ahihud S Shelomi | אחיהודבנישלמי | אחיהודבלי | A/thirteen | אחיהודבשירא 13-8-15-4(1) | 14-1-7; 15-1-5(1) |

## Coding in Psalm 51

| Item | English | Hebrew | Hebrew Athbash | Value/ Spellings | First Sequence, Span, (Interval) | Other Spellings Verse-Word (Interval) |
|---|---|---|---|---|---|---|
| 10 | Ahihud S Shelomi | אחיהודבשלמי | אתיכהואלשבמל | A/four | לאשרבוהורשו 6-2-7-2(1) | 6-3-5(1) |
| 11 | Ahihud S Shelomi | אחיהודבשלמי | אתיכהואלשבמל | A/ten | והבראחכולעט 18-5-19-8(1) | 18-6-8; 19-1-6(1) |
| 12 | Ahihud S Shelomi | אחיהודבשלמי | אתיכהואלשבמל | AAA/one | הכטואתהרגעם 6-11-12-2(3) | |
| 13 | Ahihud S Shelomi | אחיהודבשלמי | אתיכהואלשבמל | AAA/one | לבנותאאמהחו 5-6-10-2(3) | |
| 14 | Amariah S Hezekiah | אמריהבחזקיה | הטרץבלפמשרקת | AAA/one | סהואשפלברנתב 8-3-13-5(3) | |
| 15 | Amariah S Hezekiah | אמריהבחזקיה | הטרץבלפמשרקת | AAA/one | בסלפתפצטרירד 5-6-6-11(1) | |
| 16 | Amariah S Hezekiah | אמריהבחזקיה | הטרץבלפמשרקת | AAA/one | קיופנתמגבהב 8-3-13-5(3) | |
| 17 | Amariah S Hezekiah | אמריהבחזקיה | הטרץבלפמשרקת | AAA/four | םתיהכבהרששגל 8-5-10-4(1) | 8-6, 7; 9-1-6(1) |
| 18 | Amariah S Hezekiah | אמריהבחזקיה | הטרץבלפמשרקת | AAA/two | שנשמצבהכהבםו 9-3-11-3(1) | 10-2(1) |

## Appendix Three

| Item | English | Hebrew | Hebrew Athbash | Value/Spellings | First Sequence, Span, (Interval) | Other Spellings Verse-Word (Interval) |
|---|---|---|---|---|---|---|
| 19 | Amariah S Hezekiah | אמריהבןחזקיה | טמגיצבןמזקיה | AAA/one | ובנהשלמהרחבעם 6-3-7-4(1) | |
| 20 | Amariah S Hezekiah | אמריהבןחזקיה | טמגיצבןמזקיה | AAA/two | שלחמתןומחנהבק 9-3-11-3(1) | 9-5(1) |
| 21 | Azariah S Zephaniah | עזריהבןצפניה | רזגיהבןהפןיצ | AAA/one | רקדתהחתמתיץ 12-4-18-8(4) | |
| 22 | Azariah S Zephaniah | עזריהבןצפניה | רזגיהבןהפןיצ | AAA/two | אסמכנבהגמרוא 8-2-10-1(1) | 8-3(1) |
| 23 | Azariah S Zephaniah | עזריהבןצפניה | רזגיהבןהפןיצ | A/two | שבנבהגסאחלוא 2-9-6-5(2) | 3-6(2) |
| 24 | Azariah S Zephaniah | עזריהבןצפניה | רזגיהבןהפןיצ | AA/three | ובנשאךחתלשצת 14-3-16-2(1) | 14-4,5(1) |
| 25 | Azariah S Zephaniah | עזריהבןצפניה | רזגיהבןהפןיצ | AAA/two | הדכמבדאכמנהר 6-8-12-2(3) | 6-11(3) |
| 26 | Azariah S Zephaniah | עזריהבןצפנהיו | נגינפצכבנצתיו | AAA/ten | ונמשליצבבתסון 1-1-10-5(5) | 2-3,8; 3-4; 4-2; 5-2, 7; 6-5, 10; 7-4(5) |
| 27 | Azariah S Zephaniah | עזריהבןצפנהיו | נגינפצכבנצתיו | AAA/two | טפוחהגלועיערץ 10-4-19-5(5) | 11-3(5) |

## Coding in Psalm 51

| Item | English | Hebrew | Hebrew Athbash | Value/ Spellings | First Sequence, Span, (Interval) | Other Spellings Verse-Word (Interval) |
|---|---|---|---|---|---|---|
| 28 | Azariah S Zephaniah | עזריהצבניה | עגריהצבמיה | AAA/two | והצבניהעזר 6-2-7-2(1) | 6-4(1) |
| 29 | Azariah Scribe | עזריההספר | עגריההמפכ | AAA/one | ספרהעזריה 6-3-11(1) | |
| 30 | Azariah Scribe | עזריההספר | עגריההמפכ | AAA/two | בהואראטשע 8-6-10-1(1) | 8-7(1) |
| 31 | Azariah Scribe | עזריההספר | עגריההמפכ | A/one | גבוונעליזב 8-7-10-2(1) | |
| 32 | Azariah Scribe | עזריההספר | עגריההמפכ | A/two | אוסבבנוגב 9-3-10-5(1) | 9-3(2) |
| 33 | Azariah Scribe | עזריההספר | עגריההמפכ | AAA/two | ואגעשיו 14-6-16-1(1) | 14-7(1) |
| 34 | Azrikam S Azel | עזריקםבןאצל | עגריקמבמאצכ | AAA/four | בכבתוהוגרעצ 8-5-10-2(1) | 8-6, 7; 9-2(1) |
| 35 | Azrikam S Azel | עזריקםבןאצל | עגריקמבמאצכ | A/seven | העשלבכרוסט 13-7-15-2(1) | 13-8; 14-1-5(1) |
| 36 | Azrikam S Azel | עזריקםבןאצל | עגריקמבמאצכ | AAA/two | אצבבכבוהנוט 8-2-9-5(1) | 8-3(1) |

# Appendix Three

| Item | English | Hebrew | Hebrew Athbash | Value/ Spellings | First Sequence, Span, (Interval) | Other Spellings Verse-Word (Interval) |
|---|---|---|---|---|---|---|
| 37 | Azrikam S Azel | עזריקםאצל | בהצנוקמטסכ | AAA/two | בהצנוקמטסכ 8-2-9-5(1) | 8-3(1) |
| 38 | Azrikam S Azel | עזריקםאצל | בהצנגבמשעל | A/five | בהצנגבמשעל 6-2-7-1(1) | 6-3-6(1) |
| 39 | Azrikam S Azel | עזריקםאצל | סהטלגבעיצן | AAA/one | סהטלגבעיצן 9-3-11-1(1) | |
| 40 | Azrikam S Azel | עזריקםאצל | לעיסמטקה | AAA/three | לעיסמטקה 3-3-6-11(3) | 3-6, 4-2(3) |
| 41 | Azrikam S Azel | עזריקםאצל | מהעיטסמל | A/three | מהעיטסמל 3-5-5-2(1) | 3-6, 4-1(1) |
| 42 | Azrikam S Azel | עזריקםאצל | מהעיטסבמכ | AAA/six | מהעיטסבמכ 7-4-8-7(1) | 7-5, 6; 8-1-3(1) |
| 43 | Azrikam S Azel | עזריקםאצל | בהוריוסמד | A/four | בהוריוסמד 8-3-9-5(1) | 8-5-7(1) |
| 44 | Azrikam S Azel | עזריקםאצל | מהעיטנבסל | A/four | מהעיטנבסל 9-6-11-3(1) | 10-1-3(1) |
| 45 | Azrikam S Azel | עזריקםאצל | יאנצאהל | A/three | יאנצאהל 18-1-19-2(1) | 18-2, 3(1) |

## Coding in Psalm 51

| Item | English | Hebrew | Hebrew Athbash | Value/ Spellings | First Sequence, Span, (Interval) | Other Spellings Verse-Word (Interval) |
|---|---|---|---|---|---|---|
| 46 | Azrikam S Azel | עזריקםבנאצל | מזרוקבםאצכ | A/four | מבנהתואצ 19-6–20-5(1) | 19-9, 10; 20-1(1) |
| 47 | Azrikam S Azel | עזריקםבנאצל | יאנצבםקירזע | A/four | יאנבמהתק 20-1–21-3(1) | 20-2, 3, 5(1) |
| 48 | Baruch | ברוך | חרוד | AAA/six | לדוך 12-4–13-7(4) | 12-6, 8; 13-1(2), 2, 3(1) |
| 49 | Baruch S Neriah | ברוכבנריהו | יהרנבכורב | AAA/one | יהרנהתחולט 14-6–19-1(3) | |
| 50 | Baruch S Neriah | ברוכבנריהו | יהרנבכורב | AAA/two | יצאנוזרטיך 15-6–17-2(1) | 16-1(1) |
| 51 | Baruch S Neriah | ברוכבנריהו | יהרנבכורב | AAA/one | ברוכנהתונ 16-2–19-10(3) | |
| 52 | Baruch S Neriah Scribe | ברוכבנריהוהספר | רפסההוירנבכורב | AAA/one | ברוכנבטירפש 13-3–20-2(4) | |
| 53 | Baruch Scribe | ברוכהספר | רפסהכורב | A/two | ברוכפס 8-6–11-1(2) | 10-2(1) |
| 54 | Berechiah Scribe | ברכיהוהספר | רפסהוהיכרב | AAA/four | סברכיהופסנ 9-3–10-6(1) | 9-6; 10-1, 2(1) |

195

## Appendix Three

| Item | English | Hebrew | Hebrew Athbash | Value/ Spellings | First Sequence, Span, (Interval) | Other Spellings Verse-Word (Interval) |
|---|---|---|---|---|---|---|
| 55 | Berechiah Scribe | ברכיהוהספר | אמכטטחוזפעמ | A/one | והספרברכיה 6-2-11(1) | |
| 56 | Chimham | כמהם | תתהת | AA/nine | המהכ 7-5-10-1(5) | 7-5(3, 4); 8-2(1, 3), 3(1, 2), 4(1, 3) |
| 57 | Chimham S Barzillai | כמהםבברזלי | תתהתככשדאל | AAA/four | ההמכבבזלרלאי 9-3-11-1(1) | 9-4-6(1) |
| 58 | Chimham S David | כמהםבדוד | תתהתככעפע | AAA/two | כמהםבדוד 5-4-7-2(2) | 5-6(2) |
| 59 | Chimham S David | כמהםבדוד | תתהתככעפע | A/three | כמהםבדוד 14-6-16-1(1) | 14-7, 15-1(1) |
| 60 | Chimham S David | כמהםבדוד | תתהתככעפע | AAA/one | כמהםבדוד 8-4-9-5(1) | |
| 61 | Chimham S David | כמהםבדוד | תתהתככעפע | AAA/ two | כמהםבדוד 18-4-21-11(4) | 19-4(2) |
| 62 | Chimham S Jehoiachin | כמהםביהויכין | תתהתככמהוככן | AAA/one | כמהםביהויכין 3-2-9-3(4) | |
| 63 | Chimham S Jehoiachin | כמהםביהויכין | תתהתככמהוככן | A/five | כמהםביהויכין 8-4-10-3(1) | 8-5-7; 9-1(1) |

## Coding in Psalm 51

| Item | English | Hebrew | Hebrew Athbash | Value/ Spellings | First Sequence, Span, (Interval) | Other Spellings Verse-Word (Interval) |
|---|---|---|---|---|---|---|
| 64 | Chimham S Jehoiachin | ומכהמככיהו | וינכמננביאוה | A/eight | ויהככממכיו 14-5-16-3(1) | 14-6,7; 15-1-5(1) |
| 65 | Chimham S Jehoiachin | ומכהמככיהו | הוינכמננבאטס | A/one | הסטבננמכניוה 14-6-16-4(1) | |
| 66 | Chimham S Jehoiachin | ומכהמככיהו | הוישתרתהתנוש | AAA/one | ושתנתהתרתשיוה 16-2-20-3(3) | |
| 67 | Chimham S King | מככיהמכלו | ינכמננבות | AAA/one | תהמננכת 6-10-9-4(2) | |
| 68 | Chimham S King | מככיהמכלו | ושתרצוזיות | AAA/one | שעזיצרתושה 19-4-21-5(2) | |
| 69 | Chimham S King | מככיהמכלו | נענגנותעט | AAA/one | בתנגונעענב 6-7-10-4(3) | |
| 70 | Chimham Messiah | מכהמרתהו | הננבתרהחחה | A/one | התתחהבננתמ 8-4-9-5(1) | |
| 71 | Chimham Messiah | מכהמרתהו | התהבמנרצי | A/one | בנפמהצ-ת 2-8-3-7(1) | |
| 72 | Chimham Sarpuhi | מכהמשבלו | הנועמנבחנס | AAA/three | ומהנבנחשמו 8-4-9-6(1) | 8-5, 6(1) |

## Appendix Three

| Item | English | Hebrew | Hebrew Athbash | Value/ Spellings | First Sequence, Span, (Interval) | Other Spellings Verse-Word (Interval) |
|---|---|---|---|---|---|---|
| 73 | Cyrus | כורש | טפשי | A/three | טפשי<br>4-3-5-4(2) | 4-3(4), 5(2) |
| 74 | Cyrus | כורש | נפבז | AA/four | נפבז<br>8-1-9-4(4) | 8-5, 7; 9-2(2) |
| 75 | Cyrus | כורש | שעטם | A/four | שעטם<br>8-6-10-5(4) | 9-1(2), 3(2, 4) |
| 76 | Cyrus K Anshan | כורשבאנשן | לבעפיבתכסץ | AAA/one | לבעפיבתכסץ<br>5-6-8-2(2) | |
| 77 | Cyrus K Anshan | כורשבאנשן | הפנוהטפםק | AAA/two | הפנוהטפםק<br>8-1-9-4(1) | 8-3(1) |
| 78 | Cyrus K Anshan | כורשבאנשן | יבהלתזמהר | AA/one | יבהלתזמהר<br>9-3-11-1(1) | |
| 79 | Cyrus K Persia | כורשבפרס | שקטסאנגתשע | AAA/four | שקטסאנגתשע<br>7-6-10-5(2) | 8-2, 4, 6(2) |
| 80 | Cyrus K Persia | כורשבפרס | סטופדראש | A/three | סטופדראש<br>8-2-9-4(1) | 8-4, 5(1) |
| 81 | Cyrus K Persia | כורשבפרס | הסטנובכב | AAA/two | הסטנובכב<br>8-4-9-6(1) | 8-5(1) |

## Coding in Psalm 51

| Item | English | Hebrew | Hebrew Athbash | Value/ Spellings | First Sequence, Span, (Interval) | Other Spellings Verse-Word (Interval) |
|---|---|---|---|---|---|---|
| 82 | Cyrus K Babylon | כורשבבלה | נבבאהכרמא | AAA/one | וכרשבבכהנו 1-1-6-10(4) | |
| 83 | Cyrus K Babylon | כורשבבלה | נבבאהכרמא | AAA/one | שוהרהבכסמ 6-6-9-2(2) | |
| 84 | Cyrus K Babylon | כורשבבלה | נבבאהכרמא | AAA/six | שטיםנבאתרהלי 6-11-10-1(2) | 7-2, 4, 6, 8-2(2); 8-4(1) |
| 85 | Cyrus K Babylon | כורשבבלה | נבבאהכרמא | AAA/three | שיבהנאכתרהלל 8-5-10-2(1) | 8-7, 9-1(1) |
| 86 | Daniel Sarpuhi | דנאלשרפוהי | שומטנראבטמד | AAA/two | בהמדבנאפס 2-8-9-1(5) | 3-4(5) |
| 87 | Daniel Sarpuhi | דנאלשרפוהי | שומטנראבטמד | AAA/four | הבמצגנעמרכ 9-1-10-5(1) | 9-2, 3, 5(1) |
| 88 | Daniel Sarpuhi | דנאלשרפוהי | שומטנראבטמד | AAA/one | מטואסמלבאהר 9-1-10-5(1) | |
| 89 | Daniel Sarpuhi | דנאלשרפוהי | שומטנראבטמד | A/three | לאגתנאלמוד 6-1-6-11(1) | 6-2, 3(1) |
| 90 | Daniel Sarpuhi | דנאלשרפוהי | שומטנראבטמד | A/two | בהלבהמוסעט 3-2-4-5(1) | 3-3(1) |

## Appendix Three

| Item | English | Hebrew | Hebrew Athbash | Value/ Spellings | First Sequence, Span, (Interval) | Other Spellings Verse-Word (Interval) |
|---|---|---|---|---|---|---|
| 91 | Daniel Sarpuhi | דניאל/שרפוהי | כנמעל/בצרפויג | AAA/one | סנמעלבצרפויג 8-2-9-5(1) | |
| 92 | Ezekiel | יחזקאל | מחזבעל | A/five | בחזקנמ 5-6-6-4(2) | 5-6, 7(1); 6-1, 3(2) |
| 93 | Ezekiel | יחזקאל | מחזבעל | A/four | בחזקנמ 14-1-15-4(2) | 14-3(2); 15-2, 3(1) |
| 94 | Ezekiel | יחזקאל | מחזבעל | A/five | בחזקנמ 8-4-10-1(2) | 8-5-7; 9-1(1) |
| 95 | Ezekiel Alternate | שוזקאל | ושחבעלד | A/two | ושחזקלי 14-3-15-2(1) | 14-5(2) |
| 96 | Ezekiel Alternate | שוזקאל | ושחבעלד | A/two | שוטלקבה 10-2-11-2(1) | 10-3(1) |
| 97 | Ezekiel Alternate | שוזקאל | בעתוחנמ | A/five | ספתחנגמ 5-5-6-10(2) | 6-2, 3, 5-7(1) |
| 98 | Ezekiel Alternate | שוזקאל | פחותבני | A/four | חותנסבמ 10-3-11-3(1) | 10-4-6(1) |
| 99 | Ezekiel Alternate | שוזקאל | בכבופק | A/two | בהכבותמ 13-3-14-7(2) | 13-5(2) |

## Coding in Psalm 51

| Item | English | Hebrew | Hebrew Athbash | Value/ Spellings | First Sequence, Span, (Interval) | Other Spellings Verse-Word (Interval) |
|---|---|---|---|---|---|---|
| 100 | Ezekiel Alternate | שחזקאל | הזוכסב | AAA/three | הזוכסב 8-4-9-3(1) | 8-5,6(1) |
| 101 | Ezekiel S Buzi | יחזקאלבנבוזי | לבנגבלאקזחי | AAA/one | לבנגבלאקזחי 4-3-7-2(2) | |
| 102 | Ezekiel S Buzi | יחזקאלבנבוזי | הסבןבהלאקץעמ | AAA/one | הסבןבהלאקץעמ 10-1-11-6(1) | |
| 103 | Ezekiel S Buzi | יחזקאלבנבוזי | הבשאקלעתיוצ | A/two | הבשאקלעתיוצ 9-2-11-1(1) | 9-3(1) |
| 104 | Ezekiel S Buzi | יחזקאלבנבוזי | הנבהיתהוחה | A/one | הנבהיתהוחה 6-3-7-3(1) | 6-4-6(1) |
| 105 | Ezekiel S Buzi | יחזקאלבנבוזי | צטפוהיהדנס | AAA/one | צטפוהיהדנס 3-3-9-4(4) | |
| 106 | Son of Man | בנאדם | משלב | A/five | משלב 8-5-10-4(3) | 8-6(2), 7; 9-1(3), 3(1) |
| 107 | Ezekiel Sarpuhi | יחזקאלפרחי | הבבהוהאטרעמ | A/two | הבבהוהאטרעמ 8-3-10-1(1) | 8-4(1) |
| 108 | Ezekiel Sarpuhi | יחזקאלפרחי | לגוהאבהקרחה | AAA/three | לגוהאבהקרחה 4-5-9-2(3) | 5-3,6(3) |

## Appendix Three

| Item | English | Hebrew | Hebrew Athbash | Value/ Spellings | First Sequence, Span, (Interval) | Other Spellings Verse-Word (Interval) |
|---|---|---|---|---|---|---|
| 109 | Ezekiel Sarpuhi | חזקיאלצרפוהי | לחשגיטלרנבטו | A/four | טבנובאריעש 8-4-10-2(1) | 8-5-7(1) |
| 110 | Ezekiel Sarpuhi | חזקיאלצרפוהי | אודיטשתאהמו | A/seven | נשאהריאתגבל 4-2-6-1(1) | 4-3-5; 5-1-3(1) |
| 111 | Ezekiel Sarpuhi | חזקיאלצרפוהי | אודיטשתאהמו | A/nine | עשויאתאלימעו 8-5-10-3(1) | 8-6, 7; 9-1-6(1) |
| 112 | Ezekiel Sarpuhi | חזקיאלצרפוהי | גהצלאסבאנמחז | AAA/one | אתהבלתיהאחד 8-7-10-5(1) | |
| 113 | Ezekiel Sarpuhi | חזקיאלצרפוהי | טלהרתשוגבנגס | A/two | כסבבננב תתרה ל 8-2-9-6(1) | 8-3(1) |
| 114 | Ezekiel Sarpuhi | חזקיאלצרפוהי | בקרהוטש ופיצ | AAA/one | דברסטופררהו 12-4-18-4(4) | |
| 115 | Ezekiel Sarpuhi | חזקיאלצרפוהי | הרפקנצבארטס | AAA/one | הלכהנצבאדרש 19-10-21-4(1) | |
| 116 | Ezra | עזרא | סבבה | A/four | בהמכ 2-6-4-2(4) | 2-8(2), 9(3); 3-3(1) |
| 117 | Ezra | עזרא | כהחט | A/ten | נתחנ 7-4-8-4(2) | 7-4(4), 5(3), 6(4); 8-2(1, 2, 3), 3(1), 4(1, 2) |

## Coding in Psalm 51

| Item | English | Hebrew | Hebrew Athbash | Value/ Spellings | First Sequence, Span, (Interval) | Other Spellings Verse-Word (Interval) |
|---|---|---|---|---|---|---|
| 118 | Ezra | עזרא | בסומ | A/four | בסומ<br>8-5-11-1(5) | 9-1-3(1) |
| 119 | Ezra | עזרא | בסמד | A/five | בסמד<br>16-8-17-3(1) | 16-8;17-1(3),<br>3(1, 2) |
| 120 | Ezra S Seraiah | עזראבשריה | בסומלוארטצ | AAA/one | בסומלוארטצ<br>5-6-9-5(3) | |
| 121 | Ezra S Seraiah | עזראבשריה | בסומלבהטצ | AAA/one | בסומלבהטצ<br>3-4-9-6(5) | |
| 122 | Ezra S Seraiah | עזראבשריה | בסומלבהטצ | AAA/one | בסומלבהטצ<br>8-3-9-5(1) | |
| 123 | Ezra S Seraiah | עזראבשריה | בסומלבהטצ | AAA/two | בסומלבהטצ<br>10-6-12-4(1) | |
| 124 | Ezra S Seraiah | עזראבשריה | בסומלות | AAA/one | בסומלות<br>8-2-9-4(1) | 8-3(1) |
| 125 | Ezra Priest Scribe | עזראהכהנהספר | בסומאהכהנאצפט | AAA/one | בסומאהכהנאצפט<br>2-9-7-3(3) | |
| 126 | Ezra Priest Scribe | עזראהכהנהספר | בסומאהכהנאצפט | AAA/one | בסומאהכהנאצפט<br>6-11-10-3(2) | |

## Appendix Three

| Item | English | Hebrew | Hebrew Athbash | Value/ Spellings | First Sequence, Span, (Interval) | Other Spellings Verse-Word (Interval) |
|---|---|---|---|---|---|---|
| 127 | Ezra Priest Scribe | עזראהכהןהספר | אטזרגהלגמגהמפז | AAA/four | בסהנוטשטפא 11-2-15-5(3) | 11-5, 12-2(3), 14-1(1) |
| 128 | Ezra Priest Scribe | עזראהכהןהספר | אטזרגהלגמגהמפז | AAA/one | שטפאבסהנוט 14-1-15-5(1) | |
| 129 | Ezra Priest Scribe | עזראהכהןהספר | אטזרגהלגמגהמפז | AAA/one | בסהנוטשטפאג 9-5-12-9(2) | |
| 130 | Ezra Priest | עזראהכהן | שטגרגאת | AA/seven | שטגרגאת 14-3-16-4(2) | 14-3, 4, 6, 7; 15-1, 2(1) |
| 131 | Ezra Scribe | עזראהספר | המפזרגאת | AAA/six | המפזרגאת 8-4-10-5(2) | 8-4-7; 9-1(1) |
| 132 | Ezra Scribe | עזראהספר | המפזרגאת | AA/four | המפזרגאת 8-5-9-5(1) | 8-6, 7; 9-1(1) |
| 133 | Israel | ישראל | מטרגאת | A/one | מטרגאת 8-3-9-4(2) | |
| 134 | Israel S Shelomoth | ישראלבןשלמות | הסכצאגברלנומט | A/four | הסכצאגברלנומט 8-4-10-2(1) | 8-5, 6; 9-1(1) |
| 135 | Israel S Shelomoth | ישראלבןשלמות | הסכצאגברלנומט | A/four | הסכצאגברלנומט 14-4-16-2(1) | 14-5-7(1) |

## Coding in Psalm 51

| Item | English | Hebrew | Hebrew Athbash | Value/ Spellings | First Sequence, Span, (Interval) | Other Spellings Verse-Word (Interval) |
|---|---|---|---|---|---|---|
| 136 | Israel S Shelomoth | ישראלבןשלמות | בגרשאלבןחלנוט | AAA/four | בשראלבןשלמות 4-1-6-11(2) | 4-3, 5; 5-2(2) |
| 137 | Israel S Shelomoth | ישראלבןשלמות | בגרשאלבןחלנוט | AAA/one | בגרשאלבןחלנוט 8-3-10-1(1) | |
| 138 | Israel S Shelomoth | ישראלבןשלמות | טוכןהבלאעגי | AAA/two | חהנבעטלבנ2-9-6(1) | 8-3(1) |
| 139 | Israel S Shelomoth | ישראלבןשלמות | שראבןשלמוה | A/four | שראבןשלמוה 19-1-20-2(1) | 19-2-4(1) |
| 140 | Jacob S Isaac | יעקבבןיצחק | סאגחאטביצן | AAA/two | אסבגטםאוס 8-2-9-4(1) | 8-3(1) |
| 141 | Jacob S Isaac | יעקבבןיצחק | הבתקהןתוקפ | AAA/two | לבתקהןתוקפ 12-4-17-6(4) | 13-3(4) |
| 142 | Jacob S Isaac | יעקבבןיצחק | שנתודרילרע | AAA/four | לרעינודרותש 16-1-17-3(1) | 16-2-4(1) |
| 143 | Jacob S Isaac | יעקבבןיצחק | גמותההלבגע | A/one | גמותההלבגע 8-7-10-4(1) | |
| 144 | Jacob S Isaac | יעקבבןיצחק | בלהנונותל | AAA/one | בלהנונותל 6-2-11(1) | |

# Appendix Three

| Item | English | Hebrew | Hebrew Athbash | Value/ Spellings | First Sequence, Span, (Interval) | Other Spellings Verse-Word (Interval) |
|---|---|---|---|---|---|---|
| 145 | Jacob S Isaac | יעקבבןיצחק | סוסנבנדרעט | AAA/one | ובתחתיות 8-1-9-4(1) | |
| 146 | Jacob Prophet | יעקבנביא | סוסנמטמא | AAA/one | ובנסעתה 6-5-8-4(2) | |
| 147 | Jacob Prophet | יעקבנביא | סוסנמטמא | A/one | ובנמרתפס 10-1-11-3(1) | |
| 148 | Jacob | יעקב | בנסט | AA/ten | בעלה 2-6-3-6(3) | 2-8(4), 9(3); 3-3(2), 4(1, 2), 5(1, 2), 6(1); 4-1(1) |
| 149 | Jacob | יעקב | בנסט | A/four | כאלם 3-7-6-3(5) | 4-3, 5(2); 5-2(1) |
| 150 | Jacob | יעקב | בנסט | A/nine | הכבע 6-1-7(2) | 6-1(1, 5), 2(1, 4), 3(2, 4), 7(3), 9(2) |
| 151 | Jacob | יעקב | בנסט | A/three | בספא 6-7-8-2(4) | 6-11(2), 8-1(1) |
| 152 | Jacob | יעקב | חנטן | A/twelve | החן 7-4-9-6(5) | 7-4(3), 5(3, 5); 8-1, 2, 4, 5(3), (1); 9-1(1, 2), 3(1) |
| 153 | Jacob | יעקב | מטסא | A/five | אספו 7-6-10-2(5) | 8-2(3); 9-1-3(1) |

## Coding in Psalm 51

| Item | English | Hebrew | Hebrew Athbash | Value/ Spellings | First Sequence, Span, (Interval) | Other Spellings Verse-Word (Interval) |
|---|---|---|---|---|---|---|
| 154 | Jacob | יעקב | לשפט | A/four | ביעקב 15-5-16-8(3) | 15-5,6; 16-7(1) |
| 155 | House of Jacob | ביעקב | בלשפט | AA/three | בהבעצג 3-4-4-3(1) | 3-7, 4-1(1) |
| 156 | House of Jacob | ביעקב | בלשפט | AAA/two | סבגבאא 4-4-5-5(1) | 4-5(1) |
| 157 | House of Jacob | ביעקב | בלשפט | AAA/one | סבסבאא 6-3-9-3(4) | |
| 158 | Seed of Jacob | זרעיעקב | דריעקב | AAA/two | דריעקב 6-4-10(1) | 6-5(1) |
| 159 | Seed of Jacob | זרעיעקב | דריעקבט | A/three | 'דריעקבט 7-5-9-4(2) | 8-1(2), 3(1) |
| 160 | Sons of Jacob | בןיעקב | קגאנבגב | AAA/one | קגאנבגב 3-2-7-2(5) | |
| 161 | Sons of Jacob | בןיעקב | שבמנתרט | AAA/one | שבמנתרט 6-6-10-6(5) | |
| 162 | Sons of Jacob | בןיעקב | התנתוט | A/two | התנתוט 10-4-11-4(1) | 10-5(1) |

## Appendix Three

| Item | English | Hebrew | Hebrew Athbash | Value/ Spellings | First Sequence, Span, (Interval) | Other Spellings Verse-Word (Interval) |
|---|---|---|---|---|---|---|
| 163 | Jacob S Shelomoth | יעקבשלמות | העשמנאכבסט | AAA/five | במבאנצמעט 8-4-11-5(2) | 8-6(2); 9-1(1, 2), 3(2) |
| 164 | Jacob S Shelomoth | יעקבשלמות | העצמלבדדה | A/five | המצבדרהב 6-2-7-1(1) | 6-3, 5-7(1) |
| 165 | Jacob S Shelomoth | יעקבשלמות | העצמלבדדה | A/four | בכבמעיטנף 9-2-10-6(1) | 9-4-6(1) |
| 166 | Jacob S Shelomoth | יעקבשלמות | העצמלבדדה | A/four | במהרהמעב 2-9-4-3(1) | 3-1-3(1) |
| 167 | Jacob S Shelomoth | יעקבשלמות | סמבגנהבשת | AAA/two | סמבגאהבמכף 9-4-11-2(1) | 9-5(1) |
| 168 | Jacob S Shelomoth | יעקבשלמות | בצהריושגת | A/four | יצטרבהתנה 6-5-7-4(1) | 6-6-8(1) |
| 169 | Jehizkiah S Shallum | יחזקיהושלם | החצאידסבגנ | AAA/three | הנבגדסבאכסיט 8-1-9-5(1) | 8-2, 3(1) |
| 170 | Jehizkiah S Shallum | יחזקיהושלם | החזדויאסמט | AAA/two | החזדויאהמטנכב 8-2-9-6(1) | 8-3(1) |
| 171 | Jehizkiah S Shallum | יחזקיהושלם | החזדויאסמט | AAA/one | דהגבבכבאטנחמיו 4-2-9-2(3) | |

## Coding in Psalm 51

| Item | English | Hebrew | Hebrew Athbash | Value/Spellings | First Sequence, Span, (Interval) | Other Spellings Verse-Word (Interval) |
|---|---|---|---|---|---|---|
| 172 | Jehizkiah S Shallum | יחזקיהובשלם | רגזעיהובשלא | AAA/one | לשבטיאסתרומ 3-4-12-3(5) | |
| 173 | Jehizkiah S Shallum | יחזקיהובשלם | רגזעיהובשלא | A/one | מםלבטעבמד 14-6-16-3(1) | |
| 174 | Jehizkiah S Shallum | יחזקיהובשלם | רגזעיהובשלא | AAA/five | הנבטבצבנוטם 6-1-11(1) | 6-2, 5-7(1) |
| 175 | Jehizkiah S Shallum | יחזקיהובשלם | רגזעיהובשלא | A/five | חטבנבעקרדה 6-3-7-2(1) | 6-4-7(1) |
| 176 | Jehizkiah S Shallum | יחזקיהובשלם | רגזעיהובשלא | AAA/four | תנוטגהוצאושח 8-6-10-4(1) | 8-7; 9-1, 2(1) |
| 177 | Jehizkiah S Shallum | יחזקיהובשלם | רגזעיהובשלא | A/two | קבדגהנרלה 16-6-18-3(1) | 16-7(1) |
| 178 | Jehizkiah S Shallum | יחזקיהובשלם | רגזעיהובשלא | A/one | םהסבטוחרה 8-1-9-5(1) | |
| 179 | Jehizkiah S Shallum | יחזקיהובשלם | רגזעיהובשלא | A/seven | הרכבושט 6-2-7-2(1) | 6-3-8(1) |
| 180 | Jehizkiah S Shallum | יחזקיהובשלם | רגזעיהובשלא | AAA/five | לשטהנואתבסט 8-4-10-2(1) | 8-5, 7; 9-1, 2(1) |

## Appendix Three

| Item | English | Hebrew | Hebrew Athbash | Value/ Spellings | First Sequence, Span, (Interval) | Other Spellings Verse-Word (Interval) |
|---|---|---|---|---|---|---|
| 181 | Jehoiachin S Jehoiakim | יהויכיןיהויקים | התוכךןהתוכמט | AAA/one | יהויכיןיהויקיםטו 7-3-9-3(1) | |
| 182 | Jehoiachin S Eliakim | יהויכיןאליקים | התוכךןאלוכמט | AAA/two | תאכמטןיכיוהי 7-6-9-5(1) | 8-1(1) |
| 183 | Jehoiachin S Eliakim | יהויכיןאליקים | התוכךןאלוכמט | AAA/two | התוכךןאליקית 8-6-10-5(1) | 9-1(1) |
| 184 | Jehoiachin | יכניה | פוממט | AAA/one | החנוכ 7-4-9-3(3) | |
| 185 | Jehoiachin | יכניה | התנוש | A/two | החנות 14-5-15-3(1) | 14-6(1) |
| 186 | Jehoiachin | יכניה | מלכבץ | A/one | מלכבץ 19-2-20-4(3) | |
| 187 | Jehoiachin (Coniah) | כניהו | אתנבץ | A/two | אתנבץ 15-2-16-8(3) | 15-5(3) |
| 188 | Jehoiachin (Coniah) | כניהו | התנכם | A/six | כנומה 8-2-9-3(2) | 8-3, 4(1), 4, 6(2); 9-1(2) |
| 189 | Jehoiachin Sarpuhi | שלהויכינו | הבכנתהטופ | AAA/one | הבכנתהטופ 3-2-4-5(1) | |

## Coding in Psalm 51

| Item | English | Hebrew | Hebrew Athbash | Value/ Spellings | First Sequence, Span, (Interval) | Other Spellings Verse-Word (Interval) |
|---|---|---|---|---|---|---|
| 190 | Jehoiachin Sarpuhi | יהויכינצרפוהי | האטיכמרציעטדי | AAA/one | לצרפוהיכין 6-1-11(1) | |
| 191 | Jehoiachin Sarpuhi | שיהויכינצרפוהי | בצטיכמרציעטדר | AAA/three | הסבטנמכתהרו 8-4-11-5(2) | 8-6, 9-1(2) |
| 192 | Jehoiachin Sarpuhi | יהויכנצרפוהי | האטיכרציעטדי | AAA/two | וסבנצעמט״י 9-1-12-1(2) | 9-6(1) |
| 193 | Jehoiachin Sarpuhi | יהויכינהצרפוהי | האטיכמרהציעטדי | A/four | יהבמרהונטאוי 14-6-16-5(1) | 14-7; 15-1, 2(1) |
| 194 | Jehoiachin Sarpuhi | יהויכינהצרפוהי | האטיכמרהציעטדי | A/three | יהוהרישיענב 15-4-17-2(1) | 15-5, 6(1) |
| 195 | Jehoiachin Sarpuhi | שיהויכינצרפוהי | בצטיכמרציעטדר | A/five | יהויבהש״ש 15-6-17-2(1) | 16-1-4(1) |
| 196 | Jehoiachin Sarpuhi | שיהויכינהצרפוהי | בצטיכמרהציעטדר | AAA/two | הסבטנמכתאל״רהוי 20-5-21-9(1) | 20-7(1) |
| 197 | Jeremiah | ירמיהו | הבמטאנ | A/two | הבמיה 3-6-4-4(1) | 3-7 (1) |
| 198 | Jeremiah | ירמיהו | הבמטאנ | A/three | הטסמב 8-4-10-1(2) | 8-6, 9-1(2) |

## Appendix Three

| Item | English | Hebrew | Hebrew Athbash | Value/ Spellings | First Sequence, Span, (Interval) | Other Spellings Verse-Word (Interval) |
|---|---|---|---|---|---|---|
| 199 | Jeremiah | ירמיהו | באכחמט | AAA/four | בהמצכא 3-1-4-4(2) | 3-2(1), 3, 5(2) |
| 200 | Jeremiah | ירמיה | הרמצכ | A/three | יבהרמ 17-2-6(1) | 17-3(1, 2) |
| 201 | Jeremiah S Hilkiah | ירמיהובןחלקיה | הרמצכובמגלוצכה | AAA/one | וחלקיהבןירמיהו 5-6-10-5(3) | |
| 202 | Jeremiah S Hilkiah | ירמיהובןחלקיא | הרמצכובמגלוצכא | AAA/five | בןחלקיהוירמיהו 4-4-10-1(3) | 7-6; 8-1-3(1) |
| 203 | Jeremiah Prophet | ירמיהונביא | הרמצכטמבצא | AAA/one | ירמיהוהנביא 6-1-6-11(1) | |
| 204 | Jeremiah Prophet | ירמיהונביא | הרמצכטמבצא | AAA/two | הנביאירמיהו 3-2-10-3(5) | 3-7(5) |
| 205 | Nabonidus | נבנאיד | מבמגיל | AAA/two | נאבוניד 10-4-11-4(1) | 10-5(1) |
| 206 | Nabonidus | נבנאיד | מבמגיל | A/two | לנבוניד 6-2-8-3(3) | 7-3(1) |
| 207 | Nabonidus | נבנאיד | מבמגיל | A/one | נבונידו 20-1-21-6(2) | |

## Coding in Psalm 51

| Item | English | Hebrew | Hebrew Athbash | Value/ Spellings | First Sequence, Span, (Interval) | Other Spellings Verse-Word (Interval) |
|---|---|---|---|---|---|---|
| 208 | King Nabonidus | מלכנבנאד | בנכנאנתנד | AAA/four | סמנתאנבכ 8-4-9-6(1) | 8-5-7(1) |
| 209 | King Nabonidus | מלכנבנאד | בנכנאנתנד | AAA/one | אטנבנאכתנ 5-3-6-5(1) | |
| 210 | King Nabonidus | מלכנבנאד | בנכנאנתנד | A/three | הנבמטילש 8-5-10-1(1) | 8-6,7(1) |
| 211 | King Nabonidus | מלכנבנאד | בנכנאנתנד | AAA/four | לשמוטענב 9-6-11-3(1) | 10-1,2,4(1) |
| 212 | Belshazzr | בלשאנצר | וגחהב | תחהנג 8-4-10-1(2) | 8-7; 9-2-6(1) |
| 213 | Belshazzr | בלשאנצר | וגחהב | A/one | הצגבד 7-5-9-2(2) | |
| 214 | Belshazzr | בלשאנצר | לחובה | AA/five | להסמט 10-4-12-2(2) | 10-6(2); 11-1-3(1) |
| 215 | Belshazzr | בלשאנצר | לחובה | A/three | הנצבמטיל 8-2-9-5(2) | 8-4,6(2) |
| 216 | King Belshazzr | מלכבלשאנ | אנתסבכלה | A/four | הנסאטבמלה 8-6-10-1(1) | 8-7; 9-2,3(1) |

## Appendix Three

| Item | English | Hebrew | Hebrew Athbash | Value/ Spellings | First Sequence, Span, (Interval) | Other Spellings Verse-Word (Interval) |
|---|---|---|---|---|---|---|
| 217 | King Belshazzr | בלשאצר | סבצארהן | AAA/two | מבלתאזרן 8-5-9-6(1) | 8-6(1) |
| 218 | Nebuchad-nezzar | נבכדראצר | קביכדרהטר | A/three | הלרטיבם 5-7-6-8(1) | 6-3, 6(1) |
| 219 | Nebuchad-nezzar | נבכדראצר | קביכדרהטר | AAA/two | בוראנכבנ 6-2-6-10(1) | 6-3(1) |
| 220 | Nebuchad-nezzar | נבכדראצר | קביכדרהטר | A/six | הנבכנבל 8-5-9-6(1) | 8-6, 7; 9-1, 2, 4(1) |
| 221 | Nebuchad-nezzar | נבכדראצר | קביכדרהטר | AAA/two | רעבנקד 6-2-6-10(1) | 6-4(1) |
| 222 | Nebuchad-nezzar | נבכדראצר | קביכדרהטר | A/two | לנבכנוהת 6-7-7-4(1) | 6-8(1) |
| 223 | Nebuchad-nezzar | נבכדראצר | קביכדרהטר | AA/five | קנאדטר 14-3-15-3(1) | 14-4-6; 15-1(1) |
| 224 | Shecaniah S Jahaziel | שכניהוחזיאל | הלכציונרבגפכנ | AAA/two | כנבלהנצצגיטיה 5-6-7-1(1) | 5-7(1) |
| 225 | Shecaniah S Jahaziel | שכניהוחזיאל | הטחשוחניתזרטב | AAA/one | סמהתחותחתרהוה 3-3-10-6(4) | |

## Coding in Psalm 51

| Item | English | Hebrew | Hebrew Athbash | Value/ Spellings | First Sequence, Span, (Interval) | Other Spellings Verse-Word (Interval) |
|---|---|---|---|---|---|---|
| 226 | Shecaniah S Jahaziel | שכניהובןיחזיאל | עכנטהוחנטחזטאל | AAA/two | טאכנטהוחנטחז 8-1-10-1(1) | 8-4(1) |
| 227 | Shecaniah S Jahaziel | שכניהובןיחזיאל | קעכנטהובניחזט | AAA/one | קעכנטהובניחזטחוט 13-4-21-9(5) | |
| 228 | Shelemiah S Abdeel | שלמיהובןעבדאל | שלמטהובנעבדאל | A/four | לשבנעובדאהט 1-1-2-9(1) | 1-2, 3; 2-1(1) |
| 229 | Shelemiah S Abdeel | שלמיהובןעבדאל | שלמטהובנעבדאל | A/four | בנעאדהובלט 8-4-10-2(1) | 8-5-7(1) |
| 230 | Shelemiah S Abdeel | שלמיהובןעבדאל | שלמטהובנעבדאל | AA/four | שלמטהובאנעבדט 14-4-16-2(1) | 14-5-7(1) |
| 231 | Shelemiah S Abdeel | שלמיהובןעבדאל | שלמטהובניא | AAA/two | קנהבלעצאנבהוט 16-8-21-2(3) | 20-2(1) |
| 232 | Shelemiah S Abdeel | שלמיהובןעבדאל | שלמטהובניאטל | AAA/three | אנובלעאסטנ 3-3-7-6(3) | 3-6, 4-2(3) |
| 233 | Shelemiah S Abdeel | שלמיהובןעבדאל | שלמטהובנעבדקה | AAA/one | בהבלקרנבאטוט 6-2-11-2(3) | |
| 234 | Shelemiah S Abdeel | שלמיהובןעבדאל | שלמטהובנא | A/seven | טנהבבנהלטמש 8-6-10-4(1) | 8-7; 9-1-5(1) |

## Appendix Three

| Item | English | Hebrew | Hebrew Athbash | Value/Spellings | First Sequence, Span, (Interval) | Other Spellings Verse-Word (Interval) |
|---|---|---|---|---|---|---|
| 235 | Shelemiah S Abdeel | שלמיהובנעבדאל | וסנרשיבוהבנגדאם | AAA/one | ובנעבדאלמשת 9-4-11-4(1) | |
| 236 | Shelemiah S Abdeel | שלמיהובנעבדאל | וסנרשיבוהבנגדאם | AAA/one | בכרעשבטלמשחוקפת 13-3-19-8(4) | |
| 237 | Solomon S Bathshb | שלמהבנבתשבע | ולשחהבנבשתע | A/six | הבמעלהבכרעלש 8-4-10-1(1) | 8-5-7; 9-1, 2(1) |
| 238 | Solomon S David | שלמהבנדוד | ונשחהבנפוף | AAA/two | ותתאעשמוט 8-4-9-5(1) | 8-6(1) |
| 239 | Solomon S David | שלמהבנדוד | ונשחהבנפוף | AA/five | וסנשאאמנבנ 8-6-10-1(1) | 8-7; 9-1-3(1) |
| 240 | Solomon S David | שלמהבנדוד | ונשחהבנפוף | AAA/three | אסודמנו 8-3-10-6(2) | 8-6, 7(1) |
| 241 | Solomon S David | שלמהבנדוד | ונשחהבנפוף | A/one | מהסאלבגן 8-7-10-2(1) | |
| 242 | Solomon S David | שלמהבנדוד | ונשחהבנפוף | AAA/four | בטנאהככב 5-1-6-2(1) | 5-2, 4, 5(1) |
| 243 | Solomon S David | שלמהבנדוד | ונשחהבנפוף | A/two | בטנאהככב 8-5-9-6(1) | 8-6(1) |

## Coding in Psalm 51

| Item | English | Hebrew | Hebrew Athbash | Value/ Spellings | First Sequence, Span, (Interval) | Other Spellings Verse-Word (Interval) |
|---|---|---|---|---|---|---|
| 244 | Solomon S David | שלמהבןדוד | בעלסגאזדוד | AAA/two | ובצעמעשה 7-6-12-2(3) | 8-3(3) |
| 245 | Solomon S David | שלמהבןדוד | בעלסגאזדוד | AAA/two | בפשעסמים 8-2-9-4(1) | 8-3(1) |
| 246 | Solomon S David | שלמהבןדוד | בעלסגאזדוד | AAA/one | נאהבתוכמשע 14-6-20-6(5) | |
| 247 | Zedekiah | צדקיהו | אסצמפו | AAA/eleven | נבמטם 7-6-8-5(1) | 8-1-7; 9-1-3(1) |
| 248 | Zedekiah K Judah | צדקיהומלךיהודה | אסצמפוהנלךמפוסמ | AAA/three | אסצמפוהנלךכב 7-6-9-6(1) | 8-1, 2(1) |
| 249 | Zedekiah K Judah | צדקיהומלךיהודה | אסצמפוהנלךכמפוסמ | AAA/four | נהמפסותונכסאן 8-1-10-1(1) | 8-2, 3, 5(1) |
| 250 | Zedekiah K Judah | צדקיהומלךיהודה | אסצמפוהנלךכמפוסמ | AAA/two | חתאנגסוףנמפוסאו 7-3-9-3(1) | 7-4(1) |
| 251 | King Zedekiah | צדקיהומלך | אסצמפוהנלך | AAA/five | נבמסותואס 8-1-9-3(1) | 8-2-5(1) |
| 252 | King Zedekiah | צדקיהומלך | אסצמפוהנלך | AA/six | סנותואנטש 8-3-9-5(1) | 8-5-7; 9-1, 2(1) |

217

## Appendix Three

| Item | English | Hebrew | Hebrew Athbash | Value/ Spellings | First Sequence, Span, (Interval) | Other Spellings Verse-Word (Interval) |
|---|---|---|---|---|---|---|
| 253 | King Zedekiah | צדקיהמלך | פטראתהיוכנב | AAA/one | בנכויהתארטפ 8-3-9-5(1) | |
| 254 | King Zedekiah | צדקיהמלך | הןאטביסעפ | AAA/three | פעסביטאןה 7-2-8-5(1) | 7-4,5(1) |
| 255 | King Zedekiah | צדקיהמלך | אסטמבנהות | AAA/seven | תוהנבמטסא 7-6-9-2(1) | 8-1,3-7(1) |
| 256 | King Zedekiah | צדקיהמלך | ותסטבאנש | AAA/one | שנאבטסתו 6-4-10-1(3) | |
| 257 | King Zedekiah | צדקיהמלך | שאנבתסעט | AAA/one | טעסתבנאש 8-3-9-5(1) | |
| 258 | King Zedekiah | צדקיהמלך | שאנבתסעט | AAA/one | שאנבתסעט 9-6-11-3(1) | |
| 259 | Zedekiah Sarpuhi | צדקיהשרפוהי | שןלתקראתןח | AAA/one | שבהקראתלחן 16-5-20-6(3) | |
| 260 | Zedekiah Sarpuhi | צדקיהשרפוהי | הוקאתןכבוטן | AAA/two | הטובכנתאקוה 8-5-10-3(1) | 8-6(1) |
| 261 | Zedekiah Sarpuhi | צדקיהשרפוהי | הוקאתוכבוטן | AAA/one | בנוטיטעאנתה 4-1-5-7(1) | |

## Coding in Psalm 51

| Item | English | Hebrew | Hebrew Athbash | Value/ Spellings | First Sequence, Span, (Interval) | Other Spellings Verse-Word (Interval) |
|---|---|---|---|---|---|---|
| 262 | Zedekiah Sarpuhi | צדקיהוספרי | אטקיהוספרף | AAA/six | וספרהוטאסדנפ 6-5-11-2(3) | 6-8,11; 7-3, 6; 8-3(3) |
| 263 | Zedekiah Sarpuhi | צדקיהוספרי | אטקיהוספרף | A/four | וספרהוטאסדנפ 8-4-10-2(1) | 8-5-7(1) |
| 264 | Zephaniah | צפניה | הקנץל | A/two | לקנץ 6-2-10(2) | 6-6(1) |
| 265 | Zephaniah | צפניה | הקנץל | AA/three | השנכט 10-1-11-3(2) | 10-2(3), 3(2) |
| 266 | Zephaniah | צפניהו | הקנץלו | AAA/four | הגמצת 10-1-6(1) | 10-2-4(1) |
| 267 | Zephaniah | צפניה | הקנץל | A/seven | להטון 14-2-14-5(1) | 14-4, 5, 7; 15-1, 3, 4(1) |
| 268 | Zephaniah | צפניהו | הקנץלו | A/two | םהוטצ 8-3-10-5(3) | 8-6(3) |
| 269 | Zephaniah | צפניה | הקנץל | A/seven | הסנה 8-1-9-6(3) | 8-2(2), 4(1, 3), 5-7(1) |
| 270 | Zephaniah | צפניה | הקנץל | A/four | הנקם 6-11-8-6(3) | 8-1-3(1) |

| Item | English | Hebrew | Hebrew Athbash | Value/ Spellings | First Sequence, Span, (Interval) | Other Spellings Verse-Word (Interval) |
|---|---|---|---|---|---|---|
| 271 | Zephaniah | צפניה | הפטיץ | A/three | סופין<br>9-3-10-5(2) | 10-1, 3(2) |
| 272 | Zephaniah S Cushi | צפניהבנכושי | אבטיהבנמהפטיס | AAA/two | בכמהפטנאמטסטה<br>6-5-9-3(2) | 6-7(2) |
| 273 | Zephaniah S Cushi | צפניהבנכושי | אבטיהבנמהפטיס | AAA/one | אבטיהבנמהפטסט<br>3-2-4-5(1) | |
| 274 | Zephaniah S Cushi | צפניהבנכושי | הזדחוהבצנאבכה | AAA/one | וצנאבכההזדחות<br>16-7-18-4(1) | |

# Appendix Four—Coding of Exilic Names in Hebrew Scripture

This shows chi-square analyses of coding points for thirty-six exilic names divided by chapter text words for all OT chapters. Any P value ≤ .01 is a statistically significant result. The symbol # indicates ≤ .01 ≥ 9 x $10^{-7}$, while + indicates ≤ 9 x $10^{-7}$. The symbol / stands for "son of." Shading shows names, BCE years, and codes that could help to establish dates. Shaded chapter numbers indicate probable School of Daniel origin.

## Appendix Four

| Book, Chapter | Ahaziah/Jehoram: 175 hits | Ahihud/Shelomi: 153 | Amariah/Hezekiah: 191 | Azariah/Amaziah: 185 | Azariah/Zephaniah: 147 | Azrikam/Azel: 161 | Baruch: 194 | Chimham/Jehoiachin: 204 | Chimham-Sarpuhi: 152 | Cyrus: 155 | Daniel: 249 | Daniel-Sarpuhi: 177 | Ezekiel-Son of Man: 174 | Ezra: 191 | Gemariah/Shaphan: 157 | Jacob-Israel: 198 | Jehizkiah/Shallum: 171 | Jehoiachin: 183 |
|---|---|---|---|---|---|---|---|---|---|---|---|---|---|---|---|---|---|---|
| Gen |  |  |  |  |  |  |  |  |  |  |  |  |  |  |  |  |  |  |
| 1 |  |  |  |  |  |  |  |  |  |  |  |  |  |  |  |  |  |  |
| 2 |  |  |  |  |  |  |  |  | # |  |  |  |  |  |  |  |  |  |
| 3 |  |  |  |  |  | # |  |  |  |  |  |  |  |  |  |  |  |  |
| 4 |  |  |  |  |  |  |  |  |  |  |  |  |  |  |  |  |  |  |
| 5 |  |  |  |  |  |  |  |  |  |  |  |  |  |  |  |  |  |  |
| 6 |  |  |  |  |  |  |  |  |  |  |  |  |  |  |  |  |  |  |
| 7 |  |  |  |  |  |  |  |  |  |  |  |  |  |  |  |  |  |  |
| 8 |  |  |  |  |  |  |  |  |  |  |  |  |  |  |  |  |  |  |
| 9 |  |  |  |  |  |  |  |  |  |  |  |  |  |  |  |  |  |  |
| 10 |  |  |  |  |  |  |  | # |  |  |  |  | + | # |  |  |  | # |
| 11 |  |  |  |  |  |  |  |  |  |  |  |  |  |  |  |  |  |  |
| 12 |  |  |  |  |  |  |  |  | # |  |  |  |  |  |  |  |  |  |
| 13 |  |  | + | # |  |  | # |  |  |  |  |  |  |  |  |  |  |  |
| 14 |  |  |  |  |  |  |  |  |  |  |  |  |  |  |  |  |  |  |
| 15 |  |  |  |  |  |  |  |  |  |  |  |  |  |  |  |  |  |  |
| 16 |  |  |  |  |  |  |  |  |  |  |  |  |  |  |  |  |  |  |
| 17 |  |  |  |  |  |  |  |  |  |  |  |  |  |  |  |  |  |  |
| 18 |  |  | # |  | # |  |  |  |  |  |  |  |  |  |  |  | # |  |
| 19 |  |  | # | # |  | + | # |  |  | + |  | + | # |  |  |  |  |  |
| 20 |  |  |  |  |  |  |  |  |  |  |  |  |  |  |  |  |  |  |
| 21 |  |  |  |  |  |  |  |  |  |  |  |  |  |  |  |  |  |  |
| 22 |  |  |  |  |  |  |  |  |  |  |  |  |  |  |  |  |  |  |
| 23 |  |  |  |  |  |  |  |  |  |  |  |  |  |  |  |  |  |  |
| 24 |  |  |  |  | # |  |  |  |  |  |  |  |  |  |  |  |  |  |

## Coding of Exilic Names in Hebrew Scripture

| Book, Chapter | Jehoiakim-Sarpuhi: 146 Hits | Jeremiah: 194 | Seraiah/Tanhumeth: 172 | Shecaniah/Jahaziel: 179 | Shelemiah/Abdeel: 148 | Shelemiah/Kore: 223 | Shenazzar/Jehoiachin: 165 | Shephatiah/David: 189 | Solomon/David: 165 | Substitute King: 138 | Zedekiah: 184 | Zedekiah-Sarpuhi: 175 | Zephaniah: 184 | Nebchdnzr: 168 (605–562) | Ezekiel-Sarpuhi: 179 (569) | Jehoiachin-Sarp: 160 (561) | Nab–Belshzr: 186 (556–39) | Cyrus K Bab: 159 (539–30) | Chapter Hits, Book Percent |
|---|---|---|---|---|---|---|---|---|---|---|---|---|---|---|---|---|---|---|---|
| Gen |   |   |   |   |   |   |   |   |   |   |   |   |   |   |   |   |   |   | 7% |
| 1 | # |   |   |   |   |   |   |   |   |   |   |   |   |   |   |   |   |   | 1 |
| 2 |   |   |   |   |   |   |   |   |   |   |   |   |   |   |   |   |   |   | 1 |
| 3 |   |   |   |   |   |   |   |   |   |   |   |   |   |   |   |   |   |   | 1 |
| 4 |   |   |   |   |   |   |   |   |   |   |   |   |   |   |   |   |   |   |   |
| 5 |   |   |   |   |   |   |   |   |   |   |   |   |   |   |   |   |   |   |   |
| 6 |   |   |   |   |   |   |   |   |   |   |   |   |   |   |   |   |   |   |   |
| 7 |   |   |   |   |   |   |   | # |   |   |   |   |   |   |   |   |   |   | 1 |
| 8 |   |   |   |   |   |   |   |   |   |   |   |   |   |   |   |   |   |   |   |
| 9 |   |   |   |   |   |   |   |   |   |   |   |   |   |   |   |   |   |   |   |
| 10 | + |   |   |   | # |   |   | + |   | # |   | # |   |   | + | # | + |   | 12 |
| 11 |   |   |   |   |   |   |   |   |   |   |   |   |   |   |   |   |   |   |   |
| 12 | # |   |   |   |   |   |   |   |   |   |   |   |   |   |   |   |   | # | 3 |
| 13 |   |   |   | + |   |   |   | # |   |   |   |   |   |   |   |   |   |   | 5 |
| 14 | + |   |   |   |   |   |   |   |   |   |   |   |   |   |   |   |   |   | 1 |
| 15 |   |   |   |   |   |   |   |   |   |   |   |   |   |   |   | # |   |   | 1 |
| 16 |   |   |   |   |   |   |   |   |   |   |   |   |   |   |   |   |   |   |   |
| 17 |   |   |   |   |   |   |   |   |   |   |   |   |   |   |   |   |   |   |   |
| 18 |   |   |   |   |   |   |   |   |   |   |   |   |   |   |   |   |   |   | 3 |
| 19 | # |   | # |   |   | + |   | # |   |   |   | # |   |   |   |   |   |   | 12 |
| 20 |   |   |   |   |   |   |   |   |   |   |   |   |   |   |   |   |   |   |   |
| 21 |   |   | # |   |   |   |   |   |   |   |   |   |   |   |   |   |   |   | 1 |
| 22 |   |   |   |   |   |   |   |   |   |   |   |   |   |   |   |   |   |   |   |
| 23 |   | # |   |   |   |   |   |   |   |   |   |   |   |   |   |   |   |   | 1 |
| 24 |   |   |   |   |   |   |   |   |   |   |   |   |   |   |   |   |   |   | 1 |

## Appendix Four

| Book, Chapter | Ahaziah/Jehoram: 175 hits | Ahihud/Shelomi: 153 | Amariah/Hezekiah: 191 | Azariah/Amaziah: 185 | Azariah/Zephaniah: 147 | Azrikam/Azel: 161 | Baruch: 194 | Chimham/Jehoiachin: 204 | Chimham–Sarpuhi: 152 | Cyrus: 155 | Daniel: 249 | Daniel–Sarpuhi: 177 | Ezekiel–Son of Man: 174 | Ezra: 191 | Gemariah/Shaphan: 157 | Jacob-Israel: 198 | Jehizkiah/Shallum: 171 | Jehoiachin: 183 |
|---|---|---|---|---|---|---|---|---|---|---|---|---|---|---|---|---|---|---|
| 25 | | | | | | | | | | | | | | | | | | |
| 26 | | | | | | | | | | | | # | | | | | | |
| 27 | | | | | | | | | | | | | | | | | | |
| 28 | | | | | | | | | | | | | # | | | | | |
| 29 | | | | | | | | | | | | | | | | | | |
| 30 | | | # | | | | | | | | | | # | | | | | |
| 31 | | | | | | | | | | | | | | | | | | |
| 32 | | | | | | | | | | | | | | | | | | |
| 33 | | | | | | | | | | | | | # | | | | | |
| 34 | | | | | | | | | | | | | | | | | | |
| 35 | | | | | | | | | | | | | | | | | | |
| 36 | | | | | | | | | | | | | | | | | | |
| 37 | | | | | | | | | | | | | # | | | | | |
| 38 | | | | | | | | | | | | # | | | | | | |
| 39 | | | | | | | | | | | | | + | | | | | # |
| 40 | | | | | | | | + | | | | | | | # | | | |
| 41 | | | | # | | | | | | | | | | | | | | |
| 42 | | | | | | | | | | | | | | | | | | |
| 43 | # | | + | # | | # | | | | | | | | | + | | | |
| 44 | # | | | | | | | | | | | | | | | | | |
| 45 | | | | | | | | # | | | | | | | # | | # | |
| 46 | | # | | | | | | | | | | | | | | | | |
| 47 | | + | | | | + | # | | | | | | | | # | # | # | |
| 48 | | | | | | | | | | | | | | | | | | |
| 49 | | | + | + | | | | | # | | # | | | | | | | |
| 50 | | | | | | | | | | | | | # | | | | + | |

# Coding of Exilic Names in Hebrew Scripture

| Book, Chapter | Jehoiakim-Sarpuhi: 146 Hits | Jeremiah: 194 | Seraiah/Tanhumeth: 172 | Shecaniah/Jahaziel: 179 | Shelemiah/Abdeel: 148 | Shelemiah/Kore: 223 | Shenazzar/Jehoiachin: 165 | Shephatiah/David: 189 | Solomon/David: 165 | Substitute King: 138 | Zedekiah: 184 | Zedekiah-Sarpuhi: 175 | Zephaniah: 184 | Nebchdnzr: 168 (605–562) | Ezekiel-Sarpuhi: 179 (569) | Jehoiachin-Sarp: 160 (561) | Nab-Belshzr: 186 (556–39) | Cyrus K Bab: 159 (539–30) | Chapter Hits, Book Percent |
|---|---|---|---|---|---|---|---|---|---|---|---|---|---|---|---|---|---|---|---|
| 25 |  | # |  |  |  |  |  |  |  |  |  |  |  |  |  |  |  |  | 1 |
| 26 | # |  |  |  |  |  |  |  |  |  |  |  |  |  |  |  |  |  | 2 |
| 27 |  |  |  | # |  |  |  |  |  |  |  |  |  |  |  |  |  |  | 1 |
| 28 |  |  |  |  |  |  |  |  |  |  |  |  |  |  |  |  |  |  | 1 |
| 29 |  |  |  |  |  |  |  |  |  |  |  |  |  |  |  |  |  |  |  |
| 30 |  |  |  |  |  |  |  |  | # |  | # | + | # |  |  |  |  |  | 6 |
| 31 |  |  |  |  |  |  |  |  |  |  |  |  |  |  |  |  |  |  |  |
| 32 |  | # |  |  |  |  |  |  |  |  |  |  |  |  |  |  |  |  | 1 |
| 33 |  |  |  |  |  |  |  |  |  |  |  |  |  |  |  |  |  | # | 2 |
| 34 |  |  |  |  |  |  |  |  |  |  |  |  |  |  |  |  |  |  |  |
| 35 |  |  |  |  |  |  |  |  |  |  |  |  |  |  |  |  |  |  |  |
| 36 |  |  |  |  |  |  |  |  |  |  |  |  |  |  |  | # |  |  | 1 |
| 37 |  |  | + |  |  |  |  |  |  |  | # |  |  |  |  |  |  |  | 3 |
| 38 |  |  |  |  |  |  |  | # |  |  |  |  |  |  |  |  |  |  | 2 |
| 39 |  |  |  |  |  |  |  |  |  |  |  |  |  | + | # |  | # |  | 5 |
| 40 |  |  | + |  |  |  | + | # |  | + |  |  |  |  | # |  |  |  | 7 |
| 41 |  |  |  |  |  |  |  |  |  |  |  |  |  |  |  |  |  |  | 1 |
| 42 |  |  |  |  |  |  |  |  |  |  |  |  |  |  |  |  |  |  |  |
| 43 |  |  |  |  |  |  |  | # | # |  |  |  |  |  | + |  | # |  | 9 |
| 44 | + |  | + |  |  |  |  |  |  |  |  |  |  |  |  |  |  | + | 4 |
| 45 |  |  | # |  | # |  |  |  | # |  |  |  |  |  |  |  |  |  | 6 |
| 46 |  |  |  |  |  |  |  |  |  |  |  |  |  |  |  |  |  |  | 1 |
| 47 |  | # |  |  |  |  |  |  |  | # |  |  |  |  |  |  |  |  | 8 |
| 48 |  | # | + |  |  |  |  |  |  |  |  |  |  |  |  |  |  |  | 2 |
| 49 |  | + |  |  |  |  | + |  |  |  |  | + |  |  |  |  | # |  | 8 |
| 50 |  | # | # |  |  |  |  |  |  |  |  |  |  |  |  |  |  |  | 4 |

# Appendix Four

| Book, Chapter | Ahaziah/Jehoram: 175 hits | Ahihud/Shelomi: 153 | Amariah/Hezekiah: 191 | Azariah/Amaziah: 185 | Azariah/Zephaniah: 147 | Azrikam/Azel: 161 | Baruch: 194 | Chimham/Jehoiachin: 204 | Chimham–Sarpuhi: 152 | Cyrus: 155 | Daniel: 249 | Daniel-Sarpuhi: 177 | Ezekiel–Son of Man: 174 | Ezra: 191 | Gemariah/Shaphan: 157 | Jacob–Israel: 198 | Jehizkiah/Shallum: 171 | Jehoiachin: 183 |
|---|---|---|---|---|---|---|---|---|---|---|---|---|---|---|---|---|---|---|
| Exod | | | | | | | | | | | | | | | | | | |
| 1 | | | | | | | | | | | | | | | # | | | |
| 2 | | | # | | | | | | | | | | | | | | | # |
| 3 | | | | | | | | | | | | | | | | | | |
| 4 | | | | | | | | | | | | | | | | | | |
| 5 | | | | | | | | | | | | | | | | | | |
| 6 | # | | | | # | | | | | | | | | | # | # | + | |
| 7 | | | | | | | | | | | | | | | | | | |
| 8 | | | # | | | | | | | | | | | | | | | |
| 9 | | | | | | # | | | | | | | | + | | | | |
| 10 | | | | | | | | | | | | | | | | | | |
| 11 | | | | | | | | | | | | | | | | | | |
| 12 | | # | # | | + | | | | | | | + | | | | | # | |
| 13 | | | # | | | | | | # | | | | | | | | | |
| 14 | | | | | | | | | | | | | | | | | | |
| 15 | | + | # | | | | | | | | | # | | | | | | |
| 16 | | | # | | | | | # | | | | | | | | | | |
| 17 | | | | | | | | | | | | | # | | | | | |
| 18 | | | | | | | | | | | | | | | | | | |
| 19 | | | | | | | | | | | | | | | | | | |
| 20 | | | | | | | | | | | | | | | | | | |
| 21 | | | | | | | | | | | | | | | | | | |
| 22 | # | # | | | | | | | | | | | | | | | | |
| 23 | | | | | | | + | | | | # | # | | | # | | | |
| 24 | | + | | | + | | | | | | | | | | | | # | |
| 25 | + | + | # | | | + | + | | | + | + | | + | # | | + | + | + |

## Coding of Exilic Names in Hebrew Scripture

| Book, Chapter | Jehoiakim-Sarpuhi: 146 Hits | Jeremiah: 194 | Seraiah/Tanhumeth: 172 | Shecaniah/Jahaziel: 179 | Shelemiah/Abdeel: 148 | Shelemiah/Kore: 223 | Shenazzar/Jehoiachin: 165 | Shephatiah/David: 189 | Solomon/David: 165 | Substitute King: 138 | Zedekiah: 184 | Zedekiah-Sarpuhi: 175 | Zephaniah: 184 | Nebchdnzr: 168 (605–562) | Ezekiel-Sarpuhi: 179 (569) | Jehoiachin-Sarp: 160 (561) | Nab–Belshzr: 186 (556–39) | Cyrus K Bab: 159 (539–30) | Chapter Hits, Book Percent |
|---|---|---|---|---|---|---|---|---|---|---|---|---|---|---|---|---|---|---|---|
| Exod | | | | | | | | | | | | | | | | | | | 15% |
| 1 | | | | + | | | | | | | | | | | | | | | 2 |
| 2 | | | | | | | | | | | | | | | | | | | 2 |
| 3 | | | | | | | | | | | | | | | | | | | |
| 4 | | | | | | | | | | | | | | | | | | | |
| 5 | | | | | | | | | | | | | | | # | | | | 1 |
| 6 | | | | | | | | | | | | | | # | | | | | 6 |
| 7 | | | | | | | | | | | | | | | | | | | |
| 8 | | | | | | | | | | | | | | | | | | | 1 |
| 9 | | | | | # | | | | | | | | | | | | | # | 4 |
| 10 | | | | | | | | | | | | | | | | | | | |
| 11 | | | | | | | | | | | | | | | | | | | |
| 12 | | | # | | # | | | | # | | | # | # | # | # | + | + | | 14 |
| 13 | | | | | | | | | | | | | # | | | | | | 3 |
| 14 | | | | | | | | | | | | | | | | | | | |
| 15 | | | | | | | | | | | | | | | | | | | 3 |
| 16 | | | | | | | | | | | | | | | | | | | 2 |
| 17 | | | | | | | | | | | | | | | | | | | 1 |
| 18 | | | | | | | | | | | | | | | | | | | |
| 19 | | | | | | | | | | | | | | | | | | | |
| 20 | | | | | | | | | | | | | | | | | | | |
| 21 | | | | | | | | | | | | | | | | | | | |
| 22 | | | | | | | | | | | | | | | | | | | 2 |
| 23 | | + | # | | + | | + | | | | | | | + | # | # | + | | 12 |
| 24 | | | | | | | | | # | | | | | | | # | | | 5 |
| 25 | + | + | + | | + | + | | # | # | + | + | # | + | | + | | + | + | 26 |

## APPENDIX FOUR

| Book, Chapter | Ahaziah/Jehoram: 175 hits | Ahihud/Shelomi: 153 | Amariah/Hezekiah: 191 | Azariah/Amaziah: 185 | Azariah/Zephaniah: 147 | Azrikam/Azel: 161 | Baruch: 194 | Chimham/Jehoiachin: 204 | Chimham-Sarpuhi: 152 | Cyrus: 155 | Daniel: 249 | Daniel-Sarpuhi: 177 | Ezekiel-Son of Man: 174 | Ezra: 191 | Gemariah/Shaphan: 157 | Jacob-Israel: 198 | Jehizkiah/Shallum: 171 | Jehoiachin: 183 |
|---|---|---|---|---|---|---|---|---|---|---|---|---|---|---|---|---|---|---|
| 26 |   |   |   | + | # |   |   | + |   | + | # | # |   |   |   | + | + | + |
| 27 | + |   | # | + | # | # | # | + | # | # | + | # |   |   |   | + | + |   |
| 28 |   |   |   |   |   | # |   |   |   |   |   |   |   |   |   |   |   |   |
| 29 | + |   |   |   |   |   |   |   |   |   |   |   |   |   |   |   |   |   |
| 30 | + |   |   | # |   |   |   | # |   |   |   |   |   |   |   |   | # |   |
| 31 |   |   |   |   |   |   |   |   |   |   |   |   |   |   |   |   |   |   |
| 32 |   |   |   |   |   |   |   |   |   |   |   |   |   |   |   |   |   |   |
| 33 |   |   |   |   |   |   |   |   |   |   |   |   |   |   |   |   | # |   |
| 34 |   |   |   |   |   |   |   |   |   |   |   |   |   |   |   |   |   |   |
| 35 |   |   |   |   |   |   |   |   | # |   |   |   |   |   |   |   |   |   |
| 36 |   |   |   |   |   |   | + | + |   |   | + |   |   |   |   | # | + | # |
| 37 | + | # | + |   |   |   | + | + |   | + | + |   | + | + |   | + | + | # |
| 38 | + | + | # |   |   | # | # | + | # | + | + |   | + |   |   | + | + | + |
| 39 |   |   |   |   |   |   |   |   |   |   |   |   |   |   |   |   |   |   |
| 40 |   |   |   |   |   |   |   |   |   |   |   |   |   |   |   |   |   |   |
| Lev |   |   |   |   |   |   |   |   |   |   |   |   |   |   |   |   |   |   |
| 1 |   |   |   |   |   |   |   |   |   |   |   |   | # |   |   | # |   | # |
| 2 |   |   |   |   |   | # |   |   |   |   |   |   |   |   |   |   |   |   |
| 3 | + |   | # |   |   |   |   |   |   |   |   |   | # |   |   | # | # | + |
| 4 | # |   | # | # | + |   |   | + |   | # |   |   | + |   |   | + | # |   |
| 5 |   |   |   |   |   |   |   |   |   |   |   |   |   |   |   | # |   | # |
| 6 |   |   | # | + |   |   |   |   |   |   |   |   |   | + | + |   |   |   |
| 7 |   |   |   |   |   |   |   |   |   |   |   |   |   |   |   |   |   |   |
| 8 |   |   | # |   |   |   |   |   |   |   |   |   |   |   |   |   |   |   |
| 9 |   | # |   |   |   | # | # |   |   |   |   |   | # |   |   | + |   |   |
| 10 |   |   |   |   |   |   |   |   |   |   |   |   |   |   |   |   |   |   |

## Coding of Exilic Names in Hebrew Scripture

| Book, Chapter | Jehoiakim-Sarpuhi: 146 Hits | Jeremiah: 194 | Seraiah/Tanhumeth: 172 | Shecaniah/Jahaziel: 179 | Shelemiah/Abdeel: 148 | Shelemiah/Kore: 223 | Shenazzar/Jehoiachin: 165 | Shephatiah/David: 189 | Solomon/David: 165 | Substitute King: 138 | Zedekiah: 184 | Zedekiah-Sarpuhi: 175 | Zephaniah: 184 | Nebchdnzr: 168 (605–562) | Ezekiel-Sarpuhi: 179 (569) | Jehoiachin-Sarp: 160 (561) | Nab–Belshzr: 186 (556–39) | Cyrus K Bab: 159 (539–30) | Chapter Hits, Book Percent |
|---|---|---|---|---|---|---|---|---|---|---|---|---|---|---|---|---|---|---|---|
| 26 |   |   |   |   | # |   |   | + | + | # | + |   |   | + |   |   |   | + | 16 |
| 27 |   |   | + |   | + |   |   | # | # | + |   |   |   | + | + |   |   | + | 21 |
| 28 | # |   |   |   |   |   |   |   |   |   | + |   |   | # |   | + | # | + | 7 |
| 29 |   |   |   |   |   |   |   |   |   |   | # |   |   |   |   |   |   |   | 2 |
| 30 |   |   |   |   |   |   |   |   | + | # |   |   | + |   |   |   |   | # | 8 |
| 31 |   |   |   |   | # |   |   |   |   |   |   |   |   |   |   |   |   | + | 2 |
| 32 |   |   |   |   |   |   |   |   |   |   |   |   |   |   |   |   |   |   |   |
| 33 |   |   |   |   |   |   |   | # |   |   |   |   |   |   |   |   |   |   | 2 |
| 34 |   |   |   |   | + |   |   |   |   |   |   |   |   |   |   |   |   | + | 2 |
| 35 |   |   |   |   | # |   |   |   |   |   | # |   |   |   |   |   |   | + | 4 |
| 36 |   |   |   |   |   |   | # | # |   |   |   |   |   |   | # |   | # |   | 10 |
| 37 | + | + | + |   | # |   | # | + | + | + | + | + |   | + |   |   | + | # | 26 |
| 38 | # | + |   | + | + |   |   | + |   | # | + | # |   | + | # | # | # | # | 27 |
| 39 |   | + |   |   |   |   | # |   |   |   |   |   |   |   | + |   |   | # | 4 |
| 40 |   |   |   |   | # |   |   |   | # |   |   |   |   |   |   |   |   | + | 3 |
| Lev |   |   |   |   |   |   |   |   |   |   |   |   |   |   |   |   |   |   | 13% |
| 1 |   |   |   |   |   |   |   | # |   |   |   |   |   |   | + |   |   | # | 6 |
| 2 |   |   |   | # |   |   |   |   | + |   |   |   |   |   |   |   |   |   | 3 |
| 3 |   |   |   |   | + | + |   | # |   |   |   | # | # |   |   |   |   |   | 11 |
| 4 | # |   |   |   | + | # | + |   |   | + |   | + |   |   |   |   |   | + | 16 |
| 5 |   |   |   |   |   |   | + |   | # |   |   | + |   |   |   |   |   | # | 6 |
| 6 | # |   |   | # |   |   | # |   |   |   | # |   |   | # |   |   |   |   | 9 |
| 7 |   |   |   |   |   |   |   |   |   |   |   | # |   |   |   |   |   |   | 1 |
| 8 |   |   |   |   |   |   |   |   |   |   |   |   |   |   |   |   |   |   | 1 |
| 9 |   |   | # |   |   |   |   | + |   | # |   | + | # |   |   |   |   | + | 11 |
| 10 |   |   |   |   |   |   |   |   |   |   |   |   |   |   |   |   |   |   |   |

| Book, Chapter | Ahaziah/Jehoram: 175 hits | Ahihud/Shelomi: 153 | Amariah/Hezekiah: 191 | Azariah/Amaziah: 185 | Azariah/Zephaniah: 147 | Azrikam/Azel: 161 | Baruch: 194 | Chimham/Jehoiachin: 204 | Chimham–Sarpuhi: 152 | Cyrus: 155 | Daniel: 249 | Daniel–Sarpuhi: 177 | Ezekiel–Son of Man: 174 | Ezra: 191 | Gemariah/Shaphan: 157 | Jacob–Israel: 198 | Jehizkiah/Shallum: 171 | Jehoiachin: 183 |
|---|---|---|---|---|---|---|---|---|---|---|---|---|---|---|---|---|---|---|
| 11 | | | | | | | | | | | | | # | | | # | | # |
| 12 | | | | | | | | # | + | | | | | | | | | |
| 13 | | | | # | | | | | | | | | | | # | | | |
| 14 | | | | | | | | | | | | | | | | | | # |
| 15 | | | # | | | # | | + | | # | | | + | # | + | | # | # |
| 16 | # | | + | + | # | | | # | | + | | # | | # | | | | # |
| 17 | | | | | | | | | | # | | | | | | | | # |
| 18 | | | | | | | | | | | | | | | | | | |
| 19 | | | | | | | | | | | | | | | | | | |
| 20 | | | | | | | | | | | | | | | | | | |
| 21 | | | | | | | | | | | | | | | | | | |
| 22 | | | | | | | | | | | | | | | | | | |
| 23 | | | | | | | | | | | | | | | | | | |
| 24 | | | | | | | | | | | | | | | | | | |
| 25 | | | | | | | | | | | | | | | | | | |
| 26 | | | | | | | | | | | | | | + | # | | | |
| 27 | | | | | | | | | | | | | | | # | | | |
| Num | | | | | | | | | | | | | | | | | | |
| 1 | + | + | | | # | | # | # | | | | # | + | | + | + | | + |
| 2 | # | | | | | | + | # | # | + | + | | | + | # | + | # | + |
| 3 | # | # | | | | | | # | | + | # | | | | | # | | |
| 4 | | | | | | | | | | | | | | | | | | |
| 5 | | | | | | | | | | | | | | | | | | |
| 6 | | | | | | | | | | | | | | | | | | |
| 7 | + | | | + | | | # | + | | # | | | | | # | + | + | |
| 8 | # | | | | | | | | | | | | | | | | | |

## Coding of Exilic Names in Hebrew Scripture

| Book, Chapter | Jehoiakim-Sarpuhi: 146 Hits | Jeremiah: 194 | Seraiah/Tanhumeth: 172 | Shecaniah/Jahaziel: 179 | Shelemiah/Abdeel: 148 | Shelemiah/Kore: 223 | Shenazzar/Jehoiachin: 165 | Shephatiah/David: 189 | Solomon/David: 165 | Substitute King: 138 | Zedekiah: 184 | Zedekiah-Sarpuhi: 175 | Zephaniah: 184 | Nebchdnzr: 168 (605–562) | Ezekiel-Sarpuhi: 179 (569) | Jehoiachin-Sarp: 160 (561) | Nab–Belshzr: 186 (556–39) | Cyrus K Bab: 159 (539–30) | Chapter Hits, Book Percent |
|---|---|---|---|---|---|---|---|---|---|---|---|---|---|---|---|---|---|---|---|
| 11 | # | # |   |   | + |   |   |   |   |   |   |   |   |   |   |   | + |   | 7 |
| 12 |   |   |   |   |   |   |   |   |   |   |   |   |   |   |   |   |   |   | 2 |
| 13 |   |   |   |   | # |   |   |   |   |   |   | + |   |   |   |   |   |   | 4 |
| 14 |   | # |   |   |   |   |   |   |   |   |   |   |   |   |   |   |   |   | 2 |
| 15 |   |   | # |   |   | + | + |   |   |   |   | + |   |   |   |   |   |   | 13 |
| 16 |   | + |   | # | # | + |   | + |   | # |   | # | + |   | # |   | # |   | 19 |
| 17 | # |   |   |   |   |   |   |   |   |   |   |   |   |   |   |   |   |   | 3 |
| 18 |   |   |   | # |   |   |   |   |   |   |   |   |   |   |   |   |   | + | 2 |
| 19 |   |   |   |   |   |   |   |   |   |   |   |   |   |   |   |   |   |   |   |
| 20 |   |   |   |   |   |   |   |   |   |   |   |   |   |   |   |   |   |   |   |
| 21 |   |   |   |   |   |   |   |   |   |   |   |   |   |   |   |   |   |   |   |
| 22 |   |   |   |   |   |   |   |   |   |   |   |   |   |   |   |   | # |   | 1 |
| 23 |   |   |   |   |   |   |   |   |   |   |   |   |   |   |   |   |   |   |   |
| 24 |   |   |   |   |   |   |   |   |   |   |   |   |   |   |   |   |   |   |   |
| 25 |   | # |   |   |   |   |   |   |   |   |   |   |   |   |   |   |   | # | 2 |
| 26 |   |   |   | + |   |   | # | + |   |   |   | # |   |   |   |   | # |   | 7 |
| 27 |   |   |   |   |   |   |   |   |   |   |   |   |   |   |   |   |   |   | 1 |
| Num |   |   |   |   |   |   |   |   |   |   |   |   |   |   |   |   |   |   | 19% |
| 1 | # | + | + | # |   | + | + |   | + | + | + |   | + | # | + | + | # |   | 25 |
| 2 | + | + |   | # | + | + | # | # |   | # | + | + | # |   | # | + |   | + | 25 |
| 3 |   | + |   |   |   |   |   | + |   |   | # |   | + |   |   |   |   |   | 10 |
| 4 |   |   |   |   |   |   |   |   |   |   |   |   |   |   |   |   |   |   |   |
| 5 |   |   |   |   |   |   |   |   |   |   |   |   |   |   |   |   |   |   |   |
| 6 |   |   |   |   |   |   |   |   |   |   |   | # |   |   |   |   |   | # | 2 |
| 7 |   | + |   |   | + | # | + | + |   | + | + | + |   | + |   |   |   |   | 18 |
| 8 |   |   |   |   |   |   |   |   |   |   |   |   |   |   |   |   |   |   | 1 |

# Appendix Four

| Book, Chapter | Ahaziah/Jehoram: 175 hits | Ahihud/Shelomi: 153 | Amariah/Hezekiah: 191 | Azariah/Amaziah: 185 | Azariah/Zephaniah: 147 | Azrikam/Azel: 161 | Baruch: 194 | Chimham/Jehoiachin: 204 | Chimham–Sarpuhi: 152 | Cyrus: 155 | Daniel: 249 | Daniel-Sarpuhi: 177 | Ezekiel–Son of Man: 174 | Ezra: 191 | Gemariah/Shaphan: 157 | Jacob–Israel: 198 | Jehizkiah/Shallum: 171 | Jehoiachin: 183 |
|---|---|---|---|---|---|---|---|---|---|---|---|---|---|---|---|---|---|---|
| 9 | # |   |   |   | + |   |   | # |   |   |   |   |   |   |   |   |   |   |
| 10 |   |   |   |   |   | + |   | + |   |   | + | # |   |   |   | # |   |   |
| 11 |   |   |   |   |   |   |   |   |   |   |   |   |   |   |   |   |   |   |
| 12 |   |   |   |   |   |   |   | # |   |   |   |   |   |   |   |   |   |   |
| 13 |   |   |   | # |   |   |   |   |   |   |   |   |   |   |   |   |   |   |
| 14 |   |   |   |   |   |   |   |   |   |   |   |   |   |   |   |   |   |   |
| 15 |   |   |   |   |   |   |   |   |   |   |   |   |   |   |   |   |   |   |
| 16 |   |   |   |   |   |   |   | # |   |   |   |   |   | # |   |   |   |   |
| 17 |   |   |   |   |   |   |   |   |   |   |   |   |   |   |   |   |   |   |
| 18 |   |   |   |   |   |   |   |   |   |   |   |   |   |   |   |   |   |   |
| 19 |   |   |   |   |   |   | # |   | # |   |   |   |   |   |   | # |   |   |
| 20 |   |   |   |   |   |   |   |   |   |   |   |   |   |   |   |   |   |   |
| 21 |   |   |   |   |   |   |   |   |   |   |   |   |   |   |   |   |   |   |
| 22 |   |   |   |   |   |   |   |   |   |   |   |   |   |   |   |   |   |   |
| 23 |   |   |   |   |   |   |   |   |   |   |   |   |   |   |   |   |   |   |
| 24 |   |   |   | + |   |   |   |   |   |   |   |   |   |   |   |   |   |   |
| 25 |   |   |   |   |   |   |   |   |   |   |   |   |   |   |   |   |   |   |
| 26 |   |   |   |   |   |   | + | + |   |   | # | + |   | + | # | + |   | + |
| 27 |   |   |   |   |   |   |   |   |   |   |   |   |   |   | # |   |   |   |
| 28 |   |   | # |   |   |   | + |   |   |   |   |   |   | # |   | # |   | # |
| 29 |   |   |   |   |   |   | + | + | + |   | + | # | + | + |   | + | + | + |
| 30 |   |   |   |   |   |   | + |   |   |   |   |   |   |   |   |   |   |   |
| 31 |   |   |   |   |   |   |   |   |   |   |   | # |   |   |   |   |   | + |
| 32 |   |   |   |   |   |   |   |   |   |   |   |   | # |   |   |   | # |   |
| 33 |   |   |   |   |   |   |   | # |   |   |   |   | + |   |   |   |   |   |
| 34 |   |   | # |   |   |   | + |   |   |   | + | # | # |   |   | # |   | + |

## Coding of Exilic Names in Hebrew Scripture

| Book, Chapter | Jehoiakim-Sarpuhi: 146 Hits | Jeremiah: 194 | Seraiah/Tanhumeth: 172 | Shecaniah/Jahaziel: 179 | Shelemiah/Abdeel: 148 | Shelemiah/Kore: 223 | Shenazzar/Jehoiachin: 165 | Shephatiah/David: 189 | Solomon/David: 165 | Substitute King: 138 | Zedekiah: 184 | Zedekiah-Sarpuhi: 175 | Zephaniah: 184 | Nebchdnzr: 168 (605–562) | Ezekiel-Sarpuhi: 179 (569) | Jehoiachin-Sarp: 160 (561) | Nab-Belshzr: 186 (556–39) | Cyrus K Bab: 159 (539–30) | Chapter Hits, Book Percent |
|---|---|---|---|---|---|---|---|---|---|---|---|---|---|---|---|---|---|---|---|
| 9  |   |   | + |   |   |   |   |   |   |   |   |   |   |   |   |   |   |   | 4 |
| 10 |   | # |   | # | + | # |   | + | + | # |   | # | # | # |   | + |   |   | 16 |
| 11 |   |   |   |   |   |   |   |   |   | # |   |   |   |   |   |   | # |   | 2 |
| 12 |   |   |   |   |   |   |   |   |   |   |   |   |   |   |   |   |   |   | 1 |
| 13 |   |   |   | # |   |   |   |   |   |   |   |   |   |   |   | # |   |   | 3 |
| 14 |   |   |   |   |   |   |   |   |   |   |   |   |   |   |   |   |   |   |   |
| 15 |   |   |   | # |   |   |   |   |   |   |   |   |   |   |   |   |   |   | 1 |
| 16 |   |   |   |   |   |   |   |   |   |   |   |   |   |   |   |   |   |   | 2 |
| 17 |   |   |   |   |   |   |   | + | # | # |   |   |   |   |   |   |   | # | 4 |
| 18 |   |   |   | # |   |   |   |   | # |   |   |   |   |   |   |   |   |   | 2 |
| 19 |   | # |   | # | + | # |   | # |   |   |   | + | # |   |   | # | + | + | 13 |
| 20 |   |   |   |   |   |   |   |   |   | + |   |   |   |   |   |   |   |   | 1 |
| 21 |   |   |   |   |   |   |   |   |   |   | # |   |   |   |   |   |   |   | 1 |
| 22 |   |   |   |   |   |   |   |   |   |   |   |   |   |   |   |   |   |   |   |
| 23 |   |   |   |   |   |   |   |   |   |   |   |   |   |   |   |   |   |   |   |
| 24 |   |   |   |   |   | # |   |   |   |   |   |   |   |   |   |   |   |   | 2 |
| 25 |   |   |   |   |   |   |   |   |   |   |   |   |   |   |   |   |   |   |   |
| 26 | + | + |   |   |   |   |   | # |   |   |   | # | + |   |   | + | # | # | 16 |
| 27 |   |   |   |   |   |   |   |   |   | # |   |   |   |   |   |   |   |   | 2 |
| 28 |   | # |   |   |   |   |   | # |   |   |   |   |   |   |   | # |   |   | 8 |
| 29 | # |   |   | + |   | + | + | + |   | + | + |   |   | + |   | + |   | + | 20 |
| 30 |   |   |   |   |   |   |   |   |   |   |   |   |   |   |   | + |   |   | 2 |
| 31 |   |   |   | # |   |   |   |   |   |   |   |   |   |   |   |   | # | + | 5 |
| 32 |   |   |   |   | + |   |   |   | # |   |   |   |   |   |   | # |   |   | 5 |
| 33 |   |   | # |   |   |   |   |   | # |   |   |   |   |   |   | # | # |   | 6 |
| 34 | # | + | + |   |   |   |   | # | + | # | # | # | # |   |   | # | + |   | 18 |

# Appendix Four

| Book, Chapter | Ahaziah/Jehoram: 175 hits | Ahihud/Shelomi: 153 | Amariah/Hezekiah: 191 | Azariah/Amaziah: 185 | Azariah/Zephaniah: 147 | Azrikam/Azel: 161 | Baruch: 194 | Chimham/Jehoiachin: 204 | Chimham–Sarpuhi: 152 | Cyrus: 155 | Daniel: 249 | Daniel–Sarpuhi: 177 | Ezekiel–Son of Man: 174 | Ezra: 191 | Gemariah/Shaphan: 157 | Jacob–Israel: 198 | Jehizkiah/Shallum: 171 | Jehoiachin: 183 |
|---|---|---|---|---|---|---|---|---|---|---|---|---|---|---|---|---|---|---|
| 35 | | | | | | | | | | | | | | | | | | |
| 36 | + | # | # | # | # | # | + | | # | | # | | | + | # | # | | # |
| Deut | | | | | | | | | | | | | | | | | | |
| 1 | | | | | | | | | | | | | | | | | | |
| 2 | | | | | | | | | | | | | | | | | | |
| 3 | | | | | | | | | | | | | | | | | | |
| 4 | | | | | | | | | | | | | | | | | | |
| 5 | | | | | | | | | | | | | | | | | | |
| 6 | | | + | | | # | | | | | | | | | | | | |
| 7 | | | | | | | | # | | | # | | | | | | # | |
| 8 | | | | | # | | | | | | | | # | | | | | |
| 9 | | | | | | | | | | | | | | | | | | |
| 10 | | | | | | | | | | | | | | | | | | |
| 11 | | | | | | | | | | | | | | | | | | |
| 12 | | | | | | | | | | | | | | | | | | |
| 13 | | | | | | | | | | | | | | | | | | |
| 14 | | | | | | | | | | | | | | | | | | |
| 15 | | | | | | | | | | | | | | | | | | |
| 16 | | | # | | | | | | | | | | | | | # | | # |
| 17 | | | | | | | | | | | | | | | | | | |
| 18 | | | | | | | | | | | | | | | | | | |
| 19 | | | | | | | | | | | | | | | | | | |
| 20 | | | | | | | | | | | | | | | | | | |
| 21 | | | | | | | | | | | | | | | | | | |
| 22 | | | | | | | | | | | | | | | | | | |
| 23 | | | | | | | | | | | | | | | | | | |

## Coding of Exilic Names in Hebrew Scripture

| Book, Chapter | Jehoiakim-Sarpuhi: 146 Hits | Jeremiah: 194 | Seraiah/Tanhumeth: 172 | Shecaniah/Jahaziel: 179 | Shelemiah/Abdeel: 148 | Shelemiah/Kore: 223 | Shenazzar/Jehoiachin: 165 | Shephatiah/David: 189 | Solomon/David: 165 | Substitute King: 138 | Zedekiah: 184 | Zedekiah-Sarpuhi: 175 | Zephaniah: 184 | Nebchdnzr: 168 (605–562) | Ezekiel-Sarpuhi: 179 (569) | Jehoiachin–Sarp: 160 (561) | Nab–Belshzr: 186 (556–39) | Cyrus K Bab: 159 (539–30) | Chapter Hits, Book Percent |
|---|---|---|---|---|---|---|---|---|---|---|---|---|---|---|---|---|---|---|---|
| 35 | | | | | | | | | | | | | | | | | # | | 1 |
| 36 | | # | # | | | | + | | + | | + | + | | | + | | | | 21 |
| Deut | | | | | | | | | | | | | | | | | | | 5% |
| 1 | | | | | | | | | | | | | | | | | | # | 1 |
| 2 | | | | | | | | | | | | | | | | | | | |
| 3 | | | | | | | | | | | | | | | | | | | |
| 4 | | | | | | | | | | | | | | | | | | | |
| 5 | | | | | | | | | | | | | | | | | | | |
| 6 | | | | | | | | | | | | | | | # | | | | 3 |
| 7 | | | | | + | | | | | | | | | | | # | | | 5 |
| 8 | | | | + | | | | | | | | | | | | + | | | 4 |
| 9 | | # | | | | | | | # | | | | | | | | | | 2 |
| 10 | | | | | | | | | | | | | | | | | | | |
| 11 | | | + | | | | | | | | | | | | | | | | 1 |
| 12 | | | | | | | | | | | | | | | | | | | |
| 13 | | | | | | | | | | | | | | | | | | | |
| 14 | | | | | | | | | | | | | | | | | | | |
| 15 | | | | | | | | | | | | | | | | | | | |
| 16 | | | + | # | | | | + | | | # | | | | | | | | 7 |
| 17 | | | | | | | | | | | | | | | | | | | |
| 18 | | | | | | | | | | | | | | | | | | | |
| 19 | | | | | | | | # | | | | | | | | | | | 1 |
| 20 | | | | | | | | | | | | | | | | | | | |
| 21 | | | | | | | | | | | | | | | | | | | |
| 22 | | | | | | | | | # | | | | | | | | | | 1 |
| 23 | | | | | | | | | | | | | | | | | | | |

## Appendix Four

| Book, Chapter | Ahaziah/Jehoram: 175 hits | Ahihud/Shelomi: 153 | Amariah/Hezekiah: 191 | Azariah/Amaziah: 185 | Azariah/Zephaniah: 147 | Azrikam/Azel: 161 | Baruch: 194 | Chimham/Jehoiachin: 204 | Chimham–Sarpuhi: 152 | Cyrus: 155 | Daniel: 249 | Daniel–Sarpuhi: 177 | Ezekiel–Son of Man: 174 | Ezra: 191 | Gemariah/Shaphan: 157 | Jacob–Israel: 198 | Jehizkiah/Shallum: 171 | Jehoiachin: 183 |
|---|---|---|---|---|---|---|---|---|---|---|---|---|---|---|---|---|---|---|
| 24 | | | | | | | | | | | | | | | | | | |
| 25 | | | | | | | | | | | | | | | | | | |
| 26 | | | | | | | | | | | | | | | | | | |
| 27 | | | | | | | | | | | | | | | | | | |
| 28 | | | | | | | | | | | | | | | | | | |
| 29 | | | | | | | | | | | | | | | | | # | |
| 30 | | | | | | | | | | | | | | | | | | |
| 31 | | + | | | | | | | | | | | | | | | | |
| 32 | # | # | | # | | | | | | | | # | # | | | | + | # |
| 33 | # | + | + | # | # | # | | | | | | + | # | | # | # | # | |
| 34 | | | | | | | | | | | | | | | | | | |
| Josh | | | | | | | | | | | | | | | | | | |
| 1 | | | | | | | | | | | | | | | | | | |
| 2 | | | | | | | | | | | | | | | | | | |
| 3 | | | | | | | | # | | | | | | | | | | |
| 4 | | | | | | | | | | | | | + | | | | | |
| 5 | | | | | | | | | | | | | | | | | | |
| 6 | | | | | | | # | | | | | | | | | | | |
| 7 | + | | | + | # | | + | # | | | | | + | | | # | | |
| 8 | | | | | | | | | | | | | | | | | | |
| 9 | | | | | | | | | # | | | | | | | | | |
| 10 | | | | | | | | | | | | | | | | | | |
| 11 | | | | | | | | | | | | | | | | | | |
| 12 | + | | # | | + | # | | # | | + | | | + | | + | | | # |
| 13 | # | + | + | | + | + | # | # | + | + | + | + | # | # | # | + | + | + |
| 14 | | | | | | | | # | | | | | | | | | | |

## Coding of Exilic Names in Hebrew Scripture

| Book, Chapter | Jehoiakim-Sarpuhi: 146 Hits | Jeremiah: 194 | Seraiah/Tanhumeth: 172 | Shecaniah/Jahaziel: 179 | Shelemiah/Abdeel: 148 | Shelemiah/Kore: 223 | Shenazzar/Jehoiachin: 165 | Shephatiah/David: 189 | Solomon/David: 165 | Substitute King: 138 | Zedekiah: 184 | Zedekiah-Sarpuhi: 175 | Zephaniah: 184 | Nebchdnzr: 168 (605–562) | Ezekiel-Sarpuhi: 179 (569) | Jehoiachin–Sarp: 160 (561) | Nab–Belshzr: 186 (556–39) | Cyrus K Bab: 159 (539–30) | Chapter Hits, Book Percent |
|---|---|---|---|---|---|---|---|---|---|---|---|---|---|---|---|---|---|---|---|
| 24 | | | | | | | | | | | | | | | | | | | |
| 25 | | | | # | | | | # | | | | | | | | | | # | 3 |
| 26 | | | | | | | | | # | | | | | | | | + | | 2 |
| 27 | | | | | | | | | | | | | | | | | | | |
| 28 | | | | | | | | | | | | | | | | | | | |
| 29 | | | | | | | | | # | | | | | | | # | | | 3 |
| 30 | | | | | | | | | | | | | | | | | | | |
| 31 | | | | | | | | | | | | | | | | | | | 1 |
| 32 | | | | | + | | | | | | | | | | | | | | 8 |
| 33 | | # | | | # | | | # | | | # | + | # | # | # | | | + | 20 |
| 34 | | | | | | | | | | | | | | | | | | | |
| Josh | | | | | | | | | | | | | | | | | | | 21% |
| 1 | | | | # | | | | | | | | | | | | | | | 1 |
| 2 | | | | | | | | | | | | | | | | | | | |
| 3 | | | | | | | | | | | | | | | # | | | | 2 |
| 4 | | | | | | | | | | | | | | | | | | | 1 |
| 5 | | | | | | | | | | | | | | | | | | | |
| 6 | | | | | | | | | | | | | | | | | | | 1 |
| 7 | | + | | | | + | # | | # | # | | # | | | # | | | | 14 |
| 8 | | | | | | | | | | | | | | | | | | | |
| 9 | | | | | | | | | | | | | | | | | | | 1 |
| 10 | | | | | | | | | | | | | | | | | | | |
| 11 | | | | | | | | | | | | | | | | | | | |
| 12 | # | # | # | # | | + | | | # | | | # | # | | | + | # | | 19 |
| 13 | | + | + | # | # | + | | + | + | # | | + | + | + | + | # | + | # | 32 |
| 14 | | # | | | | | | | | | | | | | | | | | 2 |

## Appendix Four

| Book, Chapter | Ahaziah/Jehoram: 175 hits | Ahihud/Shelomi: 153 | Amariah/Hezekiah: 191 | Azariah/Amaziah: 185 | Azariah/Zephaniah: 147 | Azrikam/Azel: 161 | Baruch: 194 | Chimham/Jehoiachin: 204 | Chimham–Sarpuhi: 152 | Cyrus: 155 | Daniel: 249 | Daniel–Sarpuhi: 177 | Ezekiel–Son of Man: 174 | Ezra: 191 | Gemariah/Shaphan: 157 | Jacob–Israel: 198 | Jehizkiah/Shallum: 171 | Jehoiachin: 183 |
|---|---|---|---|---|---|---|---|---|---|---|---|---|---|---|---|---|---|---|
| 15 | + | + | # |   | + | + | + | + | + | + | + | + | + | + | + | + | + | + |
| 16 |   |   |   | + |   |   | # |   | # | + | # |   |   | # |   | + | + | # |
| 17 |   |   |   |   |   |   |   |   |   |   |   |   |   | # |   |   |   |   |
| 18 |   |   |   | + |   |   | # |   |   |   | # |   |   |   |   |   |   |   |
| 19 | + | + | + | # | + | + | + | + | + | + | + | + | + | + | + | + | + | + |
| 20 |   |   |   |   |   |   |   |   |   |   |   |   |   |   |   |   |   |   |
| 21 | # |   |   | + |   | + |   |   |   |   |   |   |   |   | # |   |   | + |
| 22 |   |   |   |   |   |   |   |   |   |   |   |   |   |   |   |   |   |   |
| 23 |   |   |   |   |   |   |   |   |   |   |   |   |   |   |   |   |   |   |
| 24 |   |   |   |   |   |   |   |   |   |   |   |   |   |   |   |   |   |   |
| Judg |   |   |   |   |   |   |   |   |   |   |   |   |   |   |   |   |   |   |
| 1 |   |   |   |   |   |   |   |   |   |   |   |   |   |   |   |   |   |   |
| 2 |   |   |   |   |   |   |   |   |   |   |   |   |   |   |   |   |   |   |
| 3 |   |   |   |   |   |   |   |   |   |   |   |   |   |   |   |   |   |   |
| 4 | # |   |   |   |   |   |   |   |   |   |   |   | + |   |   |   |   |   |
| 5 |   |   |   | + |   | + |   |   |   |   |   |   |   |   |   | + |   | # |
| 6 |   |   |   |   |   |   |   |   |   |   |   |   |   |   |   |   |   |   |
| 7 |   |   |   |   |   |   |   | # |   |   |   |   |   |   | # |   |   |   |
| 8 |   | # |   |   | # |   |   | # |   | # |   |   |   |   |   |   |   |   |
| 9 |   |   |   |   |   |   |   |   |   |   |   |   |   |   |   |   |   |   |
| 10 |   |   |   |   |   |   | # |   |   |   |   |   |   |   | # |   |   | # |
| 11 |   |   |   |   |   |   |   |   |   |   |   |   |   |   |   |   |   |   |
| 12 |   |   |   |   | # |   |   |   |   |   |   |   |   |   |   |   |   |   |
| 13 |   |   |   |   |   |   |   |   |   |   |   |   |   |   |   |   |   |   |
| 14 |   |   |   |   |   |   |   |   |   |   |   |   |   |   |   |   |   |   |
| 15 |   |   |   |   |   |   | + |   |   |   |   |   |   |   |   |   |   |   |

## Coding of Exilic Names in Hebrew Scripture

| Book, Chapter | Jehoiakim-Sarpuhi: 146 Hits | Jeremiah: 194 | Seraiah/Tanhumeth: 172 | Shecaniah/Jahaziel: 179 | Shelemiah/Abdeel: 148 | Shelemiah/Kore: 223 | Shenazzar/Jehoiachin: 165 | Shephatiah/David: 189 | Solomon/David: 165 | Substitute King: 138 | Zedekiah: 184 | Zedekiah-Sarpuhi: 175 | Zephaniah: 184 | Nebchdnzr: 168 (605–562) | Ezekiel-Sarpuhi: 179 (569) | Jehoiachin-Sarp: 160 (561) | Nab-Belshzr: 186 (556–39) | Cyrus K Bab: 159 (539–30) | Chapter Hits, Book Percent |
|---|---|---|---|---|---|---|---|---|---|---|---|---|---|---|---|---|---|---|---|
| 15 | # | + | + | # | + | + | + | + | + | + | + | + | + | + | + | + | + | + | 35 |
| 16 |   | + | # | + |   | + | + | + | + |   |   | # | # | + | # | + | + | # | 23 |
| 17 |   |   |   |   |   |   |   |   |   |   |   |   |   | # |   |   |   |   | 2 |
| 18 |   |   |   |   |   |   |   |   | # |   |   |   |   |   |   |   |   |   | 4 |
| 19 | + | + | + | + | + | + | + | + |   |   | + | + | + | + | + | + | + | + | 33 |
| 20 |   |   | # |   |   |   |   |   |   |   |   |   |   |   |   |   |   |   | 1 |
| 21 |   | + |   |   |   |   |   | # |   | # |   |   | # | # |   |   | + | # | + | 13 |
| 22 |   |   |   |   |   |   |   |   |   |   |   |   |   |   |   |   |   |   |   |
| 23 | # |   |   |   |   |   |   |   |   |   |   |   |   |   |   |   |   |   | 1 |
| 24 |   |   |   |   |   |   |   |   |   |   |   |   |   |   |   |   |   |   |   |
| Judg |   |   |   |   |   |   |   |   |   |   |   |   |   |   |   |   |   |   | 7% |
| 1 |   |   |   |   |   |   |   |   |   |   |   |   |   |   |   |   |   |   |   |
| 2 |   |   |   |   |   |   |   |   |   |   |   |   |   |   |   |   |   |   |   |
| 3 |   |   |   |   |   |   |   |   |   |   |   |   |   |   |   |   |   |   |   |
| 4 |   |   |   |   |   |   |   |   |   |   |   |   |   |   |   |   | # |   | 3 |
| 5 |   | + |   | # |   |   |   | # |   |   |   |   |   | # |   | # | + | + | 11 |
| 6 | # |   |   |   |   |   |   |   |   |   |   |   |   |   |   |   |   |   | 1 |
| 7 |   |   |   |   |   |   |   |   |   |   |   |   |   |   |   |   |   |   | 2 |
| 8 |   |   | # | # |   | # | # | + | # |   | # |   |   |   |   |   | + | # | 13 |
| 9 |   |   |   |   |   |   |   |   |   |   |   |   |   |   |   |   |   |   |   |
| 10 |   |   |   |   |   |   |   |   |   |   |   |   |   |   |   |   | # | # | 5 |
| 11 |   |   |   |   |   |   |   |   |   |   |   |   |   |   |   |   |   |   |   |
| 12 |   | # |   |   |   |   | + |   |   |   |   | + |   | # |   | # | + |   | 7 |
| 13 |   |   |   |   |   |   |   |   |   |   |   |   |   |   |   |   |   |   |   |
| 14 |   |   |   |   |   |   |   |   |   |   |   |   |   |   |   |   |   |   |   |
| 15 | # |   |   |   |   |   |   | # |   |   |   |   |   |   |   |   |   |   | 3 |

## Appendix Four

| Book, Chapter | Ahaziah/Jehoram: 175 hits | Ahihud/Shelomi: 153 | Amariah/Hezekiah: 191 | Azariah/Amaziah: 185 | Azariah/Zephaniah: 147 | Azrikam/Azel: 161 | Baruch: 194 | Chimham/Jehoiachin: 204 | Chimham–Sarpuhi: 152 | Cyrus: 155 | Daniel: 249 | Daniel–Sarpuhi: 177 | Ezekiel–Son of Man: 174 | Ezra: 191 | Gemariah/Shaphan: 157 | Jacob–Israel: 198 | Jehizkiah/Shallum: 171 | Jehoiachin: 183 |
|---|---|---|---|---|---|---|---|---|---|---|---|---|---|---|---|---|---|---|
| 16 | # |   | # |   | + | + |   |   | # |   |   |   | # |   |   |   |   |   |
| 17 |   |   |   |   |   |   |   |   |   |   |   |   |   |   |   |   |   |   |
| 18 |   |   |   |   |   |   |   |   | # |   |   |   |   |   |   |   |   |   |
| 19 |   |   |   |   |   |   |   |   |   |   |   |   |   |   |   |   |   |   |
| 20 |   |   |   |   |   |   |   |   |   |   |   |   |   |   |   |   |   |   |
| 21 |   |   |   |   |   |   |   |   |   |   |   |   |   |   |   |   |   |   |
| Ruth |   |   |   |   |   |   |   |   |   |   |   |   |   |   |   |   |   |   |
| 1 |   | + |   |   |   |   |   |   |   |   |   |   |   |   |   |   |   |   |
| 2 |   | + |   | # |   | # | + |   | + | + | # | # |   |   |   |   |   | + |
| 3 |   |   |   |   |   |   |   |   | # |   |   |   |   |   |   |   |   |   |
| 4 |   | # |   |   |   |   |   |   |   |   |   |   | # |   |   |   |   |   |
| 1 Sa |   |   |   |   |   |   |   |   |   |   |   |   |   |   |   |   |   |   |
| 1 |   |   |   |   |   |   |   |   |   |   |   |   |   |   |   |   |   |   |
| 2 |   |   |   |   |   |   |   |   |   |   |   |   |   |   |   |   |   |   |
| 3 |   |   |   |   |   |   |   |   |   |   |   |   |   |   |   |   |   |   |
| 4 |   |   |   |   |   |   |   |   |   |   |   |   |   |   |   | # |   |   |
| 5 |   |   | # |   |   |   | + |   |   |   |   |   |   |   |   |   |   |   |
| 6 | # |   | + | # |   |   |   |   |   |   |   |   |   |   |   |   |   | + |
| 7 |   |   |   |   |   |   |   |   |   |   |   |   |   |   |   |   |   |   |
| 8 |   |   | # |   |   |   | + |   |   | + |   |   |   |   |   |   | # | # |
| 9 |   |   |   |   |   |   |   |   | # |   |   |   |   |   |   |   |   |   |
| 10 |   |   |   |   |   |   |   |   |   |   |   |   |   |   |   |   |   |   |
| 11 |   |   |   |   |   |   |   |   |   |   |   |   |   |   |   |   |   |   |
| 12 |   |   |   |   |   |   |   |   |   |   |   |   |   |   |   |   |   |   |
| 13 |   |   |   | # |   | # |   |   |   |   |   |   |   |   |   |   |   |   |
| 14 |   |   |   |   |   |   |   |   |   |   |   |   |   |   |   |   |   |   |

## Coding of Exilic Names in Hebrew Scripture

| Book, Chapter | Jehoiakim-Sarpuhi: 146 Hits | Jeremiah: 194 | Seraiah/Tanhumeth: 172 | Shecaniah/Jahaziel: 179 | Shelemiah/Abdeel: 148 | Shelemiah/Kore: 223 | Shenazzar/Jehoiachin: 165 | Shephatiah/David: 189 | Solomon/David: 165 | Substitute King: 138 | Zedekiah: 184 | Zedekiah-Sarpuhi: 175 | Zephaniah: 184 | Nebchdnzr: 168 (605–562) | Ezekiel-Sarpuhi: 179 (569) | Jehoiachin–Sarp: 160 (561) | Nab–Belshzr: 186 (556–39) | Cyrus K Bab: 159 (539–30) | Chapter Hits, Book Percent |
|---|---|---|---|---|---|---|---|---|---|---|---|---|---|---|---|---|---|---|---|
| 16 |  |  |  | + | # |  |  | + |  |  |  |  |  |  | # |  |  |  | 10 |
| 17 |  |  |  |  |  |  |  |  |  | # |  |  |  |  |  |  |  |  | 1 |
| 18 |  |  |  |  |  |  |  |  |  |  |  |  |  |  |  |  |  |  | 1 |
| 19 |  |  |  |  |  |  |  |  |  |  |  |  |  |  |  |  |  |  |  |
| 20 |  |  |  |  |  |  |  |  |  |  |  |  |  |  |  |  |  |  |  |
| 21 |  |  |  |  |  |  |  |  |  |  |  |  |  |  |  |  |  |  |  |
| Ruth |  |  |  |  |  |  |  |  |  |  |  |  |  |  |  |  |  |  | 15% |
| 1 |  |  |  |  |  |  |  |  |  |  |  |  |  |  |  |  |  |  | 1 |
| 2 |  | + |  |  | + |  |  |  |  |  | + | + |  | # | # |  | # |  | 16 |
| 3 | # |  |  |  |  |  |  |  |  |  |  |  |  |  |  |  |  |  | 2 |
| 4 |  |  |  |  |  |  |  |  |  |  |  |  |  |  |  |  |  |  | 2 |
| 1 Sa |  |  |  |  |  |  |  |  |  |  |  |  |  |  |  |  |  |  | 4% |
| 1 |  |  |  |  |  |  |  |  |  |  |  |  |  |  |  |  |  |  |  |
| 2 |  |  |  |  |  |  |  |  |  |  | # |  |  |  |  |  |  |  | 1 |
| 3 |  |  |  |  |  |  |  |  |  |  |  |  |  |  |  |  |  |  |  |
| 4 |  |  |  |  |  |  |  |  |  |  |  | # |  |  |  | # | # |  | 4 |
| 5 |  |  |  |  |  |  |  |  |  |  |  | # |  |  |  | # |  |  | 4 |
| 6 | # |  |  |  |  | + |  |  |  |  |  |  |  |  |  | # | # |  | 8 |
| 7 |  |  |  |  |  |  |  |  |  |  |  |  |  |  |  |  |  |  |  |
| 8 | + | + |  |  |  |  |  | # | # |  |  |  |  | + | # |  | + |  | 12 |
| 9 |  |  |  |  |  |  |  |  |  |  |  |  |  |  |  | # |  | # | 3 |
| 10 |  |  |  |  |  |  |  |  |  |  |  |  |  |  |  |  |  |  |  |
| 11 |  |  |  |  |  |  |  |  |  |  |  |  |  |  |  |  |  |  |  |
| 12 |  |  |  |  |  |  |  |  |  |  |  |  |  |  |  |  |  |  |  |
| 13 |  |  |  |  |  |  | # |  |  |  |  |  |  |  |  |  |  |  | 3 |
| 14 |  |  |  |  |  |  |  |  |  |  |  |  |  |  |  |  |  |  |  |

# Appendix Four

| Book, Chapter | Ahaziah/Jehoram: 175 hits | Ahihud/Shelomi: 153 | Amariah/Hezekiah: 191 | Azariah/Amaziah: 185 | Azariah/Zephaniah: 147 | Azrikam/Azel: 161 | Baruch: 194 | Chimham/Jehoiachin: 204 | Chimham–Sarpuhi: 152 | Cyrus: 155 | Daniel: 249 | Daniel–Sarpuhi: 177 | Ezekiel–Son of Man: 174 | Ezra: 191 | Gemariah/Shaphan: 157 | Jacob–Israel: 198 | Jehizkiah/Shallum: 171 | Jehoiachin: 183 |
|---|---|---|---|---|---|---|---|---|---|---|---|---|---|---|---|---|---|---|
| 15 | | | # | | | | | | | | | | | | | | | |
| 16 | | | | | | | | | | | | | | | | | | |
| 17 | | | | | | | | | | | | | | | | | | |
| 18 | | | | | | | | | | | | | | | | | | |
| 19 | | | | | | | | | | | | | | | | | | |
| 20 | | | | | | | | | | | | | | | | | | |
| 21 | | | | | | | | | | | | | | | | | | |
| 22 | | | | | | | | | | | | | | | | | | |
| 23 | | | | | | | | | | | | | | | | | | |
| 24 | | | | | | | | | | | | | | | | | | |
| 25 | | | | | | | | | | | | | | | | | | |
| 26 | | | | | | | | | | | | | | | | | | |
| 27 | # | | | | | | | | # | | | | | | | | | |
| 28 | | | | | | | | | | | | | | | | | | |
| 29 | | | | | | | | | # | | | | | | | | | |
| 30 | | | | | | | | | | | | | | | | | | |
| 31 | | | | | | | | | | | | | | | | | | |
| 2 Sa | | | | | | | | | | | | | | | | | | |
| 1 | | + | | | | | | | | | | | | | | | | |
| 2 | | | # | | | | | | | | | | | | | | | |
| 3 | | | | | | | | | | | | | | | | | | |
| 4 | | | | | | | | | | | | | | | | | | |
| 5 | | | | | | | | | | | | | | | | | | |
| 6 | | | | | | | | | | | | | | | | | | |
| 7 | | | | | | | | | | | | | | | | | | |
| 8 | | | | | | | | | | | | | | | | | | |

## Coding of Exilic Names in Hebrew Scripture

| Book, Chapter | Jehoiakim-Sarpuhi: 146 Hits | Jeremiah: 194 | Seraiah/Tanhumeth: 172 | Shecaniah/Jahaziel: 179 | Shelemiah/Abdeel: 148 | Shelemiah/Kore: 223 | Shenazzar/Jehoiachin: 165 | Shephatiah/David: 189 | Solomon/David: 165 | Substitute King: 138 | Zedekiah: 184 | Zedekiah-Sarpuhi: 175 | Zephaniah: 184 | Nebchdnzr: 168 (605–562) | Ezekiel-Sarpuhi: 179 (569) | Jehoiachin-Sarp: 160 (561) | Nab–Belshzr: 186 (556–39) | Cyrus K Bab: 159 (539–30) | Chapter Hits, Book Percent |
|---|---|---|---|---|---|---|---|---|---|---|---|---|---|---|---|---|---|---|---|
| 15 | # | | | | | | | | | | | | | | | | | | 2 |
| 16 | | | | | | | | | | | | | | | | | | | |
| 17 | | # | | | | | | | | | | | | | | | | | 1 |
| 18 | # | | | | | | | | | | | | | | | | | | 1 |
| 19 | | | | | | | | | | | | | | | | | | | |
| 20 | | | | | | | | | | | | | | | | | | | |
| 21 | | | | | | | | | | | | | | | | | | | |
| 22 | | | | # | | | | | | | | | | | | | | | 1 |
| 23 | | | | | | | | | | | | | | | | | | | |
| 24 | # | | | | | | | | | | | | | | | | | | 1 |
| 25 | | | | | | | | | | | | | | | | | | | |
| 26 | | | | | | | | | | | | | | | | | | | |
| 27 | | | # | | | | | | | | | | | | | | | | 3 |
| 28 | | | | | | | | | | | | | | | | | | | |
| 29 | | | | | | | | # | | | | | | | | | | | 2 |
| 30 | | | | | | | | | | | | | | | | | | | |
| 31 | | # | | | | | | | | # | | | | | | | | | 2 |
| 2 Sa | | | | | | | | | | | | | | | | | | | 5% |
| 1 | | | | | | | | | | | | | | | | | | | 1 |
| 2 | | | | | | | | | | | | | | | | | | | 1 |
| 3 | | | | | | | | | | | | | | | | | | | |
| 4 | | | | | | | + | # | | | | | | | | | | | 2 |
| 5 | | | | | | | | | | | | | | | | | | | |
| 6 | | | | | | | | | | | | | | | | | | | |
| 7 | | | | | | | | | # | | | | | | | | | | 1 |
| 8 | | + | | | | | | | | | | | | | | | | | 1 |

## Appendix Four

| Book, Chapter | Ahaziah/Jehoram: 175 hits | Ahihud/Shelomi: 153 | Amariah/Hezekiah: 191 | Azariah/Amaziah: 185 | Azariah/Zephaniah: 147 | Azrikam/Azel: 161 | Baruch: 194 | Chimham/Jehoiachin: 204 | Chimham–Sarpuhi: 152 | Cyrus: 155 | Daniel: 249 | Daniel–Sarpuhi: 177 | Ezekiel–Son of Man: 174 | Ezra: 191 | Gemariah/Shaphan: 157 | Jacob–Israel: 198 | Jehizkiah/Shallum: 171 | Jehoiachin: 183 |
|---|---|---|---|---|---|---|---|---|---|---|---|---|---|---|---|---|---|---|
| 9 | | | | | | | | | | | | | | | | | | |
| 10 | | | | | | | | | | | | | | | | | | |
| 11 | | | | | | | | | | | | | | | | | | |
| 12 | | | | | | | | | | | | | | | | | | |
| 13 | | | | | | | | | | | | | | | | | | |
| 14 | | | | | | | | | | | | | | | | | | # |
| 15 | | | | | | | | | | | | | | | | | | |
| 16 | | | | | | | | | | | | | | | | | | |
| 17 | | | # | | | | | | | | | # | | | # | | | |
| 18 | | | | | | | | | | | | | | | | | | |
| 19 | | | | | | | | | | | | | | | | | | |
| 20 | | | # | | | | | | | | | | | | | | | |
| 21 | | | | | | | | | | | | | | | | | | |
| 22 | | | # | | | | # | | # | + | | | # | | + | | # | |
| 23 | | | | # | | | | | # | | | | | | | | | |
| 24 | | | | | | | | | | | | | | | | | | |
| 1 Ki | | | | | | | | | | | | | | | | | | |
| 1 | | | | | | | | | | | | | | | | | | |
| 2 | | | | | | | | | | | | | | | | | | |
| 3 | | | | | | | | | | | | | | | | | | |
| 4 | | | | | | | | | | + | | | | | | | | |
| 5 | | | | | | | | | | | | | | | | | | |
| 6 | | + | | + | | + | # | # | | # | + | + | + | | + | + | + | |
| 7 | # | + | | | + | | + | | | + | + | # | # | | + | # | + | + |
| 8 | | | | | | | | | | | | | | | | | | |
| 9 | | | | | | | | | | | | | | | | | | |

## Coding of Exilic Names in Hebrew Scripture

| Book, Chapter | Jehoiakim-Sarpuhi: 146 Hits | Jeremiah: 194 | Seraiah/Tanhumeth: 172 | Shecaniah/Jahaziel: 179 | Shelemiah/Abdeel: 148 | Shelemiah/Kore: 223 | Shenazzar/Jehoiachin: 165 | Shephatiah/David: 189 | Solomon/David: 165 | Substitute King: 138 | Zedekiah: 184 | Zedekiah-Sarpuhi: 175 | Zephaniah: 184 | Nebchdnzr: 168 (605–562) | Ezekiel-Sarpuhi: 179 (569) | Jehoiachin-Sarp: 160 (561) | Nab–Belshzr: 186 (556–39) | Cyrus K Bab: 159 (539–30) | Chapter Hits, Book Percent |
|---|---|---|---|---|---|---|---|---|---|---|---|---|---|---|---|---|---|---|---|
| 9 |   |   |   |   |   |   |   |   |   |   |   |   |   |   |   |   |   |   |   |
| 10 | # |   |   | # |   |   |   |   |   |   |   |   |   |   |   |   |   |   | 2 |
| 11 |   |   |   |   |   |   |   |   |   |   |   |   |   |   |   |   |   |   |   |
| 12 |   |   |   |   |   |   |   |   |   |   |   |   |   |   |   |   |   |   |   |
| 13 |   |   |   |   |   |   |   |   |   |   |   |   |   |   |   |   |   |   |   |
| 14 |   |   |   |   |   |   |   |   |   |   |   |   |   |   |   |   |   |   | 1 |
| 15 |   |   |   |   |   |   |   |   |   |   |   |   |   |   |   |   |   |   |   |
| 16 |   |   |   |   |   |   |   |   |   |   |   |   |   |   |   |   |   |   |   |
| 17 |   | + | + |   | + | # |   | # |   |   |   |   |   |   |   |   |   |   | 8 |
| 18 |   |   |   |   |   |   |   |   |   |   |   |   |   |   |   |   |   |   |   |
| 19 |   |   |   |   |   |   |   |   |   |   |   |   |   |   |   |   |   |   |   |
| 20 |   |   |   |   | # |   |   |   |   |   |   |   |   |   |   |   |   |   | 2 |
| 21 |   |   |   |   |   |   |   |   |   |   |   |   |   |   |   |   |   |   |   |
| 22 |   | # | + |   | # | + |   | + |   |   |   |   |   | # | + |   |   |   | 14 |
| 23 | # |   |   | # |   |   |   |   |   |   |   |   |   |   |   | # | # |   | 6 |
| 24 |   |   |   |   |   |   |   |   |   |   |   |   |   |   |   |   |   |   |   |
| 1 Ki |   |   |   |   |   |   |   |   |   |   |   |   |   |   |   |   |   |   | 9% |
| 1 |   |   |   |   |   |   |   |   |   |   |   |   |   |   |   |   |   |   |   |
| 2 |   |   |   |   |   |   |   |   |   |   |   |   |   |   |   |   |   |   |   |
| 3 |   |   |   |   |   |   |   |   |   |   |   |   |   |   |   |   |   |   |   |
| 4 |   |   |   |   |   |   |   |   |   |   |   |   |   |   |   |   |   |   | 1 |
| 5 |   |   |   |   |   |   |   |   |   |   |   |   |   |   |   |   |   |   |   |
| 6 |   | + | + |   | # | # | # | + | + |   | + | # | + | # | # | # | # | + | 27 |
| 7 |   | # | # | + | # | # | # | # | # | # | # | # | + | # |   | # | # |   | 28 |
| 8 |   |   |   |   |   |   |   |   |   |   |   |   |   |   |   |   |   |   |   |
| 9 |   |   |   |   |   |   |   |   |   |   |   |   |   |   |   |   |   |   |   |

## Appendix Four

| Book, Chapter | Ahaziah/Jehoram: 175 hits | Ahihud/Shelomi: 153 | Amariah/Hezekiah: 191 | Azariah/Amaziah: 185 | Azariah/Zephaniah: 147 | Azrikam/Azel: 161 | Baruch: 194 | Chimham/Jehoiachin: 204 | Chimham–Sarpuhi: 152 | Cyrus: 155 | Daniel: 249 | Daniel–Sarpuhi: 177 | Ezekiel–Son of Man: 174 | Ezra: 191 | Gemariah/Shaphan: 157 | Jacob–Israel: 198 | Jehizkiah/Shallum: 171 | Jehoiachin: 183 |
|---|---|---|---|---|---|---|---|---|---|---|---|---|---|---|---|---|---|---|
| 10 | | | | | | | | | | | | | | | | | | |
| 11 | | | | | | | | | | | | | | | | | | |
| 12 | | | | | | | | | | | | | | | | # | | |
| 13 | | | | | | | | | | | | | | | | | | |
| 14 | | | | | | | | | | | | | | | | | | |
| 15 | | | | | | | | | | | | # | | | | | | |
| 16 | | | | | | | | # | | | | | | | | | | |
| 17 | | | | | | | | | | | | | | | | | | |
| 18 | | | | | | | | | | | | | | | | | | |
| 19 | | | | | | | | | | | | | | | | | | |
| 20 | | | | | | | | | | | | | | | | | | |
| 21 | | | # | | | | | | | | | | | | | | # | |
| 22 | | | | # | | | | # | | | | | | | | | | |
| 2 Ki | | | | | | | | | | | | | | | | | | |
| 1 | | | | | | | | | | | | | | | | | | |
| 2 | | | | | | | | | | | | | | | | | | |
| 3 | | | | | | | | | | | | | | | | | | |
| 4 | | | | | | | | | | | | | | | | | | |
| 5 | + | | + | + | + | | | # | | | | # | | + | # | | + | |
| 6 | | | | | | | | | | | | | | | | | | |
| 7 | | | | | | | | | | | | | | | | | # | |
| 8 | | | | | | | | | | | | | | | | | | |
| 9 | | | | | | | | | | | | | | | | | | |
| 10 | | | | | | | | | | | | | | | | | | |
| 11 | | | | | | | | | | | | | | | | | | |
| 12 | | | | | | | | | | | | | | | | | | |

## Coding of Exilic Names in Hebrew Scripture

| Book, Chapter | Jehoiakim-Sarpuhi: 146 Hits | Jeremiah: 194 | Seraiah/Tanhumeth: 172 | Shecaniah/Jahaziel: 179 | Shelemiah/Abdeel: 148 | Shelemiah/Kore: 223 | Shenazzar/Jehoiachin: 165 | Shephatiah/David: 189 | Solomon/David: 165 | Substitute King: 138 | Zedekiah: 184 | Zedekiah–Sarpuhi: 175 | Zephaniah: 184 | Nebchdnzr: 168 (605–562) | Ezekiel–Sarpuhi: 179 (569) | Jehoiachin–Sarp: 160 (561) | Nab–Belshzr: 186 (556–39) | Cyrus K Bab: 159 (539–30) | Chapter Hits, Book Percent |
|---|---|---|---|---|---|---|---|---|---|---|---|---|---|---|---|---|---|---|---|
| 10 | | | | | | | | | | | | | | | | | | # | 1 |
| 11 | | # | | | | | | | | | | | | | | | | | 1 |
| 12 | | | | | | | | | | | | | | | | | | | 1 |
| 13 | | | | | | | | | | | | | | | | | | | |
| 14 | | | | | | | | | | | | | | | | | | | |
| 15 | | | | | | | | | | | | | | | | | | | 1 |
| 16 | | | | | | | | | | | | | | | | | | | 1 |
| 17 | | | | | | | | | | | | | | | | | | | |
| 18 | # | | | | | | | | | | | | | | | | | | 1 |
| 19 | | | | # | | | | | | | | | | | | | | | 1 |
| 20 | | | | | | | | | | | | | | | | | | | |
| 21 | | | | | | | | | # | # | + | | | | | | | | 5 |
| 22 | | | | | | | | | | | | | | | | | | | 2 |
| 2 Ki | | | | | | | | | | | | | | | | | | | 5% |
| 1 | | | | | | | | | | | | | | | | | | | |
| 2 | | | | | | | | | | | | | | | | | | | |
| 3 | | | | | | | | | | | | | | | | | | | |
| 4 | | | | # | | | | | | | | | | | | | | | 1 |
| 5 | | | | | | # | | # | | # | | | | | # | | | | 13 |
| 6 | | | | | | | | | | | | | | | | | | | |
| 7 | | | | | | | | | | | | | | | | | | | 1 |
| 8 | | | + | | | | | | | | | | | | | | | | 1 |
| 9 | | | | | | | | | | | | | | | | | | | |
| 10 | | | | | | | | | | | | | | | | | | | |
| 11 | | | | # | | | | | | | | | | | | | | | 1 |
| 12 | | + | | | | | | | | | | | | | | | | + | 2 |

## Appendix Four

| Book, Chapter | Ahaziah/Jehoram: 175 hits | Ahihud/Shelomi: 153 | Amariah/Hezekiah: 191 | Azariah/Amaziah: 185 | Azariah/Zephaniah: 147 | Azrikam/Azel: 161 | Baruch: 194 | Chimham/Jehoiachin: 204 | Chimham-Sarpuhi: 152 | Cyrus: 155 | Daniel: 249 | Daniel-Sarpuhi: 177 | Ezekiel–Son of Man: 174 | Ezra: 191 | Gemariah/Shaphan: 157 | Jacob–Israel: 198 | Jehizkiah/Shallum: 171 | Jehoiachin: 183 |
|---|---|---|---|---|---|---|---|---|---|---|---|---|---|---|---|---|---|---|
| 13 | | | | | | | | | | | | | | | | | | |
| 14 | # | | | | | | | | | | | | | | | | | |
| 15 | | | # | | | | | | | | | | | | + | | | |
| 16 | | # | | | | | | | | | | | | | | | | |
| 17 | | | | | | | | | | | | | | | | | | |
| 18 | | # | | | | | | | | | | | | | | | | |
| 19 | + | | | | + | | | | | | | | # | | | | | # |
| 20 | | | | # | | | | | | | | | | | | | | |
| 21 | | | | | | | | | | | | | | | | | | |
| 22 | | # | | | | | | | | | | | | | + | | | |
| 23 | | | | | | | | | | | | | | | | | | |
| 24 | | | | | | | | | | | | | | | | | | |
| 25 | # | | | | | | | | | | | | | | | | | |
| 1 Ch | | | | | | | | | | | | | | | | | | |
| 1 | | | | # | | + | | + | | # | | # | | | | # | | |
| 2 | | | | | | | | | | | | | | | | | | |
| 3 | | | | | | | # | + | + | + | # | | # | | | | | # |
| 4 | | | | | | | # | | | | | # | | | | | | |
| 5 | # | | + | | # | + | + | # | # | + | + | | # | | | | | + |
| 6 | # | # | | # | | | | + | | # | + | | | | # | # | | # |
| 7 | | | | | | + | | | | | | | | | | | | |
| 8 | | | | | | | | | | | | | | | | | | |
| 9 | | | | | | | | # | | | | | | | | | | |
| 10 | | | | | | | | | | | | | | | | | | |
| 11 | | | | | | | | | | | | | | | | | | |
| 12 | | # | | | | | # | # | + | | + | | + | + | + | # | | |

248

## Coding of Exilic Names in Hebrew Scripture

| Book, Chapter | Jehoiakim-Sarpuhi: 146 Hits | Jeremiah: 194 | Seraiah/Tanhumeth: 172 | Shecaniah/Jahaziel: 179 | Shelemiah/Abdeel: 148 | Shelemiah/Kore: 223 | Shenazzar/Jehoiachin: 165 | Shephatiah/David: 189 | Solomon/David: 165 | Substitute King: 138 | Zedekiah: 184 | Zedekiah-Sarpuhi: 175 | Zephaniah: 184 | Nebchdnzr: 168 (605–562) | Ezekiel-Sarpuhi: 179 (569) | Jehoiachin–Sarp: 160 (561) | Nab–Belshzr: 186 (556–39) | Cyrus K Bab: 159 (539–30) | Chapter Hits, Book Percent |
|---|---|---|---|---|---|---|---|---|---|---|---|---|---|---|---|---|---|---|---|
| 13 | | | | | | | | | | | | | | | | | | | |
| 14 | | # | | | | | | | | | | | | | | | | | 2 |
| 15 | | | | | | | | | | | | | | | | # | | | 3 |
| 16 | | | | | | | | | | + | # | | | | | | | | 3 |
| 17 | | | | | | | | | | | | | | | | | | | |
| 18 | | # | | | | | | # | | # | | | | | | | | | 4 |
| 19 | | | | | | | # | | | # | # | | | | | | | | 7 |
| 20 | | | | | | | | | | | | | | | | | | | 1 |
| 21 | | | | | | | | | | | | | | | | | | | |
| 22 | | | | | | | | | | | | # | | | | | # | | 4 |
| 23 | | | | | | | | | | | | | | | | | | # | 1 |
| 24 | | | | | | | | | | | | | | | | | | | |
| 25 | | | | # | | | | | | | | | | | | | | | 2 |
| 1 Ch | | | | | | | | | | | | | | | | | | | 19% |
| 1 | + | + | | | | # | | # | | | # | | | | | | # | | 12 |
| 2 | | | | | | | | | | | | | | | | | | | |
| 3 | + | # | # | + | | | # | # | | + | # | | | | | + | | | 16 |
| 4 | | | | | | | | | | | | | | | | # | | | 3 |
| 5 | | | # | | # | | # | | | # | | | | | # | | | | 16 |
| 6 | + | + | | | # | | | | | | # | + | # | | | + | | # | 17 |
| 7 | | | | | # | | | # | | | | | | | | | | | 3 |
| 8 | | + | | | | | | | | | | | | | | | # | | 2 |
| 9 | | | | | | | | | | | | | | | | # | | | 2 |
| 10 | # | | | | | | | | | | | | | | | | | | 1 |
| 11 | # | | | | | | | | | | | | | | # | | | | 2 |
| 12 | | # | | + | | | + | + | # | | # | # | | # | | # | | 18 |

## Appendix Four

| Book, Chapter | Ahaziah/Jehoram: 175 hits | Ahihud/Shelomi: 153 | Amariah/Hezekiah: 191 | Azariah/Amaziah: 185 | Azariah/Zephaniah: 147 | Azrikam/Azel: 161 | Baruch: 194 | Chimham/Jehoiachin: 204 | Chimham–Sarpuhi: 152 | Cyrus: 155 | Daniel: 249 | Daniel–Sarpuhi: 177 | Ezekiel–Son of Man: 174 | Ezra: 191 | Gemariah/Shaphan: 157 | Jacob–Israel: 198 | Jehizkiah/Shallum: 171 | Jehoiachin: 183 |
|---|---|---|---|---|---|---|---|---|---|---|---|---|---|---|---|---|---|---|
| 13 |   | # |   |   |   |   |   |   |   |   |   |   |   |   |   |   | # |   |
| 14 |   |   |   |   | # |   |   |   |   |   |   |   | + | + |   |   |   |   |
| 15 |   | # |   |   | + |   |   | + |   |   |   |   | # |   |   |   |   |   |
| 16 |   |   |   |   |   |   |   |   |   |   |   | # |   |   |   |   | # |   |
| 17 |   |   |   |   |   |   |   |   |   |   |   |   |   |   |   |   |   |   |
| 18 |   | # |   | # | # |   |   |   |   |   |   |   |   |   | # |   |   |   |
| 19 |   |   |   |   |   |   |   | # |   |   |   |   |   |   |   |   |   |   |
| 20 |   |   |   |   |   |   |   |   |   |   |   | # |   |   |   |   |   |   |
| 21 |   |   |   |   |   |   |   |   |   |   |   |   |   |   |   |   |   |   |
| 22 |   |   |   |   |   |   |   |   |   |   |   |   |   |   |   | # |   |   |
| 23 |   |   |   |   |   |   |   |   |   |   |   |   |   |   |   |   |   | + |
| 24 | # |   |   |   |   |   |   |   |   |   |   |   | + |   |   | # |   | # |
| 25 |   |   |   |   |   |   | # |   |   | # | # | # |   |   |   |   |   |   |
| 26 |   |   |   | + |   |   |   | + | # |   |   |   | # |   | # |   | # | + |
| 27 |   | # |   | # |   | # | # | # | + | # | + |   |   | + |   | + |   | + |
| 28 |   |   |   |   |   | + | # | + | + | # |   |   | # |   |   | + |   |   |
| 29 |   |   |   | + |   |   |   |   |   | # |   |   |   |   |   |   |   |   |
| 2 Ch |   |   |   |   |   |   |   |   |   |   |   |   |   |   |   |   |   |   |
| 1 |   |   |   |   |   |   |   |   |   |   |   |   |   |   |   |   |   |   |
| 2 | + | # | # | # | # |   | + |   | # |   |   |   |   | # | # | + |   | # |
| 3 |   |   |   |   | + |   |   |   |   | # | + |   |   |   |   | # | # |   |
| 4 | + |   | # |   |   |   | + | + |   | # | + | # | + |   | + | + | # | # |
| 5 |   |   |   |   |   |   |   |   |   |   |   |   |   |   |   | # |   |   |
| 6 |   |   |   |   |   |   |   |   |   |   |   |   |   |   |   |   |   |   |
| 7 |   |   |   |   |   |   |   |   |   |   |   |   |   |   |   |   |   |   |
| 8 |   |   |   |   | # |   |   |   |   |   |   |   |   |   |   |   |   |   |

## Coding of Exilic Names in Hebrew Scripture

| Book, Chapter | Jehoiakim-Sarpuhi: 146 Hits | Jeremiah: 194 | Seraiah/Tanhumeth: 172 | Shecaniah/Jahaziel: 179 | Shelemiah/Abdeel: 148 | Shelemiah/Kore: 223 | Shenazzar/Jehoiachin: 165 | Shephatiah/David: 189 | Solomon/David: 165 | Substitute King: 138 | Zedekiah: 184 | Zedekiah-Sarpuhi: 175 | Zephaniah: 184 | Nebchdnzr: 168 (605–562) | Ezekiel-Sarpuhi: 179 (569) | Jehoiachin-Sarp: 160 (561) | Nab-Belshzr: 186 (556–39) | Cyrus K Bab: 159 (539–30) | Chapter Hits, Book Percent |
|---|---|---|---|---|---|---|---|---|---|---|---|---|---|---|---|---|---|---|---|
| 13 |  |  |  | + |  |  |  |  |  |  |  |  |  |  |  |  |  |  | 3 |
| 14 | # |  |  |  |  |  | # |  |  |  |  | # |  |  |  |  |  |  | 6 |
| 15 |  |  |  |  |  | + |  |  |  |  |  |  |  |  |  | # |  |  | 6 |
| 16 |  | + |  |  |  |  |  | # |  |  |  |  |  | # |  |  |  | # | 6 |
| 17 |  |  |  |  |  |  |  |  |  |  |  |  |  |  |  |  |  |  |  |
| 18 |  |  |  |  |  |  |  |  |  |  |  |  |  | # |  |  |  |  | 5 |
| 19 |  |  |  |  |  |  |  |  |  |  |  |  |  |  |  |  |  |  | 1 |
| 20 |  |  |  | # |  |  |  |  |  |  |  |  |  |  |  |  |  |  | 2 |
| 21 |  |  |  |  |  |  |  |  |  |  |  |  |  |  |  |  |  |  |  |
| 22 |  | # |  |  |  |  |  |  |  |  | # |  |  |  |  |  |  |  | 3 |
| 23 |  |  |  | # |  |  |  |  |  | # |  |  |  |  |  |  |  |  | 3 |
| 24 |  |  |  |  |  |  |  |  |  |  |  |  |  |  |  |  |  |  | 4 |
| 25 |  |  |  |  |  | # |  |  |  | # | # |  |  |  |  |  |  |  | 7 |
| 26 | + | # | + | + |  |  | # | + |  |  | + | + |  |  | # | + |  |  | 17 |
| 27 |  | + |  | # |  | # |  | + | + | + | + | + |  |  | + | + | + |  | 21 |
| 28 |  | + | + |  |  |  |  | + | + | + | # | # |  | + | + | # | # | # | 19 |
| 29 | # |  |  |  |  |  |  | + |  |  | # | # | # |  |  |  |  | # | 8 |
| 2 Ch |  |  |  |  |  |  |  |  |  |  |  |  |  |  |  |  |  |  | 14% |
| 1 |  |  |  |  |  |  |  |  |  | # |  |  |  |  |  |  |  |  | 1 |
| 2 |  | + |  |  | # |  | + |  | # |  |  |  |  | # |  |  | # |  | 17 |
| 3 |  | # |  |  |  |  | # | + |  | # | # |  |  | + | + |  |  |  | 12 |
| 4 | # | + |  | # |  | + | + | + | + | + | # |  |  | + | + | + |  |  | 25 |
| 5 |  |  | # |  |  |  | # |  | + |  |  |  |  |  |  |  |  | # | 5 |
| 6 |  |  |  |  |  |  |  |  |  |  |  | + |  |  |  | + |  |  | 2 |
| 7 |  |  |  |  |  |  |  |  |  |  |  |  |  |  |  |  |  |  |  |
| 8 |  |  |  |  |  |  |  |  |  |  |  |  |  |  |  |  |  |  | 1 |

# Appendix Four

| Book, Chapter | Ahaziah/Jehoram: 175 hits | Ahihud/Shelomi: 153 | Amariah/Hezekiah: 191 | Azariah/Amaziah: 185 | Azariah/Zephaniah: 147 | Azrikam/Azel: 161 | Baruch: 194 | Chimham/Jehoiachin: 204 | Chimham–Sarpuhi: 152 | Cyrus: 155 | Daniel: 249 | Daniel–Sarpuhi: 177 | Ezekiel–Son of Man: 174 | Ezra: 191 | Gemariah/Shaphan: 157 | Jacob–Israel: 198 | Jehizkiah/Shallum: 171 | Jehoiachin: 183 |
|---|---|---|---|---|---|---|---|---|---|---|---|---|---|---|---|---|---|---|
| 9  |   |   |   |   |   |   |   |   |   |   |   |   |   |   |   |   |   |   |
| 10 |   |   |   |   |   |   |   |   |   |   |   |   |   |   | # |   |   |   |
| 11 |   |   |   |   |   |   |   |   |   |   |   |   |   |   |   |   |   |   |
| 12 |   |   |   |   |   |   |   |   |   |   |   |   |   |   |   |   |   |   |
| 13 |   |   |   |   |   |   |   |   |   |   |   |   |   |   |   |   |   |   |
| 14 |   |   |   |   |   |   |   |   |   |   |   |   | # |   |   |   |   |   |
| 15 |   | # | # |   |   |   |   |   |   |   |   |   |   |   |   |   |   |   |
| 16 |   |   |   |   |   |   |   |   |   |   |   |   |   |   |   |   |   |   |
| 17 |   |   |   | # |   | + |   |   |   |   |   |   |   |   | # | + |   | # |
| 18 |   |   |   |   |   |   |   |   |   |   |   |   |   |   |   |   |   |   |
| 19 |   |   | # |   |   | + |   |   |   |   |   |   |   |   |   |   |   |   |
| 20 |   |   |   |   |   |   |   |   | + |   |   |   |   |   |   |   |   |   |
| 21 |   |   |   |   |   |   |   |   |   |   |   |   |   |   |   |   |   |   |
| 22 |   |   |   |   |   |   |   |   |   |   |   |   |   |   |   |   |   |   |
| 23 |   |   |   |   |   |   |   |   |   |   |   |   |   |   |   |   |   |   |
| 24 |   |   |   |   |   |   |   |   |   |   |   |   |   |   |   |   |   | # |
| 25 |   |   |   |   |   |   |   |   |   |   |   |   |   | # |   |   |   |   |
| 26 |   | + | # |   |   | + |   | + |   |   | + | + | + | + |   | + |   |   |
| 27 |   |   |   |   |   |   |   |   |   |   |   |   |   |   |   |   |   |   |
| 28 |   |   |   |   |   |   |   |   |   |   |   |   |   |   | # |   |   |   |
| 29 |   |   |   | + | # | + |   |   |   |   | # | # |   |   |   |   |   |   |
| 30 |   |   |   |   |   |   |   |   |   |   |   |   |   | # |   |   |   |   |
| 31 |   |   |   | # |   | + | # |   | # |   |   |   |   |   | # |   | # | # |
| 32 |   |   |   | # |   | # |   |   | # |   |   |   |   |   | # | # | + | # |
| 33 |   |   |   |   |   | # |   |   |   |   |   |   |   |   |   |   |   |   |
| 34 | + |   |   |   |   | + | + | + |   |   | # | + |   | # | # | + |   |   |

## Coding of Exilic Names in Hebrew Scripture

| Book, Chapter | Jehoiakim-Sarpuhi: 146 Hits | Jeremiah: 194 | Seraiah/Tanhumeth: 172 | Shecaniah/Jahaziel: 179 | Shelemiah/Abdeel: 148 | Shelemiah/Kore: 223 | Shenazzar/Jehoiachin: 165 | Shephatiah/David: 189 | Solomon/David: 165 | Substitute King: 138 | Zedekiah: 184 | Zedekiah-Sarpuhi: 175 | Zephaniah: 184 | Nebchdnzr: 168 (605–562) | Ezekiel-Sarpuhi: 179 (569) | Jehoiachin–Sarp: 160 (561) | Nab–Belshzr: 186 (556–39) | Cyrus K Bab: 159 (539–30) | Chapter Hits, Book Percent |
|---|---|---|---|---|---|---|---|---|---|---|---|---|---|---|---|---|---|---|---|
| 9 | | | | | | | | | | | | | | | | | | # | 1 |
| 10 | # | | | | | | | | | | | | | | | | | | 2 |
| 11 | | | | | | | | | | | | | | | | | | | |
| 12 | | | | | | | | | | | | | | | | | | | |
| 13 | | # | | | | | | | | | | | | | | | | | 1 |
| 14 | | | | | # | | | | | | | | | | | | | | 2 |
| 15 | | # | | | | | | # | | | | | | | | | | | 4 |
| 16 | | | | | | | | | | | | | | | | | | | |
| 17 | # | | # | | | | # | + | | | | | | | | | | # | 10 |
| 18 | | | | | | | | | | | | | | | | | | | |
| 19 | | | | | | | | | | | | | | | | # | | | 3 |
| 20 | | # | | | | | | | | | + | | | # | # | | | | 5 |
| 21 | | | | | | | | | | | | | | | | | | | |
| 22 | | | | | | | | | | | | | | | | | | | |
| 23 | | | | | | | | | | | | | | | | | | | |
| 24 | | | | | | | | | | | | | | | | | | | 1 |
| 25 | | | | | | | | | | | | | | | | | | | 1 |
| 26 | | + | | + | # | + | + | + | | + | | | | # | + | # | + | | 19 |
| 27 | | | | | | | | | | | | | | | | | | | |
| 28 | | | | | | | | | | | | | | | | | | | 1 |
| 29 | | # | | | # | | | | + | + | | # | | + | | | | | 11 |
| 30 | | | # | | | | # | | | | | | | | | | | | 3 |
| 31 | | + | | | | | | | # | | | | | | | | | | 9 |
| 32 | | # | | | | | | | | | | | # | | | | | | 9 |
| 33 | | | # | | | | | | | | | | | | | | | | 2 |
| 34 | # | # | # | | | | + | | | | + | | | + | + | | | | 16 |

## Appendix Four

| Book, Chapter | Ahaziah/Jehoram: 175 hits | Ahihud/Shelomi: 153 | Amariah/Hezekiah: 191 | Azariah/Amaziah: 185 | Azariah/Zephaniah: 147 | Azrikam/Azel: 161 | Baruch: 194 | Chimham/Jehoiachin: 204 | Chimham–Sarpuhi: 152 | Cyrus: 155 | Daniel: 249 | Daniel–Sarpuhi: 177 | Ezekiel–Son of Man: 174 | Ezra: 191 | Gemariah/Shaphan: 157 | Jacob–Israel: 198 | Jehizkiah/Shallum: 171 | Jehoiachin: 183 |
|---|---|---|---|---|---|---|---|---|---|---|---|---|---|---|---|---|---|---|
| 35 | + |  |  | + | + | # | # | + | + | + |  |  |  |  | # | # | + |  |
| 36 |  |  |  |  |  |  |  |  |  |  |  |  |  |  |  |  |  |  |
| Ezra |  |  |  |  |  |  |  |  |  |  |  |  |  |  |  |  |  |  |
| 1 | # |  |  |  |  | + | # | + |  | + | # |  |  |  | + | + | + |  |
| 2 |  |  |  |  |  | # |  |  |  |  | # |  | + |  |  |  |  |  |
| 3 |  |  |  |  |  |  |  | # |  |  |  |  |  |  |  | # |  | # |
| 4 |  |  |  |  |  |  |  | # |  |  |  |  | + | + |  | # |  |  |
| 5 |  |  |  |  |  |  |  |  |  |  |  |  |  |  |  |  |  |  |
| 6 |  |  |  |  |  | # |  |  |  |  | # |  |  |  |  |  |  |  |
| 7 | # |  |  |  |  | # | + |  |  |  |  |  |  |  | + |  |  | + |
| 8 |  |  |  |  |  | # |  |  | + | # |  |  |  |  | # |  |  |  |
| 9 |  |  | # |  |  | + | + |  |  | # | # |  |  |  | + |  | # |  |
| 10 |  |  |  |  |  | + |  |  |  |  |  |  |  |  |  |  |  |  |
| Neh |  |  |  |  |  |  |  |  |  |  |  |  |  |  |  |  |  |  |
| 1 |  |  | # |  |  | # |  |  |  |  |  |  |  |  | # |  |  |  |
| 2 |  |  |  |  |  |  |  | + |  |  |  |  |  |  |  |  |  |  |
| 3 | + | + | + |  | # | + | + | + |  | + | + | # | + |  | + | + | + | + |
| 4 |  |  |  |  |  | # | + |  |  |  |  |  | # |  |  | # | + |  |
| 5 |  |  |  |  |  |  |  |  |  |  |  |  |  |  |  |  |  |  |
| 6 |  | # |  |  |  |  |  |  |  |  |  |  |  |  |  |  |  |  |
| 7 |  |  |  |  |  | # |  | + | + | + |  | + |  |  |  |  |  | # |
| 8 |  |  |  | # |  |  |  |  |  |  |  |  |  |  |  |  |  |  |
| 9 |  | + |  |  |  |  |  |  |  |  |  |  |  |  |  |  |  |  |
| 10 |  |  |  | # | + | + | + |  | # |  |  | + | + | # |  | # |  |  |
| 11 |  |  |  |  | # |  | # | # |  |  |  |  |  |  | # |  |  |  |
| 12 |  |  | # |  | # | + | + | + |  | + | + | # | # |  | # |  | + |  |

## Coding of Exilic Names in Hebrew Scripture

| Book, Chapter | Jehoiakim-Sarpuhi: 146 Hits | Jeremiah: 194 | Seraiah/Tanhumeth: 172 | Shecaniah/Jahaziel: 179 | Shelemiah/Abdeel: 148 | Shelemiah/Kore: 223 | Shenazzar/Jehoiachin: 165 | Shephatiah/David: 189 | Solomon/David: 165 | Substitute King: 138 | Zedekiah: 184 | Zedekiah-Sarpuhi: 175 | Zephaniah: 184 | Nebchdnzr: 168 (605–562) | Ezekiel-Sarpuhi: 179 (569) | Jehoiachin-Sarp: 160 (561) | Nab-Belshzr: 186 (556–39) | Cyrus K Bab: 159 (539–30) | Chapter Hits, Book Percent |
|---|---|---|---|---|---|---|---|---|---|---|---|---|---|---|---|---|---|---|---|
| 35 |   |   | + |   | + |   | + |   | + | # |   | + |   | + | + |   | # | # | 20 |
| 36 |   |   |   |   |   |   |   |   |   |   |   |   |   |   |   |   |   |   |   |
| Ezra |   |   |   |   |   |   |   |   |   |   |   |   |   |   |   |   |   |   | 24% |
| 1 |   | # | + |   | # | # | # |   |   |   |   | # | # |   |   |   |   |   | 16 |
| 2 |   |   |   |   |   |   |   |   |   |   |   |   |   |   |   | + |   |   | 4 |
| 3 |   |   | + | # |   |   |   |   |   |   |   |   |   |   |   |   |   | + | 6 |
| 4 | + | # |   |   | + |   | + | + |   | # |   | # |   |   |   |   | # | # | 13 |
| 5 |   |   |   |   |   |   |   |   |   | + |   |   |   |   |   |   | + |   | 2 |
| 6 |   |   | # | + |   |   | # |   |   |   |   | # |   |   |   |   | # | # | 8 |
| 7 |   | + | # |   |   |   |   | + | # |   |   |   |   | # |   |   | # | + | 12 |
| 8 | + |   |   |   |   |   | # |   |   |   |   |   |   | # |   |   |   | # | 8 |
| 9 |   |   | + |   | + |   |   | # |   | # | + |   |   |   |   |   | # | # | 14 |
| 10 |   |   |   |   |   |   |   |   | + |   |   |   |   |   |   |   |   |   | 2 |
| Neh |   |   |   |   |   |   |   |   |   |   |   |   |   |   |   |   |   |   | 24% |
| 1 |   | + |   |   |   |   |   |   |   |   |   |   |   | # |   |   |   | # | 6 |
| 2 |   |   |   |   |   |   | # |   |   |   |   |   |   |   |   | + |   |   | 3 |
| 3 | + | # | + | # | + | + | + | + | # | + | + | + |   | + | + |   | + | # | 30 |
| 4 |   | # |   |   |   |   |   | # |   |   |   |   |   |   |   | # |   | # | 9 |
| 5 |   |   |   |   |   |   |   |   |   |   |   |   |   |   |   |   |   |   |   |
| 6 |   |   | + |   |   |   | # |   |   |   | + | # |   |   |   |   | # |   | 6 |
| 7 | # |   | # |   |   |   |   |   |   |   |   |   |   | # | # | # |   |   | 11 |
| 8 | # |   |   |   |   |   |   |   |   |   |   |   |   |   |   |   |   |   | 2 |
| 9 |   |   |   | # |   |   |   |   |   |   |   |   |   |   |   |   |   | # | 3 |
| 10 |   |   | + |   |   |   | # |   | # |   |   | + |   |   |   |   | # |   | 14 |
| 11 | # | # |   |   |   |   |   |   |   |   |   |   |   |   |   |   |   |   | 6 |
| 12 | # | # | # | # |   |   |   | + |   | + | # | # |   | + |   |   | # | # | 22 |

## Appendix Four

| Book, Chapter | Ahaziah/Jehoram: 175 hits | Ahihud/Shelomi: 153 | Amariah/Hezekiah: 191 | Azariah/Amaziah: 185 | Azariah/Zephaniah: 147 | Azrikam/Azel: 161 | Baruch: 194 | Chimham/Jehoiachin: 204 | Chimham–Sarpuhi: 152 | Cyrus: 155 | Daniel: 249 | Daniel–Sarpuhi: 177 | Ezekiel–Son of Man: 174 | Ezra: 191 | Gemariah/Shaphan: 157 | Jacob–Israel: 198 | Jehizkiah/Shallum: 171 | Jehoiachin: 183 |
|---|---|---|---|---|---|---|---|---|---|---|---|---|---|---|---|---|---|---|
| 13 | | | | | | | | | | | | | | | | | | |
| Esth | | | | | | | | | | | | | | | | | | |
| 1 | # | | | | | | | | | | # | # | | | | | | |
| 2 | | | | | | | | | | | | | | | | | | |
| 3 | | | | | | | | # | # | | | | # | | # | | | |
| 4 | | | | | | | # | | # | | | | | | | | | |
| 5 | | | | | | | | | | | | | | | # | | | # |
| 6 | | | | | | | | | | | | | | | | | | |
| 7 | | | | | | | | | | | | + | | + | # | # | # | |
| 8 | | | | | | | | | | | | | | | | | | |
| 9 | | | | | | | | | | + | # | | | | | | | |
| 10 | | | | | | | | | | | | | | | | | | |
| Job | | | | | | | | | | | | | | | | | | |
| 1 | | | | | | | | | | | | | | + | | | | |
| 2 | | | | | | | | | | | | | | | | | | |
| 3 | | # | | | | | | | | | + | | # | | | | | |
| 4 | # | # | | # | | # | | | | | # | # | | # | # | # | # | |
| 5 | | # | | # | + | # | | | | | # | | | | | # | | |
| 6 | | | # | | # | | | # | | | # | | | | | | # | |
| 7 | | | | | | | | | | | | | | | | | | |
| 8 | | # | + | | | | | | | | | + | | | | # | | |
| 9 | | # | | | | | | | | + | | # | | | | # | # | |
| 10 | + | + | + | + | | | + | | | + | | | | + | | | | |
| 11 | | # | | | | | | | | | # | # | | | | | | |
| 12 | # | | # | # | + | + | | | | | # | # | # | | # | + | # | + |
| 13 | | | | | | | | | | | | | | | | | | |

## Coding of Exilic Names in Hebrew Scripture

| Book, Chapter | Jehoiakim-Sarpuhi: 146 Hits | Jeremiah: 194 | Seraiah/Tanhumeth: 172 | Shecaniah/Jahaziel: 179 | Shelemiah/Abdeel: 148 | Shelemiah/Kore: 223 | Shenazzar/Jehoiachin: 165 | Shephatiah/David: 189 | Solomon/David: 165 | Substitute King: 138 | Zedekiah: 184 | Zedekiah–Sarpuhi: 175 | Zephaniah: 184 | Nebchdnzr: 168 (605–562) | Ezekiel–Sarpuhi: 179 (569) | Jehoiachin–Sarp: 160 (561) | Nab–Belshzr: 186 (556–39) | Cyrus K Bab: 159 (539–30) | Chapter Hits, Book Percent |
|---|---|---|---|---|---|---|---|---|---|---|---|---|---|---|---|---|---|---|---|
| 13 | | | | | | | | | | | | # | | | | | | | 1 |
| Esth | | | | | | | | | | | | | | | | | | | 14% |
| 1 | | | | | # | | | # | | | | | | # | | | | | 6 |
| 2 | # | # | + | | | | | | + | | | | | | | | | | 4 |
| 3 | | | | # | | # | | | | | | | | # | | | # | | 8 |
| 4 | # | | # | + | | | | # | | | # | | # | | | | | | 8 |
| 5 | | | | + | | | | | | | | | | | | | | # | 4 |
| 6 | | | | | | # | | | | | | | | | | | | | 1 |
| 7 | | | | # | | | + | | | | | | | | | | | # | 3 |
| 8 | # | + | | # | + | | # | | | | | # | | | | | # | | 12 |
| 9 | | | | | | | | | | | | | | | | | | | |
| 10 | | | | | | | | | | | | | | | | | | | 2 |
| Job | | | | | | | | | | | | | | | | | | | 25% |
| 1 | | | # | | | | | | | | # | | | | | | | | 3 |
| 2 | | | | | | | | | | | | | # | | | | | | 1 |
| 3 | | | | + | | | | | | # | | | | | | | | | 5 |
| 4 | | # | | # | # | | # | # | | # | | | | + | | | | | 17 |
| 5 | | | | # | | | | | | | | | | | | | | | 7 |
| 6 | | # | | + | | | | | | | | # | | | | | | | 8 |
| 7 | | | | # | | | | | | | | # | | | | | | | 2 |
| 8 | | # | | | | | # | # | | | | | | | | | # | | 8 |
| 9 | | | | + | | | | # | | | # | + | | | | + | | | 9 |
| 10 | | # | # | | + | # | | | | # | + | # | | # | | # | # | | 15 |
| 11 | | | # | | | | # | # | | | | | | | | | | | 6 |
| 12 | | + | + | + | # | # | | + | + | | | + | + | | | | # | | 22 |
| 13 | | | | | | | | | | | | | | | | # | | | 1 |

## Appendix Four

| Book, Chapter | Ahaziah/Jehoram: 175 hits | Ahihud/Shelomi: 153 | Amariah/Hezekiah: 191 | Azariah/Amaziah: 185 | Azariah/Zephaniah: 147 | Azrikam/Azel: 161 | Baruch: 194 | Chimham/Jehoiachin: 204 | Chimham–Sarpuhi: 152 | Cyrus: 155 | Daniel: 249 | Daniel–Sarpuhi: 177 | Ezekiel–Son of Man: 174 | Ezra: 191 | Gemariah/Shaphan: 157 | Jacob–Israel: 198 | Jehizkiah/Shallum: 171 | Jehoiachin: 183 |
|---|---|---|---|---|---|---|---|---|---|---|---|---|---|---|---|---|---|---|
| 14 | # |   | + | # | # |   |   | # | # | # |   |   |   |   | # |   |   | # |
| 15 |   |   | # |   |   |   |   |   |   |   |   |   |   |   |   |   |   |   |
| 16 |   |   |   |   |   |   |   | # |   |   |   |   |   |   |   |   |   | # |
| 17 | # | + | # |   |   |   |   |   |   |   |   |   |   |   | # |   |   |   |
| 18 |   | # | + | + |   |   | + | + | + |   | + | # | # |   | + | + | + |   |
| 19 |   |   | + |   | # | + |   |   |   |   | + |   | # |   |   | # | # | + |
| 20 |   | # |   |   | + |   |   |   | + |   | # |   |   |   | + |   |   |   |
| 21 | + | # | # |   | + | + | + |   | + |   | + | + | + |   | # | # | # | + |
| 22 | # |   | + |   | + |   |   |   |   |   | # |   |   |   | # | # |   |   |
| 23 |   |   | # |   |   |   |   |   |   | # |   |   |   | # |   | # |   |   |
| 24 |   |   |   |   | + |   |   | + |   | + |   |   | # | # |   |   | # | # |
| 25 |   |   |   |   | + |   |   |   |   |   |   |   |   |   |   |   |   |   |
| 26 |   |   |   |   |   |   |   |   |   |   |   |   |   |   |   |   |   |   |
| 27 |   | # |   | # |   |   |   |   |   |   |   |   | # |   |   |   |   |   |
| 28 |   |   |   | # | + |   |   |   |   | # |   |   |   |   | # |   |   | # |
| 29 | + |   | + | # |   | + |   |   |   | + | + |   |   |   | # | + | + |   |
| 30 |   |   |   |   |   |   |   | # |   |   |   |   |   |   |   |   |   |   |
| 31 |   |   | # |   |   |   |   |   | # |   |   |   |   |   |   |   |   |   |
| 32 |   |   |   |   |   |   |   |   |   |   |   |   |   |   |   |   |   |   |
| 33 |   | # |   |   |   |   |   | # |   |   |   |   |   |   |   |   |   |   |
| 34 |   |   |   |   |   |   |   |   |   |   |   |   |   | # |   |   |   |   |
| 35 | # |   |   |   |   |   |   |   |   |   |   |   |   |   |   |   |   |   |
| 36 |   |   |   | # |   |   |   |   | # |   |   |   |   |   | # |   |   |   |
| 37 |   | # |   |   | # |   |   |   |   |   |   |   | # |   |   |   | + | # |
| 38 |   | + | + | + |   | + |   | # | # | # | # |   | + | # |   |   | + |   |
| 39 |   | # |   |   |   |   |   |   |   |   |   |   | # |   |   |   |   | + |

## Coding of Exilic Names in Hebrew Scripture

| Book, Chapter | Jehoiakim-Sarpuhi: 146 Hits | Jeremiah: 194 | Seraiah/Tanhumeth: 172 | Shecaniah/Jahaziel: 179 | Shelemiah/Abdeel: 148 | Shelemiah/Kore: 223 | Shenazzar/Jehoiachin: 165 | Shephatiah/David: 189 | Solomon/David: 165 | Substitute King: 138 | Zedekiah: 184 | Zedekiah-Sarpuhi: 175 | Zephaniah: 184 | Nebchdnzr: 168 (605–562) | Ezekiel-Sarpuhi: 179 (569) | Jehoiachin–Sarp: 160 (561) | Nab–Belshzr: 186 (556–39) | Cyrus K Bab: 159 (539–30) | Chapter Hits, Book Percent |
|---|---|---|---|---|---|---|---|---|---|---|---|---|---|---|---|---|---|---|---|
| 14 | # |   | # |   | + |   |   |   |   |   | + | # | # |   |   |   | # |   | 16 |
| 15 |   |   |   |   | # |   |   |   |   |   | # |   | # |   |   |   |   |   | 4 |
| 16 |   | # |   | # | # |   |   |   | + |   |   |   |   |   |   |   |   |   | 6 |
| 17 |   |   |   |   |   |   |   | # |   |   |   |   |   |   | + |   |   |   | 6 |
| 18 |   |   | # |   | # |   | # | # |   |   | + | # | # |   | # |   |   |   | 20 |
| 19 | # |   | + |   | # | + |   | # | + | # |   | + | + |   | # |   |   |   | 18 |
| 20 |   |   | # | + |   |   |   |   | + |   |   |   |   | # | + |   |   |   | 10 |
| 21 | # | + |   | # |   | + |   | # | # |   |   | # | # |   |   | + |   |   | 23 |
| 22 |   |   |   |   | # |   |   |   |   |   |   | # |   |   |   |   |   |   | 8 |
| 23 |   |   |   |   |   | + |   |   | # |   |   | # |   | # |   |   | # |   | 9 |
| 24 |   |   | # |   | # |   |   | # | + |   |   | # |   | + |   |   | # |   | 14 |
| 25 |   |   |   |   |   |   |   |   |   |   |   |   |   |   |   |   |   |   | 1 |
| 26 |   |   |   |   |   |   |   |   |   |   |   |   |   |   |   |   |   |   |   |
| 27 |   | # |   |   |   |   |   |   | + |   |   |   |   |   |   |   |   |   | 5 |
| 28 |   | + | # | + | # |   |   |   |   | # | + |   |   |   | + |   |   |   | 12 |
| 29 | + |   |   | # |   |   |   |   | # |   |   |   |   |   |   | + |   |   | 13 |
| 30 |   |   |   |   |   |   |   |   |   |   |   |   |   |   |   |   |   |   | 1 |
| 31 |   |   |   |   |   |   |   |   |   |   |   |   |   |   |   |   |   |   | 2 |
| 32 |   |   |   |   |   |   |   |   |   |   |   |   |   |   |   |   |   |   |   |
| 33 |   |   | # |   |   |   |   |   |   |   |   |   |   |   |   |   |   |   | 3 |
| 34 | # |   |   |   | + |   | # |   |   |   |   |   |   |   |   |   |   |   | 4 |
| 35 |   |   |   |   |   |   |   |   |   |   |   |   |   |   | + |   |   |   | 2 |
| 36 |   |   |   |   | + |   |   |   |   |   | + |   |   | + |   |   | # |   | 7 |
| 37 |   |   | + | # | + | # |   |   |   |   |   | # |   |   |   |   | # |   | 12 |
| 38 | + | + | + |   | + |   |   | + | + |   |   | + |   |   |   |   |   |   | 18 |
| 39 |   |   |   |   |   | + | # | # |   | # |   |   |   |   |   |   | # | # | 9 |

## Appendix Four

| Book, Chapter | Ahaziah/Jehoram: 175 hits | Ahihud/Shelomi: 153 | Amariah/Hezekiah: 191 | Azariah/Amaziah: 185 | Azariah/Zephaniah: 147 | Azrikam/Azel: 161 | Baruch: 194 | Chimham/Jehoiachin: 204 | Chimham-Sarpuhi: 152 | Cyrus: 155 | Daniel: 249 | Daniel-Sarpuhi: 177 | Ezekiel–Son of Man: 174 | Ezra: 191 | Gemariah/Shaphan: 157 | Jacob–Israel: 198 | Jehizkiah/Shallum: 171 | Jehoiachin: 183 |
|---|---|---|---|---|---|---|---|---|---|---|---|---|---|---|---|---|---|---|
| 40 | # |   | # |   |   | + | # | + | # | + | + | + | # | # | + | + | + | + |
| 41 | + | + | # | + | + | + | + | + |   | # | + | # | + | + | # |   | + | # |
| 42 |   |   |   |   |   |   |   |   |   |   |   |   |   |   |   |   |   |   |
| Ps |   |   |   |   |   |   |   |   |   |   |   |   |   |   |   |   |   |   |
| 1 |   |   |   |   |   |   |   |   |   |   |   |   |   |   |   |   |   |   |
| 2 |   | + |   | # |   | + |   |   | # | + | + | + | + | + | + | + | + |   |
| 3 |   |   |   |   |   | # |   |   |   |   |   |   |   |   |   |   |   |   |
| 4 |   |   | + | # |   |   |   |   |   |   |   |   |   |   |   | + |   | # |
| 5 |   |   |   |   |   | # |   |   | # |   |   |   |   |   |   |   |   |   |
| 6 |   |   |   |   |   |   |   |   |   |   |   |   |   |   |   |   |   |   |
| 7 | # |   | + |   |   | # |   |   |   |   | + | # | + |   |   | + |   |   |
| 8 |   |   | # | # |   |   |   |   |   |   | + |   |   |   |   |   |   |   |
| 9 |   |   | + | + |   | # |   | # |   |   | + |   | + |   |   | + |   |   |
| 10 | + |   | + | + |   |   | # | + |   |   | + |   | + | + | + | + |   | + |
| 11 |   |   | # |   |   |   |   | # |   |   | + |   |   | + |   | # |   | # |
| 12 | # |   |   | # | + |   |   |   |   | # |   | + | # |   |   | # |   |   |
| 13 |   |   |   | + |   |   |   |   |   |   |   |   |   |   |   |   |   |   |
| 14 |   |   |   |   |   |   |   |   |   |   |   |   |   |   |   |   |   |   |
| 15 |   |   | # |   |   |   |   |   |   |   |   |   |   |   | + |   |   |   |
| 16 |   |   | # |   |   |   | + |   |   |   | # |   |   |   |   |   |   |   |
| 17 | + | + | + | + | + | + | + |   | + | + | + | + | + | # | + | + | + |
| 18 |   |   |   |   | # | # | # | # |   | + | # | # | + | # |   | + |   |   |
| 19 | # |   | # | + |   | # |   |   |   |   |   |   | # | + |   | # | # |   |
| 20 | # |   |   | + |   |   |   |   | + |   |   |   | # |   |   |   |   |   |
| 21 |   |   | # |   |   |   | # |   |   |   |   |   |   |   |   |   |   |   |
| 22 |   |   |   | # |   |   | # |   |   |   |   |   | + |   | # |   | + |   |

## Coding of Exilic Names in Hebrew Scripture

| Book, Chapter | Jehoiakim-Sarpuhi: 146 Hits | Jeremiah: 194 | Seraiah/Tanhumeth: 172 | Shecaniah/Jahaziel: 179 | Shelemiah/Abdeel: 148 | Shelemiah/Kore: 223 | Shenazzar/Jehoiachin: 165 | Shephatiah/David: 189 | Solomon/David: 165 | Substitute King: 138 | Zedekiah: 184 | Zedekiah-Sarpuhi: 175 | Zephaniah: 184 | Nebchdnzr: 168 (605–562) | Ezekiel-Sarpuhi: 179 (569) | Jehoiachin-Sarp: 160 (561) | Nab–Belshzr: 186 (556–39) | Cyrus K Bab: 159 (539–30) | Chapter Hits, Book Percent |
|---|---|---|---|---|---|---|---|---|---|---|---|---|---|---|---|---|---|---|---|
| 40 |  |  | + | + | # | # |  | + | # | # |  | + | + |  | + | + |  |  | 26 |
| 41 | + | + | + |  |  | + | # | + | + | + |  | + | + |  | + | + |  |  | 28 |
| 42 |  |  |  |  |  |  |  | # |  |  |  |  |  |  |  |  |  |  | 1 |
| Ps |  |  |  |  |  |  |  |  |  |  |  |  |  |  |  |  |  |  | 26% |
| 1 |  |  |  |  |  |  |  |  |  |  |  |  |  |  |  |  |  |  |  |
| 2 |  |  | + | + |  | + |  | + | # |  | + |  |  |  |  | # |  |  | 18 |
| 3 |  |  |  |  |  |  |  | # |  |  |  |  |  |  |  |  |  |  | 2 |
| 4 |  |  |  |  |  |  | + |  |  |  |  | # |  |  |  |  |  |  | 6 |
| 5 |  |  |  | # |  |  |  |  |  |  |  |  |  |  | # |  |  |  | 4 |
| 6 |  |  |  |  |  |  |  |  |  |  |  | # |  |  |  |  |  |  | 1 |
| 7 |  |  |  |  |  |  |  |  |  |  |  | # |  |  |  |  |  |  | 8 |
| 8 |  |  |  |  | # | + |  |  |  |  | # | # |  |  |  |  |  | # | 8 |
| 9 | # | # |  |  | # | # |  | # |  | # |  |  |  | + | # | + | + |  | 17 |
| 10 | # |  | # |  |  | + | + | + |  | # | + |  |  | + | # |  |  | # | 21 |
| 11 |  |  |  |  |  | + |  |  | + |  |  |  |  |  | # |  |  | + | 10 |
| 12 |  |  |  |  |  |  |  |  |  |  |  | # |  |  |  |  |  |  | 8 |
| 13 |  |  |  | # |  | # |  |  |  |  |  |  |  |  |  |  |  |  | 3 |
| 14 |  |  |  | + |  |  |  |  |  |  |  |  |  |  |  |  |  |  | 1 |
| 15 |  |  |  |  |  |  |  | # |  |  |  |  |  |  |  |  |  |  | 3 |
| 16 |  |  |  |  |  | + | # |  |  |  |  |  |  |  |  |  |  |  | 5 |
| 17 | + | + | # | # | + | + | + | + | + |  | + | + | # | + | + | + | + | # | 34 |
| 18 |  |  | + | + |  | # |  |  |  | # |  |  |  |  | + | # |  |  | 16 |
| 19 | + | + | + |  |  |  |  | + | # | # |  | + |  |  | + |  |  |  | 16 |
| 20 |  | + |  |  |  | # |  |  |  |  |  | # |  |  |  |  |  | + | 8 |
| 21 |  |  |  |  |  |  |  |  |  | + |  |  |  |  |  |  | # |  | 4 |
| 22 | # |  | + |  |  | + |  |  | + |  |  | # |  |  |  | # |  | # | 12 |

## Appendix Four

| Book, Chapter | Ahaziah/Jehoram: 175 hits | Ahihud/Shelomi: 153 | Amariah/Hezekiah: 191 | Azariah/Amaziah: 185 | Azariah/Zephaniah: 147 | Azrikam/Azel: 161 | Baruch: 194 | Chimham/Jehoiachin: 204 | Chimham–Sarpuhi: 152 | Cyrus: 155 | Daniel: 249 | Daniel–Sarpuhi: 177 | Ezekiel–Son of Man: 174 | Ezra: 191 | Gemariah/Shaphan: 157 | Jacob–Israel: 198 | Jehizkiah/Shallum: 171 | Jehoiachin: 183 |
|---|---|---|---|---|---|---|---|---|---|---|---|---|---|---|---|---|---|---|
| 23 |   |   |   |   |   |   |   |   |   |   |   |   |   | + |   |   | + |   |
| 24 |   |   |   | # |   |   |   |   | # |   |   |   |   |   |   |   |   |   |
| 25 |   |   |   |   |   |   |   | + |   |   |   |   |   |   |   | + |   | # |
| 26 |   |   |   |   |   |   |   |   |   |   |   |   |   | + |   | + |   |   |
| 27 |   |   |   |   | # |   |   |   |   |   |   |   |   |   |   | + |   | + |
| 28 |   |   |   | # |   |   |   |   |   |   |   |   |   |   |   |   |   |   |
| 29 |   |   |   |   |   |   |   |   |   |   |   |   |   |   |   |   |   |   |
| 30 | # |   | # | # |   |   |   |   |   |   |   | # |   | # |   |   |   |   |
| 31 |   |   |   | # |   |   |   |   | # | + |   |   | + | # |   | + | + |   |
| 32 |   |   | # | + |   |   |   |   |   |   |   | # |   | + | # | # | # | + |
| 33 |   |   |   |   |   |   |   |   |   |   |   |   |   |   |   |   |   |   |
| 34 |   |   |   | # |   |   |   |   | # |   |   |   | + | # |   |   |   |   |
| 35 |   |   |   |   |   |   |   | # | + | # | + |   | # | + |   | + |   |   |
| 36 |   |   |   | # |   |   |   |   |   |   |   |   | + | + | + | # |   |   |
| 37 | # |   | + | + | # |   |   |   | # | # | + | + |   | + |   | # | + | # |
| 38 |   |   | + |   |   |   |   | # |   | # |   |   | # |   |   |   |   |   |
| 39 |   |   |   |   |   |   |   |   |   |   |   |   | # |   | # |   | # | # |
| 40 |   |   | + | # |   | # | + |   | # | # | + | # | + |   | + | + |   |   |
| 41 |   |   | # |   |   |   |   |   |   |   |   |   |   |   |   |   |   |   |
| 42 |   |   |   |   |   |   |   |   |   |   |   |   |   |   |   | # |   |   |
| 43 |   |   |   |   |   |   |   |   |   |   |   |   |   | + |   | + |   |   |
| 44 |   |   | # |   | # |   |   | # |   | + | + | + | # | + |   | + | + | # |
| 45 |   |   |   |   |   |   |   | # |   |   | # |   |   |   |   |   |   |   |
| 46 |   | # | + |   | + |   | # |   | + | # |   |   | + |   |   |   | + |   |
| 47 |   |   |   |   |   |   |   |   |   |   |   |   |   | # |   |   |   |   |
| 48 | + |   | # | # | + | + |   | + |   | + | + | + | + | + | + | + | + |   |

## Coding of Exilic Names in Hebrew Scripture

| Book, Chapter | Jehoiakim-Sarpuhi: 146 Hits | Jeremiah: 194 | Seraiah/Tanhumeth: 172 | Shecaniah/Jahaziel: 179 | Shelemiah/Abdeel: 148 | Shelemiah/Kore: 223 | Shenazzar/Jehoiachin: 165 | Shephatiah/David: 189 | Solomon/David: 165 | Substitute King: 138 | Zedekiah: 184 | Zedekiah-Sarpuhi: 175 | Zephaniah: 184 | Nebchdnzr: 168 (605–562) | Ezekiel-Sarpuhi: 179 (569) | Jehoiachin–Sarp: 160 (561) | Nab-Belshzr: 186 (556–39) | Cyrus K Bab: 159 (539–30) | Chapter Hits, Book Percent |
|---|---|---|---|---|---|---|---|---|---|---|---|---|---|---|---|---|---|---|---|
| 23 | | | | | | | | | | | | | | | | | | | 2 |
| 24 | | | | + | | | # | | | | | | | | | | | | 4 |
| 25 | | | | | | | | | | | | | | | | | | | 3 |
| 26 | | | | | | | | | | | | | | | | | | | 2 |
| 27 | | | | | | # | # | | | | | # | # | | | | | | 7 |
| 28 | | | | | | | | | | | | | | | | | | | 1 |
| 29 | | | | | | | | | | | | | | | | | | | |
| 30 | | | | | | | | + | | | | | | | | | | | 6 |
| 31 | | | + | | + | # | | | | | | + | | + | + | # | | + | 15 |
| 32 | | | + | | + | # | | | | | | | | | | + | | | 14 |
| 33 | # | | | | | | | | | | | | | | | | | | 1 |
| 34 | | + | | | # | | + | # | | | | # | | | | | | | 9 |
| 35 | | | # | | | | | | | | | # | | | | # | + | | 11 |
| 36 | | | | | # | | | # | | | | # | | | # | # | | | 10 |
| 37 | # | # | # | + | + | | + | # | + | + | # | + | + | + | | | | | 25 |
| 38 | | | | | | | | | | | | | | | | # | | | 5 |
| 39 | | | | + | | | # | # | # | | | | | | | | + | # | 10 |
| 40 | | + | + | + | | + | # | | | | | + | + | | + | # | # | + | 22 |
| 41 | | | # | | | | # | | | | | | | | | | | + | 4 |
| 42 | | | # | | | | | # | | | | | | | | | | | 3 |
| 43 | | | | | | # | | | # | | + | | # | | | | | | 6 |
| 44 | | + | + | | | + | + | | | + | + | # | # | + | | + | | | 21 |
| 45 | | | | # | + | | | + | | # | | | | | # | | # | | 8 |
| 46 | | + | | # | | # | | + | # | + | | # | | | | # | # | | 19 |
| 47 | | | | | | | | | | | | | | | | | | | 1 |
| 48 | | | + | # | # | + | | # | + | + | + | # | + | + | + | | | + | 27 |

# Appendix Four

| Book, Chapter | Ahaziah/Jehoram: 175 hits | Ahihud/Shelomi: 153 | Amariah/Hezekiah: 191 | Azariah/Amaziah: 185 | Azariah/Zephaniah: 147 | Azrikam/Azel: 161 | Baruch: 194 | Chimham/Jehoiachin: 204 | Chimham-Sarpuhi: 152 | Cyrus: 155 | Daniel: 249 | Daniel-Sarpuhi: 177 | Ezekiel-Son of Man: 174 | Ezra: 191 | Gemariah/Shaphan: 157 | Jacob-Israel: 198 | Jehizkiah/Shallum: 171 | Jehoiachin: 183 |
|---|---|---|---|---|---|---|---|---|---|---|---|---|---|---|---|---|---|---|
| 49 |   |   |   |   |   |   |   |   |   |   |   |   |   |   |   | # |   |   |
| 50 | # | # |   | # | # |   |   | # |   |   | # | + |   | + |   | + |   |   |
| 51 | + | + | + | + | + | + | + | + | # | + | + | + | + | + | + | + | + | + |
| 52 | + |   | + | # |   |   |   | # | # |   | + | + | # | + |   | # | # | # |
| 53 |   |   |   |   |   |   |   |   |   |   |   |   |   |   |   |   |   |   |
| 54 |   |   |   |   |   |   |   | # |   |   |   | + |   | + |   | + |   |   |
| 55 |   |   | # |   |   |   |   |   |   |   |   |   |   | # | # |   |   |   |
| 56 |   | # |   |   |   |   |   | # |   |   |   |   |   |   |   |   |   |   |
| 57 |   |   |   |   |   | + | # |   |   | + |   |   | # |   | + |   |   |   |
| 58 | + |   | # | + | + |   | # | + | + | + | # | + |   | # | + | # | + |   |
| 59 |   | # |   |   |   |   | + |   | + |   |   | + |   |   | + |   |   |   |
| 60 | + | + |   |   |   | # | + |   |   | + | # | # | # | + |   | + |   | + |
| 61 |   |   |   |   |   |   |   | # |   | # |   |   |   | # |   |   |   |   |
| 62 |   |   |   |   |   |   |   |   |   |   |   |   |   |   |   |   | # | # |
| 63 |   |   |   |   |   |   |   |   |   |   |   |   |   |   |   |   |   |   |
| 64 |   |   |   |   | + |   |   |   |   |   |   |   |   |   |   |   |   |   |
| 65 | + |   | + | + | + | # | # | + | + |   | + |   | # | + | + | + | # | # |
| 66 |   |   |   |   |   |   |   |   |   |   |   |   | + | # |   |   |   |   |
| 67 |   |   |   |   |   |   |   |   |   |   |   |   |   |   |   |   |   |   |
| 68 |   |   | # | + |   | + | # |   |   | + |   | # | + |   | + | + | + |   |
| 69 | + |   | # | + |   | # |   |   |   |   |   |   | + |   | # |   |   |   |
| 70 |   |   |   |   |   | + | + |   | + | # |   |   | + |   |   |   |   |   |
| 71 | # |   | # | + | # |   | # | # | + |   | + | # | # | + | # |   | + |   |
| 72 |   |   |   |   | # | # | # |   | # |   | # |   |   | # |   |   |   |   |
| 73 |   | # | # |   | # | # |   |   |   |   |   |   |   |   | # | # |   |   |
| 74 | + | # |   | # |   |   |   |   |   |   | # |   |   | # |   |   |   |   |

## Coding of Exilic Names in Hebrew Scripture

| Book, Chapter | Jehoiakim-Sarpuhi: 146 Hits | Jeremiah: 194 | Seraiah/Tanhumeth: 172 | Shecaniah/Jahaziel: 179 | Shelemiah/Abdeel: 148 | Shelemiah/Kore: 223 | Shenazzar/Jehoiachin: 165 | Shephatiah/David: 189 | Solomon/David: 165 | Substitute King: 138 | Zedekiah: 184 | Zedekiah-Sarpuhi: 175 | Zephaniah: 184 | Nebchdnzr: 168 (605–562) | Ezekiel-Sarpuhi: 179 (569) | Jehoiachin-Sarp: 160 (561) | Nab-Belshzr: 186 (556–39) | Cyrus K Bab: 159 (539–30) | Chapter Hits, Book Percent |
|---|---|---|---|---|---|---|---|---|---|---|---|---|---|---|---|---|---|---|---|
| 49 | | | | # | | | | # | | | | | | | | | | | 3 |
| 50 | # | # | # | | | | | # | | | + | # | | | | | | | 15 |
| 51 | | + | + | + | + | + | + | + | + | | + | + | + | + | + | + | + | + | 34 |
| 52 | | + | | | # | | | # | | | | | | | # | # | | + | 18 |
| 53 | | | | | | | | | | | | | | | # | | | | 1 |
| 54 | | | + | # | | | | | | | | | | | | | | | 6 |
| 55 | + | # | | | | | | | | | | | | | | | | | 5 |
| 56 | | | | | | | | # | | | | | | | | | | | 3 |
| 57 | | | # | | | | | | + | | | | | | | | | | 7 |
| 58 | | | + | # | + | + | | # | | | + | | | | | | | + | 21 |
| 59 | | # | | | # | | # | | | | | | | + | | | | # | 11 |
| 60 | | # | | | | | | # | # | | + | | | + | + | | # | | 18 |
| 61 | | # | + | | | | | | + | + | | | | | | | | | 7 |
| 62 | + | | # | | | | | + | # | | | | | | # | | | + | 8 |
| 63 | | | | | | + | | | | | | | | | # | | | + | 3 |
| 64 | | + | | # | + | | | # | | | | | | | # | | | | 6 |
| 65 | | + | | # | # | + | | # | + | # | + | # | # | + | | + | + | + | 27 |
| 66 | # | | # | + | + | # | + | | # | # | | | | + | | | # | | 12 |
| 67 | | | | | | | | | | | | | | | | | | | |
| 68 | # | + | # | # | | # | | + | | | # | | # | | # | | # | + | 22 |
| 69 | + | | | | | # | | + | # | | # | # | # | | | | # | | 14 |
| 70 | | | + | | | | | | | | | | | | | | | | 6 |
| 71 | | | + | + | + | | # | # | + | + | | | + | | + | # | # | # | 25 |
| 72 | | | | | | | | | | | | | | | # | | | | 6 |
| 73 | | | | | | | | + | | | # | | | | | | | | 8 |
| 74 | | | | # | # | | | # | # | | # | + | # | # | | | | | 13 |

## Appendix Four

| Book, Chapter | Ahaziah/Jehoram: 175 hits | Ahihud/Shelomi: 153 | Amariah/Hezekiah: 191 | Azariah/Amaziah: 185 | Azariah/Zephaniah: 147 | Azrikam/Azel: 161 | Baruch: 194 | Chimham/Jehoiachin: 204 | Chimham–Sarpuhi: 152 | Cyrus: 155 | Daniel: 249 | Daniel-Sarpuhi: 177 | Ezekiel–Son of Man: 174 | Ezra: 191 | Gemariah/Shaphan: 157 | Jacob-Israel: 198 | Jehizkiah/Shallum: 171 | Jehoiachin: 183 |
|---|---|---|---|---|---|---|---|---|---|---|---|---|---|---|---|---|---|---|
| 75 |   |   |   |   |   |   |   |   |   |   |   |   |   | # |   |   |   |   |
| 76 |   |   | # | + |   |   | # | # |   |   |   |   |   | + |   |   | # |   |
| 77 | # |   |   | + | + |   |   | # |   |   | + | # | # |   |   | + |   |   |
| 78 |   | + | # | + | # | # | + | + |   | + | # | + | + | # | + | # | + | + |
| 79 | + | + |   | # | + |   | + |   |   |   | # |   |   | # |   | # | # | + |
| 80 | + | + | # | + | + |   | + | + |   |   | + | + | + | + |   | + | + | # |
| 81 |   |   |   | # |   | # |   |   |   |   | # | # |   |   |   | + | # | # |
| 82 |   |   | # |   |   |   |   |   |   |   |   | + |   |   |   |   |   |   |
| 83 | # | # | + | # | # |   |   | # |   | + | + | + | # | + |   | + |   | # |
| 84 |   |   | # | + |   |   |   | # |   |   | # |   | # | # |   | + | + |   |
| 85 |   | + |   |   |   | + | + |   |   |   |   |   | + | # |   |   | # | + |
| 86 |   |   |   |   |   |   | + |   |   |   |   |   |   |   |   |   |   |   |
| 87 | + | # |   |   |   |   |   |   |   |   |   |   |   |   |   |   |   |   |
| 88 |   | # |   | # | # | + | + |   |   |   | + | # | + | + |   | + |   | + |
| 89 | + | # | + | + | + | + | + | # |   | # | + | + |   | + | # |   | + | + |
| 90 |   |   |   |   |   |   |   |   |   |   |   |   |   |   |   |   |   |   |
| 91 |   |   |   |   |   |   | # |   | # |   | # |   |   | + |   |   |   |   |
| 92 |   | + | # | # |   |   | # | # |   |   |   |   |   | + |   | # |   |   |
| 93 |   |   |   |   |   |   |   |   |   |   |   |   |   | # |   |   |   |   |
| 94 |   |   |   |   |   | + |   |   | # |   | # | + |   |   |   | + | + |   |
| 95 |   |   |   |   |   |   |   |   |   |   |   |   |   |   | + |   |   |   |
| 96 |   |   |   |   |   |   |   |   |   |   |   |   |   |   |   |   | # |   |
| 97 | # |   |   | # |   |   | + |   |   |   | + | # | # | + |   | + | + | + |
| 98 |   | # |   | + |   |   | # | # |   |   |   |   | + | + |   |   | + |   |
| 99 |   |   |   |   |   |   |   |   |   | # |   |   |   |   |   |   |   |   |
| 100 |   |   |   |   |   |   |   |   |   |   |   |   |   | # |   |   |   | # |

## Coding of Exilic Names in Hebrew Scripture

| Book, Chapter | Jehoiakim-Sarpuhi: 146 Hits | Jeremiah: 194 | Seraiah/Tanhumeth: 172 | Shecaniah/Jahaziel: 179 | Shelemiah/Abdeel: 148 | Shelemiah/Kore: 223 | Shenazzar/Jehoiachin: 165 | Shephatiah/David: 189 | Solomon/David: 165 | Substitute King: 138 | Zedekiah: 184 | Zedekiah-Sarpuhi: 175 | Zephaniah: 184 | Nebchdnzr: 168 (605–562) | Ezekiel-Sarpuhi: 179 (569) | Jehoiachin-Sarp: 160 (561) | Nab-Belshzr: 186 (556–39) | Cyrus K Bab: 159 (539–30) | Chapter Hits, Book Percent |
|---|---|---|---|---|---|---|---|---|---|---|---|---|---|---|---|---|---|---|---|
| 75 |  |  | + |  |  |  |  | # |  |  | # |  |  |  |  |  |  |  | 4 |
| 76 |  |  | # | # |  |  | + |  | # | # |  | # |  | + |  |  |  |  | 13 |
| 77 |  | # | + | + |  | + | # |  | # | + | + | + | # | + | # |  | # | + | 22 |
| 78 |  | + | # | + | + | + |  | + | + |  |  | # | + | + | # | # |  |  | 28 |
| 79 |  | + |  |  |  | # |  | # |  |  |  |  |  | + | # | # |  |  | 16 |
| 80 | + | + | + | + |  | + | + | + | + | + | # | + | # | # | # | # | + | + | 31 |
| 81 | + | + |  | + |  | # |  |  |  |  |  | + |  | + | # |  |  |  | 14 |
| 82 |  | # |  | + | + |  |  |  |  | + |  | # |  |  |  |  |  |  | 7 |
| 83 |  | + | + | # | + | # |  | + |  |  | # |  |  |  |  |  | # |  | 21 |
| 84 |  | + | + | # |  |  |  |  |  |  | # |  |  | + |  |  |  |  | 13 |
| 85 | + |  |  |  | + |  |  | # | + |  |  | # |  | + |  | + |  |  | 14 |
| 86 |  |  |  |  |  |  |  |  |  |  |  |  |  | # |  |  |  |  | 2 |
| 87 |  | # |  |  |  |  |  |  | # |  |  |  |  |  |  |  |  |  | 4 |
| 88 | + | + |  | + |  | # | + | # |  |  | # | # | # | # | # | # | # | + | 24 |
| 89 |  | + | + | + | # | + | + | # | + | + | + | + | + | + | + |  |  | + | 31 |
| 90 |  |  |  |  |  |  |  |  |  |  |  |  |  |  |  |  |  |  |  |
| 91 | + |  | # |  |  |  |  | + |  |  | # |  |  |  |  |  |  |  | 8 |
| 92 |  | # | # | # |  | + | # |  |  |  |  |  |  |  | # |  |  |  | 13 |
| 93 |  |  |  |  |  |  |  |  |  |  |  |  |  |  |  |  |  |  | 1 |
| 94 |  |  | # |  | # | # |  |  |  |  |  |  |  |  |  | + |  | + | 11 |
| 95 |  |  | # |  |  |  |  |  |  |  |  |  |  |  |  |  |  |  | 2 |
| 96 |  |  |  |  |  |  |  |  |  | + | # |  | # |  |  |  |  |  | 4 |
| 97 |  | + | # | # |  | + |  |  | + |  | + | + |  | + |  | + |  | + | 20 |
| 98 |  |  |  |  |  |  |  |  |  |  |  |  |  |  |  |  | + |  | 8 |
| 99 |  |  |  |  |  |  |  |  |  |  |  |  |  |  |  |  |  |  | 1 |
| 100 |  |  |  |  |  |  |  |  |  |  |  |  |  |  |  |  |  |  | 2 |

## Appendix Four

| Book, Chapter | Ahaziah/Jehoram: 175 hits | Ahihud/Shelomi: 153 | Amariah/Hezekiah: 191 | Azariah/Amaziah: 185 | Azariah/Zephaniah: 147 | Azrikam/Azel: 161 | Baruch: 194 | Chimham/Jehoiachin: 204 | Chimham–Sarpuhi: 152 | Cyrus: 155 | Daniel: 249 | Daniel-Sarpuhi: 177 | Ezekiel-Son of Man: 174 | Ezra: 191 | Gemariah/Shaphan: 157 | Jacob-Israel: 198 | Jehizkiah/Shallum: 171 | Jehoiachin: 183 |
|---|---|---|---|---|---|---|---|---|---|---|---|---|---|---|---|---|---|---|
| 101 | | | | | | | | | | | | | | | | | | |
| 102 | | | | | # | | # | # | | | | | | # | | | | |
| 103 | | | + | | # | # | | # | | + | + | | # | | | | | |
| 104 | | | | # | | + | + | # | | + | + | # | # | # | | + | + | |
| 105 | | | | # | | # | # | # | # | # | # | | # | | | # | | |
| 106 | + | | | + | + | | + | + | # | + | + | | + | + | | + | # | # |
| 107 | | | # | + | + | + | # | + | # | # | # | + | # | + | | + | | + |
| 108 | # | + | + | # | | + | | | | | | # | | | | | | |
| 109 | | | | # | | # | # | # | | | + | # | | | | # | | |
| 110 | | | | | | + | | | | | | | | | | | + | |
| 111 | | | | | | | | + | | | | # | | + | | | # | # |
| 112 | + | + | | | | | | + | | | | | | | | | | + |
| 113 | | | | | | | | | | | | | | # | | | | |
| 114 | | | | | | + | | | | | | # | | + | | | | # |
| 115 | | | | | | | | | | | | | | | | | | # |
| 116 | | | | | | | | | | | | | | | | | | |
| 117 | | | | | | | | | | | | | | | | | | |
| 118 | | | | | | | | | | | | | | + | | | # | |
| 119 | + | + | + | + | + | | + | + | # | # | + | + | + | + | + | + | + | + |
| 120 | | | | | | | | | | | | | | | | | | |
| 121 | | | | | | | | | | | | | | | | | | |
| 122 | | | | | | | # | | | | | | | | | | | |
| 123 | | | | | | | | | | | | | | | | | | |
| 124 | | | # | | # | | + | | + | | | # | | + | | + | + | # |
| 125 | | | | | | | | # | | | | | + | | | | # | |
| 126 | | | | | | | | # | | | | | # | + | | | # | |

## Coding of Exilic Names in Hebrew Scripture

| Book, Chapter | Jehoiakim-Sarpuhi: 146 Hits | Jeremiah: 194 | Seraiah/Tanhumeth: 172 | Shecaniah/Jahaziel: 179 | Shelemiah/Abdeel: 148 | Shelemiah/Kore: 223 | Shenazzar/Jehoiachin: 165 | Shephatiah/David: 189 | Solomon/David: 165 | Substitute King: 138 | Zedekiah: 184 | Zedekiah-Sarpuhi: 175 | Zephaniah: 184 | Nebchdnzr: 168 (605–562) | Ezekiel-Sarpuhi: 179 (569) | Jehoiachin-Sarp: 160 (561) | Nab-Belshzr: 186 (556–39) | Cyrus K Bab: 159 (539–30) | Chapter Hits, Book Percent |
|---|---|---|---|---|---|---|---|---|---|---|---|---|---|---|---|---|---|---|---|
| 101 | | | | | | | | | | | | | | | | | | | |
| 102 | | | | + | | # | | + | | | | | | | | | | | 7 |
| 103 | | + | | | # | # | | | # | + | | | | | | | | # | 13 |
| 104 | # | | | # | | + | | # | | + | | # | + | | | # | # | | 19 |
| 105 | | # | | | | | | | | | | | | | | | | | 10 |
| 106 | # | | # | | + | + | + | # | | + | # | # | # | + | + | # | # | | 27 |
| 107 | + | + | | | | + | | + | # | + | + | | | + | | | # | # | 24 |
| 108 | | | | | # | | | | | | | | | + | | | + | | 9 |
| 109 | | | | + | | | | | | | | + | | | | | | | 10 |
| 110 | | | | | | | | | # | | | | | | | # | | | 4 |
| 111 | | + | | # | | # | | | | | | | | + | | | | | 9 |
| 112 | | | | | | | | + | | | | | | # | | | # | | 7 |
| 113 | | | | | | | | | | | | | | | | | | | 1 |
| 114 | | # | | | | | | | # | | | | | | | | | | 6 |
| 115 | | + | | + | | | | | | | | | | # | | | | | 4 |
| 116 | | # | | | | | | | | | | | | | | # | | | 2 |
| 117 | | | | | | | | | | | | | | | | | | | |
| 118 | | | | | | | | | | | | | | | | | | | 2 |
| 119 | | + | + | + | + | + | + | + | + | + | + | + | + | + | + | + | # | + | 32 |
| 120 | | | | | | | | | | | | | | | | | | | |
| 121 | | | | | | | | | | | | | | | | | | | |
| 122 | | | | | | | | | | | | | | | | | | | 1 |
| 123 | | | | | | | | | | | | | | | | | | | |
| 124 | | + | | | + | | + | | # | | | + | | | + | | + | | 16 |
| 125 | | | | | | + | | | | | | | + | # | | | | | 6 |
| 126 | | | # | | | | # | | | | | | | | | | | | 6 |

269

## Appendix Four

| Book, Chapter | Ahaziah/Jehoram: 175 hits | Ahihud/Shelomi: 153 | Amariah/Hezekiah: 191 | Azariah/Amaziah: 185 | Azariah/Zephaniah: 147 | Azrikam/Azel: 161 | Baruch: 194 | Chimham/Jehoiachin: 204 | Chimham–Sarpuhi: 152 | Cyrus: 155 | Daniel: 249 | Daniel–Sarpuhi: 177 | Ezekiel–Son of Man: 174 | Ezra: 191 | Gemariah/Shaphan: 157 | Jacob–Israel: 198 | Jehizkiah/Shallum: 171 | Jehoiachin: 183 |
|---|---|---|---|---|---|---|---|---|---|---|---|---|---|---|---|---|---|---|
| 127 | | | | | | | | | | | | | | # | | | | |
| 128 | | | | | | | | | | | | | | | | | | # |
| 129 | | | | | # | | | | | | | | | | | | # | |
| 130 | | | | | | | | | | | | | | | | | # | |
| 131 | | | | | | | | | | | | | | | | | | |
| 132 | | | | | | | | | | | | | | | | | | |
| 133 | | | | | | | | | | | | | | | | | | |
| 134 | | | | | | | | | | | | | | | | | | |
| 135 | | | | | | | | | | | | | | | | | | |
| 136 | | | | | | + | + | # | + | | | | | | | | # | + |
| 137 | | | | | | | | | | | | | | | | | | |
| 138 | | | | | | | | # | | | | | | | | | | |
| 139 | | | | | | | | # | | | | | | | | | # | |
| 140 | # | | | | | | | # | | | | | | # | # | | | |
| 141 | | | | | | | | # | | | | # | | | | | | |
| 142 | | | + | + | + | | | + | + | | + | | | | # | + | # | |
| 143 | + | | # | # | | # | | | | | + | # | | + | | + | | + |
| 144 | | | | + | | | | | | + | # | | # | + | | | + | |
| 145 | # | | + | + | | + | + | # | + | | | | + | + | | + | + | + |
| 146 | | | | | | | | | | | | | | # | | | | |
| 147 | + | | # | + | + | # | + | | + | | | | | + | | + | + | + |
| 148 | | | | # | | | | | | | | | + | # | | | | |
| 149 | . | | | | | | | | | | | | | | | | | |
| 150 | | | | | | # | | | | | | | | | | | | |
| Prov | | | | | | | | | | | | | | | | | | |
| 1 | | | + | # | + | | # | | | | | | | | | | | |

## Coding of Exilic Names in Hebrew Scripture

| Book, Chapter | Jehoiakim-Sarpuhi: 146 Hits | Jeremiah: 194 | Seraiah/Tanhumeth: 172 | Shecaniah/Jahaziel: 179 | Shelemiah/Abdeel: 148 | Shelemiah/Kore: 223 | Shenazzar/Jehoiachin: 165 | Shephatiah/David: 189 | Solomon/David: 165 | Substitute King: 138 | Zedekiah: 184 | Zedekiah-Sarpuhi: 175 | Zephaniah: 184 | Nebchdnzr: 168 (605–562) | Ezekiel-Sarpuhi: 179 (569) | Jehoiachin-Sarp: 160 (561) | Nab-Belshzr: 186 (556–39) | Cyrus K Bab: 159 (539–30) | Chapter Hits, Book Percent |
|---|---|---|---|---|---|---|---|---|---|---|---|---|---|---|---|---|---|---|---|
| 127 |   |   |   |   |   | # |   |   |   |   |   |   |   |   |   |   |   |   | 2 |
| 128 |   |   |   |   |   |   |   |   |   |   |   |   |   |   |   |   |   |   | 1 |
| 129 |   |   |   |   |   |   |   | # |   | # |   |   |   |   |   |   |   |   | 4 |
| 130 |   |   |   |   |   |   |   |   |   |   |   |   |   |   |   |   |   |   | 1 |
| 131 |   |   |   |   |   |   |   |   |   |   |   |   |   |   |   |   |   |   |   |
| 132 |   |   |   |   |   |   |   |   |   |   |   | # |   |   |   |   |   |   | 1 |
| 133 |   |   |   |   |   |   |   |   |   |   |   | + |   |   |   |   |   |   | 1 |
| 134 |   |   |   |   |   |   |   |   |   |   |   |   |   |   |   |   |   |   |   |
| 135 |   |   |   |   |   |   |   |   |   |   |   |   |   |   | + |   |   |   | 1 |
| 136 |   |   |   |   | # |   |   |   | # |   |   |   |   | # |   |   | + |   | 10 |
| 137 |   |   |   |   |   |   |   |   |   |   |   |   |   |   |   |   |   |   |   |
| 138 |   |   |   |   |   |   |   |   |   |   |   |   |   |   |   |   |   |   | 1 |
| 139 |   |   |   | # |   |   |   |   |   |   |   |   |   |   |   |   |   | + | 4 |
| 140 |   | # | # |   | # |   |   |   | # | + | # |   |   |   |   |   |   |   | 10 |
| 141 |   | # |   |   |   |   |   |   |   |   |   |   |   |   |   |   |   |   | 3 |
| 142 |   |   | + | # |   |   |   | # |   |   | + |   |   | # | + |   |   |   | 15 |
| 143 |   |   |   | # | + | # |   |   | # |   |   |   |   |   | # | + | + |   | 16 |
| 144 |   |   | # | # |   |   |   | + | # |   | + |   | # |   | # |   |   |   | 13 |
| 145 |   |   | + | + |   | + | # |   | + | # | # |   |   | + | # |   |   | + | 22 |
| 146 |   |   |   |   |   |   |   |   |   |   |   |   |   |   |   |   |   |   | 1 |
| 147 | + |   |   | + |   |   | + | # |   | # | # | # |   | + | # | + | # | + | 23 |
| 148 |   |   |   |   |   |   |   |   |   |   |   |   |   |   |   |   |   |   | 3 |
| 149 |   |   |   |   | + | + |   |   | # |   |   |   |   | # |   |   | # |   | 6 |
| 150 |   |   |   |   |   |   |   |   |   |   |   |   |   |   |   |   |   |   | 1 |
| Prov |   |   |   |   |   |   |   |   |   |   |   |   |   |   |   |   |   |   | 41% |
| 1 |   |   |   | # | + |   |   |   |   |   |   |   |   | + |   |   |   | + | 8 |

## Appendix Four

| Book, Chapter | Ahaziah/Jehoram: 175 hits | Ahihud/Shelomi: 153 | Amariah/Hezekiah: 191 | Azariah/Amaziah: 185 | Azariah/Zephaniah: 147 | Azrikam/Azel: 161 | Baruch: 194 | Chimham/Jehoiachin: 204 | Chimham-Sarpuhi: 152 | Cyrus: 155 | Daniel: 249 | Daniel–Sarpuhi: 177 | Ezekiel–Son of Man: 174 | Ezra: 191 | Gemariah/Shaphan: 157 | Jacob–Israel: 198 | Jehizkiah/Shallum: 171 | Jehoiachin: 183 |
|---|---|---|---|---|---|---|---|---|---|---|---|---|---|---|---|---|---|---|
| 2 |   | + | + | + | + | # | + | + |   | # | + | + | + | + |   | # | + |   |
| 3 | # |   |   | + |   |   |   |   | # |   |   |   |   |   |   | # |   | # |
| 4 |   |   |   |   | # |   |   |   | # |   |   | # |   | + |   | # |   | # |
| 5 |   |   | + |   |   |   | + | + |   | + | # | # | # |   |   |   | # |   |
| 6 |   |   | # |   | + |   |   | # |   |   |   |   | # |   |   |   | + |   |
| 7 |   | + |   | # | + |   |   | + |   |   | + |   |   | + |   |   |   |   |
| 8 |   | + | + | + | # |   | # |   | # | + |   | + |   |   | + | + |   | + |
| 9 |   |   | # | # |   |   |   | + |   |   |   |   |   | # | + |   |   |   |
| 10 | + | + |   | + | + | # | + | + |   | + | + | + | # | # | + |   | + | + |
| 11 |   | + |   | + |   |   |   | + |   | + | + | + | + | # |   | + |   | + |
| 12 |   | + |   |   | + | + |   | + | # |   | + |   | + |   | # |   | + |   |
| 13 |   |   | + |   |   |   | + |   | # |   | + | + |   |   |   | # | # | # |
| 14 |   | + | # | + | # | + |   |   |   |   | + | + | + |   | + | + |   | + |
| 15 |   | # |   | # |   |   |   |   | + | # | + |   |   |   |   | # |   |   |
| 16 | + |   | + | # | # |   | # | + |   | + | + | + | + |   | + |   |   | + |
| 17 | + | # | + | # | # | # | # | # |   | # | # | # |   |   |   |   | # |   |
| 18 |   | + |   | + | + | # | # |   | + | + |   | + | # |   |   | + | + |   |
| 19 |   |   |   |   | + |   |   |   |   |   |   |   |   |   |   |   |   |   |
| 20 |   | + | # | + | # | # |   |   |   |   |   |   |   | + |   | + |   |   |
| 21 | + |   | + | + | + | + |   | + | + |   | + | + | + |   |   | + | # | # |
| 22 |   | + |   |   |   |   | # |   |   |   |   | # |   |   |   |   |   |   |
| 23 |   |   | # |   |   |   |   |   |   |   |   |   |   |   |   |   |   |   |
| 24 |   |   | # |   |   |   |   |   |   | + | # | + |   |   |   |   |   |   |
| 25 |   | # |   |   |   | # |   |   |   |   | # | # |   |   |   |   |   |   |
| 26 |   |   |   |   | # |   | # |   |   | # | + | + |   |   | + | # | # |   |
| 27 | + | + | + | + | # | + | # | + |   |   | + | + |   |   | + | + |   |   |

## Coding of Exilic Names in Hebrew Scripture

| Book, Chapter | Jehoiakim-Sarpuhi: 146 Hits | Jeremiah: 194 | Seraiah/Tanhumeth: 172 | Shecaniah/Jahaziel: 179 | Shelemiah/Abdeel: 148 | Shelemiah/Kore: 223 | Shenazzar/Jehoiachin: 165 | Shephatiah/David: 189 | Solomon/David: 165 | Substitute King: 138 | Zedekiah: 184 | Zedekiah-Sarpuhi: 175 | Zephaniah: 184 | Nebchdnzr: 168 (605–562) | Ezekiel-Sarpuhi: 179 (569) | Jehoiachin-Sarp: 160 (561) | Nab–Belshzr: 186 (556–39) | Cyrus K Bab: 159 (539–30) | Chapter Hits, Book Percent |
|---|---|---|---|---|---|---|---|---|---|---|---|---|---|---|---|---|---|---|---|
| 2 |  | + | # |  | + | + | + | + | + |  | + | + | + | + | + | # | + |  | 28 |
| 3 |  |  |  | + |  | + |  |  |  |  |  |  |  |  | + |  |  | + | 9 |
| 4 |  |  |  | # |  | # | # | # | # |  |  |  |  |  |  |  |  |  | 11 |
| 5 |  | + |  | + | + | # |  | + | + |  | # |  | + | + |  | + |  |  | 18 |
| 6 |  | # |  |  |  |  |  |  | # |  |  |  |  |  |  |  |  |  | 7 |
| 7 |  |  | + |  | + |  | # |  |  |  | # | # |  | + |  |  | # | # | 14 |
| 8 |  | + | + | + | # | + |  | + |  |  | + |  | # | # |  |  | # |  | 21 |
| 9 |  | # |  |  | # |  |  |  |  |  | # |  |  |  |  |  |  |  | 8 |
| 10 | + | + | + | + |  | + | + |  | # | + | + | + | + | + |  | + |  | # | 30 |
| 11 | + | + | + | + |  | + |  | # | + |  | + | + | + |  | # | + | + |  | 24 |
| 12 | + |  | + |  | + |  | # |  |  |  |  | # | + | + |  |  | + | # | 18 |
| 13 |  | + | # |  |  | + | + | # | + |  |  |  |  |  |  |  |  |  | 14 |
| 14 | + | # | + | + |  | + | # |  |  |  | # | + | # |  | + |  |  |  | 21 |
| 15 |  | # |  |  |  | + |  |  | # |  |  |  |  | + | # | # |  |  | 13 |
| 16 | # | + | # |  |  | + | + | + |  | # |  | + | # | # | + | # | + |  | 25 |
| 17 | # | # | + |  | # | + | + | # |  |  | + |  | + |  | + |  |  | + | 23 |
| 18 |  | + |  | + |  | + | # |  | # |  | # | + |  | + |  |  | + |  | 19 |
| 19 | # |  | # |  |  | # |  |  |  |  |  | # |  |  |  |  |  | # | 6 |
| 20 |  | # | # |  |  |  | + |  |  |  |  | + | + | + |  |  | + |  | 14 |
| 21 |  | + | + |  | + | + | + |  | + |  |  | + | + |  |  | + | # |  | 23 |
| 22 |  |  |  | # |  |  |  |  |  |  |  |  |  |  |  |  |  |  | 4 |
| 23 |  |  |  | # |  |  |  |  |  |  |  |  |  |  |  |  |  |  | 2 |
| 24 |  |  |  | # |  |  |  |  | # |  | # |  |  |  | + |  |  | # | 9 |
| 25 |  | + |  |  |  | # | # |  | # |  | # |  |  |  | # |  |  | # | 11 |
| 26 | # |  | + | # |  |  |  |  |  |  |  |  |  | + |  |  |  |  | 13 |
| 27 |  | + | # | + | + | + | + |  |  |  |  |  |  |  | + | # | + | # | 22 |

## Appendix Four

| Book, Chapter | Ahaziah/Jehoram: 175 hits | Ahihud/Shelomi: 153 | Amariah/Hezekiah: 191 | Azariah/Amaziah: 185 | Azariah/Zephaniah: 147 | Azrikam/Azel: 161 | Baruch: 194 | Chimham/Jehoiachin: 204 | Chimham-Sarpuhi: 152 | Cyrus: 155 | Daniel: 249 | Daniel-Sarpuhi: 177 | Ezekiel-Son of Man: 174 | Ezra: 191 | Gemariah/Shaphan: 157 | Jacob-Israel: 198 | Jehizkiah/Shallum: 171 | Jehoiachin: 183 |
|---|---|---|---|---|---|---|---|---|---|---|---|---|---|---|---|---|---|---|
| 28 |   |   | # |   |   |   | + |   | + |   | # |   | # |   |   |   |   |   |
| 29 | + | + | + |   | # |   |   |   |   | # |   | # |   |   |   |   |   |   |
| 30 |   |   |   | # |   |   |   |   |   |   |   |   |   |   |   |   | # |   |
| 31 | # |   | + | + | + | + | # |   |   | + | + | + | + |   | + |   | # |   |
| Eccl |   |   |   |   |   |   |   |   |   |   |   |   |   |   |   |   |   |   |
| 1 |   |   |   |   |   |   |   |   |   |   |   |   |   |   |   |   |   |   |
| 2 |   |   |   |   |   |   |   |   |   | # |   |   |   |   |   |   |   |   |
| 3 |   |   |   |   | # |   |   |   |   |   |   |   |   |   |   |   |   |   |
| 4 |   |   |   |   |   |   |   |   |   |   |   |   |   |   |   |   |   | # |
| 5 |   |   |   | # |   |   |   |   |   |   |   |   |   |   |   |   |   |   |
| 6 |   |   |   |   |   |   |   |   |   |   |   |   |   |   |   |   |   |   |
| 7 |   |   |   |   |   |   |   |   |   |   |   |   |   |   |   |   | + |   |
| 8 |   |   |   |   |   |   |   |   |   |   |   |   |   |   |   |   |   |   |
| 9 |   |   | + |   |   | + |   | # | # | + |   |   | + |   |   |   |   |   |
| 10 | + |   |   |   | # |   |   | + |   |   |   |   |   |   |   |   | # | + |
| 11 |   |   |   |   |   |   |   | + |   |   |   |   | + |   |   |   |   |   |
| 12 | + | # | + | + | + | + | # | + |   | + | + |   | + |   |   |   | # | # |
| Song |   |   |   |   |   |   |   |   |   |   |   |   |   |   |   |   |   |   |
| 1 | + |   | + |   |   |   |   |   |   |   |   | # | # |   |   |   |   |   |
| 2 | + |   | + | # | + | + |   |   | # |   | + | + | + |   |   | # | # | # |
| 3 | + |   | # | # | + |   | # | + |   |   |   |   |   | + | # |   | + | # |
| 4 |   |   | # | + |   | + |   | + |   |   | + |   | + | + |   | + |   |   |
| 5 | + |   | + | # | # | # | # |   |   |   | + |   |   |   |   |   |   |   |
| 6 |   |   | # |   |   | # |   |   |   |   | # |   | + |   |   |   |   |   |
| 7 | + | + | + |   | # | + |   |   | # | + | # |   | + | + | # |   |   | + |
| 8 |   |   |   |   |   |   |   |   |   |   |   |   |   |   |   |   | # |   |

## Coding of Exilic Names in Hebrew Scripture

| Book, Chapter | Jehoiakim-Sarpuhi: 146 Hits | Jeremiah: 194 | Seraiah/Tanhumeth: 172 | Shecaniah/Jahaziel: 179 | Shelemiah/Abdeel: 148 | Shelemiah/Kore: 223 | Shenazzar/Jehoiachin: 165 | Shephatiah/David: 189 | Solomon/David: 165 | Substitute King: 138 | Zedekiah: 184 | Zedekiah-Sarpuhi: 175 | Zephaniah: 184 | Nebchdnzr: 168 (605–562) | Ezekiel-Sarpuhi: 179 (569) | Jehoiachin–Sarp: 160 (561) | Nab-Belshzr: 186 (556–39) | Cyrus K Bab: 159 (539–30) | Chapter Hits, Book Percent |
|---|---|---|---|---|---|---|---|---|---|---|---|---|---|---|---|---|---|---|---|
| 28 |  |  | # |  |  | + |  | # |  |  |  |  |  |  |  | # |  |  | 9 |
| 29 |  |  |  |  |  | + |  | + |  |  |  |  |  | # | # |  |  |  | 11 |
| 30 |  |  |  |  |  |  |  |  |  |  |  |  |  |  |  |  |  |  | 2 |
| 31 | # |  | + |  | # | + | + | + |  |  | # |  | + | + | # | + |  | + | 24 |
| Eccl |  |  |  |  |  |  |  |  |  |  |  |  |  |  |  |  |  |  | 15% |
| 1 |  |  |  |  |  |  |  |  |  |  |  |  |  |  |  |  |  |  |  |
| 2 |  |  |  |  |  |  |  |  |  |  |  | # | # |  |  |  |  |  | 3 |
| 3 |  |  |  |  |  |  |  |  |  |  |  |  |  |  |  |  |  |  | 1 |
| 4 |  |  | # |  |  |  |  |  |  |  |  |  | # |  |  |  |  |  | 3 |
| 5 |  |  |  |  |  |  |  |  |  |  |  |  |  |  |  |  |  |  | 1 |
| 6 |  |  |  |  |  |  |  |  |  |  |  |  |  |  |  |  |  |  |  |
| 7 |  |  | # |  |  | # |  |  |  |  |  |  |  |  |  |  |  |  | 3 |
| 8 |  |  |  |  |  |  |  |  |  |  |  |  |  |  |  |  |  |  |  |
| 9 |  |  | + | + | # |  | # | # |  | + | # |  |  | + |  |  | + |  | 15 |
| 10 |  |  | # |  |  |  |  |  |  |  |  |  |  |  | # |  |  | # | 8 |
| 11 | + |  |  |  |  |  |  | # |  |  |  | + |  |  |  |  |  |  | 5 |
| 12 |  | + | + | # | + | + |  | + | + |  |  |  |  | # | + | # | # | # | 25 |
| Song |  |  |  |  |  |  |  |  |  |  |  |  |  |  |  |  |  |  | 42% |
| 1 |  |  | # |  | # |  |  |  |  |  |  |  |  |  |  | + |  |  | 7 |
| 2 |  |  | # |  | # | + |  | # | + | # |  | # |  |  |  |  | + |  | 20 |
| 3 | + | # |  | + |  | # | + | + |  | + | # |  | # |  |  |  | + | + | 21 |
| 4 |  | + |  |  | + | + | + |  | # | + | + | + |  | # | # | # | # |  | 20 |
| 5 |  |  | + |  | # | # |  | # | # |  |  | # | # |  |  |  |  |  | 14 |
| 6 | + |  | + |  |  |  | # |  | # | # | + |  | # | # | # | # | + |  | 14 |
| 7 |  |  | + | # |  | + | + | + |  |  | + |  | + |  | + | # | + | # | 25 |
| 8 |  |  |  |  |  |  |  |  |  |  |  |  |  |  |  |  |  |  | 1 |

# Appendix Four

| Book, Chapter | Ahaziah/Jehoram: 175 hits | Ahihud/Shelomi: 153 | Amariah/Hezekiah: 191 | Azariah/Amaziah: 185 | Azariah/Zephaniah: 147 | Azrikam/Azel: 161 | Baruch: 194 | Chimham/Jehoiachin: 204 | Chimham-Sarpuhi: 152 | Cyrus: 155 | Daniel: 249 | Daniel-Sarpuhi: 177 | Ezekiel-Son of Man: 174 | Ezra: 191 | Gemariah/Shaphan: 157 | Jacob-Israel: 198 | Jehizkiah/Shallum: 171 | Jehoiachin: 183 |
|---|---|---|---|---|---|---|---|---|---|---|---|---|---|---|---|---|---|---|
| Isa | | | | | | | | | | | | | | | | | | |
| 1 | + | | | + | | + | # | + | # | + | + | + | # | + | | + | # | # |
| 2 | | # | | | + | | + | # | # | + | # | + | # | + | | # | + | # |
| 3 | + | + | + | + | + | + | + | | + | + | + | + | + | + | + | + | + | + |
| 4 | | | | + | | | | | | | | | | + | | | | |
| 5 | + | + | + | + | + | + | # | # | + | # | + | + | + | # | + | + | | + |
| 6 | | | | | # | # | | | | | | # | | | | | | |
| 7 | | | | | | | | | | | | | | | | | | |
| 8 | | | | | | | | | | | | | | | | | | # |
| 9 | | | | | # | | | | | + | | # | | | | | | |
| 10 | # | # | + | | + | | + | # | | | + | | # | | + | | | # |
| 11 | | | | | | | + | | + | | | | # | | | + | # | + |
| 12 | | | | | | | | | | | | | | | | | | |
| 13 | + | | | | # | # | + | + | | | # | | | | + | + | # | + |
| 14 | | | | | | | # | # | | | | | # | + | | + | | + |
| 15 | | # | # | | | | | | | | | | | # | | | | |
| 16 | # | | | + | | | | # | | | | | | | | | | |
| 17 | | + | | | + | # | | + | + | | + | + | + | | | + | | # |
| 18 | # | | | # | | + | | | + | + | + | | # | + | | | # | |
| 19 | # | | | | | | | | | | | | | | | | # | |
| 20 | # | + | | # | | | | | | | | | + | | | + | # | + |
| 21 | | | | | | # | | # | | | # | | | | # | | | |
| 22 | # | | + | | | # | | # | | | | | | | # | | | |
| 23 | # | | | | # | | | | | | | | # | | # | | + | # |
| 24 | | | | | | | | | | | | | | | | | | |
| 25 | + | | | | | | + | | | # | | | | | | | + | |

276

## Coding of Exilic Names in Hebrew Scripture

| Book, Chapter | Jehoiakim-Sarpuhi: 146 Hits | Jeremiah: 194 | Seraiah/Tanhumeth: 172 | Shecaniah/Jahaziel: 179 | Shelemiah/Abdeel: 148 | Shelemiah/Kore: 223 | Shenazzar/Jehoiachin: 165 | Shephatiah/David: 189 | Solomon/David: 165 | Substitute King: 138 | Zedekiah: 184 | Zedekiah–Sarpuhi: 175 | Zephaniah: 184 | Nebchdnzr: 168 (605–562) | Ezekiel–Sarpuhi: 179 (569) | Jehoiachin–Sarp: 160 (561) | Nab–Belshzr: 186 (556–39) | Cyrus K Bab: 159 (539–30) | Chapter Hits, Book Percent |
|---|---|---|---|---|---|---|---|---|---|---|---|---|---|---|---|---|---|---|---|
| Isa | | | | | | | | | | | | | | | | | | | 33% |
| 1 | + | # | + | | | + | # | + | # | + | + | + | + | | | | # | | 26 |
| 2 | + | | | | | + | | | | + | + | | | # | + | | | # | 20 |
| 3 | + | + | + | + | + | + | + | + | + | + | + | + | + | + | + | + | | + | 33 |
| 4 | | | | | | | # | | | | | # | + | | | | | + | 6 |
| 5 | # | # | | + | # | + | | + | | # | + | # | # | # | # | + | | | 30 |
| 6 | | | | | # | | | | | | | | | # | | | | | 5 |
| 7 | | | | | | | | | | | | | | | | | | | |
| 8 | | | | | | | | # | | | | | | | + | | | | 3 |
| 9 | | # | | | | # | | | | | | # | | | | # | | | 7 |
| 10 | + | # | | + | # | | + | # | # | # | # | + | # | | # | # | | | 22 |
| 11 | | | | + | | | # | | + | | + | | | + | | | + | # | 14 |
| 12 | | | | | | | | | | | | | | | | | | | |
| 13 | | # | | # | | + | # | + | | # | | # | # | | + | # | + | | 21 |
| 14 | | | # | | | | # | | | | # | | # | | # | | # | + | 12 |
| 15 | | # | | | + | | | # | | | | | | | | | | | 6 |
| 16 | | | + | # | # | | | + | | | | | | # | | | | | 8 |
| 17 | | | | | | + | + | | | # | # | # | | | | | | | 14 |
| 18 | | + | # | | + | + | | | # | | # | # | + | | + | | | # | 19 |
| 19 | | | | | | | | | | | | | | | | | | | 2 |
| 20 | | # | | | | | + | | | | | | | | | # | | | 10 |
| 21 | | | | | | | | | | | | | | | | | | | 4 |
| 22 | | # | | + | | | | | # | # | | | | | | + | | | 10 |
| 23 | | | | | | | # | | | | | | | # | | | # | | 8 |
| 24 | | | | + | | | # | # | # | | | | | + | | # | # | | 7 |
| 25 | | | | # | | # | | | | | | # | | | | | | | 7 |

277

## Appendix Four

| Book, Chapter | Ahaziah/Jehoram: 175 hits | Ahihud/Shelomi: 153 | Amariah/Hezekiah: 191 | Azariah/Amaziah: 185 | Azariah/Zephaniah: 147 | Azrikam/Azel: 161 | Baruch: 194 | Chimham/Jehoiachin: 204 | Chimham-Sarpuhi: 152 | Cyrus: 155 | Daniel: 249 | Daniel-Sarpuhi: 177 | Ezekiel–Son of Man: 174 | Ezra: 191 | Gemariah/Shaphan: 157 | Jacob–Israel: 198 | Jehizkiah/Shallum: 171 | Jehoiachin: 183 |
|---|---|---|---|---|---|---|---|---|---|---|---|---|---|---|---|---|---|---|
| 26 |   | # |   | # |   | + |   | + | # | + | + |   |   |   | # |   |   |   |
| 27 |   | # |   |   |   |   |   | + |   |   |   |   |   |   |   |   |   |   |
| 28 | + | # | + | + | + | + | + | + | + | # | + | + | + | + | + | + | + | + |
| 29 | + | + |   |   |   |   | + |   |   | # | + | # |   |   |   |   |   | + |
| 30 | + | + | # | # |   | # | # | # |   |   | # | + | # | + |   |   | # |   |
| 31 |   |   |   |   | # |   | # |   |   |   |   |   |   |   | # |   | # | # |
| 32 |   | + | # | # |   |   | # |   | + | # | + |   |   |   |   | + |   | + |
| 33 | + |   | + | + | # | # | # |   |   |   | # |   | + |   | + | + | + | # |
| 34 |   |   | # | + |   |   |   |   |   |   | # |   | # |   | # |   |   |   |
| 35 |   | # | + |   |   |   |   |   |   |   |   |   | # |   |   |   |   |   |
| 36 |   | # | + | # |   |   |   |   |   |   |   |   |   |   |   |   |   |   |
| 37 | # | # |   | # |   | # |   |   |   | # |   |   | # | + |   |   |   | # |
| 38 |   |   |   |   | + |   |   |   |   |   |   |   |   |   |   |   |   |   |
| 39 |   |   |   |   |   |   |   |   |   |   |   |   |   |   | # |   |   |   |
| 40 |   |   |   | # |   | # | # |   |   |   | + | + |   | # |   | # | + |   |
| 41 | + | + | # | + |   |   | + | + |   | + | # |   | + | # | # | + | + |   |
| 42 |   | # | # |   | # |   |   |   | # |   | + |   |   |   |   |   | # | # |
| 43 |   | # | # | + | + | + |   |   | # |   |   | + | # |   | + |   | + | + |
| 44 | # |   |   |   |   | # |   |   |   |   |   | + |   |   |   |   |   |   |
| 45 | # |   |   | # | # |   |   | # |   |   |   | # |   |   |   |   |   |   |
| 46 | # |   |   | + | # | # | # |   |   | # | # |   | # |   | # | + |   |   |
| 47 |   |   | + |   |   |   |   | # |   |   |   | # |   |   |   |   | # |   |
| 48 |   | + | + | + | + | + | # | + | # |   |   | + | + | # | # | + | + | + |
| 49 |   |   |   |   |   |   |   | + | # |   |   | + |   |   |   |   | + |   |
| 50 |   |   |   |   |   |   |   |   |   |   |   |   |   |   |   |   |   |   |
| 51 | # |   |   | # |   |   |   |   |   | + |   | # |   |   |   |   |   |   |

## Coding of Exilic Names in Hebrew Scripture

| Book, Chapter | Jehoiakim-Sarpuhi: 146 Hits | Jeremiah: 194 | Seraiah/Tanhumeth: 172 | Shecaniah/Jahaziel: 179 | Shelemiah/Abdeel: 148 | Shelemiah/Kore: 223 | Shenazzar/Jehoiachin: 165 | Shephatiah/David: 189 | Solomon/David: 165 | Substitute King: 138 | Zedekiah: 184 | Zedekiah-Sarpuhi: 175 | Zephaniah: 184 | Nebchdnzr: 168 (605–562) | Ezekiel-Sarpuhi: 179 (569) | Jehoiachin-Sarp: 160 (561) | Nab-Belshzr: 186 (556–39) | Cyrus K Bab: 159 (539–30) | Chapter Hits, Book Percent |
|---|---|---|---|---|---|---|---|---|---|---|---|---|---|---|---|---|---|---|---|
| 26 |   | # |   |   | + |   |   |   | + | + |   |   |   |   |   |   | # | # | 14 |
| 27 |   |   | + |   |   |   |   |   |   |   |   |   |   |   |   |   |   |   | 3 |
| 28 | # | + | + | # |   | + | + | # |   | # | + | + | + | + | + | # | + | + | 34 |
| 29 |   |   |   |   |   |   |   |   |   | # | # |   |   |   |   |   |   |   | 9 |
| 30 |   |   |   | # |   | # | + |   | + |   |   |   |   |   | # |   | # |   | 18 |
| 31 | # |   | + | # |   |   |   |   |   |   | # |   |   |   |   |   |   |   | 9 |
| 32 | # |   |   |   | # | + | + |   |   |   |   | + | + | + | # |   |   |   | 18 |
| 33 |   |   | + | + | + | # | + |   |   | # |   |   |   |   | + |   |   | # | 20 |
| 34 | # |   | # |   | # |   |   | # |   |   |   | # |   |   |   |   |   |   | 10 |
| 35 |   |   |   | # | # |   | # |   |   |   |   |   |   |   |   |   |   |   | 6 |
| 36 |   | # | # |   | # |   | # |   |   |   | + |   | # |   |   |   |   |   | 9 |
| 37 | # |   |   |   |   |   | # |   |   | # | # |   |   |   |   |   |   |   | 12 |
| 38 |   |   |   |   |   |   |   |   |   |   |   |   |   |   |   |   |   |   | 1 |
| 39 |   |   |   |   |   |   |   |   |   |   |   |   |   |   |   |   |   |   | 1 |
| 40 |   | + | # | # | # | + |   |   | + |   | + |   |   |   | + | # | + |   | 19 |
| 41 | + | + | # |   | # |   |   | # |   |   |   | # | + |   |   |   |   |   | 20 |
| 42 | + |   | + |   | # |   |   | + | + |   |   |   |   |   |   |   |   | # | 13 |
| 43 |   | + | # | + | + | + | # | + | + | # | + | + |   | # | + | + | # |   | 26 |
| 44 |   | # |   |   |   |   |   | # |   |   |   |   |   |   | # |   |   |   | 6 |
| 45 |   |   |   | # |   |   |   | # |   |   |   |   |   |   |   |   |   |   | 7 |
| 46 |   | + |   | + |   |   |   | # | + |   |   |   |   |   |   |   | # | + | 17 |
| 47 |   | + |   |   |   | + | # |   |   |   |   |   |   |   |   |   |   |   | 7 |
| 48 |   |   | + |   | + |   |   | # | # |   | + |   | + | # | + | # | # | + | 26 |
| 49 |   | # |   |   |   |   |   | # |   |   | # |   | # |   |   | # |   |   | 8 |
| 50 |   |   |   |   |   |   |   |   |   |   |   |   |   |   |   |   |   |   |   |
| 51 |   |   |   |   |   |   |   |   |   |   |   | # |   |   |   |   |   |   | 5 |

## Appendix Four

| Book, Chapter | Ahaziah/Jehoram: 175 hits | Ahihud/Shelomi: 153 | Amariah/Hezekiah: 191 | Azariah/Amaziah: 185 | Azariah/Zephaniah: 147 | Azrikam/Azel: 161 | Baruch: 194 | Chimham/Jehoiachin: 204 | Chimham–Sarpuhi: 152 | Cyrus: 155 | Daniel: 249 | Daniel–Sarpuhi: 177 | Ezekiel–Son of Man: 174 | Ezra: 191 | Gemariah/Shaphan: 157 | Jacob–Israel: 198 | Jehizkiah/Shallum: 171 | Jehoiachin: 183 |
|---|---|---|---|---|---|---|---|---|---|---|---|---|---|---|---|---|---|---|
| 52 |   |   |   |   |   |   |   | # |   |   |   |   | + |   |   |   |   |   |
| 53 |   |   |   | # |   |   |   |   |   | # |   |   |   |   |   |   |   |   |
| 54 | + | # | + | # | + | + |   | # | # |   | + | + | + | # | # | + | + | + |
| 55 | + |   | # |   |   | # |   |   |   |   |   |   | + |   |   |   |   |   |
| 56 |   |   |   |   |   |   |   |   |   |   |   |   |   |   |   |   |   |   |
| 57 | + |   | + | # | # |   |   | # | + | # | # |   | # |   |   |   |   |   |
| 58 | + | + | + | + | # |   | + | # | + |   | + | + | + | # | + | + | # | # |
| 59 | + | + | + |   |   | + | # |   | + | + | + |   |   |   | # | + | + | + |
| 60 |   | + | + | # |   | # |   |   |   |   |   | + | + |   | # |   |   | # |
| 61 |   |   |   |   |   | + |   |   |   |   |   |   |   |   |   |   |   |   |
| 62 |   |   |   |   |   |   |   | # | + |   |   |   |   |   |   |   |   | + |
| 63 |   | # |   |   |   |   |   |   |   |   |   |   |   |   |   |   | # | # |
| 64 | + |   | # | + |   |   |   |   |   |   | # |   |   |   |   |   |   |   |
| 65 |   | # |   |   | # |   |   |   |   |   |   |   | # |   |   |   |   |   |
| 66 |   |   |   |   |   |   |   |   |   |   |   |   |   |   |   |   |   |   |
| Jer |   |   |   |   |   |   |   |   |   |   |   |   |   |   |   |   |   |   |
| 1 |   |   |   |   |   |   |   |   |   |   |   |   |   |   | # |   |   |   |
| 2 |   |   |   |   |   |   |   | # |   |   |   |   |   |   |   |   |   |   |
| 3 |   |   |   |   |   |   |   |   |   |   |   |   |   |   |   |   |   |   |
| 4 |   | # |   |   |   |   |   |   |   |   |   |   |   |   |   |   | # |   |
| 5 |   |   |   |   |   |   |   |   |   |   | # | # |   |   |   |   |   |   |
| 6 |   | # |   |   |   |   |   |   |   |   |   |   |   |   | # |   |   |   |
| 7 |   |   | # |   |   |   |   |   | # |   |   |   |   |   |   |   |   |   |
| 8 |   |   |   |   |   |   |   |   |   |   |   |   |   |   |   |   |   |   |
| 9 |   |   |   |   |   |   |   |   |   |   |   |   |   |   |   |   |   |   |
| 10 | # |   | + |   |   | # |   |   |   |   |   |   | # | + | # |   | + |   |

## Coding of Exilic Names in Hebrew Scripture

| Book, Chapter | Jehoiakim-Sarpuhi: 146 Hits | Jeremiah: 194 | Seraiah/Tanhumeth: 172 | Shecaniah/Jahaziel: 179 | Shelemiah/Abdeel: 148 | Shelemiah/Kore: 223 | Shenazzar/Jehoiachin: 165 | Shephatiah/David: 189 | Solomon/David: 165 | Substitute King: 138 | Zedekiah: 184 | Zedekiah–Sarpuhi: 175 | Zephaniah: 184 | Nebchdnzr: 168 (605–562) | Ezekiel-Sarpuhi: 179 (569) | Jehoiachin–Sarp: 160 (561) | Nab–Belshzr: 186 (556–39) | Cyrus K Bab: 159 (539–30) | Chapter Hits, Book Percent |
|---|---|---|---|---|---|---|---|---|---|---|---|---|---|---|---|---|---|---|---|
| 52 | | | | # | | # | | | | | | | | | | | | | 4 |
| 53 | | # | | | | | | | | | | | | | | | | # | 4 |
| 54 | # | + | + | | + | + | | + | + | | + | | | | + | | + | # | 27 |
| 55 | | | | | | | | | | | | | | | | | | | 4 |
| 56 | | | | | | | | | | | | | | | | | | | |
| 57 | # | | + | # | | # | | | | | | | | | # | | | | 14 |
| 58 | + | + | # | | + | + | + | + | # | # | # | | | + | # | + | + | # | 31 |
| 59 | + | + | + | + | + | + | + | # | + | + | + | + | + | + | + | + | | | 30 |
| 60 | | # | | | # | | + | # | + | | | | # | | | | | | 15 |
| 61 | | | | | + | | | + | # | + | # | | | # | | # | | | 8 |
| 62 | | | | | | | | | + | | | | | + | | | | # | 6 |
| 63 | | # | + | | # | + | + | | | | | | | | | # | + | | 10 |
| 64 | + | # | | | | | + | | | # | | | | + | # | | | | 10 |
| 65 | | | | # | | | # | | | | | | | | | | | | 5 |
| 66 | | | + | | | | | | | | | # | | | | | | | 2 |
| Jer | | | | | | | | | | | | | | | | | | | 9% |
| 1 | | | | | | | | | | | | | | | | | # | | 2 |
| 2 | | | | | | | | | | | | | | | | | | | 1 |
| 3 | | | | | | | | | | | | | | | | | | | |
| 4 | | | | | | | | | | | | | | | | | | | 2 |
| 5 | | | | | | | | # | # | | | | | | | | | | 4 |
| 6 | | | | # | | | | | | | | | | | | | | | 3 |
| 7 | | | | | | | | + | | | | | | | | | | | 3 |
| 8 | | | # | | | | | | # | | | | | | | | | | 2 |
| 9 | | | | | | | | | | | | | | | | | | | |
| 10 | | | # | | # | | | | | | | | # | | + | | | | 11 |

## Appendix Four

| Book, Chapter | Ahaziah/Jehoram: 175 hits | Ahihud/Shelomi: 153 | Amariah/Hezekiah: 191 | Azariah/Amaziah: 185 | Azariah/Zephaniah: 147 | Azrikam/Azel: 161 | Baruch: 194 | Chimham/Jehoiachin: 204 | Chimham–Sarpuhi: 152 | Cyrus: 155 | Daniel: 249 | Daniel–Sarpuhi: 177 | Ezekiel–Son of Man: 174 | Ezra: 191 | Gemariah/Shaphan: 157 | Jacob–Israel: 198 | Jehizkiah/Shallum: 171 | Jehoiachin: 183 |
|---|---|---|---|---|---|---|---|---|---|---|---|---|---|---|---|---|---|---|
| 11 |  |  | # |  |  |  |  |  |  |  |  |  |  | + |  |  |  |  |
| 12 |  |  | # |  |  |  |  | # |  |  |  |  |  |  |  |  |  |  |
| 13 |  | + |  | + | # | # |  |  | # | # | + |  | # |  |  |  | # |  |
| 14 |  |  |  |  |  |  |  |  |  |  |  |  |  |  |  |  |  |  |
| 15 |  |  |  |  |  |  |  |  |  |  |  |  |  |  | # |  |  |  |
| 16 |  |  |  |  |  |  |  |  |  |  |  |  |  |  |  |  | + |  |
| 17 |  |  |  |  |  |  |  |  |  |  |  |  |  |  |  |  |  |  |
| 18 |  |  |  |  |  |  |  |  |  |  |  |  |  |  |  |  |  |  |
| 19 |  |  | + |  |  |  |  | # |  |  |  |  |  |  |  |  |  |  |
| 20 |  |  |  | # |  |  |  |  |  |  |  |  |  |  |  |  |  |  |
| 21 | # |  |  | + |  |  |  |  |  |  |  | + |  |  |  |  | # |  |
| 22 | # |  | # |  |  |  |  |  |  |  |  |  |  |  |  |  |  |  |
| 23 |  |  |  |  |  |  |  |  |  |  |  |  |  |  |  |  |  |  |
| 24 |  |  |  |  |  |  |  |  |  |  |  |  |  |  |  |  |  |  |
| 25 |  |  |  |  |  |  |  |  |  |  |  |  |  |  |  |  |  |  |
| 26 |  |  |  |  |  |  |  |  |  |  |  |  |  |  |  |  |  |  |
| 27 |  |  |  |  |  |  |  |  |  |  |  |  |  |  |  |  |  |  |
| 28 |  |  |  |  |  |  |  |  | # |  |  |  |  |  |  |  |  |  |
| 29 |  |  |  |  |  |  |  |  |  |  |  |  |  |  |  |  |  |  |
| 30 |  |  |  |  |  |  |  |  |  |  |  |  |  |  |  |  |  |  |
| 31 |  |  |  |  |  |  |  |  |  |  |  |  | # |  |  |  |  |  |
| 32 | # |  |  |  |  |  |  | # |  |  |  | # |  |  |  |  |  |  |
| 33 |  |  |  |  |  |  |  |  |  |  |  |  |  |  |  |  |  |  |
| 34 |  |  |  |  |  |  |  |  |  |  |  |  |  |  |  |  |  |  |
| 35 |  |  |  |  |  |  |  |  |  |  |  |  |  |  |  |  |  |  |
| 36 |  |  |  | # |  |  |  |  |  |  |  |  |  |  |  |  |  |  |

## Coding of Exilic Names in Hebrew Scripture

| Book, Chapter | Jehoiakim-Sarpuhi: 146 Hits | Jeremiah: 194 | Seraiah/Tanhumeth: 172 | Shecaniah/Jahaziel: 179 | Shelemiah/Abdeel: 148 | Shelemiah/Kore: 223 | Shenazzar/Jehoiachin: 165 | Shephatiah/David: 189 | Solomon/David: 165 | Substitute King: 138 | Zedekiah: 184 | Zedekiah–Sarpuhi: 175 | Zephaniah: 184 | Nebchdnzr: 168 (605–562) | Ezekiel-Sarpuhi: 179 (569) | Jehoiachin–Sarp: 160 (561) | Nab–Belshzr: 186 (556–39) | Cyrus K Bab: 159 (539–30) | Chapter Hits, Book Percent |
|---|---|---|---|---|---|---|---|---|---|---|---|---|---|---|---|---|---|---|---|
| 11 | + |   |   |   |   |   |   |   | # |   |   |   |   |   | # | # |   |   | 6 |
| 12 |   |   |   |   |   |   |   |   | # |   |   |   |   |   |   |   | # | + | 5 |
| 13 |   |   | # |   | + | # | # | # | # |   |   | # |   | # | # |   |   |   | 18 |
| 14 |   |   |   |   |   |   |   |   |   |   |   |   |   |   |   |   |   |   |   |
| 15 |   |   |   |   |   |   |   |   |   |   |   |   |   |   |   |   | # |   | 2 |
| 16 | + |   |   |   |   |   |   |   |   |   |   |   |   |   |   |   |   |   | 2 |
| 17 |   |   |   | # |   | # |   |   |   |   |   |   |   |   |   | # |   |   | 3 |
| 18 |   |   |   |   |   |   |   |   |   |   |   | # |   |   |   |   | # |   | 2 |
| 19 |   |   |   |   |   |   |   |   |   |   |   |   |   |   |   |   |   |   | 2 |
| 20 |   |   |   |   |   |   |   |   |   |   |   |   |   |   | + |   |   |   | 2 |
| 21 |   |   |   | # |   | + |   |   |   |   |   |   |   |   |   |   |   |   | 6 |
| 22 |   |   |   |   |   |   |   |   |   |   |   |   |   |   |   |   |   |   | 2 |
| 23 |   |   |   |   |   |   |   |   |   |   |   |   |   |   |   |   |   |   |   |
| 24 |   |   |   |   |   |   |   |   |   |   |   |   |   |   |   |   |   |   |   |
| 25 |   |   |   |   |   |   |   |   |   | # |   |   |   |   |   |   |   |   | 1 |
| 26 |   |   |   |   |   |   |   |   |   |   |   |   |   |   |   |   |   |   |   |
| 27 |   |   |   |   |   |   |   |   |   |   |   |   |   |   |   |   |   |   |   |
| 28 |   |   |   |   |   |   |   |   |   |   |   |   |   |   |   |   |   |   | 1 |
| 29 |   |   |   |   |   |   |   |   |   |   |   |   |   |   |   | # |   |   | 1 |
| 30 |   |   |   |   |   |   |   |   |   |   |   |   |   |   |   |   |   |   |   |
| 31 |   |   |   |   |   |   |   |   | + |   |   |   |   |   |   |   |   |   | 2 |
| 32 |   |   | + | # |   |   |   |   |   |   |   | # | # |   | + | # |   |   | 9 |
| 33 |   |   |   |   |   |   |   |   |   |   |   |   |   |   |   |   |   |   |   |
| 34 |   |   |   |   |   |   |   |   |   |   |   |   |   |   |   |   |   |   |   |
| 35 |   |   |   |   |   |   |   |   |   |   |   |   |   |   |   |   |   |   |   |
| 36 |   |   |   |   |   |   |   |   |   |   |   |   |   |   |   |   |   |   | 1 |

## Appendix Four

| Book, Chapter | Ahaziah/Jehoram: 175 hits | Ahihud/Shelomi: 153 | Amariah/Hezekiah: 191 | Azariah/Amaziah: 185 | Azariah/Zephaniah: 147 | Azrikam/Azel: 161 | Baruch: 194 | Chimham/Jehoiachin: 204 | Chimham–Sarpuhi: 152 | Cyrus: 155 | Daniel: 249 | Daniel–Sarpuhi: 177 | Ezekiel–Son of Man: 174 | Ezra: 191 | Gemariah/Shaphan: 157 | Jacob–Israel: 198 | Jehizkiah/Shallum: 171 | Jehoiachin: 183 |
|---|---|---|---|---|---|---|---|---|---|---|---|---|---|---|---|---|---|---|
| 37 | | | | | | | | | | | | | | | | | | |
| 38 | | | | | | | | | | | | | | | | | | |
| 39 | | | | | | | | + | | | | | | | | | | + |
| 40 | | | | | | | | | + | # | | | | | | | | |
| 41 | | | | | | | | | # | | | | | | | | | |
| 42 | | | | | | | | | | | | | | | | | | |
| 43 | | | # | # | | | | | # | | | | | | + | | | |
| 44 | | | | | | | | | # | | | | | | # | # | # | |
| 45 | | | | | | | | | | | | | | | | | | |
| 46 | | # | | | | | | # | + | | | # | | | # | | + | # |
| 47 | | | + | | # | | | | + | # | # | | | | | | + | |
| 48 | | # | | # | # | | | | | | | | + | | | | # | |
| 49 | | | # | | + | | | | | | + | | # | | | | | |
| 50 | | | | | | | | | | | | | | | | | | |
| 51 | | | + | # | | | | | | | | | | | | | | |
| 52 | | | # | + | | | | # | | # | # | | | | | # | | |
| Lam | | | | | | | | | | | | | | | | | | |
| 1 | | | | | | | | # | | | | | | | | | | |
| 2 | | # | | | | | | | | | # | # | | | | | + | |
| 3 | | | # | | # | | | # | # | # | # | | | | | | # | |
| 4 | | # | + | # | # | # | | | # | + | | | + | + | + | | | # |
| 5 | # | | | | | + | + | + | | | | # | | | + | | | + |
| Ezek | | | | | | | | | | | | | | | | | | |
| 1 | | | | | | | | | | | | | | | # | | | |
| 2 | | | | | | | | | | | | | | | | | | |
| 3 | | | | | | | | | | | | | | | | | | |

## Coding of Exilic Names in Hebrew Scripture

| Book, Chapter | Jehoiakim-Sarpuhi: 146 Hits | Jeremiah: 194 | Seraiah/Tanhumeth: 172 | Shecaniah/Jahaziel: 179 | Shelemiah/Abdeel: 148 | Shelemiah/Kore: 223 | Shenazzar/Jehoiachin: 165 | Shephatiah/David: 189 | Solomon/David: 165 | Substitute King: 138 | Zedekiah: 184 | Zedekiah-Sarpuhi: 175 | Zephaniah: 184 | Nebchdnzr: 168 (605–562) | Ezekiel-Sarpuhi: 179 (569) | Jehoiachin-Sarp: 160 (561) | Nab-Belshzr: 186 (556–39) | Cyrus K Bab: 159 (539–30) | Chapter Hits, Book Percent |
|---|---|---|---|---|---|---|---|---|---|---|---|---|---|---|---|---|---|---|---|
| 37 | | | | | | | | | | | | | | | | | | | |
| 38 | | | | | | | | | | | | | | | | | | | |
| 39 | | | | | | | | | | | | | | | | | | | 2 |
| 40 | | | | # | | | | | | | | | | | | | | | 3 |
| 41 | | | | | | # | | | # | | | | | | | | | + | 4 |
| 42 | | | | | | | | | | | | | | | | | | | |
| 43 | # | | | | | | | # | | | | | | | | # | # | | 8 |
| 44 | | | | # | | | | | # | | | | | | | | | + | 7 |
| 45 | | | | | | | | | | | | | | | | | | | |
| 46 | | | | | | | | | | | | # | | | | | # | | 9 |
| 47 | | | | | # | | | | | | | # | | | | | | | 8 |
| 48 | # | | # | | # | | | | | | | | | | # | | | | 9 |
| 49 | | | | | | + | | # | # | # | + | | | | | | # | # | 11 |
| 50 | | | | # | | | | | | | | | | | | | | | 1 |
| 51 | | | | | | | | | | | | | | | | | | | 2 |
| 52 | # | | | | + | | | | # | | | | # | | | | | | 10 |
| Lam | | | | | | | | | | | | | | | | | | | 32% |
| 1 | | | | | | | | | | | | | | | | | | | 1 |
| 2 | | + | | | # | + | | | # | | | | | | | | + | | 9 |
| 3 | | | # | # | + | | | | | # | + | | | | # | + | | | 14 |
| 4 | + | | # | # | | + | # | # | | | # | | | + | + | # | + | | 22 |
| 5 | + | | + | | | | | | # | | | | | | | # | # | | 12 |
| Ezek | | | | | | | | | | | | | | | | | | | 19% |
| 1 | # | | | | | | | | | | | | | | | | | | 2 |
| 2 | | | | | | | | | | | | | | | | | | | |
| 3 | | | | | | | | | | | | | | | | | | | |

## Appendix Four

| Book, Chapter | Ahaziah/Jehoram: 175 hits | Ahihud/Shelomi: 153 | Amariah/Hezekiah: 191 | Azariah/Amaziah: 185 | Azariah/Zephaniah: 147 | Azrikam/Azel: 161 | Baruch: 194 | Chimham/Jehoiachin: 204 | Chimham–Sarpuhi: 152 | Cyrus: 155 | Daniel: 249 | Daniel–Sarpuhi: 177 | Ezekiel–Son of Man: 174 | Ezra: 191 | Gemariah/Shaphan: 157 | Jacob–Israel: 198 | Jehizkiah/Shallum: 171 | Jehoiachin: 183 |
|---|---|---|---|---|---|---|---|---|---|---|---|---|---|---|---|---|---|---|
| 4 | | | | | | | + | | | | | | | | | | | |
| 5 | # | | # | | | # | # | | + | | | | # | | # | + | | |
| 6 | | | # | | | # | + | | # | | | | | | + | # | | + |
| 7 | | | | | | | | | | | # | | | | # | + | | |
| 8 | # | | | | | | # | | | | | | | | | | | |
| 9 | | + | + | | | + | | | | | # | | | | | | | |
| 10 | | | | | | | | | | | # | | | # | | | | |
| 11 | # | | # | | + | | | | | | | # | | | | | | |
| 12 | | | | | | | | | | | | | | | | | | |
| 13 | | + | + | | | | | | | | # | | + | | + | | # | |
| 14 | | | | | | | | | | | | | | | | | | |
| 15 | | | | | | | | | | | | | | | | | | |
| 16 | # | | | | | + | | + | | | # | + | # | + | # | | # | # |
| 17 | # | | | | | | | | | | | # | + | | # | | | |
| 18 | | | | | | | | | | | | | | + | | | | |
| 19 | | | + | | | | | # | | | # | # | | | | | # | |
| 20 | | # | | | | | | | | | | | | | | | | |
| 21 | | | + | | | | | | | | | | | | | | | |
| 22 | + | + | + | + | # | + | + | # | | + | + | | + | | | + | # | + |
| 23 | + | + | + | + | | + | + | | | + | + | # | # | + | # | | # | |
| 24 | # | | | | | | # | | | | | | | | | | | |
| 25 | | | | | | | | | | | | | | | | | | |
| 26 | + | | + | | | + | # | | | | + | + | | | | | | + |
| 27 | + | | | | # | + | # | # | # | + | # | | | | # | + | | + |
| 28 | | | | | | | | | | | | | + | | | | | |
| 29 | | | | | | | | | | | | | | | | | | |

## Coding of Exilic Names in Hebrew Scripture

| Book, Chapter | Jehoiakim-Sarpuhi: 146 Hits | Jeremiah: 194 | Seraiah/Tanhumeth: 172 | Shecaniah/Jahaziel: 179 | Shelemiah/Abdeel: 148 | Shelemiah/Kore: 223 | Shenazzar/Jehoiachin: 165 | Shephatiah/David: 189 | Solomon/David: 165 | Substitute King: 138 | Zedekiah: 184 | Zedekiah-Sarpuhi: 175 | Zephaniah: 184 | Nebchdnzr: 168 (605–562) | Ezekiel-Sarpuhi: 179 (569) | Jehoiachin–Sarp: 160 (561) | Nab-Belshzr: 186 (556–39) | Cyrus K Bab: 159 (539–30) | Chapter Hits, Book Percent |
|---|---|---|---|---|---|---|---|---|---|---|---|---|---|---|---|---|---|---|---|
| 4 |  |  |  |  |  |  |  |  | # |  |  |  |  |  |  |  |  |  | 2 |
| 5 | + |  | # |  | + |  | # |  | # | + |  | + | + |  | # | # |  |  | 18 |
| 6 |  | # |  |  |  | # |  | # | # | + |  |  |  | + | # |  |  |  | 14 |
| 7 |  | # |  | # |  |  | # | # |  |  |  |  |  |  |  |  |  | + | 8 |
| 8 |  |  | # |  |  |  |  |  |  |  |  |  |  |  |  |  |  |  | 3 |
| 9 |  |  |  |  |  |  |  |  | # |  |  |  |  |  | # |  |  |  | 6 |
| 10 |  |  |  |  |  |  |  |  | # |  |  |  |  |  |  |  |  |  | 3 |
| 11 |  |  |  |  |  |  |  |  |  |  |  |  |  |  |  |  |  |  | 4 |
| 12 |  |  |  |  |  |  |  |  |  |  |  |  |  |  |  |  |  |  |  |
| 13 |  | # | + |  | + | # |  | # |  |  |  | # |  |  | + | # |  |  | 14 |
| 14 |  |  |  |  |  |  |  |  |  |  |  |  |  |  |  |  |  |  |  |
| 15 |  |  |  |  |  |  |  |  |  |  |  |  |  |  |  |  |  |  |  |
| 16 |  | # |  | + | + | # |  | + | # | + | # |  |  | + | # | + | + | + | 23 |
| 17 | # |  |  |  |  |  |  |  |  |  |  | # |  |  |  |  |  |  | 6 |
| 18 |  |  |  |  |  |  |  |  |  |  |  |  |  |  |  |  | # |  | 2 |
| 19 | # | # | # | + | # | + |  | # |  |  | + | + | + |  | # |  |  |  | 16 |
| 20 |  | # |  |  |  |  |  |  |  |  |  | # |  |  |  |  |  |  | 3 |
| 21 |  |  |  | + |  |  |  |  |  |  |  | # |  |  |  |  |  |  | 3 |
| 22 |  | + | + | # |  | + | + | + | # |  |  | # | # |  | + | + |  |  | 25 |
| 23 | # | + | + | + | + | + | # | # | # |  | # | + |  | + | + | + | + |  | 28 |
| 24 |  |  |  |  |  |  |  |  |  |  |  |  |  | # |  |  |  |  | 3 |
| 25 |  |  |  |  |  |  |  |  |  |  |  |  |  |  |  |  |  |  |  |
| 26 | # | + | # | + |  | + |  |  | # |  |  |  |  | + | # | # | # |  | 17 |
| 27 |  |  | + |  |  | + |  |  | # | # |  | + | + | + |  |  | + | + | 20 |
| 28 |  |  |  |  |  |  |  |  |  |  |  |  |  |  |  |  |  |  | 1 |
| 29 |  |  |  |  |  |  |  |  |  |  |  |  |  |  |  |  |  |  |  |

## Appendix Four

| Book, Chapter | Ahaziah/Jehoram: 175 hits | Ahihud/Shelomi: 153 | Amariah/Hezekiah: 191 | Azariah/Amaziah: 185 | Azariah/Zephaniah: 147 | Azrikam/Azel: 161 | Baruch: 194 | Chimham/Jehoiachin: 204 | Chimham–Sarpuhi: 152 | Cyrus: 155 | Daniel: 249 | Daniel–Sarpuhi: 177 | Ezekiel–Son of Man: 174 | Ezra: 191 | Gemariah/Shaphan: 157 | Jacob–Israel: 198 | Jehizkiah/Shallum: 171 | Jehoiachin: 183 |
|---|---|---|---|---|---|---|---|---|---|---|---|---|---|---|---|---|---|---|
| 30 | | | | | | + | | | | | # | # | | | | | | |
| 31 | | + | | | | | | | | | | | | | | | | |
| 32 | | | | | | | | | | | | | | | | | | |
| 33 | | | | | | | | | | | | | | | | | | |
| 34 | | | | | # | | | # | | # | | | | | | # | | |
| 35 | | | | | | | | | | | | | | | | | | |
| 36 | | | | | # | # | | # | | | | | + | # | | | | |
| 37 | | | | | | | | | | | | | | | | | | |
| 38 | # | | | | | # | | | | | | | | | | | | |
| 39 | | | | | | | | | | | | | | | | | | |
| 40 | | | | | | | | | | | | | | | | | | + |
| 41 | # | # | | | | # | # | | | + | # | | | | + | # | | + |
| 42 | | | # | | | # | | | | | | | | + | | + | | + |
| 43 | | | | | | + | + | | | | # | # | | | # | # | | |
| 44 | | | | | | | | | | | | | | | | | | |
| 45 | | # | | + | | + | | | | | | | | | # | | | |
| 46 | | | | | | | | | | | | | | | # | + | | |
| 47 | # | | | | | + | | | | | + | | # | + | # | | | + |
| 48 | | | | | | + | | | | | | | # | # | | | | + |
| Dan | | | | | | | | | | | | | | | | | | |
| 1 | | | | | | | | | | | # | | | | | | | |
| 2 | | + | | # | | + | + | | | | # | # | # | | # | | | |
| 3 | + | + | + | + | + | + | + | + | + | + | + | + | + | + | + | + | + | + |
| 4 | # | # | + | # | + | + | + | | | # | + | # | + | | | # | | # |
| 5 | | | | | | # | + | | # | | + | # | | | | # | | # |
| 6 | | | # | | | # | | | | + | # | | # | | | # | # | |

## Coding of Exilic Names in Hebrew Scripture

| Book, Chapter | Jehoiakim-Sarpuhi: 146 Hits | Jeremiah: 194 | Seraiah/Tanhumeth: 172 | Shecaniah/Jahaziel: 179 | Shelemiah/Abdeel: 148 | Shelemiah/Kore: 223 | Shenazzar/Jehoiachin: 165 | Shephatiah/David: 189 | Solomon/David: 165 | Substitute King: 138 | Zedekiah: 184 | Zedekiah-Sarpuhi: 175 | Zephaniah: 184 | Nebchdnzr: 168 (605–562) | Ezekiel-Sarpuhi: 179 (569) | Jehoiachin-Sarp: 160 (561) | Nab–Belshzr: 186 (556–39) | Cyrus K Bab: 159 (539–30) | Chapter Hits, Book Percent |
|---|---|---|---|---|---|---|---|---|---|---|---|---|---|---|---|---|---|---|---|
| 30 |   |   |   |   |   |   |   |   |   | + |   | # | # |   |   | # | # |   | 8 |
| 31 | # |   |   |   |   |   |   |   |   |   |   |   |   |   |   |   |   |   | 2 |
| 32 |   |   |   |   |   |   |   |   |   |   |   |   |   |   |   |   |   |   |   |
| 33 |   |   |   |   |   |   |   |   |   |   |   |   |   |   |   |   |   |   |   |
| 34 |   | + |   | + |   | # |   | # |   |   | # |   |   |   |   |   |   | # | 10 |
| 35 |   |   |   |   |   |   |   |   |   |   |   |   |   |   |   |   |   |   |   |
| 36 |   |   |   | # |   |   | # |   | # |   |   |   |   |   |   |   | # |   | 9 |
| 37 |   |   |   |   |   |   |   |   |   |   |   |   |   |   |   |   |   |   |   |
| 38 |   |   |   |   |   |   |   |   |   |   |   |   |   |   |   |   |   |   | 2 |
| 39 |   |   |   |   |   |   |   |   |   |   |   |   |   |   |   |   |   |   |   |
| 40 |   |   |   |   |   |   |   |   |   |   |   |   |   |   |   |   |   |   | 1 |
| 41 |   |   |   | + |   | # | + |   |   |   |   |   |   |   | + |   | + | + | 15 |
| 42 |   | # |   |   |   |   |   |   | + |   |   |   |   | + |   |   | # |   | 9 |
| 43 |   |   | + | # |   | # |   |   | # | # | # | # |   |   | + |   |   |   | 14 |
| 44 |   |   |   |   |   |   |   |   |   |   |   |   |   |   |   |   |   |   |   |
| 45 |   |   |   | # |   |   |   |   |   |   |   | + |   |   | # |   |   |   | 7 |
| 46 | # |   |   |   |   |   | # |   |   |   |   |   |   |   |   | + |   | # | 6 |
| 47 | # |   |   |   |   |   |   | # | # | + |   |   |   |   | # |   | # |   | 13 |
| 48 | # |   |   |   |   | + |   |   |   |   |   |   |   |   |   |   |   |   | 6 |
| Dan |   |   |   |   |   |   |   |   |   |   |   |   |   |   |   |   |   |   | 44% |
| 1 |   |   |   |   |   |   |   |   |   |   |   |   |   |   |   |   |   | + | 2 |
| 2 |   | # |   | # | + | # | # | + | + | + | + | + | + | + |   |   |   |   | 20 |
| 3 | + | + | + | + | + | + | + | + | + | + | + | + | + | + | + | + | + | + | 35 |
| 4 |   | + | # |   | # | + | # | # | + |   | + | + | + | + |   | + |   |   | 26 |
| 5 |   | # |   | # |   |   |   |   | + | # | # |   |   |   | # |   | + | # | 15 |
| 6 | # | # | # | + |   |   |   |   | + | # |   | + |   |   |   |   | + |   | 16 |

## Appendix Four

| Book, Chapter | Ahaziah/Jehoram: 175 hits | Ahihud/Shelomi: 153 | Amariah/Hezekiah: 191 | Azariah/Amaziah: 185 | Azariah/Zephaniah: 147 | Azrikam/Azel: 161 | Baruch: 194 | Chimham/Jehoiachin: 204 | Chimham–Sarpuhi: 152 | Cyrus: 155 | Daniel: 249 | Daniel–Sarpuhi: 177 | Ezekiel–Son of Man: 174 | Ezra: 191 | Gemariah/Shaphan: 157 | Jacob–Israel: 198 | Jehizkiah/Shallum: 171 | Jehoiachin: 183 |
|---|---|---|---|---|---|---|---|---|---|---|---|---|---|---|---|---|---|---|
| 7 | # |   |   | # |   | + | # |   |   | # |   | # |   |   |   |   |   |   |
| 8 |   |   |   | + |   |   | # |   | # |   | # |   |   |   |   | + |   |   |
| 9 | + |   | # |   | + |   | + | + | + |   | + |   | # | + |   | + |   |   |
| 10 | # |   |   |   |   | # |   |   |   |   |   |   |   |   |   |   |   |   |
| 11 | # | + | # | + |   | + | + | + | + |   | + | + | + |   |   | + | # | + |
| 12 |   | # |   | # |   |   |   | # | # |   |   | # |   |   |   | # |   |   |
| Hos |   |   |   |   |   |   |   |   |   |   |   |   |   |   |   |   |   |   |
| 1 |   |   |   |   |   |   |   |   |   |   |   |   |   |   |   |   |   |   |
| 2 |   |   |   | # |   |   |   |   |   |   |   | # |   |   |   |   |   |   |
| 3 |   |   |   |   |   |   |   |   |   |   |   |   |   |   |   |   |   |   |
| 4 |   | # |   |   |   |   |   |   |   |   |   |   |   |   |   |   |   |   |
| 5 |   |   | # |   |   |   |   | + |   |   | # | + | # |   |   |   | # |   |
| 6 |   |   | + | # |   | + | # |   |   |   |   | + | # |   |   | + | + |   |
| 7 |   |   |   | + | # |   |   |   |   |   | # | # |   |   |   |   |   |   |
| 8 |   | + |   |   |   |   | # |   |   |   |   |   |   |   |   |   | # |   |
| 9 |   |   | # | # | + | + | # |   |   |   |   | # |   |   | # |   |   |   |
| 10 |   | + |   |   |   |   | + |   |   |   | # | # |   |   | + | # |   |   |
| 11 | + | + | + | # | # | # | + | # |   |   | # | # | + |   |   |   |   |   |
| 12 |   | # |   |   | # |   |   |   |   |   |   |   |   |   |   |   |   |   |
| 13 |   |   |   |   |   |   |   |   |   | # | # |   |   |   |   |   |   |   |
| 14 |   |   |   |   |   |   |   |   |   |   |   |   |   |   |   | # |   |   |
| Joel |   |   |   |   |   |   |   |   |   |   |   |   |   |   |   |   |   |   |
| 1 | # |   |   |   |   |   |   |   |   |   |   |   | + |   |   |   |   |   |
| 2 |   | + | + |   |   | # | + | # |   |   | + | # | # |   |   | # | # |   |
| 3 |   |   | # | # |   |   |   |   |   |   |   |   |   |   |   |   |   |   |
| 4 | + |   | + |   |   |   |   |   |   |   | + | # | # |   |   | + |   |   |

## Coding of Exilic Names in Hebrew Scripture

| Book, Chapter | Jehoiakim-Sarpuhi: 146 Hits | Jeremiah: 194 | Seraiah/Tanhumeth: 172 | Shecaniah/Jahaziel: 179 | Shelemiah/Abdeel: 148 | Shelemiah/Kore: 223 | Shenazzar/Jehoiachin: 165 | Shephatiah/David: 189 | Solomon/David: 165 | Substitute King: 138 | Zedekiah: 184 | Zedekiah-Sarpuhi: 175 | Zephaniah: 184 | Nebchdnzr: 168 (605–562) | Ezekiel-Sarpuhi: 179 (569) | Jehoiachin-Sarp: 160 (561) | Nab-Belshzr: 186 (556–39) | Cyrus K Bab: 159 (539–30) | Chapter Hits, Book Percent |
|---|---|---|---|---|---|---|---|---|---|---|---|---|---|---|---|---|---|---|---|
| 7 |  |  | # |  |  | # | # |  |  |  |  |  |  |  |  |  |  |  | 9 |
| 8 | # |  |  |  |  | + | + |  |  |  | # | + | # |  |  |  |  |  | 11 |
| 9 |  | # |  |  |  | # | # | + | # |  |  | # |  |  |  | + |  | # | 18 |
| 10 |  |  |  |  |  |  |  |  |  |  |  |  |  |  |  |  |  |  | 2 |
| 11 | + | + | + |  |  |  | # |  |  | + |  | # |  |  | # | + | + |  | 23 |
| 12 | + | # |  |  | # | # |  |  |  |  |  | # |  | + |  | # |  |  | 13 |
| Hos |  |  |  |  |  |  |  |  |  |  |  |  |  |  |  |  |  |  | 21% |
| 1 |  |  | # |  |  |  |  |  |  |  | # |  |  |  |  |  |  |  | 2 |
| 2 | # |  |  | + |  |  |  |  |  |  |  |  |  |  |  |  | # |  | 5 |
| 3 |  |  |  |  |  |  |  |  |  |  |  |  |  |  |  |  |  |  |  |
| 4 |  |  |  |  |  |  |  |  |  |  |  |  |  | # |  | + |  |  | 3 |
| 5 |  | # |  |  |  | + |  | + |  | # | # | # |  |  |  |  | # |  | 13 |
| 6 |  | # |  | # | + | + |  | # |  |  |  | + |  |  |  | # |  |  | 15 |
| 7 |  |  |  |  |  | # |  |  |  |  |  |  |  |  |  | # |  |  | 6 |
| 8 |  |  |  | # |  |  |  |  |  |  |  |  |  |  | # | + | # |  | 7 |
| 9 |  | # |  |  |  | # |  | # |  |  |  | # | + |  |  | # |  |  | 13 |
| 10 |  | + |  |  | # | # | + | # |  |  |  |  |  |  | # |  | + |  | 13 |
| 11 |  |  |  |  |  | + |  | + |  |  | + |  |  | # | # |  |  |  | 17 |
| 12 |  |  | + |  |  |  |  |  |  |  |  |  |  | # |  |  |  |  | 4 |
| 13 |  | + |  |  |  |  |  | # |  |  |  |  |  | # |  |  |  |  | 5 |
| 14 |  |  |  |  |  |  |  |  | # |  |  |  |  |  |  |  |  |  | 2 |
| Joel |  |  |  |  |  |  |  |  |  |  |  |  |  |  |  |  |  |  | 28% |
| 1 |  |  |  |  |  |  |  |  | # |  |  |  |  |  | # |  |  |  | 4 |
| 2 |  | # | # | + | + | + | # | # |  | # | + |  |  |  | # |  | # |  | 21 |
| 3 |  |  |  |  |  |  |  |  |  |  |  |  |  | # |  |  |  |  | 3 |
| 4 |  |  | # | # |  | # | # | # |  |  | + |  |  | # |  |  |  |  | 13 |

## Appendix Four

| Book, Chapter | Ahaziah/Jehoram: 175 hits | Ahihud/Shelomi: 153 | Amariah/Hezekiah: 191 | Azariah/Amaziah: 185 | Azariah/Zephaniah: 147 | Azrikam/Azel: 161 | Baruch: 194 | Chimham/Jehoiachin: 204 | Chimham–Sarpuhi: 152 | Cyrus: 155 | Daniel: 249 | Daniel–Sarpuhi: 177 | Ezekiel–Son of Man: 174 | Ezra: 191 | Gemariah/Shaphan: 157 | Jacob–Israel: 198 | Jehizkiah/Shallum: 171 | Jehoiachin: 183 |
|---|---|---|---|---|---|---|---|---|---|---|---|---|---|---|---|---|---|---|
| Amo | | | | | | | | | | | | | | | | | | |
| 1 | # | | # | | | | | # | | | | | | | | | | + |
| 2 | | | | | # | | | # | | | | | | | # | | | + |
| 3 | | | | | | | | | | | | | | | | | | |
| 4 | | | | | # | | | | | | | + | | | | | | # |
| 5 | + | | | + | | | | | | | | # | | | | | | |
| 6 | | + | | + | # | | + | | | | | + | + | # | + | + | | # |
| 7 | | | | | | | | | | | | | | | | | | |
| 8 | | | | # | + | | | # | | | | | | | # | | | |
| 9 | + | | # | | # | + | # | | | | | # | | | | | | |
| Oba | | | | | | | | | | | | | | | | | | |
| 1 | | | | | | | | | | | | | | | | | | |
| Jon | | | | | | | | | | | | | | | | | | |
| 1 | | | | | | | | | | | | | | | | | | |
| 2 | # | | # | | | | | | | | | # | | | | | | |
| 3 | + | | + | | # | | # | | | | # | # | # | | | | | # |
| 4 | | | | | | | | | | | | | | | | | | |
| Mic | | | | | | | | | | | | | | | | | | |
| 1 | | | # | | # | # | | | | | | + | | | | | | # |
| 2 | # | # | | + | # | | | + | + | | | | | | | | | |
| 3 | | | | | | + | # | + | | | # | # | | | # | | | # |
| 4 | | # | | + | # | # | | | | | | | | | | | + | |
| 5 | | | | | | | | | | | | | | | | | | |
| 6 | | | + | + | # | | # | | + | | # | # | # | + | | | | + |
| 7 | | # | + | # | | | | | # | | | | + | | | | | |
| Nah | | | | | | | | | | | | | | | | | | |

## Coding of Exilic Names in Hebrew Scripture

| Book, Chapter | Jehoiakim-Sarpuhi: 146 Hits | Jeremiah: 194 | Seraiah/Tanhumeth: 172 | Shecaniah/Jahaziel: 179 | Shelemiah/Abdeel: 148 | Shelemiah/Kore: 223 | Shenazzar/Jehoiachin: 165 | Shephatiah/David: 189 | Solomon/David: 165 | Substitute King: 138 | Zedekiah: 184 | Zedekiah–Sarpuhi: 175 | Zephaniah: 184 | Nebchdnzr: 168 (605–562) | Ezekiel-Sarpuhi: 179 (569) | Jehoiachin–Sarp: 160 (561) | Nab–Belshzr: 186 (556–39) | Cyrus K Bab: 159 (539–30) | Chapter Hits, Book Percent |
|---|---|---|---|---|---|---|---|---|---|---|---|---|---|---|---|---|---|---|---|
| Amo | | | | | | | | | | | | | | | | | | | 29% |
| 1 | # | | | + | | | | | | | | | | | | | | | 6 |
| 2 | # | | + | | | + | + | | | | | | | | + | + | | | 10 |
| 3 | | | | | | | | | | | | | | | | | | | |
| 4 | | | | | # | | | | | | | | | # | | | | + | 6 |
| 5 | | | + | | # | # | | + | + | | | # | | # | # | | | | 11 |
| 6 | | | + | + | # | | + | | + | | | | # | + | | # | # | # | + | 21 |
| 7 | | | | | | | | | | | | | | | | | | | |
| 8 | | | + | | + | | | | | | | | | | # | | # | | 8 |
| 9 | | | # | | | # | # | | | # | | | | | | | + | | 11 |
| Oba | | | | | | | | | | | | | | | | | | | 0% |
| 1 | | | | | | | | | | | | | | | | | | | |
| Jon | | | | | | | | | | | | | | | | | | | 17% |
| 1 | | | | | | | | | | | | | | | | | | | |
| 2 | | # | + | | | | | | | | | | | + | | | # | + | 8 |
| 3 | + | | | | | | | | | | | | | # | + | + | # | # | 15 |
| 4 | # | | | | | | | | | | | | | # | | | | | 2 |
| Mic | | | | | | | | | | | | | | | | | | | 32% |
| 1 | | # | | | | | | | + | | | | | # | | # | | | 9 |
| 2 | | + | | | # | + | # | | | | | | + | # | | | | | 12 |
| 3 | | | # | + | + | # | | | | | | | # | + | # | | | # | 15 |
| 4 | | | # | # | | | # | # | | # | # | | | | | | | | 11 |
| 5 | | # | | | | # | | | | | | | | | | | | | 2 |
| 6 | | | # | | + | | | | + | + | | | + | | # | | | | 17 |
| 7 | | # | | | + | + | # | | # | | | + | # | | # | # | # | | 15 |
| Nah | | | | | | | | | | | | | | | | | | | 64% |

# Appendix Four

| Book, Chapter | Ahaziah/Jehoram: 175 hits | Ahihud/Shelomi: 153 | Amariah/Hezekiah: 191 | Azariah/Amaziah: 185 | Azariah/Zephaniah: 147 | Azrikam/Azel: 161 | Baruch: 194 | Chimham/Jehoiachin: 204 | Chimham–Sarpuhi: 152 | Cyrus: 155 | Daniel: 249 | Daniel–Sarpuhi: 177 | Ezekiel–Son of Man: 174 | Ezra: 191 | Gemariah/Shaphan: 157 | Jacob–Israel: 198 | Jehizkiah/Shallum: 171 | Jehoiachin: 183 |
|---|---|---|---|---|---|---|---|---|---|---|---|---|---|---|---|---|---|---|
| 1 | + | + |   |   |   | + |   |   |   |   | # | + | # |   |   |   | # |   |
| 2 |   | + | + | + | + | # | + | + |   | + | + |   | # | # | + | + |   | # |
| 3 | # | + | + |   | # | # | + | # | + | # | + | + |   | + | + | + |   | + |
| Hab |   |   |   |   |   |   |   |   |   |   |   |   |   |   |   |   |   |   |
| 1 |   | # |   | + |   |   |   | # | # |   | # |   | + |   |   |   |   |   |
| 2 | + | # |   |   |   |   |   |   |   |   | # | # |   |   |   |   |   |   |
| 3 | + | + | + | # |   | + |   | + | # |   | + |   | + |   |   | + | + | + |
| Zeph |   |   |   |   |   |   |   |   |   |   |   |   |   |   |   |   |   |   |
| 1 |   |   |   |   |   |   |   |   |   |   |   |   |   |   |   |   |   |   |
| 2 |   |   | # |   |   |   |   |   |   |   |   | # |   |   |   |   |   |   |
| 3 |   |   |   | + |   | + | # |   |   |   |   |   |   |   | # |   | # | # |
| Hag |   |   |   |   |   |   |   |   |   |   |   |   |   |   |   |   |   |   |
| 1 |   |   |   |   |   |   |   |   |   |   |   |   |   |   |   |   |   |   |
| 2 |   |   |   |   |   |   |   |   |   |   |   |   |   |   |   |   |   |   |
| Zech |   |   |   |   |   |   |   |   |   |   |   |   |   |   |   |   |   |   |
| 1 |   |   |   |   |   |   |   |   |   |   |   |   |   |   |   |   |   |   |
| 2 |   |   |   |   |   |   |   |   |   |   |   |   |   |   |   |   |   |   |
| 3 |   |   |   |   |   |   |   |   |   |   |   |   |   |   |   |   | # |   |
| 4 |   |   |   |   |   |   |   |   |   |   |   |   |   |   |   |   |   |   |
| 5 |   |   |   |   |   |   |   |   |   |   |   |   |   |   |   |   |   |   |
| 6 | + |   | + |   |   |   |   | # |   |   |   |   |   |   | # |   |   |   |
| 7 |   |   |   |   |   |   |   |   |   |   |   |   |   |   |   |   |   |   |
| 8 |   |   |   |   |   |   |   |   |   |   |   |   |   |   |   |   |   |   |
| 9 | + | # | + | # |   | + |   |   | # | + | # |   |   |   | + | + |   | + |
| 10 |   |   |   |   | # |   |   |   |   |   |   |   |   | # |   |   |   |   |
| 11 |   |   |   |   |   |   |   |   |   |   |   |   |   |   |   |   |   |   |

## Coding of Exilic Names in Hebrew Scripture

| Book, Chapter | Jehoiakim-Sarpuhi: 146 Hits | Jeremiah: 194 | Seraiah/Tanhumeth: 172 | Shecaniah/Jahaziel: 179 | Shelemiah/Abdeel: 148 | Shelemiah/Kore: 223 | Shenazzar/Jehoiachin: 165 | Shephatiah/David: 189 | Solomon/David: 165 | Substitute King: 138 | Zedekiah: 184 | Zedekiah-Sarpuhi: 175 | Zephaniah: 184 | Nebchdnzr: 168 (605–562) | Ezekiel-Sarpuhi: 179 (569) | Jehoiachin-Sarp: 160 (561) | Nab–Belshzr: 186 (556–39) | Cyrus K Bab: 159 (539–30) | Chapter Hits, Book Percent |
|---|---|---|---|---|---|---|---|---|---|---|---|---|---|---|---|---|---|---|---|
| 1 |  |  | + |  |  |  |  |  |  |  |  |  | + |  |  |  | + | # | 11 |
| 2 | + | + | + |  |  | + | # | # | + | + | + |  | # |  | # | # | + | + | 28 |
| 3 | + | # | + | + | + |  | # | + | # |  | + | + | # | + | # | + | + |  | 30 |
| Hab |  |  |  |  |  |  |  |  |  |  |  |  |  |  |  |  |  |  | 37% |
| 1 | # | # |  |  |  |  | # |  |  |  | # |  |  | # |  |  |  | # | 12 |
| 2 |  |  |  | # |  |  |  |  |  |  |  |  |  |  | # |  | + |  | 7 |
| 3 |  |  | + | # | + |  | + |  | # | + |  | + |  |  | # | # |  |  | 21 |
| Zeph |  |  |  |  |  |  |  |  |  |  |  |  |  |  |  |  |  |  | 16% |
| 1 |  |  |  |  |  |  |  |  |  |  |  |  | # |  |  |  |  |  | 1 |
| 2 |  | # | + |  |  | + |  |  |  |  |  |  |  |  |  |  |  |  | 5 |
| 3 |  |  | + | # |  |  |  | # |  |  |  | # |  | # |  |  |  |  | 11 |
| Hag |  |  |  |  |  |  |  |  |  |  |  |  |  |  |  |  |  |  | 2% |
| 1 |  |  |  |  |  |  |  |  |  |  |  |  |  |  |  |  |  |  |  |
| 2 |  |  |  | # |  |  |  |  |  |  |  |  |  |  |  |  |  |  | 1 |
| Zech |  |  |  |  |  |  |  |  |  |  |  |  |  |  |  |  |  |  | 9% |
| 1 |  |  |  |  |  |  |  |  |  |  | # |  |  |  |  |  |  |  | 1 |
| 2 |  |  |  |  |  |  |  |  |  |  |  |  |  |  |  |  |  |  |  |
| 3 | # |  |  |  |  |  |  |  |  |  |  |  |  |  |  |  |  |  | 2 |
| 4 |  |  |  |  |  |  |  |  |  |  |  |  |  |  |  |  |  |  |  |
| 5 |  |  |  |  |  |  |  |  |  |  |  |  |  |  |  |  |  |  |  |
| 6 |  | + |  |  |  |  |  |  |  |  | # |  |  |  |  |  |  |  | 6 |
| 7 |  |  |  | # |  |  |  |  |  |  |  |  |  |  |  |  |  |  | 1 |
| 8 |  |  |  |  |  |  |  |  |  |  |  |  |  |  |  |  |  |  |  |
| 9 |  |  |  | # | # | + |  | # |  | # |  |  |  |  | # | # |  |  | 18 |
| 10 |  |  |  |  |  |  |  |  |  |  |  |  |  |  |  | # |  |  | 3 |
| 11 |  |  |  |  |  |  |  |  |  |  |  |  |  |  |  |  |  |  |  |

## Appendix Four

| Book, Chapter | Ahaziah/Jehoram: 175 hits | Ahihud/Shelomi: 153 | Amariah/Hezekiah: 191 | Azariah/Amaziah: 185 | Azariah/Zephaniah: 147 | Azrikam/Azel: 161 | Baruch: 194 | Chimham/Jehoiachin: 204 | Chimham–Sarpuhi: 152 | Cyrus: 155 | Daniel: 249 | Daniel–Sarpuhi: 177 | Ezekiel–Son of Man: 174 | Ezra: 191 | Gemariah/Shaphan: 157 | Jacob–Israel: 198 | Jehizkiah/Shallum: 171 | Jehoiachin: 183 |
|---|---|---|---|---|---|---|---|---|---|---|---|---|---|---|---|---|---|---|
| 12 |  | # | # |  |  |  |  | # |  | # | + |  |  |  |  |  |  | + |
| 13 |  |  |  |  |  |  |  |  |  |  |  |  |  |  |  |  |  |  |
| 14 |  |  |  |  |  |  |  | # |  |  |  |  |  |  |  |  |  |  |
| Mal |  |  |  |  |  |  |  |  |  |  |  |  |  |  |  |  |  |  |
| 1 |  |  |  |  |  |  |  |  |  |  |  |  |  |  | # |  |  | # |
| 2 |  |  |  |  |  | # |  |  |  |  |  |  |  |  |  |  |  | # |
| 3 | # | # |  |  |  | # | # |  |  |  |  |  | # |  |  |  |  |  |

## Coding of Exilic Names in Hebrew Scripture

| Book, Chapter | Jehoiakim-Sarpuhi: 146 Hits | Jeremiah: 194 | Seraiah/Tanhumeth: 172 | Shecaniah/Jahaziel: 179 | Shelemiah/Abdeel: 148 | Shelemiah/Kore: 223 | Shenazzar/Jehoiachin: 165 | Shephatiah/David: 189 | Solomon/David: 165 | Substitute King: 138 | Zedekiah: 184 | Zedekiah-Sarpuhi: 175 | Zephaniah: 184 | Nebchdnzr: 168 (605–562) | Ezekiel-Sarpuhi: 179 (569) | Jehoiachin–Sarp: 160 (561) | Nab–Belshzr: 186 (556–39) | Cyrus K Bab: 159 (539–30) | Chapter Hits, Book Percent |
|---|---|---|---|---|---|---|---|---|---|---|---|---|---|---|---|---|---|---|---|
| 12 | | | | | # | | + | | | | # | | | # | + | | # | | 12 |
| 13 | | | | | | | | | | | | # | | | | | | | 1 |
| 14 | | | + | | | | | | | | | # | | | | | | | 3 |
| Mal | | | | | | | | | | | | | | | | | | | 13% |
| 1 | | | | | | | | # | | | | | | | | | | | 3 |
| 2 | # | | | | | | | | # | | | | | | | | | | 4 |
| 3 | | | | # | | | | | | # | | | | | | | | | 7 |

# Bibliography

Abba, Raymond. "Name." In *IDB* 3:500–508.
Aberbach, Moses. "Jacob In the Aggadah." In *EncJud* 9:1198–1201.
Achtemeier, Elizabeth R. "Seraiah." In *IDB* 4:278–79.
Ackroyd, Peter R. *Exile and Restoration: A Study of Hebrew Thought of the Sixth Century B.C.* Old Testament Library. Philadelphia: Westminster, 1968.
Albright, William F. "King Joiachin in Exile." *BA* 5 (1942) 50–55.
———. "The Seal of Eliakim and the Latest Preexilic History of Judah, with Some Observations on Ezekiel." *JBL* 51 (1932) 77–106.
Althann, Robert. "Josiah." In *ABD* 3:1015–18.
———. "Zedekiah." In *ABD* 6:1068–71.
Avigad, Nahman. *Hebrew Bullae from the Time of Jeremiah.* Jerusalem: Israel Exploration Society, 1986.
Barkay, Gabriel. "The Priestly Benediction on Silver Plaques from Ketef Hinnom in Jerusalem." *TA* 19 (1992) 139–92.
———, et al. "The Amulets from Ketef Hinnom: A New Edition and Evaluation." *BASOR* 334 (2004) 41–71.
Beaulieu, Paul-Alain. "Antiquarianism and the Concern for the Past in the Neo-Babylonian Period." *Canadian Society for Mesopotamian Studies* 28 (1994) 37–42.
———. "The Reign of Nabonidus, King of Babylon (556–539 B.C.)." Ph.D. dissertation, Yale University, 1985.
Berridge, John M. "Jehoiachin." In *ABD* 3:663.
Black, Matthew. *The Book of Enoch or I Enoch: A New English Edition with Commentary and Textual Notes.* Studia in Veteris Testamenti Pseudepigrapha 7. Leiden: Brill, 1985.
Blank, Sheldon H. "Book of Proverbs." In *IDB* 3:936–40.
Boling, Robert G. "Book of Judges." In *ABD* 3:1107–17.
Bowman, Raymond. "An Aramaic Religious Text in Cryptogram." *JNES* 3 (1944) 219–27.
Brown, Frances, et al. *The New Brown-Driver-Briggs-Gesenius Hebrew and English Lexicon.* Peabody, MA: Hendrickson, 1979.
Clay, Albert T. "Cylinder of Nabonidus." In *Miscellaneous Inscriptions.* Yale Oriental Series 45. New Haven: Yale University Press, 1915.
Clifford, Richard J. "Second Isaiah." In *ABD* 3:490–501.
Collins, John J. "Book of Daniel." In *ABD* 2:29–37.
Cross, Frank Moore. *Canaanite Myth and Hebrew Epic: Essays in the History of the Religion of Israel.* Cambridge: Harvard University Press, 1973.
Dahood, Mitchell. *Psalms II.* AB 17. Garden City, NY: Doubleday, 1968.

# Bibliography

Day, John. "Inner-biblical Interpretation in the Prophets." In *"The Place Is Too Small for Us": The Israelite Prophets in Recent Scholarship*, edited by Robert P. Gordon, 230–46. Sources for Biblical and Theological Study 5. Winona Lake, IN: Eisenbrauns, 1995.

Deist, F. E. "The Punishment of the Disobedient Zedekiah." *JNES* 1 (1971) 71–72.

Dendai [*pseudo.*] "The Mezuzah Cryptogram." *The Cryptogram: Journal of the American Cryptogram Association* 45 (1979) 88.

Driver, G. R. "Isaiah 52:13—53:12: the Servant of the Lord." In *In Memoriam Paul Kahle*, edited by Georg Fohrer, 90–105. BZAW 103. Berlin: Töpelmann, 1968.

Drosnin, Michael. *The Bible Code*. New York: Simon & Schuster, 1997.

Eslinger, Lyle. "Inner-Biblical Exegesis and Inner-Biblical Allusion: The Question of Category." *VT* 42 (1992) 47–58.

Fales, F. M., and J. N. Postgate, editors. *Imperial Administrative Records, Part I: Palace and Temple Administration*. State Archives of Assyria 7. Helsinki: Helsinki University Press, 1992.

Freedman, David Noel. "The Book of Ezekiel." *Int* 8 (1954) 446–71.

Freedman, H., translator. *Genesis Rabbah*. London: Soncino, 1939.

Friedman, Theodore. "Isaiah." In *EncJud* 9:44–49.

Fishbane, Michael. *Biblical Interpretation in Ancient Israel*. New York: Oxford University Press, 1985.

Funk, Robert W., et al. *The Five Gospels*. San Francisco: HarperSanFrancisco, 1997.

Gadd, C. J. "The Harran Inscriptions of Nabonidus." *AnSt* 8 (1958) 35–92.

———, and R. Campbell Thompson. "A Middle-Babylonian Chemical Text." *Iraq* 3 (1936) 87–96.

Garbini, Giovanni. *History and Ideology in Ancient Israel*. Translated by John Bowden. New York: Crossroad, 1988.

Ginzberg, Louis. *Legends of the Jews*. Philadelphia: Jewish Publication Society, 1913.

Grayson, A. K. Babylonian Historical-Literary Texts. Toronto Semitic Texts and Studies 3. Toronto: University of Toronto Press, 1975.

Greenberg, Moshe. "Ezekiel." In *EncJud* 6: 1078–95.

Hicks, R. Lansing. "Patriarchs." In *IDB* 3:677–78.

Hollenberg, D. E. "Nationalism and 'the Nations' in Isaiah XL–LV." *VT* 19 (1969) 23–36.

Jastrow, Marcus. *Dictionary of the Targumim, the Talmud Babli and Jerushalmi, and the Midrashic Literature*. 1903. Reprinted, New York: Judaica, 1985.

Kahn, David. *The Codebreakers: The Story of Secret Writing*. Rev. ed. New York: Macmillan, 1996.

Kavanagh, Preston. "The Jehoiachin Code in Scripture's Priestly Benediction." *Bib* 88 (2007) 234–44.

———. *Secrets of the Jewish Exile*. Tarentum, PA: Word Association, 2005.

Klouda, Sheri L. "Isaiah's Use of Psalm 97 in Isaiah 60 and 62." Presentation to the November 2005 convention of the Society for Biblical Literature.

Kraetzschmar, Richard. *Das Buch Ezechiel*. Handkommentar zum Alten Testament. Göttingen: Vandenhoeck & Ruprecht, 1900.

Kudlek, Manfred, and Erich H. Mickler. *Solar and Lunar Eclipses of the Ancient Near East from 3000 B.C. to 0*. AOAT Sonderreihe 1. Kevelaer: Butzon & Bercker, 1971.

Lambert, W. G. "A Part of a Ritual for the Substitute King." *AfO* 18 (1957–58) 109–12.

Langdon, Stephen. "Accadian Prayer to Shemesh." In *Babylonian Penitential Psalms*. Oxford Editions of Cuneiform Texts 6. Paris: Geuthner, 1927.

# Bibliography

———. "Nebuchadnezzar XVII." In *Building Inscriptions of the Neo-Babylonian Empire. Part 1: Nabopolassar to Nebuchadnezzar*. Paris: Leroux, 1905.
Leichty, Erle. "The Colophon." In *Studies Presented to A. Leo Oppenheim*, edited by R. D. Briggs and J. A. Brinkman, 147–54. Chicago: Oriental Institute, 1964.
Levine, Baruch A. "Book of Leviticus." In *ABD* 4:311–20.
Levenson, Jon D. *Resurrection and the Restoration of Israel*. New Haven: Yale University Press, 2006.
———, interviewed by Sharon Goldman. "The World Repaired, Remade." *Harvard Divinity Bulletin* 35 (2007) 76–83.
Limburg, James. "Book of Psalms." In *ABD* 5:522–36.
Lipinski, Edward. "Jeremiah." In *EncJud* 9:1346–59.
Lundbom, Jack R. "Baruch." In *ABD* 1:617.
———. "Book of Jeremiah." In *ABD* 3:706–21.
MacLean, Hugh B. "Josiah." In *IDB* 2:996–999.
Malamat, A. "The Twilight of Judah: in the Egyptian-Babylonian Maelstrom." In *Congress Volume: Edinburgh 1974*, edited by J. A. Emerton, 123–45. VTSup 28. Leiden: Brill, 1975.
Mallowan, Max. "Cyrus the Great (558–529 B.C.)." *Iran* 10 (1972) 1–17.
McFall, Leslie. "The Evidence for a Logical Arrangement of the Psalter." *WTJ* 62 (2000) 223–56.
McKay, Brendan, et al. "Solving the Bible Code Puzzle." *StatSci* 14 (1999) 150–73.
McKensie, John L. *Second Isaiah*. AB 20. Garden City, NY: Doubleday, 1968.
McKnight, Scot. *Jesus and His Death*. Waco: Baylor University Press, 2005.
Mendenhall, George E., and Gary A. Herion. "Covenant." In *ABD* 1:1179–1202.
Millard, Alan R. "The Question of Israelite Literacy." *BR* 3 (1987) 22–31.
Murphy, Roland E. "Book of Song of Songs." In *ABD* 6:150–55.
Noegel, Scott B. "Atbash (אתבש) in Jeremiah and Its Literary Significance." *JBQ* 24 (1996) 82–89, 160–66, 247–50.
North, Christopher R. "Isaiah." In *IDB* 2:731–44.
———. *The Suffering Servant in Deutero-Isaiah*. 2nd ed. London: Oxford University Press, 1956.
North, Robert. "Ezra." In *ABD* 2:726–8.
Noth, Martin. *The Deuteronomistic History*. 2nd ed. Journal for the Study of the Old Testament Supplements 15. Sheffield: JSOT Press, 1991.
Olmstead, A. T. *History of the Persian Empire*. Chicago: University of Chicago Press, 1948.
Pallis, Svend Aage. *The Babylonian Akitu Festival*. Historisk-filologiske meddelelser 12.1. Copenhagen: Bianco Lunos, 1926.
Parker, Richard A., and Waldo H. Dubberstein. *Babylonian Chronology: 626 B.C.–A.D. 75*. Brown University Studies 19. Providence: Brown University Press, 1956.
Parpola, Simo. *Assyrian Prophecies*. State Archives of Assyria 9. Helsinki: Helsinki University Press, 1997.
———. "The Babylonian Substitute King Ritual and the Ideology of the Innocent Suffering of Jesus." Presentation (in Finnish) on November 25, 1985, to the Finnish Exegetical Society.
———. *Letters from Assyrian Scholars to the Kings Esarhaddon and Assurbanipal: Texts*. AOAT 5. Kevalaer: Butzon & Bercker, 1970.
———. *Letters from Assyrian Scholars to the Kings Esarhaddon and Assurbanipal: Commentary and Appendices*. AOAT 5. Kevalaer: Butzon & Bercker, 1983.

# Bibliography

Pritchard, James B., editor. *Ancient Near Eastern Texts Relating to the Old Testament.* 3rd ed. Princeton: Princeton University Press, 1969.
Rad, Gerhard von. "The Royal Ritual in Judah." In *From Genesis to Chronicles: Explorations in Old Testament Theology*, edited by K. C. Hanson, 167-73. Translated by E. W. Trueman Dicken. Fortress Classics in Biblical Studies. Minneapolis: Fortress, 2005.
Reiner, Erica, editor. *The Assyrian Dictionary.* Chicago: Oriental Institute of the University of Chicago, 1971-.
Renz, Johannes, and Wolfgang Röllig. *Handbuch der althebräischen Epigraphik.* Darmstadt: Wissenschaft Buchgesellshaft, 1995.
Roberts, Bleddyn J. "Athbash." In *IDB* 1:306-7.
Rogerson, John, and Philip R. Davies. "Was the Siloam Tunnel Built by Hezekiah?" *BA* 59 (1996) 138-48.
Rosenbaum, M., and A. M. Silbermann, translators. *Pentateuch with Targum Onkelos, Haphtaroth, and Rashi's Commentary.* London: Shapiro, 1929.
Rowley, H. H. *The Servant of the Lord and Other Essays on the Old Testament.* London: Lutterworth, 1952.
Sack, Ronald H. "Evil-Merodach." In *ABD* 2:679.
Saldarini, Anthony J., translator. *Avot of Rabbi Nathan*, Version B. Leiden: Brill, 1975.
Sarna, Nahum M. "The Patriarchs." In *EncJud* 13: 181-83.
Schoville, Kieth N. "Song of Songs." In *EncJud* 15:144-52.
Scott, Robert B. Y. "Book of Proverbs." In *EncJud* 13:1268-73.
Shamasastry, R., trans. *Kautilya's Arthasastra.* 4th ed. Mysore: Sri Raghuveer Printing Press, 1951.
Smith, Sidney. *Isaiah Chapters XL-LV.* London: Oxford University Press, 1944.
Tadmor, Hayim. "The Inscriptions of Nabunaid." In *Studies in Honor of Benno Landsberger*, 351-64. Assyriological Studies 16. Chicago: University of Chicago Press, 1965.
Thomas, D. Winton. "Miscellanea: A Consideration of Isaiah LIII in the Light of Recent Textual and Philological Study." *ETL* 44 (1968) 79-86.
———. "The Sixth Century B.C.: A Creative Epoch in the History of Israel." *JSS* 6 (1961) 33-46.
Toorn, Karel van der. "Judges xvi 21 in the Light of the Akkadian Sources." *VT* 36 (1986) 248-53.
Ussishkin, David. "Royal Judean Storage Jars and Private Seal Impressions." *BASOR* 223 (1976) 1-13.
Vermes, Geza. *The Complete Dead Sea Scrolls in English.* New York: Penguin, 1998.
Waaler, Erik. "A Revised Date for Pentateuchal Texts?" *TynBul* 53 (2002) 29-55.
Walton, John H. "The Imagery of the Substitute King Ritual in Isaiah's Fourth Servant Song." *JBL* 122 (2003) 734-43.
Weidner, Ernest F. "Jojachin, Koenig von Juda, in babylonischen Keilschrifttexten." In *Melanges Syriens offerts a M. Rene Dussaud*, edited by A. Causse, 2:923-35. Gembloux: Duculot, 1939.
Weisburg, David B. "Murashu's Sons." In *EncJud* 12:529-30.
Willoughby, Bruce E. "The Book of Amos." In *ABD* 1:203-12.
Witztum, Doron. "Equidistant Letter Sequences in the Book of Genesis." *StatSci* 9 (1994) 429-38.
Yardeni, Ada. "Remarks on the Priestly Blessing on Two Ancient Amulets from Jerusalem." *VT* 41 (1991) 176-85.
Young, T. Cuyler Jr. "Cyrus." In *ABD* 1:1231-32.

# Index of Modern Authors

Abba, R., 64
Aberbach, Moses, 66, 67
Achtemeier, E. R., 94
Ackroyd, Peter R., 93
Albright, William F., 9, 148
Althann, Robert, 99, 152
Avigad, Nahman, 8

Barkay, Gabriel, 4–6, 18
Beaulieu, Paul-Alain, 103, 108
Berridge, John M., 31
Black, Matthew, 123
Blank, S. H., 144
Boling, Robert G., 143
Bowman, Raymond, 1
Brown, Frances, 114

Clay, Albert T., 23
Clifford, Richard J., 93
Collins, John J., 166, 172
Cross, Frank Moore, 75, 141, 166, 172

Dahood, Mitchell, 85, 105
Davies, Philip R., 6
Day, John, 37
Deist, F. E., 99
Dendai [pseudo.], 27
Driver, G. R., 109, 299
Drosnin, Michael, 19, 20
Dubberstein, Waldo H., 34

Eslinger, Lyle, 37

Fales, F. M., 90
Freedman, D. N., 111

Friedman, Theodore, 62
Fishbane, Michael, 27
Funk, Robert W., 124, 127, 132

Gadd, C. J., 1, 128
Garbini, G., 93
Ginzberg, Louis, 66, 67, 95
Grayson, A. K., 48
Greenberg, Moshe, 34, 110, 111

Herion, Gary A., 78
Hicks, L., 65
Hollenberg, D. E., 112

Jastrow, Marcus, 8

Kahn, David, 1
Kavanagh, Preston, 18, 36, 98
Klouda, Sheri L., 37
Kraetzschmar, R., 110
Kudlek, M., 17, 47

Lambert, W. G., 17, 115, 127
Langdon, Stephen, 52, 115
Leichty, Erle, 1
Levine, Baruch A., 141
Levenson, Jon D., 117
Limburg, James, 157
Lipinski, Edward, 77
Lundbom, Jack R., 78, 80, 154

MacLean, H. B., 154
Malamat, A., 9
Mallowan, Max, 35
McFall, Leslie, 37
McKay, Brendan, 19

## Index of Modern Authors

McKensie, John L., 112
McNight, Scot, 132
Mendenhall, George E., 78
Mickler, E. H., 17, 47
Millard, Alan R., 90
Murphy, Roland E., 144

Noegel, Scott B., 27, 28
North, Christopher R., 93, 107, 110
North, Robert, 93
Noth, Martin, 75, 141, 143

Olmstead, A. T., 37

Pallis, Svend Aage, 125
Parker, Richard A., 34
Parpola, Simo, vii, 15, 17, 43, 52,
    54–59, 60, 107–9, 113–16,
    124, 126–29
Postgate, J. N., 90
Pritchard, James B., 110

Rad, Gerhard von, 126
Reiner, Erica, 128
Renz, Johannes, 6
Roberts, B. J., 27
Rogerson, John, 6
Rollig, Wolfgang, 6
Rosenbaum, M., 67
Rowley, H. H., 107

Sack, Ronald H., 49
Saldarini, Anthony J., 49
Sarna, Nahum M., 65
Schoville, Kieth N., 144
Scott, Robert B. Y., 144
Shamasastry, R., 1
Silbermann, A. M., 67
Smith, Sidney, 116

Tadmor, Hayim, 36
Thomas, D. Winton, 62, 109
Thompson, R. Campbell, 1
Toorn, Karel van der, 99

Ussishkin, David, 9

Vermes, Geza, 123

Waaler, Erik, 6
Walton, John H., 110
Weidner, Ernest F., 148, 156
Weisburg, David B., 2
Willoughby, Bruce E., 82
Witztum, Doron, 19

Yardeni, Ada, 5, 6
Young, T. Cuyler Jr., 36

# Index of Scripture

## HEBREW SCRIPTURE

### Genesis

| | |
|---|---|
| 1 | 54 |
| 2 | 58 |
| 3 | 53 |
| 4 | 47 |
| 6 | 46 |
| 9 | 67 |
| 10 | 140 |
| 14 | 33, 36, 140 |
| 17 | 60 |
| 18 | 53 |
| 19 | 140 |
| 24 | 50, 60 |
| 25 | 58, 62–64, 68, 70, 74 |
| 27 | 53 |
| 27–32 | 74 |
| 28 | 57 |
| 31 | 47 |
| 32 | 65, 74, 79 |
| 33 | 68 |
| 34 | 74 |
| 35 | 68, 74, 79 |
| 37 | 47, 54 |
| 40 | 59 |
| 41 | 50 |
| 43 | 58 |
| 45 | 53 |
| 46 | 74, 79 |
| 47 | 74 |
| 48 | 79 |
| 49 | 74, 79 |
| 50 | 60 |

### Exodus

| | 171, 172 |
|---|---|
| 3 | 77, 134 |
| 5 | 46 |
| 12 | 51, 60, 140 |
| 13 | 51 |
| 19 | 79 |
| 23 | 51, 53, 140 |
| 25 | 53, 171 |
| 27 | 171 |
| 29 | 54, 134 |
| 30 | 45 |
| 31 | 49 |
| 31–34 | 140 |
| 32 | 55 |
| 34 | 50 |
| 37 | 171 |
| 38 | 57, 58, 171 |

### Leviticus

| | |
|---|---|
| 3 | 76 |
| 4 | 141 |
| 7 | 51 |
| 9 | 141 |
| 10 | 60, 96 |
| 11 | 53 |
| 15 | 53, 60, 141 |
| 16 | 51, 60, 141 |
| 17 | 60 |
| 17–27 | 141 |
| 22 | 51 |
| 23 | 60 |
| 24 | 53 |
| 25 | 60 |
| 26 | 53 |

## Index of Scripture

| Numbers | 74, 172 |
|---|---|
| 2 | 171 |
| 4 | 171 |
| 6 | 5–19 |
| 7 | 141 |
| 10 | 141 |
| 11 | 53 |
| 14 | 46 |
| 19 | 58, 141 |
| 20 | 58 |
| 21–24 | 141 |
| 23 | 74, 134 |
| 24 | 54, 57, 74, 134 |
| 26 | 141 |
| 28 | 52, 53, 58 |
| 28–36 | 141 |
| 29 | 60, 171 |
| 31 | 51, 57 |

| Deuteronomy | 141, 152, 163 |
|---|---|
| 5 | 49, 114 |
| 8 | 53 |
| 9 | 50 |
| 10 | 49 |
| 14 | 57, 58 |
| 15 | 53 |
| 16 | 51 |
| 17 | 122 |
| 24 | 46 |
| 26 | 53 |
| 27 | 49, 114 |
| 28 | 55 |
| 30 | 58 |
| 31 | 46 |
| 32 | 143 |
| 33 | 74, 143, 171 |

| Joshua | 141, 163, 171, 172 |
|---|---|
| 5 | 53, 96 |
| 7 | 143, 171 |
| 12 | 143, 171 |
| 13 | 143, 151, 155, 171 |
| 13–21 | 143 |
| 14 | 143 |
| 15 | 143, 151, 155, 171 |
| 16 | 143, 171 |
| 17 | 143 |
| 18 | 143 |
| 19 | 143, 151, 155, 171 |
| 20 | 143 |
| 21 | 60, 143 |
| 23 | 44, 58 |

| Judges | 141, 163 |
|---|---|
| 3 | 49 |
| 5 | 143 |
| 6 | 96 |
| 8 | 45, 59, 143 |
| 9 | 54 |
| 11 | 52, 54 |
| 12 | 143 |
| 16 | 47, 60, 143 |
| 18 | 46 |
| 19 | 53 |

| Ruth | 151 |
|---|---|
| 1 | 50 |
| 2 | 151 |
| 4 | 53, 95, 96 |

| First Samuel | 141, 163 |
|---|---|
| 1 | 50 |
| 2 | 24, 54, 60, 61 |
| 3 | 61 |
| 5 | 74 |
| 6 | 143 |
| 8 | 143, 171 |
| 9 | 53 |
| 17 | 51, 59, 61 |
| 18 | 52 |
| 20 | 47 |
| 21 | 50 |
| 23 | 47 |
| 25 | 56 |

## Index of Scripture

| | |
|---|---:|
| 26 | 58 |
| 29 | 54 |
| 30 | 53 |

### Second Samuel   141, 163

| | |
|---|---:|
| 2 | 54 |
| 3 | 50, 54, 97 |
| 5 | 97 |
| 7 | 60 |
| 9 | 57, 58 |
| 11 | 53, 56 |
| 12 | 52 |
| 13 | 52 |
| 14 | 59 |
| 17 | 143 |
| 18 | 52 |
| 19 | 54, 57, 58, 98 |
| 20 | 59 |
| 22 | 143 |

### First Kings   136, 141, 163, 172

| | |
|---|---:|
| 1 | 49, 54, 126 |
| 1–15 | 138 |
| 2 | 54, 58 |
| 3 | 52 |
| 4 | 57, 58 |
| 5 | 57, 58, 60 |
| 6 | 143, 171 |
| 7 | 143 |
| 8 | 55, 57, 58, 75 |
| 9 | 54 |
| 10 | 57 |
| 12 | 48 |
| 13 | 46, 51 |
| 14 | 51, 57 |
| 15 | 46 |
| 16 | 46, 49 |
| 17 | 53, 57 |
| 20 | 47 |
| 21 | 49 |
| 22 | 47, 54, 57, 58 |

### Second Kings   41, 141, 163, 166, 172

| | |
|---|---:|
| 1 | 51, 61 |
| 3 | 54 |
| 4 | 52, 53, 117 |
| 5 | 45, 143 |
| 6 | 50, 96 |
| 8 | 50 |
| 9 | 54 |
| 10 | 96 |
| 11 | 126 |
| 13 | 46 |
| 15 | 46, 54 |
| 17 | 47, 79, 117 |
| 18 | 45 |
| 19 | 49, 79, 143 |
| 20 | 44, 61 |
| 22 | 153, 154 |
| 23 | 46, 61 |
| 24 | 44 |
| 25 | 17, 38, 39, 42–61, 94, 98, 109, 114 |

### First Chronicles   151, 152, 163, 171

| | |
|---|---:|
| 1 | 151 |
| 3 | 97, 151 |
| 5 | 94, 151 |
| 6 | 151 |
| 12 | 151 |
| 15 | 96 |
| 16 | 79 |
| 21 | 96 |
| 26 | 151 |
| 27 | 57, 58, 151 |
| 28 | 151 |

### Second Chronicles   151, 152, 163, 171

| | |
|---|---:|
| 2 | 46, 151 |
| 3 | 45, 151, 171, 172 |

## Index of Scripture

| | | | |
|---|---|---|---|
| 4 | 151 | 2 | 53, 58, 96 |
| 12 | 46 | 3 | 46 |
| 16 | 99 | 4 | 51 |
| 17 | 151 | 6 | 54, 55, 57 |
| 18 | 47 | 7 | 53 |
| 20 | 51 | 8 | 53, 151 |
| 21 | 52, 99 | 9 | 46, 96 |
| 22 | 51 | | |
| 23 | 61 | Job | 4, 150, 163, 172 |
| 24 | 45, 60 | 1 | 51, 55, 57, 58 |
| 26 | 151, 171, 172 | 5 | 55 |
| 29 | 151 | 7 | 58 |
| 30 | 51 | 8 | 148 |
| 31 | 53 | 10 | 171 |
| 34 | 151, 152, 153 | 12 | 148, 171 |
| 35 | 96, 151, 171 | 18 | 171 |
| 36 | 172 | 19 | 171, 172 |
| | | 21 | 171 |
| Ezra | 151, 152, 163, 171 | 39 | 148 |
| 1 | 57, 58, 61, 151 | 40 | 171 |
| 2 | 57, 58 | 41 | 171 |
| 3 | 60 | | |
| 4 | 151 | Psalms | 4, 172 |
| 7 | 61, 151 | 2 | 171 |
| 8 | 61 | 4 | 46 |
| 9 | 61, 151 | 8 | 123 |
| 10 | 50, 53, 96 | 11 | 171 |
| | | 14 | 75, 134 |
| Nehemiah | 151, 152, 163, 171 | 17 | 151, 155, 171 |
| | | 18 | 171 |
| 2 | 46, 61 | 20 | 75 |
| 3 | 150, 151, 171, 172 | 22 | 76, 128 |
| 5 | 50 | 23 | 56 |
| 7 | 57, 58, 151 | 24 | 76, 134 |
| 9 | 46 | 25 | 76, 134 |
| 10 | 60, 151 | 27 | 60 |
| 12 | 151 | 31 | 171 |
| 13 | 94 | 37 | 171 |
| | | 39 | 58 |
| Esther | 151, 171 | 41 | 75, 96 |
| | | 44 | 76 |
| 1 | 37, 53, 56 | 45 | 54 |

## Index of Scripture

| | | | |
|---|---|---|---|
| 46 | 75, 76 | 147 | 76 |
| 47 | 134 | | |
| 48 | 171 | Proverbs | 4, 132, 144, 145, |
| 51 | 85–106, 118, 134, 135, 151, | | 150, 163, 171, 172 |
| | 155, 160, 171 | | |
| 53 | 75 | 1 | 54 |
| 55 | 34, 36 | 2 | 145, 171 |
| 57 | 120 | 4 | 145 |
| 59 | 76 | 5 | 171 |
| 65 | 171, 172 | 7 | 171 |
| 68 | 75, 76 | 7–21 | 138 |
| 69 | 76 | 8 | 146, 171, 172 |
| 71 | 76 | 10 | 46, 146, 151, 171 |
| 72 | 76 | 11 | 55, 146, 171 |
| 75 | 24, 76 | 12 | 145, 171 |
| 76 | 76 | 14 | 46, 171 |
| 77 | 76, 171 | 15 | 50 |
| 78 | 75, 96, 171, 172 | 16 | 24, 57, 58, 171 |
| 79 | 76 | 17 | 46 |
| 80 | 151, 155, 171 | 18 | 53 |
| 81 | 75, 76 | 20 | 54, 147, 148 |
| 83 | 76 | 21 | 171 |
| 84 | 60, 76 | 24 | 171 |
| 87 | 76, 134 | 25 | 46 |
| 88 | 171 | 26 | 171 |
| 89 | 76, 122, 171 | 27 | 57, 58, 171 |
| 94 | 76 | 28 | 122, 146, 147, 171 |
| 98 | 76 | 30 | 54 |
| 99 | 76, 134 | 31 | 147, 171, 172 |
| 104 | 171 | | |
| 105 | 75 | Ecclesiastes | 4, 132, 151, 171 |
| 106 | 75, 171, 172 | 2 | 57 |
| 107 | 120 | 3 | 53 |
| 107–50 | 157 | 5 | 54 |
| 109 | 55 | 6 | 57, 58 |
| 110 | 33 | 7 | 57 |
| 114 | 75, 76 | 8 | 53, 58, 121 |
| 115 | 76 | 9 | 57, 121, 122, 151 |
| 118 | 126 | 10 | 57, 126 |
| 119 | 151, 155, 171 | 12 | 151, 171 |
| 132 | 76, 134 | | |
| 135 | 76 | | |
| 136 | 76 | | |
| 146 | 76, 134 | | |

## Index of Scripture

| Songs | 4, 150, 163, 171, 172 |
|---|---|
| 1–7 | 144 |
| 2 | 144, 171 |
| 4 | 144, 171 |
| 6 | 144 |
| 7 | 171 |

| Isaiah | 4, 172 |
|---|---|
| 1 | 56, 79, 171 |
| 1–39 | 73, 157, 158 |
| 2 | 61, 73, 82 |
| 3 | 50, 151, 155, 158, 171 |
| 5 | 79, 151, 158, 171, 172 |
| 6 | 54 |
| 7 | 44, 54, 158 |
| 9 | 79 |
| 10 | 73, 171 |
| 12 | 79, 158 |
| 14 | 79 |
| 17 | 73 |
| 19 | 158 |
| 20 | 44 |
| 26 | 171 |
| 27 | 79 |
| 28 | 151, 155, 158, 171 |
| 29 | 73 |
| 30 | 79 |
| 31 | 79 |
| 35 | 61 |
| 37 | 79 |
| 38 | 158 |
| 39 | 158 |
| 40 | 69, 70, 72 |
| 40–55 | 29, 62, 68–72, 75, 79, 93, 157, 158 |
| 41 | 30, 34, 35, 64, 70, 71, 72 |
| 42 | 3, 47, 70, 72, 112 |
| 42–49 | 71 |
| 43 | 24, 29, 70–72, 101, 112 |
| 44 | 24, 34, 64, 69, 70, 72, 93, 101 |
| 45 | 34, 36, 70–72, 93, 101 |
| 46 | 24, 70–72 |
| 47 | 24, 71, 72, 112 |
| 48 | 24, 69–72 |
| 49 | 25, 62–64, 68–71, 79, 112 |
| 50 | 24, 101, 158 |
| 51 | 47, 112 |
| 52 | 40, 71, 72, 109, 118–20, 161 |
| 53 | 25, 72, 107, 110–19, 121–28, 131, 132, 161 |
| 54 | 25, 30, 71, 72, 96, 171, 172 |
| 55 | 71, 72 |
| 56 | 158 |
| 56–66 | 73, 157, 158 |
| 58 | 151, 155, 158, 171 |
| 59 | 151, 171 |
| 60 | 25, 73 |
| 61 | 73 |

| Jeremiah | 163, 166 |
|---|---|
| 2 | 25, 26, 79 |
| 3 | 25, 26, 79, 80, 101 |
| 4 | 58, 72 |
| 5 | 25, 26, 31, 171 |
| 6 | 26 |
| 7 | 26 |
| 8 | 25, 31 |
| 9 | 80 |
| 10 | 79, 80 |
| 11 | 26, 39, 46, 80, 101 |
| 12 | 80 |
| 13 | 31, 101 |
| 15 | 31, 44 |
| 16 | 58, 99 |
| 17 | 44 |
| 18 | 47, 80 |
| 19 | 26 |
| 20 | 26 |
| 21 | 80 |
| 22 | 26, 52, 61, 99 |
| 23 | 26, 80 |
| 24 | 25, 44 |
| 25 | 80, 101, 161, 172 |
| 26 | 171 |
| 27 | 80 |
| 28 | 80 |

| | | | |
|---|---|---|---|
| 29 | 26, 44, 80 | 19 | 31 |
| 30 | 26, 77, 78, 80, 134 | 20 | 23, 46, 79, 81, 102 |
| 31 | 26, 77, 78, 80 | 21 | 31, 112 |
| 32 | 78, 80 | 22 | 23, 46, 162, 171 |
| 33 | 25, 61, 78, 80 | 23 | 102, 162, 171 |
| 34 | 25, 80, 98–100 | 24 | 81, 111, 122 |
| 35 | 26, 80, 101 | 26 | 23 |
| 36 | 37, 51, 52, 61 | 27 | 23, 162 |
| 37 | 47, 80 | 28 | 23 |
| 38 | 58, 80 | 29 | 23 |
| 39 | 80 | 33 | 23, 46, 81, 111, 122 |
| 40 | 56, 148 | 34 | 34, 36, 162 |
| 41 | 58, 97 | 36 | 23, 24 |
| 42 | 25 | 37 | 31, 61, 80, 117 |
| 44 | 26, 46 | 39 | 24, 31, 81 |
| 46 | 79, 80 | 41 | 56, 162 |
| 48 | 26, 80 | 44 | 46 |
| 49 | 25, 26, 171 | 46 | 162 |
| 50 | 26, 79, 80 | | |
| 51 | 26, 27, 52, 79, 80 | | |
| 52 | 17, 45, 51, 96, 99 | | |

| | | | |
|---|---|---|---|
| *Lamentations* | 151 | *Daniel* | 172 |
| 2 | 52, 79 | 1 | 50, 166 |
| 3 | 120, 151 | 2–6 | 171 |
| 4 | 151, 171 | 2–7 | 166 |
| 5 | 151 | 3 | 151, 155, 166, 167, 171 |
| | | 4 | 171 |
| *Ezekiel* | 125, 172 | 5 | 171 |
| 2 | 53 | 6 | 96 |
| 3 | 111, 122 | 7 | 122, 123, 132 |
| 4 | 50, 60, 111, 113 | 7–12 | 171 |
| 6 | 31, 81 | 8 | 53, 96 |
| 7 | 162 | 10 | 50, 122, 132 |
| 9 | 31, 32, 81, 162 | 11 | 171, 172 |
| 10 | 96 | 12 | 53, 117 |
| 11 | 96 | | |
| 12 | 81, 111 | *Hosea* | 163 |
| 13 | 81 | 1 | 61 |
| 14 | 31, 46, 81 | 2 | 51 |
| 16 | 22–24, 46, 54, 101, 162 | 6 | 81 |
| 17 | 45, 128 | 7 | 102 |
| 18 | 23, 31, 46, 81, 162 | 10 | 81 |
| | | 11 | 81 |
| | | 12 | 81 |

## Index of Scripture

| Joel | 4, 163 |
|---|---|
| 2 | 171 |

| Amos | 163 |
|---|---|
| 3 | 82 |
| 4 | 50, 72 |
| 5 | 82 |
| 6 | 82, 102, 171 |
| 7 | 82 |
| 8 | 82, 102 |
| 9 | 82 |

| Obadiah | 4, 83, 163 |
|---|---|

| Jonah | 4 |
|---|---|
| 4 | 58 |

| Micah | 163 |
|---|---|
| 1 | 82 |
| 2 | 82, 83 |
| 3 | 82, 83 |
| 4 | 61, 82 |
| 5 | 83 |
| 6 | 44, 102, 171 |
| 7 | 83 |

| Nahum | 163 |
|---|---|
| 2 | 79, 83, 171, 172 |
| 3 | 151 |

| Habakkuk | 163 |
|---|---|

| Zephaniah | 4 |
|---|---|
| 2 | 83 |
| 3 | 83 |

| Haggai | 163 |
|---|---|
| 2 | 61 |

| Zechariah | |
|---|---|
| 8 | 51, 83, 96 |
| 9 | 126, 171 |
| 12 | 61 |

| Malachi | 4 |
|---|---|
| 1 | 83 |
| 2 | 83 |
| 3 | 83, 102 |
| 4 | 127 |

## NEW TESTAMENT

| Matthew | |
|---|---|
| 4 | 125 |
| 9 | 125 |
| 11 | 126 |
| 17 | 124 |
| 24 | 128 |
| 25 | 126 |
| 27 | 126–28 |

| Mark | |
|---|---|
| 2 | 127 |
| 8 | 124–126 |
| 9 | 124, 127, 131 |
| 10 | 127, 129 |
| 11 | 126 |
| 14 | 126, 127, 131, 132 |
| 15 | 125–28 |
| 16 | 128 |

| Luke | |
|---|---|
| 4 | 127 |
| 19 | 126 |
| 22 | 126 |

| Hebrews | 123, 132 |
|---|---|
| 2 | 124 |
| 11 | 67 |

# Index of Scripture

## APOCRYPHA

*First Esdras*

| | |
|---|---|
| 4 | 123 |

*Second Esdras*

| | |
|---|---|
| 1 | 94 |
| 3 | 95 |
| 5 | 95 |
| 9 | 95 |
| 12 | 95 |

*Tobit*  132

| | |
|---|---|
| 12 | 123 |

*Wisdom*  123

| | |
|---|---|
| 9 | 123 |

*Sirach*  111, 122, 123, 132

| | |
|---|---|
| 17 | 122 |